D1314512

The 70-315 Cram Sheet

This Cram Sheet contains the distilled, key facts about developing and implementing Web applications with Microsoft Visual C# .NET and Microsoft Visual Studio .NET. Review this information as the last thing you do before you enter the testing center, paying special attention to those areas where you feel you need the most review. You can transfer any of these facts from your head onto a blank sheet of paper immediately before you begin the exam.

- Each ASPX page is dynamically converted to a class that derives its basic functionality from the System.Web.UI.Page class.

- The Page directive is used to specify page-related attributes that help compilers know how an ASP.NET page is to be compiled and executed.

- The Inherits attribute of the Page directive specifies the code-behind class for the ASPX page. The Src attribute of the Page directive specifies the path to the code-behind file. If you are precompiling the code-behind file, you don't specify the Src attribute.

- To make an HTML control run as a server control, apply the runat="server" attribute to the HTML control.

- Only some HTML server controls raise events on the server side; an HTML control can raise either a ServerClick event or ServerChange event.

- When the AutoPostBack property of the ASP.NET Web server controls is set to true, it causes an immediate postback and allows the Web server to immediately respond to change events without waiting for a click event to cause a page postback.

- The preferred way to add client-side event-handling code for Web server controls is via the the Attributes property of the Web server controls.

- To set properties on a control at runtime, you use the control.property = value syntax.

- To load controls dynamically on a Web form, create the controls and add them to the Controls collection of a container control, such as Page, Panel, or Placeholder.

- The Repeater and the DataList controls use templates to precisely format data from a collection. The DataBinder.Eval method is used to handle casts and formatting for data in a templated control.

- You can import an ActiveX control to a Visual Studio .NET project by adding it to the Toolbox.

- ActiveX controls are instantiated on the client, not the server. Any event handlers for the control must be written in a scripting language and will also execute on the client. ActiveX controls impose a performance penalty and have other drawbacks.

- The Response.Redirect() method can be used to connect to any specified URL. The specified URL can point to any resource and contain query strings. The use of Response.Redirect() causes an additional round trip to the server.

- The Server.Transfer() method performs a server-side redirection of a page and avoids an extra round trip.

- The Server.Execute() method executes the specified ASPX file and then returns execution to the calling ASPX page.

- The file specified as an argument to the Server.Execute() or the Server.Transfer() method must be an ASPX file residing on the same Web server, and the argument should not contain query string data.

- You should set the EnableViewStateMac attribute of the Page directive to false for the destination page, in case of calling the page via Server.Execute() method or Server.Transfer() method with the second argument set to true.

- ASP.NET uses a hidden input control named __VIEWSTATE to maintain state for all non-postback controls modified in the code.

- You can use the ViewState property of the Page class to store page-level values. The ViewState property enables you to store structured data as long as the data is serializable.

- You can use the Page.IsPostBack property to determine whether a page is being loaded for the first time or in response to a postback operation.

- If you add predefined installation components (for example, a `PerformanceCounter` installation component) to the Setup project, they are added to the `Installers` collection of the `ProjectInstaller` class.

- Shared assemblies are used by multiple applications on a machine. They are placed in the GAC and enjoy special priviliges, such as file security (because they are placed in the System folder), shared location, and side-by-side versioning.

- A shared assembly must be assigned a cryptographically strong name. Public/private key pairs are generated using the Strong Name tool (`sn.exe`). The pairs can then be used to digitally sign an assembly.

- A shared assembly can be added to the GAC by using Windows Explorer, the .NET Framework Configuration tool, the Global Assembly Cache Tool (`gacutil.exe`), or the Windows Installer.

- The CLR first searches the GAC to locate assemblies before looking in the files and folders where the application is installed. Thus, shared assemblies placed in the GAC are more efficient because the CLR does not look in the `<codebase>` and `<probing>` elements of the applicable configuration files.

- Delay signing enables a shared assembly to be placed in the GAC by just signing the assembly with the public key. This allows the assembly to be signed with a private key at a later stage when the development process is complete and the component or assembly is ready to be deployed.

- Merge modules enable you to create reusable components that help in deploying shared components. The merge modules cannot be directly installed; they need to be merged with installer programs of applications that use the component packed into the merge module.

- To save memory and processing time, if your page doesn't depend on session state, disable it with the `<@% Page EnableSessionState="false" %>` attribute in the `Page` directive.

- View state causes additional bytes to travel in each direction and therefore imposes a speed hit. You can avoid this penalty by setting the `EnableViewState` property of controls to `false` when you don't need their contents to persist.

- Using `StringBuilder` can help you achieve noticeable performance gains in an application using extensive string manipulations.

- Reduce the number of calls between the managed and unmanaged code, possibly by doing more work in each call rather than making frequent calls for doing small tasks.

- Use the `SqlClient` managed provider rather than the generic `OleDb` managed provider to retrieve data from the SQL Server database.

- SQL Server stored procedures are highly optimized for server-side data access, and their use usually improves data access performance significantly.

- Run SQL Server's Profiler and Index Tuning Wizard to avoid any bottlenecks because of indexing. Also, use the SQL Server Query Analyzer to optimize a query's performance.

- If you are reading a table sequentially, give preference to using `DataReader` over a `DataSet`.

- The SQL Server .NET Data provider provides connection pooling to improve performance when connecting to a database. Use the same connection strings to connect to the database to utilize the performance gains provided by connection pooling.

- You can use the `ConfigurationSettings` object to retrieve custom information from a configuration file.

- The `web.config` file can appear in multiple directories on an ASP.NET Web application server. Each `web.config` file applies settings to its own directory and all child directories below it. The `web.config` files in child directories(can override or modify settings defined in parent directories..

- The `machine.config` file contains settings that control the operation of .NET on the entire computer. For example, compiler settings for the .NET Framework are stored in this file.

- Role-based security enables you to authorize access to resources based on user identity or group membership. Identity impersonation lets the ASP.NET process act as the authenticated user.

- `OutputCache` directive enables you to cache the output of pages and user controls in a Web application. When an `OutputCache` directive is applied to an ASPX page, both the `Duration` and `VaryByParam` attributes must be specified. As opposed to this, in case of user controls, either the `VaryByParam` or `VaryByControl` attribute must be specified along with the `Duration` attribute.

- *Application data caching* refers to caching arbitrary data. You can cache any object you want in ASP.NET by calling the `Add` or `Insert` method of the `Cache` object.

- You can also register events of the Page class by defining event handlers with specific names, such as Page_Init(), Page_Load(), and so on, by setting the AutoEventWireup attribute to true in the Page directive.

- The global.asax file is the appropriate place to handle global events that are not specific to a Web form but rather apply to an application as a whole.

- Web user controls let you encapsulate common blocks of user interface functionality for reuse. They must be contained within the project in which they are used.

- Web custom controls are compiled components that offer support for almost all the features of the server controls that ship with Visual Studio .NET.

- You can create a Web custom control by combining existing controls, by deriving it from an existing control, or by inheriting it directly from the WebControl class.

- The DataSet object represents an entire relational database in memory. It's composed of DataTable, DataRelation, DataRow, and DataColumn objects.

- The DataView object provides a filtered row of the data from a DataTable.

- To persist changes from DataSet to the underlying database, you must call the Update method of the SqlDataAdapter object.

- The UpdateCommand, InsertCommand, and DeleteCommand properties of the SqlDataAdapter object specifies a SqlCommand object to be executed for updating, inserting and deleting rows respectively.

- The FileStream class treats a file as a raw, typeless stream of bytes.

- The StreamReader and StreamWriter classes are optimized for textual data, whereas the BinaryReader and BinaryWriter classes are optimized for structured binary data.

- Elements of an XML document can be represented by XmlNode objects. XmlNode objects are collected into an XmlDocument object, which is the object in the System.Xml namespace that represents an entire XML document.

- You can also treat an XML document as relational data. To do this, you can use an XmlDataDocument class, which inherits from XmlDocument. The key feature of the XmlDataDocument class is that it can be synchronized with a DataSet.

- The SqlException and SqlError objects provide the means to retrieve SQL Server[nd]specific error information.

- The System.Web.TraceContext class can be used to display trace messages in an application. These messages can be easily viewed by using the trace viewer or at the end of the page output.

- Tracing can be enabled at the application level by setting the trace element's enabled attribute to true in the applicationwide web.config file. To enable tracing for an individual page, you set the trace attribute to true in the Page directive.

- Listeners are objects that receive trace and debug output. By default, one listener, DefaultTraceListener, is attached to the Trace and Debug classes and displays the messages in the Output window.

- Debug and Trace objects share the same listeners collection. Therefore, any listener added to the Trace.Listeners collection is also added to the Debug.Listeners collection.

- Trace switches enable you to change the type of messages traced by a program depending on the value stored in the XML configuration file. You don't need to recompile the application for this change to take effect.

- The Trace and Debug classes from System.Diagnostics can be used to display informative messages in an application when the DEBUG and TRACE symbols are defined at the time of compilation.

- By default, both TRACE and DEBUG symbols are defined in the Debug Configuration for compilation, and only the TRACE symbol is defined for the Release configuration of compilation.

- Breakpoints enable you to mark code that signals the debugger to pause execution when it encour ters them.

- The various tool windows, such as Locals, Auto. Watch, and Call Stack, can be of great help in tracking the execution path and the status of variables when debugging an application in Visual Studio .NET.

- Use the Exceptions dialog box to customize how the exceptions are thrown in your program.

- You can attach a debugger to a running process (local or remote) with the help of the Processes dialog box.

- The Custom Actions Editor enables you to add custom actions to be performed during the installation process. It allows you to run .dll, .exe, assembly, and scripts files.

- The Launch Conditions editor enables you to set conditions to be evaluated when the installation begins on the target machine. If the conditions are not met, the installation stops.

- The System.Configuration.Install. Installer class works as a base class for all the custom installers in the .NET Framework. The Install() method of this class is called when the application is installed, and the Uninstall() method is called when the application is uninstalled. The Commit() method is executed if the Install() method is executed successfully; the Rollback() method is executed if the Install() method is not executed successfully.

- ASP.NET has a feature called smart navigation that can greatly enhance the user experience, such as eliminating flash and persisting control focus during postback of a Web page for users of Internet Explorer 5.0 or higher browsers.

- Session variables let you store information across multiple browser requests. The default storage location for session state is in-process memory in the ASP.NET process itself. The session state can be scaled to support multiple Web servers in a Web farm by storing the state in a separate process or in a SQL Server database.

- ASP.NET provides two ways to store global data: Application state and application data cache. The application data cache provides advanced features such as a cache expiration policy.

- Validation controls provide sophisticated validation on both the client side and the server side, depending on the validation settings and the browser's capabilities.

- The BaseValidator class serves as the base class for all the validation controls. This class provides the basic implementation of the validation controls.

- The RequiredFieldValidator control can be used to check whether the input control contains an entry.

- The RegularExpressionValidator control ensures that the associated input control's value matches a specified regular expression.

- The RangeValidator control is used to check whether the input control contains a value in the specified range.

- The CompareValidator control is used to compare the input server control's value against a data type, a fixed value, or another input control.

- The CustomValidator control enables you to specify custom validation code to be executed during validation.

- The ValidationSummary control is used to display a summary of all the validation errors of a Web page.

- To iterate through the elements of a string in a world-ready application, you should use the GetTextElementEnumerator method of the StringInfo class.

- SystemException represents the exceptions thrown by the CLR, whereas ApplicationException represents the exceptions thrown by the user programs.

- The try block consists of code that can raise an exception. A try block should be immediately followed by one or more catch blocks or a finally block.

- If multiple catch blocks are associated with a try block, the catch blocks should be arranged in the top-bottom order of specific to general exception types.

- The throw statement is used to raise an exception. Throwing exceptions is a costly operation. Don't use exceptions just to manage normal program flow.

- The finally block is used to enclose the code that needs to be run regardless of whether the exception is raised.

- Custom error pages can be configured by using the customErrors element in the web.config file.

- You can set a custom error Web page for individual pages in your application by using the ErrorPage attribute of the Page directive.

- You can handle any unhandled error that occurs in a page by using the page's Error event handler.

- Unhandled exceptions for an entire application can be trapped in the Application_Error event handler in the global.asax file.

- The Server.CreateObject() method is used to create late-bound COM components. However, not all COM components can be instantiated with Server.CreateObject(). In particular, components that use the STA threading model will not function properly in ASP.NET pages unless you add a compatability directive to the page, such as <%@Page aspcompat="true"%>.

- Using COM or COM+ components from .NET-managed code requires the creation of a runtime callable wrapper (RCW). RCWs impose a performance penalty on COM code.

- You can create an RCW for a COM component by either using the Type Library Importer or directly referencing the COM component from your .NET code.

- To use COM components you did not create, you should obtain a primary interop assembly (PIA) from the creator of the component.

- You can use PInvoke to call functions from unmanaged libraries. The DllImport attribute tells the CLR where to find the implementation of the extern method by specifying the name of the library.

- The CultureInfo object represents a culture in the .NET Framework.

- The System.Text.Encoding class and its subclasses enable you to convert text from one encoding to another.

- The .NET Framework provides partial support for mirroring through the RightToLeft property on forms and controls.

- You can respond to an event by overriding the On method corresponding to an event. When you use this method, you should be sure to call the corresponding On method for the base class so that you don't miss any of the functionality of the base class when the event is raised.

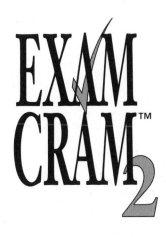

Developing and Implementing Web Applications with Visual C#® .NET and Visual Studio® .NET

Amit Kalani

Priti Kalani

CERTIFICATION

Developing and Implementing Web Applications with Visual C#® .NET and Visual Studio® .NET

International Standard Book Number: 0-7897-2901-6

Library of Congress Catalog Card Number: 2003100980

Printed in the United States of America

First Printing: August 2003

06   05   04   03   4   3   2   1

Que Certification offers excellent discounts on this book when ordered in quantity for bulk purchases or special sales. For more information, please contact

U.S. Corporate and Government Sales
1-800-382-3419
corpsales@pearsontechgroup.com

For sales outside the U.S., please contact

International Sales
1-317-581-3793
international@pearsontechgroup.com

Trademarks

All terms mentioned in this book that are known to be trademarks or service marks have been appropriately capitalized. Que Certification cannot attest to the accuracy of this information. Use of a term in this book should not be regarded as affecting the validity of any trademark or service mark.

Microsoft is a registered trademark of Microsoft Corporation.

Visual C# is a registered trademark of Microsoft Corporation.

Visual Studio is a registered trademark of Microsoft Corporation.

Warning and Disclaimer

Every effort has been made to make this book as complete and as accurate as possible, but no warranty or fitness is implied. The information provided is on an "as is" basis. The authors and the publisher shall have neither liability nor responsibility to any person or entity with respect to any loss or damages arising from the information contained in this book or from the use of the CD or programs accompanying it.

Publisher
Paul Boger

Executive Editor
Jeff Riley

Development Editor
Ginny Bess Munroe

Managing Editor
Charlotte Clapp

Project Editor
Tonya Simpson

Production Editor
Megan Wade

Indexer
John Sleeva

Proofreaders
Katie Robinson
Suzanne Thomas

Technical Editors
Steve Heckler
Greg Guntle

Team Coordinator
Pamalee Nelson

Multimedia Developer
Dan Scherf

Page Layout
Cheryl Lynch
Michelle Mitchell

CERTIFICATION

Que Certification • 201 West 103rd Street • Indianapolis, Indiana 46290

A Note from Series Editor Ed Tittel

You know better than to trust your certification preparation to just anybody. That's why you, and more than two million others, have purchased an Exam Cram book. As Series Editor for the new and improved Exam Cram 2 series, I have worked with the staff at Que Certification to ensure you won't be disappointed. That's why we've taken the world's best-selling certification product—a finalist for "Best Study Guide" in a CertCities reader poll in 2002—and made it even better.

As a "Favorite Study Guide Author" finalist in a 2002 poll of CertCities readers, I know the value of good books. You'll be impressed with Que Certification's stringent review process, which ensures the books are high-quality, relevant, and technically accurate. Rest assured that at least a dozen industry experts—including the panel of certification experts at CramSession—have reviewed this material, helping us deliver an excellent solution to your exam preparation needs.

Best Study Guides

We've also added a preview edition of PrepLogic's powerful, full-featured test engine, which is trusted by certification students throughout the world.

As a 20-year-plus veteran of the computing industry and the original creator and editor of the Exam Cram series, I've brought my IT experience to bear on these books. During my tenure at Novell from 1989 to 1994, I worked with and around its excellent education and certification department. This experience helped push my writing and teaching activities heavily in the certification direction. Since then, I've worked on more than 70 certification-related books, and I write about certification topics for numerous Web sites and for *Certification* magazine.

In 1996, while studying for various MCP exams, I became frustrated with the huge, unwieldy study guides that were the only preparation tools available. As an experienced IT professional and former instructor, I wanted "nothing but the facts" necessary to prepare for the exams. From this impetus, Exam Cram emerged in 1997. It quickly became the best-selling computer book series since "...*For Dummies*," and the best-selling certification book series ever. By maintaining an ~nse focus on subject matter, tracking errata and updates quickly, and following the co..fication market closely, Exam Cram was able to establish the dominant position in cert prep books.

You will not be disappointed in your decision to purchase this book. If you are, please contact me at etittel@jump.net. All suggestions, ideas, input, or constructive criticism are welcome!

Ed Tittel

Taking You to the MCAD/MCSD Finish Line!

MCAD/MCSD Training Guide
Amit Kalani
ISBN 0-7897-2822-2
$49.99 US/$77.99 CAN/£36.50 Net UK

Before you walk into your local testing center, make absolutely sure you're prepared to pass your exam. In addition to the Exam Cram2 series, consider our Training Guide series. Que Certification's Training Guides have exactly what you need to pass your exam:

- Exam Objectives highlighted in every chapter

- Notes, Tips, Warnings, and Exam Tips advise what to watch out for

- Step-by-Step Exercises for "hands-on" practice

- End-of-chapter Exercises and Exam Questions

- Final Review with Fast Facts, Study and Exam Tips, and another Practice Exam

- A CD that includes PrepLogic Practice Tests for complete evaluation of your knowledge

- Our authors are recognized experts in the field. In most cases, they are current or former instructors, trainers, or consultants – they know exactly what you need to know!

www.examcram.com

For Pooja and Sheetal.

About the Authors

Amit Kalani is a Microsoft Certified Application Developer (MCAD) and Microsoft Certified Solution Developer (MCSD) for the Microsoft .NET platform. Amit has long been associated with Microsoft certifications exams. In an earlier job, he managed a Microsoft Certified Technical Education Center (CTEC), where he closely worked with students to understand their requirements and guided them toward passing the certification exams.

Amit is also an author of *MCAD/MCSD Training Guides* for the 70-315, 70-316, and 70-320 exams. You can reach Amit at amit@techcontent.com.

Priti Kalani is a Microsoft Certified Application Developer (MCAD) and Microsoft Certified Solution Developer (MCSD) for the Microsoft .NET platform. Priti is a coauthor of *MCAD/MCSD Training Guide (Exam 70-320): Developing XML Web Services and Server Components with Microsoft Visual C# .NET and Microsoft .NET Framework.* She has been programming with the .NET Framework since its early beta versions and has been a technical reviewer for several popular books about the .NET Framework and related technologies. Priti welcomes your comments about the book at priti@techcontent.com.

About the Technical Editors

Steve Heckler is president of Accelebrate, an IT training and programming firm based in Atlanta. An avid ASP.NET, Java, and ColdFusion developer and trainer, Steve served more than six years as a senior manager and instructor at a leading East Coast IT training firm prior to founding Accelebrate. He holds bachelor's and master's degrees from Stanford University.

Greg Guntle is a 21-year veteran of developing PC applications using languages including C, C++, VB, Visual Basic .NET, and C# .NET. He has been technical editing computer programming books for the past 18 years. He has also coauthored several books, including *Teach Yourself Advanced C* and *Borland C++ Builder*.

Acknowledgments

Many people have worked hard to make this book possible. It is our immense pleasure to acknowledge the efforts of these fine people: Ginny Bess, Tonya Simpson, Megan Wade, Steve Heckler, Greg Guntle, Mike Gunderloy, Jeff Riley, John Sleeva, Katie Robinson, Cheryl Lynch, Michelle Mitchell, and Tammy Graham.

We would also like to extend our thanks to the development team of the *MCAD/MCSD Training Guide: Developing and Implementing Web Applications with Visual C# .NET and Visual Studio .NET*. Their efforts were instrumental in developing this book.

Contents at a Glance

Table of Contents

. . . .

Chapter 14
Deploying a Web Application **331**

We Want to Hear from You!

As the reader of this book, *you* are our most important critic and commentator. We value your opinion and want to know what we're doing right, what we could do better, what areas you'd like to see us publish in, and any other words of wisdom you're willing to pass our way.

As an executive editor for Que, I welcome your comments. You can email or write me directly to let me know what you did or didn't like about this book—as well as what we can do to make our books better.

Please note that I cannot help you with technical problems related to the *topic* of this book. We do have a User Services group, however, where I will forward specific technical questions related to the book.

When you write, please be sure to include this book's title and author as well as your name, email address, and phone number. I will carefully review your comments and share them with the author and editors who worked on the book.

Email: feedback@quepublishing.com

Mail: Jeff Riley
                Que Certification
                800 East 96th Street
                Indianapolis, IN 46240 USA

For more information about this book or another Que title, visit our Web site at www.quepublishing.com. Type the ISBN (excluding hyphens) or the title of a book in the Search field to find the page you're looking for. For information about the Exam Cram 2 series, visit www.examcram2.com.

Introduction

Welcome to the *70-315 Exam Cram 2*! Whether this is your 1st or your 15th *Exam Cram* series book, you'll find information here that will help ensure your success as you pursue knowledge, experience, and certification. This introduction explains Microsoft's certification programs in general and talks about how the *Exam Cram 2* series can help you prepare for Microsoft's developer certification exams for Microsoft .NET. Chapters 2–16 are designed to remind you of everything you'll need to know to take—and pass—the 70-315 Microsoft certification exam. Two sample exams at the end of the book (Chapters 17–20) should give you a reasonably accurate assessment of your knowledge, and we've provided the answers to the exams and their explanations. Read the book, and you'll stand a very good chance of passing the exam. Chapter 1, "Microsoft Certification Exams," includes a description of the testing environment and a discussion of test-taking strategies.

Exam Cram 2 books help you understand and appreciate the subjects and materials you need to pass Microsoft certification exams. These books are aimed strictly at test preparation and review; they do not teach you everything you need to know about a topic. Instead, we present and dissect the questions and problems you're likely to encounter on a test.

To completely prepare yourself for any Microsoft test, we recommend that you begin by taking the Self-Assessment included in this book, immediately following this Introduction. The Self-Assessment tool will help you evaluate your knowledge base against the requirements for a Microsoft Certified Application Developer (MCAD) or Microsoft Certified Solution Developer (MCSD) for Microsoft .NET.

Based on what you learn from the Self-Assessment, you might decide to begin your studies with some classroom training or background reading. On the other hand, you might decide to pick up and read one of the many study guides, such as the award-winning *MCAD/MCSD Training Guide* series from Que Publishing. We also recommend that you supplement your study program with visits to www.examcram2.com to receive additional practice questions, get advice, and track the MCAD and MCSD for Microsoft .NET program.

We also strongly recommend that you install, configure, and play around with the software that you'll be tested on because nothing beats hands-on experience and familiarity when it comes to understanding the questions you're likely to encounter on a certification test. Book learning is essential, but without a doubt, hands-on experience is the best teacher of all!

Taking a Certification Exam

After you've prepared for your exam, you need to register with a testing center. In the United States and Canada, tests are administered by Prometric and VUE. Here's how you can contact them:

> *Prometric*—You can sign up for a test through the company's Web site, at www.prometric.com. Within the United States and Canada, you can register by phone at 1-800-755-3926. If you live outside this region, you should check the Prometric Web site for the appropriate phone number.

> *VUE*—You can sign up for a test or get the phone numbers for local testing centers through the Web at www.vue.com/ms.

To sign up for a test, you must possess a valid credit card or contact either Prometric or VUE for mailing instructions to send a check (in the United States). Only when payment is verified or a check has cleared can you actually register for a test.

To schedule an exam, register online or through a telephone at least one day in advance. To cancel or reschedule an exam, you must call before 7 p.m. PST the day before the scheduled test (otherwise, you might be charged, even if you don't show up to take the test). When you want to schedule a test, you should have the following information ready:

> Your name, organization, and mailing address

> Your testing ID (if you are appearing for a Microsoft exam for the first time, you will be assigned a testing ID when you register for the exam)

> The name and number of the exam you want to take

> A method of payment, such as a credit card

After you sign up for a test, you are told when and where the test is scheduled. You should try to arrive at least 15 minutes early. You must supply two forms of identification—one of which must be a photo ID—to be admitted into the testing room.

All exams are completely closed book. In fact, you are not permitted to take anything with you into the testing area, but you are given a few blank sheets of paper and a pen or, in some cases, an erasable plastic sheet and a marker. We suggest that you immediately write down on that sheet of paper all the information you've memorized for the test. In *Exam Cram 2* books, this information appears on a tear-out sheet inside the front cover of each book. You are given some time to compose yourself, record this information, and take a sample orientation exam before you begin the real thing. We suggest that you take the orientation test before taking your first exam, but because all the certification exams are more or less identical in layout, behavior, and controls, you probably don't need to do this more than once.

When you complete a Microsoft certification exam, the software tells you whether you've passed or failed. If you need to retake an exam, you must schedule a new test with Prometric or VUE.

The first time you fail a test, you can retake the test the next day. However, if you fail a second time, you must wait 14 days before retaking that test. The 14-day waiting period remains in effect for all retakes after the second failure.

Tracking MCP Status

As soon as you pass any Microsoft exam, you attain MCP status. Microsoft generates transcripts that indicate which exams you have passed. You can view a copy of your transcript at any time by going to the MCP secured site (www.microsoft.com/traincert/mcp/mcpsecure.asp) and selecting Transcript Tool. This tool enables you to print a copy of your current transcript and confirm your certification status.

After you pass the necessary set of exams, you are certified. Microsoft sends you a Welcome Kit in about six to eight weeks. The kit contains a certificate that is suitable for framing, along with a wallet card and lapel pin. In addition, you get a number of other benefits, such as

➤ A license to use the MCP/MCAD/MCSD logo, which means you can use the logo on your letterhead and business cards (refer to the Microsoft Web site for the logo usage guidelines and terms and conditions)

➤ Access to the MCP Secure Web site to get the latest technical and product information as well as exclusive discount offers on products and services from select companies

➤ Invitations to Microsoft conferences, technical training sessions, and special events

➤ A free subscription to the *Microsoft Certified Professional Magazine Online*, which provides ongoing data about testing and certification activities, requirements, and changes to the program

Many people believe that the industry recognition of the MCP/MCAD/MCSD credential goes well beyond the perks that Microsoft provides to newly anointed members of this elite group. We're starting to see more job listings that request or require applicants to have MCP, MCAD, MCSD, and other certifications, and many individuals who complete Microsoft certification programs can qualify for increases in pay or responsibility. As an official recognition of hard work and broad knowledge, an MCP credential is a badge of honor in many IT organizations.

How to Prepare for the Exam

Preparing for Exam 70-315 requires that you obtain and study materials designed to provide comprehensive information about the .NET Framework and Visual Studio .NET and their capabilities for Web application development. The following list of materials can help you study and prepare:

➤ *The Visual Studio .NET product CD*—You can develop Web applications using the freely available .NET Framework SDK (http://msdn.microsoft.com/netframework/downloads/howtoget.asp), but I also recommend that you use Microsoft Visual Studio .NET. Several questions on the exam will test your skills on Visual Studio .NET. If do not have access to Visual Studio .NET, consider getting a trial version from http://msdn.microsoft.com/vstudio/productinfo/trial.

➤ *MSDN (Microsoft Developer Network) Online*—This Web site (http://msdn.microsoft.com) provides access to the most up-to-date product documentation, articles, product support knowledge base, and seminars.

➤ *The .NET Framework Community sites*—Sites such as www.gotdotnet.com and www.asp.net provide the latest news and announcements related to Web application development using the .NET Framework. In addition to accessing the information, you can also discuss your topics of interest with other developers.

➤ *The Exam Cram 2 Web site*—The official Exam Cram 2 Web site (www.examcram2.com) provides various exam preparation tools, such as exam preparation advice, practice tests, questions of the day, and discussion groups.

➤ *Search engines*—Search engines such as www.google.com let you easily find the information you are looking for. You can search for Microsoft-specific information using the Google's Microsoft search Web site, www.google.com/microsoft.

The Google Groups Web site (groups.google.com) requires a special mention because it not only allows you to post questions in the subject-related newsgroups such as microsoft.public.cert.exam.mcad and microsoft.public.cert.exam.mcsd, but also allows you to search the Usenet archive. You can use the Usenet archive to find out whether other developers have already posted solutions for the problems you are facing.

In addition, you might find any or all of the following materials useful in your exam preparation:

➤ *Self-Study MCAD/MCSD Training Guides*—Que Certification offers a comprehensive self-study training guide for the MCAD and the MCSD for Microsoft .NET exams. The training guides cover these subjects in much greater detail than the Exam Cram 2 books and are designed to teach you everything you need to know about the subject covered by the exam. For the 70-315 exam, refer to the *MCAD/MCSD Training Guide: Developing and Implementing Web Applications with Visual C# .NET and Visual Studio .NET (Exam 70-315)* by Amit Kalani.

➤ *Classroom training*—Although classroom training can be an expensive solution, many novice developers find classroom training useful. Many companies, including the Microsoft Certified Technical Education Centers (CTECs) and third-party training companies (such as Wintellect and DevelopMentor), offer classroom training on subjects related to the 70-315 exam.

➤ *Other publications*—There's no shortage of materials available about the .NET Framework and Visual Studio .NET. You can select the topics in which you are having difficulty and then select a book related to that topic for an in-depth study. You can find several books and sample chapters online at the InformIT Web site (www.informit.com).

What This Book Will Not Do

This book will *not* teach you everything you need to know about the .NET Framework, or even about a given topic. Nor is this book an introduction to computer programming. If you're new to applications development and are looking for an initial preparation guide, check out www.quepublishing.com, where you will find whole sections dedicated to the books about the

MCSD/MCAD certifications and computer programming. This book reviews what you need to know before you take the test, with the fundamental purpose dedicated to reviewing the information needed on the Microsoft 70-315 certification exam.

This book uses a variety of teaching and memorization techniques to analyze the exam-related topics and provide ways to input, index, and retrieve everything you'll need to know to pass the test. Once again, it is *not* an introduction to application development.

What This Book Is Designed to Do

This book is designed to be read as a pointer to the areas of knowledge on which you will be tested. In other words, you might want to read the book one time to get an insight into how comprehensive your knowledge of Web development using the .NET Framework is. The book is also designed to be read shortly before you take the actual test and to give you a distillation of the entire field of Web application development using the Microsoft .NET Framework in as few pages as possible. We think you can use this book to get a sense of the underlying context of any topic in the chapters or to skim for alerts, bullet points, summaries, and topic headings.

We've drawn on material from Microsoft's own listing of knowledge requirements, from other preparation guides, and from the exams themselves. We've also drawn from a battery of third-party test-preparation tools, technical Web sites, and our own experience with application development. Our aim is to walk you through the knowledge you will need, looking over your shoulder, so to speak, and pointing out those things that are important for the exam (study alerts, practice questions, and so on).

The 70-315 exam makes a basic assumption that you already have a strong background with Web application development and its terminology. On the other hand, because the .NET development environment is new, no one can be a complete expert. We've tried to demystify the jargon, acronyms, terms, and concepts, and wherever we think you're likely to blur past an important concept, we've defined the assumptions and premises behind that concept.

About This Book

If you're preparing for the 70-315 certification exam for the first time, we've structured the topics in this book to build on one another. Therefore, the topics covered in later chapters often refer to discussions in earlier chapters.

In our opinion, many computer manuals and reference books are essentially a list of facts. Rather than simply listing raw facts about each topic on the exam, we've tried to paint an integrated landscape in which each exam fact becomes an obvious conclusion to the problems evolving out of earlier technology.

We suggest you read this book from front to back. You won't be wasting your time: Nothing we've written is a guess about an unknown exam. What might appear to be a detour into rambling discussions is based on our many years of working with less-experienced computer users. We've had to explain certain underlying information on such a regular basis that we've included those explanations here. Time and again, we've found that, by understanding the conceptual underpinnings of a topic, our audience members were better able to recall the resulting details.

After you've read the book, you can brush up on a topic by using the index or the table of contents to go straight to the topics and questions you want to reexamine. We've tried to use the headings and subheadings to provide outline information about each given topic. After you've been certified, we think you'll find this book useful as a tightly focused reference and an essential foundation of Web application development.

Chapter Formats

Each Exam Cram 2 chapter follows a regular structure, along with graphical cues about especially important or useful material. The structure of a typical chapter includes

➤ *Opening hotlists*—Each chapter begins with a list of the terms you'll need to understand and a list of the concepts you'll need to master before you can be fully conversant with the chapter's subject matter. We follow the hotlists with a few introductory paragraphs, setting the stage for the rest of the chapter.

➤ *Topical coverage*—After the opening hotlists, each chapter covers at least three topics related to the chapter's subject.

➤ *Alerts*—Throughout the topical coverage section, we highlight material most likely to appear on the exam by using a special alert layout that looks like this:

This is what an alert looks like. An alert stresses concepts, terms, software, or activities that will most likely appear in one or more certification exam questions. For that reason, we think any information found offset in alert format is worthy of extra attentiveness on your part.

Even if material isn't flagged as an alert, *all* the content in this book is associated in some way with test-related material. What appears in the chapter content is critical knowledge.

➤ *Notes*—This book is an overall examination of computers. As such, we dip into nearly every aspect of Web application development. Where a body of knowledge is deeper than the scope of the book, we use notes to indicate areas of concern or specialty training.

> Cramming for an exam will get you through a test, but it won't make you a competent IT professional. Although you can memorize just the facts you need to become certified, your daily work in the field will rapidly put you in water over your head if you don't know the underlying principles of application development.

➤ *Tips*—We provide tips that will help you build a better foundation of knowledge or focus your attention on an important concept that will reappear later in the book. Tips are a helpful way to remind you of the context surrounding a particular area of a topic under discussion.

> You can visit **www.examcram2.com** to receive additional practice questions, get advice, and track the MCAD and MCSD for Microsoft .NET program.

➤ *Practice questions*—This section presents a short list of test questions related to the specific chapter topic. Each question has a following explanation of both correct and incorrect answers. The practice questions highlight the areas we found to be most important on the exam.

➤ *Need to know more?*—Every chapter ends with a section titled "Need to Know More?" This section provides pointers to resources we found to be helpful in offering further details on the chapter's subject matter. If you find a resource you like in this collection, use it, but don't feel compelled to use all these resources. We use this section to recommend resources we have used on a regular basis, so none of the recommendations will be a waste of your time or money. These resources might go out of print or be taken down (in the case of Web sites), so we've tried to reference widely accepted resources.

The bulk of the book follows this chapter structure, but we would like to point out a few other elements:

➤ *Sample exams*—The sample exams, which appear in Chapter 17, "Practice Exam #1," and Chapter 19, "Practice Exam #2," are very close approximations of the types of questions you are likely to see on the current 70-315 exam.

➤ *Answer keys*—Here you'll find the answers to the sample tests, with a following explanation of both the correct response and the incorrect responses.

➤ *Glossary*—This is an extensive glossary of important terms used in this book.

➤ *The Cram Sheet*—This appears as a tear-away sheet inside the front cover of this Exam Cram book. The Cram Sheet is a valuable tool that represents a collection of the most important facts we think you should memorize before taking the test. Remember, you can dump this information out of your head onto a piece of paper as soon as you enter the testing room. These are usually facts that require brute-force memorization: You need to remember this information only long enough to write it down when you walk into the test room. Be advised that you will be asked to surrender all personal belongings before you enter the exam room itself.

You might want to look at the Cram Sheet in the parking lot or lobby of the testing center just before you walk into the testing center. The Cram Sheet is separated into headings, so you can review the appropriate parts just before each test.

➤ *CD-ROM*—The CD-ROM that comes with this book contains the complete code listing of the various examples presented in the chapters. The CD also contains the *PrepLogic Practice Tests, Preview Edition* exam simulation software. The preview edition exhibits most of the full functionality of the Premium Edition but offers questions sufficient for only one practice exam. To get the complete set of practice questions and exam functionality, visit `www.preplogic.com`.

Thanks for choosing us as your personal trainers, and enjoy the book. We would wish you luck on the exam, but we know that if you read through all the chapters, you won't need luck—you'll ace the test on the strength of real knowledge!

Self-Assessment

This Self-Assessment helps you evaluate your readiness to tackle Microsoft certifications. It should also help you understand what you need to know to master the topic of this book—namely, Exam 70-315, "Developing and Implementing Web Applications with Microsoft Visual C# .NET and Microsoft Visual Studio .NET." However, before you tackle this Self-Assessment, let's talk about the developer certifications offered by Microsoft for Microsoft .NET.

Microsoft Developer Certifications for Microsoft .NET

Microsoft currently offers two levels of developer certification for Microsoft .NET—Microsoft Certified Application Developer (MCAD) and Microsoft Certified Solution Developer for Microsoft .NET (MCSD). In fact, the MCAD certification is a subset of the MCSD certification. In this section, you will learn how the two certifications are structured and what you would expect from an ideal MCAD or MCSD candidate.

The MCAD Certification

The MCAD is a certification for the developers who develop, deploy, and maintain applications and components using the Microsoft .NET Framework and Microsoft Visual Studio .NET. To get the MCAD certificate, you are required to pass three exams that include two core exams and one elective exam as listed in the following sections.

MCAD Core Exams

You must pass two of the following core exams to earn credit toward the MCAD certification:

➤ 70-305, "Developing and Implementing Web Applications with Microsoft Visual Basic .NET and Microsoft Visual Studio .NET"

OR

70-306, "Developing and Implementing Windows-based Applications with Microsoft Visual Basic .NET and Microsoft Visual Studio .NET"

OR

70-315, "Developing and Implementing Web Applications with Microsoft Visual C# .NET and Microsoft Visual Studio .NET"

OR

70-316, "Developing and Implementing Windows-based Applications with Microsoft Visual C# .NET and Microsoft Visual Studio .NET"

➤ 70-310, "Designing XML Web Services and Server Components with Microsoft Visual Basic .NET and the Microsoft .NET Framework"

OR

70-320, "Designing XML Web Services and Server Components with Microsoft Visual C# .NET and the Microsoft .NET Framework"

MCAD Elective Exams

You must pass one of the following elective exams to earn credit toward the MCAD certification:

➤ 70-229, "Designing and Implementing Databases with Microsoft SQL Server 2000 Enterprise Edition"

➤ 70-230, "Designing and Implementing Solutions with Microsoft BizTalk Server 2000 Enterprise Edition"

➤ 70-234, "Designing and Implementing Solutions with Microsoft Commerce Server 2000"

You can also count as an elective one of the four core exams: 70-305, 70-306, 70-315, and 70-316. The one you can count as an elective is the exam from the opposite technology from the exam you count as a core exam. For example, if you take the exam "Developing and Implementing Web Applications with Microsoft Visual C# .NET and Microsoft Visual Studio .NET" (70-315) as a core exam, you can either take the exam "Developing and Implementing Windows-based Applications with Microsoft Visual C# .NET and Microsoft Visual Studio .NET" (70-316) or the exam "Developing and Implementing Windows-based Applications with Microsoft Visual Basic .NET and Microsoft Visual Studio .NET" (70-306) as an elective, but you cannot take the exam "Developing and Implementing Web Applications with

Microsoft Visual Basic .NET and Microsoft Visual Studio .NET" (70-305) as an elective.

The Ideal MCAD Candidate

The ideal MCAD candidate is someone who has from one to two years of experience in developing and maintaining department-level applications, Web or desktop clients, XML Web services, and back-end data services using the Microsoft .NET Framework and Microsoft Visual Studio .NET. The ideal MCAD candidate might also be someone who works in teams that use Microsoft .NET Framework and other Microsoft technologies to develop enterprise-level applications. Typical job titles for an ideal MCAD candidate include programmer, programmer/analyst, and software developer.

The MCSD for Microsoft .NET Certification

The MCSD for Microsoft .NET certification is for those developers who design and develop enterprise-level solutions using the Microsoft .NET Framework and other Microsoft development tools and technologies. For the MCSD for Microsoft .NET certification, you must pass four core exams and one elective exam as listed in the following sections.

MCSD for Microsoft .NET Track Core Exams

You must pass four of the following core exams to earn credit toward the MCSD for Microsoft .NET certification:

➤ 70-305, "Developing and Implementing Web Applications with Microsoft Visual Basic .NET and Microsoft Visual Studio .NET"

OR

70-315, "Developing and Implementing Web Applications with Microsoft Visual C# .NET and Microsoft Visual Studio .NET"

➤ 70-306, "Developing and Implementing Windows-based Applications with Microsoft Visual Basic .NET and Microsoft Visual Studio .NET"

OR

70-316, "Developing and Implementing Windows-based Applications with Microsoft Visual C# .NET and Microsoft Visual Studio .NET"

➤ 70-310, "Designing XML Web Services and Server Components with Microsoft Visual Basic .NET and the Microsoft .NET Framework"

OR

70-320, "Designing XML Web Services and Server Components with Microsoft Visual C# .NET and the Microsoft .NET Framework"

➤ 70-300, "Analyzing Requirements and Defining .NET Solution Architectures"

MCSD for Microsoft .NET Track Elective Exams

You must pass one of the following elective exams to earn credit toward the MCSD for Microsoft .NET certification:

➤ 70-229, "Designing and Implementing Databases with Microsoft SQL Server 2000 Enterprise Edition"

➤ 70-230, "Designing and Implementing Solutions with Microsoft BizTalk Server 2000 Enterprise Edition"

➤ 70-234, "Designing and Implementing Solutions with Microsoft Commerce Server 2000"

 Exam 70-315 also qualifies as an elective toward a different certification—The Microsoft Certified Database Administrator (MCDBA) for the Microsoft SQL Server 2000 Certification.

The Ideal MCSD for Microsoft .NET Candidate

The ideal MCSD for Microsoft .NET candidate is someone who has at least two years of experience in designing and developing enterprise-level solutions with the Microsoft .NET Framework and other Microsoft technologies. An ideal MCSD for Microsoft .NET candidate should be able to work as a lead developer performing tasks such as analyzing business and technical requirements and defining solution architecture. In addition, an MCSD for Microsoft .NET candidate should also be able to perform the tasks typical to the MCAD certification, such as building, deploying, and maintaining the applications. Typical job titles for an ideal MCSD for Microsoft .NET candidate include software engineer, application analyst, application developer, and technical consultant.

Put Yourself to the Test

The following series of questions and observations is designed to help you figure out how much work you must do to pursue Microsoft certification and what types of resources you might consult on your quest.

Two things should be clear from the outset, however:

➤ Even a modest background in computer science and programming will be helpful.

➤ Hands-on experience with Microsoft products and technologies is an essential ingredient to certification success.

Following are the questions:

1. Do you have prior experience with computer programming or with the C# programming language?

Any experience with a programming language, even if it's with a different language, will help you in passing exam 70-315. However, if you do not have much experience with programming or, in particular, with the C# programming language, we recommend you read the following book:

C# How to Program by Harvey M. Deitel, et al. (Prentice Hall, 2001)

2. Do you have prior experience with Web development using HTML and JavaScript?

The 70-315 exam mostly emphasizes server-side programming. However, knowledge of HTML and JavaScript is still needed for the Web application development, especially when it comes to designing a responsive user interface. If you do not have much experience in using HTML or JavaScript, we recommend you read the following book:

Special Edition Using HTML 4, Sixth Edition by Molly E. Holzschlag (Que Publishing, 1999)

3. Do you have a general understanding of what the .NET Framework is and what it has to offer you as a developer?

The .NET Framework has a lot to offer. Even if you have been developing applications in the .NET Framework for the past few months, you might not have had the opportunity to experiment with all its features. If this is the case, we recommend you read the following book:

Understanding .NET: A Tutorial and Analysis by David Chappell (Addison Wesley Professional Publishing, 2002)

This book gives you a bird's-eye view of Microsoft .NET and how it affects you as a developer. Many questions in the 70-315 exam require you to have a high-level view of the .NET Framework and related technologies.

4. Have you installed, configured, or used Visual Studio .NET and the .NET Framework Software Development Kit (SDK)?

Experience is necessary for passing Exam 70-315. If you haven't worked with the .NET Framework SDK and Visual Studio .NET, now is the time. Before you appear for the exam, make sure you spend enough time in programming using both the Microsoft .NET Framework SDK and Visual Studio .NET.

The Microsoft .NET Framework is available as a free download from `http://msdn.microsoft.com/netframework/downloads/howtoget.asp`. Unlike the .NET Framework, you will have to buy a license for using Visual Studio .NET. Even if you do not plan to buy a license, you should at least consider ordering a trial version of Visual Studio .NET from `http://msdn.microsoft.com/vstudio/productinfo/trial`.

5. Have you reviewed the exam objectives?

If you have not reviewed the exam objectives lately, look at them when you are determining your exam readiness. The up-to-date exam objectives for the 70-315 exam are available at `http://www.microsoft.com/traincert/exams/70-315.asp`. You should review each objective and then ask yourself whether you have used Visual C# .NET and Visual Studio .NET enough to answer questions related to that particular exam objective. If you are not confident, consider studying the related topics in the following resources:

➤ `http://msdn.microsoft.com`

➤ `http://support.microsoft.com`

➤ *MCAD/MCSD Training Guide (70-315): Developing and Implementing Web Applications with Visual C# and Visual Studio.NET* by Amit Kalani (Que Certification, 2002)

6. Have you taken a few practice exams for the Exam 70-315?

This book has two sample exams in Chapter 17, "Practice Exam #1," and Chapter 19, "Practice Exam #2." You should attempt these exams to determine how ready you are. If you require additional practice, you can also take practice exams from other test providers.

Onward, Through the Fog!

After you have assessed your readiness, undertaken the right background studies, obtained the hands-on experience that will help you understand the products and technologies at work, and reviewed the many sources of information to help you prepare for a test, you will be ready to take a round of practice tests. When your scores come back positive enough to get you through the exam, you are ready to go after the real thing. If you follow our assessment regime, you will know not only what you need to study, but also when you are ready to set a test date at Prometric (www.2test.com) or VUE (www.vue.com). Good luck!

Microsoft Certification Exams

Terms you'll need to understand:

- ✓ Adaptive tests
- ✓ Build-list-and-reorder question format
- ✓ Case study
- ✓ Create-a-tree question format
- ✓ Drag-and-connect question format
- ✓ Fixed-length tests
- ✓ Multiple-choice question format
- ✓ Select-and-place question format
- ✓ Short-form tests
- ✓ Simulations

Techniques you'll need to master:

- ✓ Assessing your exam-readiness
- ✓ Answering Microsoft's varying question types
- ✓ Altering your test strategy depending on the exam format
- ✓ Practicing (to make perfect)
- ✓ Making the best use of the testing software
- ✓ Budgeting your time
- ✓ Guessing (as a last resort)

The content of this chapter is located on the enclosed CD-ROM.

Introducing Web Forms

Terms you'll need to understand:

✓ AutoEventWireup
✓ Code-behind
✓ Delegate
✓ Directives
✓ Event
✓ Event handling
✓ Namespace
✓ Property

Techniques you'll need to master:

✓ Understanding the execution of ASP.NET pages
✓ Using the ASP.NET Page directive and understanding how it affects the compilation and execution of an ASP.NET page
✓ Learning the code-behind technique to separate user interface and business logic in ASP.NET pages
✓ Learning how to handle and raise events in an ASP.NET page

The Microsoft .NET Framework enables you to create different types of programs, such as Web applications, Windows-based applications, XML Web services, and reusable components. Active Server Pages .NET (ASP.NET) is a part of the .NET Framework that enables you to develop Web Forms (programmable Web pages and Web services). This chapter introduces the basic concepts involved in developing Web Forms.

Introduction to ASP.NET

The ASP.NET infrastructure consists of two main parts:

> *A set of classes and interfaces that enables communication between the Web browser and Web server*—These classes are organized in the System.Web namespace.

> *A process that handles the Web request for ASP.NET resources*—This process is also known as the ASP.NET worker process or aspnet_wp.exe.

At a higher level, an ASP.NET Web application is executed through a series of Hypertext Transfer Protocol (HTTP) request and response messages between the client browsers and Web server (see Figure 2.1). The process occurs as follows:

1. The user requests a resource from a Web server by typing a URL in her browser. The browser sends an HTTP request to the destination Web server.

2. The Web server analyzes the HTTP request and searches for a process capable of executing this request.

3. The results of the HTTP request are returned to the client browser in the form of an HTTP response.

4. The browser reads the HTTP response and displays it as a Web page to the user.

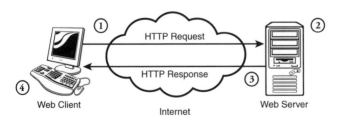

Figure 2.1 When running ASP.NET applications, user computers and the Web server communicate with each other using the HTTP protocol.

As a Web programmer, you will be more interested in knowing what goes on behind the scenes when a Web server executes a Web request for an ASP.NET page (an .aspx file). Figure 2.2 represents the process of server-side execution.

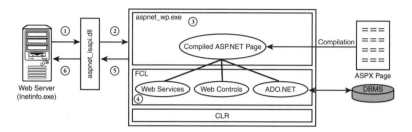

Figure 2.2   The ASP.NET worker process serves the requests to ASP.NET resources using the services provided by the .NET Framework.

Following is a description of the ASP.NET page execution:

1. When IIS (inetinfo.exe) receives an HTTP request, it uses the file-name extension of the requested resource to determine which Internet Server Application Programming Interface (ISAPI) program to run to process the request. When the request is for an ASP.NET page (an .aspx file), it passes the request to the ISAPI DLL capable of handling requests for ASP.NET pages, which is aspnet_isapi.dll.

2. The aspnet_isapi.dll process passes the request to the ASP.NET worker process (aspnet_wp.exe), which fulfills the request.

3. The ASP.NET worker process compiles the .aspx file into an assembly and instructs the CLR to execute the resulting assembly.

4. When the assembly containing the code for an ASP.NET page executes, it takes the service of various classes in the FCL to accomplish its work and generate response messages for the requesting client.

5. The ASP.NET worker process collects the response generated by the execution of the Web page, creates a response packet, and passes it to the aspnet_isapi.dll process.

6. aspnet_isapi.dll forwards the response packet to IIS, which in turn passes the response to the requesting client machine.

Creating an ASP.NET Page

To create an ASP.NET page, all you need to do is write the ASP.NET code in a text file with the `.aspx` extension and place it in an accessible virtual directory on the Web server. The following example creates a simple ASP.NET Web page that displays a Fahrenheit-to-Celsius temperature conversion chart. Here's how you do it:

1. Launch Visual Studio .NET. On the start page, click the New Project button (alternatively, you can select File, New, Project). In the New Project dialog box, select Visual C# Projects as the project type and Empty Web Project as the template. Specify the location of the project as `http://localhost/ExamCram/315C02`. This sets up the project directory (315C02) as a virtual directory (within the `ExamCram` directory) on the default Web site of the local Web server. The project directory is also set up as an IIS application.

2. Invoke the Solution Explorer window by selecting View, Solution Explorer. Right-click the name of the project and select Add, Add New Item from its shortcut menu, as shown in Figure 2.3. Alternatively, you can select Project, Add New Item from the Visual Studio .NET main menu. In the Add New Item dialog box, select the Text File template and name the file `Example2_1.aspx`.

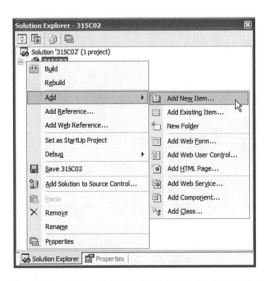

Figure 2.3 Solution Explorer allows easy access to a project and its elements.

3. Write the following code in the HTML view of `Example2_1.aspx`. (Line numbers are for reference purpose only and are not part of the code.)

```
01: <!--Example2_1.aspx -->
02: <%@ Page Language="C#" %>
03: <html><head>
04: <script runat="server">
05:     double ToCelsius(double f)
06:     {
07:         return  (5.0/9.0)*(f-32.0);
08:     }
09: </script></head>
10: <body>
11: <h2>Fahrenheit to Celsius Conversion Chart</h2>
12:     <table border="2">
13:         <tr>
14:         <th>&deg; Fahrenheit</th><th>&deg; Celsius</th>
15:         </tr>
16:         <%
17:         for (double f = 50.0; f<=100.0; f++)
18:         {
19:             // Sends formatted output to HTTP response
20:             Response.Output.Write(
21:                 "<tr><td>{0}</td><td>" +
22:                 "{1:f}</td></tr>", f, ToCelsius(f));
23:         }
24:         %>
25:     </table>
26: </body>
27: </html>
```

NOTE   The **Response** property of the **Page** class gives you access to the HTTP Response object. You can add content to the HTTP response using the **Response.Write()** and **Response.Output.Write()** methods. The only difference between the two methods is that the latter allows you to write formatted output.

4. In the Solution Explorer, right-click `Example2_1.aspx` and select View in Browser from its shortcut menu. A browser window opens in Visual Studio .NET and displays the page output shown in Figure 2.4.

In step 3's code, line 1 is the HTML comment line and line 2 is an ASP.NET directive that controls the behavior of the compiler translating the ASP.NET page to MSIL. All ASP.NET code in the page is enclosed in either the `<script runat="server">...</script>` tag (lines 4–9) or inside the `<%...%>` tag (lines 16–24).

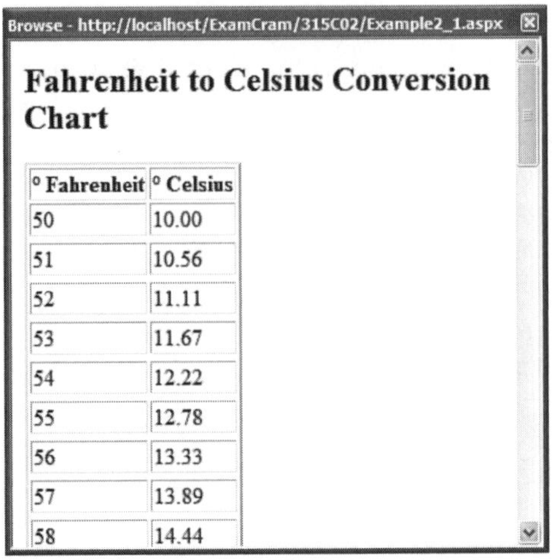

Figure 2.4 The temperature conversion chart is created by executing ASP.NET code on the Web server.

The **Page** Class

Prior to execution, each ASPX page is converted into a class. The class corresponding to the ASPX page derives most of its functionality from its base class—System.Web.UI.Page. If you look at the .NET Framework documentation, you will note that the Page class itself derives from System.Web.UI.TemplateControl, System.Web.UI.Control, and System.Object.

Because of this inheritance relationship, you can also say that a page is a control, and because the Page class derives from the TemplateControl, it derives extended capabilities for placing other controls on its surface. Table 2.1 lists important members of the Page class.

Table 2.1	Important Members of the Page Class	
Member	**Type**	**Description**
Application	Property	Returns the application state object for the current HTTP request.
Cache	Property	Returns the cache object of the application to which the page belongs.
ClientTarget	Property	Provides information about the client browser and its capabilities. You can use this information to control the rendering of a page according to particular browser clients.
Controls	Property	Returns a **ControlCollection** object that represents the collection of controls placed on the page.

(continued)

Table 2.1   Important Members of the Page Class *(continued)*

Member	Type	Description
EnableViewState	Property	Indicates whether the view state is maintained for the page and its container controls.
Error	Event	Occurs when an unhandled exception occurs in the page processing.
ErrorPage	Property	Specifies the error page where the user is redirected whenever an unhandled exception occurs in the page processing.
Init	Event	Occurs when the page is initialized. This event is the first step in the page life cycle.
IsPostBack	Property	Indicates whether the page is loaded as the result of a client postback.
IsValid	Property	Indicates whether all the validation controls on a page succeeded.
Load	Event	Occurs when the page is loaded in memory.
OnError()	Method	Raises the **Error** event. It is a protected method derived from the **TemplateControl** class.
MapPath()	Method	Returns the actual physical path corresponding to a virtual path.
OnInit()	Method	Raises the **Init** event. It is a protected method derived from the **Control** class.
OnLoad()	Method	Raises the **Load** event. It is a protected method derived from the **Control** class.
OnPreRender()	Method	Raises the **PreRender** event. It is a protected method derived from the **Control** class.
OnUnload()	Method	Raises the **Unload** event. It is a protected method derived from the **Control** class.
PreRender	Event	Occurs when a page is about to render its contents.
RenderControl()	Method	Outputs content of a page to a provided **HtmlTextWriter** object and stores tracing information about the control if tracing is enabled.
Request	Property	Returns the request object that contains information about the current HTTP request.
Response	Property	Returns the response object for the current HTTP request.
Server	Property	Provides access to the server object associated with the page.

(continued)

Table 2.1	Important Members of the Page Class *(continued)*	
Member	**Type**	**Description**
Session	Property	Returns the session state object applicable for the current HTTP request.
SmartNavigation	Property	Indicates whether smart navigation is enabled for the page.
Trace	Property	Returns the trace context object for the current HTTP request.
Unload	Event	Occurs when a page is unloaded from memory.
Validators	Property	Returns a collection of all validation controls contained in a page.
Visible	Property	Indicates whether the page should be displayed.

Stages in Page Processing

When ASP.NET processes a Web page, the page goes through distinct stages. Some of these common stages are listed in Table 2.2.

Table 2.2	The Stages of ASP.NET Page Processing
Stage	**Meaning**
Page Initialization	Page initialization is the first stage in the ASP.NET page processing. Its objective is to create the instance of an ASP.NET page. The **Init** event is raised to indicate this stage. An **Init** event handler is the best place for code that you want to be executed prior to further page processing.
User Code Initialization	At this stage, the page initialization is complete and the page is loaded into the memory. The **Page** object indicates this stage by raising the **Load** event. A method that handles the **Load** event is the best place to store initialization code for any controls specific to this page.
PreRender	The page is just about to render its contents. The **PreRender** event is raised to indicate this stage. An event handler for the **PreRender** event has the last chance to modify the page's output before it is sent to the browser.
Page Cleanup	The page has finished rendering and is ready to be discarded. The **Unload** event is raised to indicate this stage.

ASP.NET Directives

ASP.NET pages enable you to specify various options that can be used by compilers at the time of compilation. You can specify these commands and options with the help of *directives*. A directive name begins with the @ character and is enclosed in <% and %> tags. A directive can be placed anywhere in a Web page but is usually placed at the top. Directives contain one or more attribute/value pairs, which are not case sensitive and need not be placed in quotes.

Table 2.3 lists the various types of directives that can be added to an ASP.NET page.

Table 2.3 ASP.NET Page Directives	
Directive	**Description**
Assembly	Links an assembly to the application or a Web page during compilation. It is similar to the **/reference** command-line switch of the C# compiler (**csc.exe**). You can have multiple **Assembly** directives on a page to link multiple assemblies.
Control	Specifies user control-related attributes that are used by the ASP.NET compiler when the user control (ASCX file) is compiled.
Implements	Indicates that the Web page (ASPX file) or the user control (ASCX file) implements an interface specified by the **Interface** attribute of the directive.
Import	Imports a namespace into a page, a user control, or an application. It is similar to the **using** directive in C#. You can have multiple **Import** directives to import different namespaces.
OutputCache	Controls the output caching of a Web page (ASPX file) or user control (ASCX file).
Page	Specifies page-related attributes used by the ASP.NET compiler when the Web client requests the ASPX page. See Table 2.4 for a list of attributes allowed in a **Page** directive.
Reference	Indicates a Web page or user control that should be compiled and linked during compilation of the ASPX page that contains the **Reference** directive. It can contain either the **Page** attribute (ASPX file name) or **Control** attribute (ASCX file name).
Register	Registers a custom server control or a user control to be used within an ASP.NET page.

The **Page** Directive

The Page directive is used to specify page-related attributes that control how an ASP.NET page is compiled and executed. An ASP.NET page can have only one Page directive. Also, the keyword Page is optional in a Page directive. Table 2.4 lists the various attributes of the Page directive.

Table 2.4 Attributes of the Page Directive	
Attribute	**Description**
AspCompat	Indicates whether the page is to be executed on a Single-Threaded Apartment (STA) thread model for backward compatibility. The default value is **false**.
AutoEventWireUp	Indicates whether ASP.NET should automatically connect methods with specific names, such as **Page_Init()**, **Page_Load()**, and so on, with the page events. The default value is **true**. However, for Web pages created using Visual Studio .NET, the default value is **false**.
Buffer	Indicates whether the HTTP response buffer is enabled. The default value is **true**.
ClassName	Specifies the name for the dynamically generated class file for the ASPX page.
ClientTarget	Represents the target user agent (such as Mozilla/4.0) or alias (such as IE4) according to which the ASP.NET page should be rendered.
CodePage	Indicates the culture codepage value for the ASP.NET page. Supports any valid codepage value. For example, the value **932** specifies a Japanese codepage.
CompilerOptions	Indicates the compiler options and switches to be passed to the language compiler.
ContentType	Indicates the MIME type for the page response.
Culture	Indicates the culture setting for the page and supports any valid culture string, such as **en-US**, **en-GB**, and so on.
Debug	Indicates whether the compilation should include debug symbols. The default value is **false**.
Description	Represents the description of the page. The page compilers ignore this attribute.
EnableSessionState	Indicates whether the session state is enabled (**true**), read-only (**ReadOnly**), or disabled (**false**) for the page. The default value is **true**.

(continued)

Table 2.4 Attributes of the Page Directive *(continued)*	
Attribute	**Description**
EnableViewState	Indicates whether the view state is maintained for the page and its container controls. The default value is **true**.
EnableViewStateMac	Indicates whether the view state should be verified against Machine Authentication Check (MAC) to ensure that the view state is not tampered with.
ErrorPage	Specifies the error page where the user is redirected whenever an unhandled exception occurs in the page.
Explicit	Ignored when the **Language** attribute is **C#**.
Inherits	Represents the name of the code-behind class that contains code for the ASPX page and from which the dynamically generated class inherits.
Language	Represents any .NET programming language used for inline coding in the page.
LCID	Defines the 32-bit locale identifier for code in the page.
ResponseEncoding	Defines the response encoding for the page, such as **UTF7Encoding**, **UTF8Encoding**, **ASCIIEncoding**, **UnicodeEncoding**, and so on.
Src	Represents the source filename of the code-behind class that is dynamically compiled when the Web page is requested. Visual Studio .NET does not use this attribute because it precompiles the code-behind class.
SmartNavigation	Indicates whether smart navigation is enabled for the page. The smart navigation feature preserves the scroll position and element focus whenever the page is refreshed. The default value is **false**.
Strict	Ignored when the **Language** attribute is **C#**.
Trace	Indicates whether page-level tracing is enabled. The default value is **false**.
TraceMode	Indicates how trace messages are to be displayed when tracing is enabled. The default value is **SortByTime**, and the other possible value is **SortByCategory**.
Transaction	Indicates whether transactions are supported on the page. The default value is **Disabled**, and the other possible values are **NotSupported**, **Supported**, **Required**, and **RequiresNew**.
UICulture	Indicates the culture setting for the user interface of a page. Supports any valid culture string, such as **en-US**, **en-GB**, and so on.
WarningLevel	Specifies the warning level at which page compilation should be stopped. The possible values are from **0** to **4**.

The following example demonstrates how you can display information related to the execution of a page using the Trace attribute of the Page directive:

1. Add a new text file to project 315C02, and name the text file **Example2_2.aspx.**

2. Switch to the HTML view and add the following code to the Example2_2.aspx file:

```
<%@ Page Language="C#" Trace="true"%>
<html>
<body>
Trace Information
</body>
</html>
```

3. View Example2_2.aspx in the browser. Trace information enables you to analyze the execution information for a Page request.

The process of displaying execution information for an ASP.NET page is also called *tracing*. Various sections in the tracing information display a wealth of information about the page execution.

Event Handling

When you perform an action with an object, the object in turn raises events in the application. Clicking a button, for example, generates an event. Not all events are triggered by user actions, however. Changes in the environment—such as the arrival of an email message, modifications to a file, change in time, and completion of program execution—also trigger events.

Handling Events by Overriding the Virtual, Protected Method of the Base Class

When an ASP.NET page is dynamically compiled, it inherits from the Page class.

The following example demonstrates event handling by overriding the virtual, protected method of the base class:

1. Add a new text file to project 315C02 and name it **Example2_3.aspx.**

2. Switch to the HTML view and add the following code to the Example2_3.aspx file:

```
<%@ Page Language="c#"%>
<html><body>
```

```
<script runat="server">
    protected override void OnLoad(EventArgs e)
    {
        Response.Write(
            "Message from OnLoad() method.<br>");
        base.OnLoad(e);
    }
    protected override void OnInit(EventArgs e)
    {
        Response.Write(
            "Message from OnInit() method.<br>");
        base.OnInit(e);
    }
    protected override void OnPreRender(EventArgs e)
    {
        Response.Write(
            "Message from OnPreRender() method.<br>");
        base.OnPreRender(e);
    }
</script>
<hr></body>
</html>
```

3. View `Example2_3.aspx` in your browser.

When an ASP.NET Page object is created, it invokes the `OnInit()`, `OnLoad()`, and `OnPreRender()` methods to raise the `Init`, `Load`, and `PreRender` events, respectively, in that order. You can write custom code in these methods in response to the specific events.

The predefined event handlers `OnInit()` and `OnLoad()` also bootstrap the event handling process for events (`Init`, `Load`, and so on) of the `Page` class. However, you need not program this functionality again because it is already programmed in the base class. But to ensure that the base class version of an overridden method is also invoked, you need to explicitly call the base class version of a method by using the `base.MemberName` syntax.

Handling Events by Attaching a Delegate

A *delegate* is a special class whose object is capable of storing references to methods with a particular prototype. These methods are nothing but the event handlers that need to be invoked in response to an event.

Using delegates to handle events is far more flexible because of the following reasons:

➤ Delegates allow you to attach a single event handler to several events. This technique eliminates extra coding efforts when you have to take similar actions when different events occur.

➤ Delegates allow you to dynamically add and remove event handlers for an event. You can also associate multiple event handlers for an event.

➤ The class that handles the event is not required to derive from the class that publishes an event.

The following example uses delegates to display messages when various events for a Page object are raised.

1. Add a new text file to project 315C02 and name it **Example2_4.aspx**.

2. Switch to the HTML view and add the following code to the Example2_4.aspx file:

```
<%@ Page Language="c#"%>
<html><body>
<script runat="server">
    protected void Example2_4_Load(
        Object o, EventArgs e)
    {
        Response.Write(
            "Message from Load event handler.<br>");
    }
    protected void Example2_4_Init(
        Object o, EventArgs e)
    {
        Response.Write(
            "Message from Init event handler.<br>");
    }
    protected void Example2_4_PreRender(
        Object o, EventArgs e)
    {
        Response.Write(
          "Message from PreRender event handler.<br>");
    }

    protected override void OnInit(EventArgs e)
    {
        this.Load += new EventHandler(
            Example2_4_Load);
        this.PreRender += new EventHandler(
            Example2_4_PreRender);
        this.Init += new EventHandler(
            Example2_4_Init);

        base.OnInit(e);
    }
</script>
<hr></body>
</html>
```

3. View Example2_4.aspx in your browser. When an ASP.NET page is loaded for the first time, the Init, Load, and PreRender events occur in order.

Why use the OnInit() method in code? You do so because writing code in the OnInit() method ensures that the code will be executed before any other processing on the page.

The crux of the event-handling technique used in the previous example lies in the first three lines of the `OnInit()` method. Each of these three lines works in the same way. Consider the first line:

```
this.Load += new EventHandler(Example2_4_Load);
```

This looks like a complex statement, but if you examine it carefully, you can see that there are three parts to it with the following roles:

➤ *The `Load` event is raised when an ASP.NET page is loaded*—A set of event handlers can be attached to an event, and when the event is fired, it invokes all the attached event handlers. An event handler can be attached to the `Load` event only through its delegate object. The `this` keyword qualifies the `Load` event for the current instance of the Web page.

➤ `Example2_4_Load` *is the name of the method responding to the `Load` event*— When a method name is used without any argument list, it works as a reference to the actual method definition.

➤ *The delegate type of the `Load` event is `EventHandler`*—You can add event handlers to a `Load` event only by adding new instances of the delegate to it. In the Visual Studio .NET documentation, the definition of the `EventHandler` delegate looks like this:

```
public delegate void EventHandler(
    object sender, EventArgs e);
```

This means that the `EventHandler` delegate is capable of storing references to any method that has a `void` return type and that accepts two arguments: the first one of type `System.Object` and the other one of type `EventArgs`. The signature of the `Example2_4_Load()` method matches the criteria of this delegate, and hence a reference to the `Example2_4_Load()` method can be stored in an instance of a delegate of type `EventHandler`.

When you have an instance of the `EventHandler` delegate, you can attach it to the event by using the `+=` operator. The `+=` operator ensures that, if any event handlers are already attached to this event by the base class, they remain in the list.

At a later stage, when the `Load` event is raised, the `Example2_4_Load()` method is invoked through its reference that is maintained by the delegate object.

Handling Events of the **Page** Class Through **AutoEventWireup**

ASP.NET supports an additional mechanism for handling events raised by the Page class. This technique is called as AutoEventWireup.

AutoEventWireup relies on using specific names for the event handlers of Page class events. The name has to be of the type Page_*EventName*(). For example, when handling the Init, Load, and PreRender events, the name of the event handlers should be Page_Init(), Page_Load(), and Page_PreRender(), respectively.

Event handling through AutoEventWireup works only when the AutoEventWireup attribute of the Page directive is true. The AutoEventWireup attribute is true by default, so if you don't specify this attribute in the Page directive, it's assumed true by ASP.NET.

The following example demonstrates the use of predefined event handlers to handle various events of the Page class:

1. Add a new text file to project 315C02 and name it **Example2_5.aspx**.

2. Switch to the HTML view and add the following code to the Example2_5.aspx file:

```
<!--Example2_5.aspx-->
<%@ Page Language="c#"%>
<html><body>
<script runat="server">
    protected void Page_Load(Object o, EventArgs e)
    {
        Response.Write(
            "Message from Load event handler.<br>");
    }
    protected void Page_Init(Object o, EventArgs e)
    {
        Response.Write(
            "Message from Init event handler.<br>");
    }
    protected void Page_PreRender(
        Object o, EventArgs e)
    {
        Response.Write(
          "Message from PreRender event handler.<br>");
    }
</script>
<hr></body>
</html>
```

3. View Example2_5.aspx in your browser. You should see results similar to Example2_4.aspx.

`AutoEventWireup` isn't as flexible as event handling through delegates because the page event handlers are required to have specific names. Therefore, `AutoEventWireup` is set to `false` when creating Web forms using Visual Studio .NET.

Separating User Interface from Business Logic

In the ASP.NET pages created so far, you likely noted that the C# code is interspersed between the HTML code. Mixing both HTML and ASP.NET code makes the Web pages difficult to understand, maintain, and debug. HTML code represents the user interface (UI) of the application, whereas the ASP.NET code defines the business logic for that page. These are two diverse ideas that usually need to be handled differently.

ASP.NET provides a mechanism to separate the UI portion of a Web page from the business logic. This mechanism is known as *code-behind*. To implement code-behind, you write all the UI-related code in one file (.aspx) and the business logic in another file (.cs for C#) and then link these two files using the `Page` directive in the ASPX page. The linking is provided in the ASPX page instead of the CS file because the user requests the ASPX page. When ASP.NET compiles the ASPX page, it examines the `Page` directive to locate the business logic associated with the UI in the ASPX page. You can use the `Page` directive in different ways to link the code to the UI.

Using Code-behind Without Precompilation

When you write both the UI and business logic in separate files, one way to link them is via the `Src` and `Inherits` attributes of the `Page` directive. The following example uses the code of the `Example2_1.aspx` file and converts it into the code-behind version. The UI is stored in `Example2_6.aspx`, and the code is stored in `TemperatureCB.cs`. Do the following:

  1. Add a new text file to Web project 315C02, and name it **Example2_6.aspx**. Switch to its HTML view and add the following code to the Web page:

```
<!--Example2_6.aspx -->
<%@ Page Language="C#"
     Inherits="Temperature.TemperatureCB"
     Src="TemperatureCB.cs"%>
<html>
<body>
    <h2>Fahrenheit to Celsius Conversion Chart</h2>
    <table border="2">
```

```
            <tr>
                <th>&deg; Fahrenheit</th>
                <th>&deg; Celsius</th>
            </tr>
            <%CreateTemperatureTable();%>
        </table>
    </body>
</html>
```

2. Right-click the project in the Solution Explorer, and then select Add, Add New Item. This opens the Add New Item dialog box. Select the Code File template and name the file **TemperatureCB.cs**.

3. Add the following code to the TemperatureCB.cs file:

```
//TemperatureCB.cs
namespace Temperature
{
    // Define TemperatureCB class
    public class TemperatureCB : System.Web.UI.Page
    {
        double ToCelsius(double f)
        {
            // Calculate the temperature in Celsius
            return  (5.0/9.0)*(f-32.0);
        }

        public void CreateTemperatureTable()
        {
            for (double f = 50.0; f<=100.0; f++)
                Response.Output.Write(
                  "<tr><td>{0}</td><td>" +
                  "{1:f}</td></tr>", f, ToCelsius(f));
        }
    }
}
```

4. Access the Properties Window for the TemperatureCB.cs file. Set the Build Action property to None; this restricts Visual Studio .NET from automatically compiling this file.

5. Select Debug, Run to view the Example2_6.aspx file in your browser.

The Page directive in the Example2_6.aspx file provides the linking mechanism for the UI and code-behind. The Inherits attribute specifies that when the ASPX page is dynamically compiled, it inherits its functionality (such as methods and properties) from the TemperatureCB class of the Temperature namespace. In addition, the Src attribute specifies that the source code for the TemperatureCB class is stored in the TemperatureCB.cs file.

Using Code-behind with Visual Studio .NET Web Forms

Web forms are the preferred way of creating ASP.NET pages using Visual Studio .NET. They provide three distinct benefits over simple ASP.NET pages:

➤ Support code-behind by separating UI from business logic

➤ Provide an event-based programming model for designing Web pages

➤ Support RAD tools, such as Visual Studio .NET

The following example demonstrates how to create a Web form using Visual Studio .NET for displaying a temperature-conversion chart:

1. Open the Solution Explorer window for project 315C02; right-click the project name and select Add, Add Web Form. In the Add New Item dialog box, name the file `Example2_7.aspx`.

2. The Web form is in Design view. In the background of the form, you see a message asking you to select between grid layout mode and flow layout mode. Open the Properties window by selecting View, Property Pages. Then, change the Page Layout property of Document to FlowLayout.

3. In the flow layout mode, type `Fahrenheit to Celsius Conversion Chart`. Then, select the text and change its block format to Heading 2 using the Block Format combo box on the formatting toolbar.

4. Select Table, Insert, Table. In the Insert Table dialog box, select options to make a table of size 1 row and 2 columns. Set the Width attribute to 200 pixels.

5. Switch to the HTML view of the `Example2_7.aspx` file, and modify the code in the `<TABLE>` tag as shown here:

```
<TABLE id="Table1" cellSpacing="1" cellPadding="1"
        width="200" border="1">
    <TR>
        <TD>&deg; Fahrenheit</TD>
        <TD>&deg; Celsius</TD>
    </TR>
    <%CreateTemperatureTable();%>
</TABLE>
```

6. Invoke the Solution Explorer, right-click `Example2_7.aspx`, and select View Code. This opens the code-behind file `Example2_7.aspx.cs`. Add the following code just above the Web Form Designer–generated code region:

```
double ToCelsius(double f)
{
    // Calculate and return the temperature in Celsius
    return  (5.0/9.0)*(f-32.0);
}

public void CreateTemperatureTable()
{
    for (double f = 50.0; f<=100.0; f++)
        Response.Output.Write("<tr><td>{0}</td><td>" +
            "{1:f}</td></tr>", f, ToCelsius(f));
}
```

7. In the Solution Explorer, right-click Example2_7.aspx and select Set As Start Page.

8. Compile the page by selecting Build, Build 315C02; then run the page by selecting Debug, Start Without Debugging. You should see that the temperature table is created just as in the case of earlier examples.

An ASP.NET Web form is made up of two distinct pieces:

➤ The UI piece stored in the ASPX page

➤ The business logic piece stored in a CS file

Analyzing the User Interface Piece of a Web Form

In the Example2_7.aspx file, the Page directive is written as follows:

```
<%@ Page language="c#"
        Codebehind="Example2_7.aspx.cs"
        AutoEventWireup="false"
        Inherits="_315C02.Example2_7" %>
```

This usage of the Page directive has two new attributes—AutoEventWireup and Codebehind. AutoEventWireup is used for event handling. Visual Studio .NET, by default, sets the AutoEventWireup attribute to false. The Codebehind attribute, on the other hand, is used by Visual Studio .NET to track the location of the source code of the code-behind file. ASP.NET does not understand the Codebehind attribute and therefore ignores it. This attribute does not play any role in the execution of the ASP.NET page.

 In the **Page** directive, when the name of the source code file is specified using the **Src** attribute, the source code file is dynamically compiled at runtime. However, the same does not hold true for the **Codebehind** attribute, which is necessary only for design-time support in Visual Studio .NET. The **Codebehind** attribute plays no role at runtime because it is not recognized by ASP.NET.

If you are handling events in your program by attaching delegates, set the **AutoEventWireup** attribute of the **Page** directive to **false**. If you keep it **true**, as the page runs, some of the event handlers might be called twice.

To understand why, assume that you want to handle the **Load** event for the **Page** object, so you create a method named **Page_Load()** and attach it to the **Load** event of the **Page** using a delegate object. Now, because the **AutoEventWireup** attribute is **true**, based on the name of the method, the ASP.NET page framework will automatically attach **Page_Load()** as an event handler for the **Load** event of the **Page**. This results in the registration of the same event handler twice—hence, the event handler will also be invoked twice when the event is raised.

It is for this reason that Visual Studio .NET by default always sets **AutoEventWireup** to **false**.

Analyzing the Business Logic Piece of a Web Form

When you analyze the file storing the business logic piece, `Example2_7.aspx.cs`.

The class definition for the `Example2_7` class looks like this:

```
public class Example2_7 : System.Web.UI.Page
{
   ...
}
```

In the `Example2_7.aspx.cs` file, you can also write this definition as

```
public class Example2_7 : Page
{
   ...
}
```

How does the compiler locate a class if its full namespace-qualified name is not provided?

Inclusion of these `using` directives directs the C# compiler to search for each class used in the code in the namespaces specified by the `using` directives. The compiler looks up each namespace one by one, and when it finds the given class in one of the namespaces, it internally replaces the reference of the class with `NamespaceName.ClassName` in the code.

Exam Prep Questions

Question 1

You are developing a Web form to display weather information. When a user requests the Web form, the form needs to do some initializations that will change the appearance of the form and assign values to some controls. Where should you put the code?

○ A. In the **InitializeComponent()** method

○ B. In the event handler for the **Load** event of the page

○ C. In the event handler for the **Init** event of the page

○ D. In the event handler for the **PreRender** event of the page

Answer B is correct. The most appropriate place to put these types of initialization is the Load event handler. Answer A is incorrect because the InitializeComponent() method is for the use of Visual Studio .NET, and you should not modify it on your own. Answer C is incorrect because the properties of the control are available only after the page has been initialized. Answer D is incorrect because, at this stage, the page is about to be rendered and any changes to the control's properties will not have a visible effect.

Question 2

You are developing a Web form using Visual Studio .NET and have placed the initialization code in the **Page_Load()** method of the form. You then attached this method to the **Load** event of the Web form. When you execute the program, you notice that the **Page_Load()** method is executing twice instead of just once. What should you do to correct this problem?

○ A. Set **AutoEventWireup** to **true** in the **Page** directive of the Web form.

○ B. Set **AutoEventWireup** to **false** in the **Page** directive of the Web form.

○ C. Set **SmartNavigation** to **true** in the **Page** directive of the Web form.

○ D. Set **SmartNavigation** to **false** in the **Page** directive of the Web form.

Answer B is correct. You should set AutoEventWireup to false. Answer A is incorrect because, when AutoEventWireup is set to true, ASP.NET automatically registers the Page_Load() method as an event handler for the Load event of the Page class. When you use Visual Studio .NET to attach Page_Load() with the Load event, Page_Load() is registered twice for the Load event. For this reason, Page_Load() is executing twice in your programs.

Answers C and D are incorrect because the SmartNavigation property of the Page class is used for other purposes, such as eliminating the flash caused by navigation and persisting the scroll position when moving from page to page during a page postback operation.

Question 3

One of your colleagues is designing a **Changed** event for a Web page. She complains to you that her code behaves abnormally, running fine some of the time and generating errors at other times. Part of her event handling code is as listed here (line numbers are for reference purpose only):

```
01: public delegate void ChangedEventHandler(
02:     object sender, ChangedEventArgs args);
03: public event ChangedEventHandler Changed;
04: protected virtual void OnChanged(
05:     ChangedEventArgs e)
06: {
07:         Changed(this, e);
08:}
```

Which of the following suggestions will solve her problem?

- ○ A. Replace line 7 with the following code:
    ```
    if (ChangedEventHandler != null)
        ChangedEventHandler(this, e);
    ```

- ○ B. Replace line 7 with the following code:
    ```
    if (ChangedEventHandler != null)
        Changed(this, e);
    ```

- ○ C. Replace line 7 with the following code:
    ```
    if (Changed != null)
        ChangedEventHandler(this, e);
    ```

- ○ D. Replace line 7 with the following code:
    ```
    if (Changed != null)
        Changed(this, e);
    ```

Answer D is correct. When the OnChange() method is called, it notifies all the registered objects about the Changed event. The method should first check whether the event object Changed is null. If it is null, it means that no objects have registered themselves with the event. Therefore, raising events this time will cause an error. Answers A, B, and C are incorrect because you should use Changed instead of ChangedEventHandler in the if statement. ChangedEventHandler is a delegate that defines the type of event, rather than the event itself.

Question 4

Your colleague is designing an event-driven Web page that the material management group of your company will use. She needs to handle an event named **LowInventory** in the Web page and change the color of the text to red whenever a **LowInventory** event is raised. She has written the following code in an ASP.NET Web form to attach an event handler with the **LowInventory** event:

```
protected override void OnInit(EventArgs e)
{
    this.LowInventory += new
        EventHandler(Inventory_LowInventory);
}
```

When she executes the page, she notes that although the **LowInventory** event is handled properly, other events that were previously raised by the page have stopped occurring. Which of the following options would you recommend to her to resolve this problem?

○ A. Change the method definition to

```
protected override void OnLoad(EventArgs e)
{
    this.LowInventory += new
        EventHandler(Inventory_LowInventory);
}
```

○ B. Change the method definition to

```
protected override void OnLoad(EventArgs e)
{
    this.LowInventory += new
        EventHandler(Inventory_LowInventory);
    base.OnInit(e);
}
```

○ C. Change the method definition to

```
protected override void OnInit(EventArgs e)
{
    this.LowInventory += new
        EventHandler(Inventory_LowInventory);
    base.OnInit(e);
}
```

○ D. Change the method definition to

```
protected override void OnInit(EventArgs e)
{
    this.LowInventory += new
        EventHandler(Inventory_LowInventory);
    base.OnLoad(e);
}
```

Answer C is correct. When you override methods of a base class, you should call the base class version of the same method. Otherwise, you will lose the functionality offered by the method of the base class. Answers A and B are incorrect because the `OnInit()` method—instead of the `OnLoad()` method—is appropriate for attaching a delegate for event handling. Answer D is incorrect because you should call the `OnInit()` method of the base class.

Question 5

You are developing a library of useful classes that you plan to sell over the Internet to other developers. In one of the classes, **CommercePage**, you have a method named **Render()**. You want users of the library to be able to change the definition of the **Render()** method from a class that derives from **CommercePage** to one that does not. You also do not want to make the **Render()** method visible to those classes that do not derive from **CommercePage**. Which of the following modifiers should be applied to the **Render()** method while defining it in the **CommercePage** class? (Select two.)

❑ A. **public**

❑ B. **protected**

❑ C. **virtual**

❑ D. **override**

Answers B and C are correct. If you want the derived classes to override a method of base class, that method should be declared with `protected` and `virtual` modifiers in the base class. Answer A is incorrect because the `public` modifier increases the visibility of a method to all the classes and not just the derived classes. Answer D is incorrect because `override` is used only in the derived class and not in the base class.

Question 6

You want to implement your Web page using the code-behind technique. You place the UI in a file named **WeatherPage.aspx** and the business logic in another file named **WeatherPage.aspx.cs**. The **WeatherPage.aspx.cs** file contains the definition of a class that derives from the **Page** class. You want to link the UI file with the code-behind file, but you do not want to compile the business logic before you deploy it on the Web server. Which of the following attributes will you use for the **Page** directive in the **WeatherPage.aspx** file? (Select two.)

❑ A. The **Src** attribute

❑ B. The **Inherits** attribute

❑ C. The **Codebehind** attribute

❑ D. The **ClassName** attribute

Answers A and B are correct. Because you do not want to precompile the business logic file before you deploy it to the Web server, you need to specify both the `Inherits` and `Src` attributes with the `Page` directive of the `WeatherPage.aspx` file. Answer C is incorrect because the `Codebehind` attribute is ignored by ASP.NET. Answer D is incorrect because the `ClassName` attribute is used to specify the class name for the page that will automatically be dynamically compiled when the page is requested.

Question 7

You are designing a Web application that contains several Web forms. One of the Web forms, **Catalog.aspx**, displays catalogs to the users and performs several actions based on user input. You have extensively used event handling to make **Catalog.aspx** responsive to the user. When **Catalog.aspx** is loaded, you need to invoke a method named **PerformInitializations()**. Which statement should you use in the Web form to achieve this?

- A. **this.Init = EventHandler(PerformInitializations);**
- B. **this.Init = new EventHandler(PerformInitializations);**
- C. **this.Load = new EventHandler(PerformInitializations);**
- D. **this.Load += new EventHandler(PerformInitializations);**

Answer D is correct. You want to invoke `PerformInitializations()` when the Web form is loaded, so you must attach to the `Load` event of the Web form. You also want the Web form to be responsive to any previously registered event, so you should use the `+=` operator to register this event handler. Answers A and B are incorrect because the `Init` event occurs before the `Load` event. Answer C is incorrect because using the `=` operator is destructive in the sense that it deletes all the previously attached event handlers to the `Load` event.

Question 8

You want to display values of C# expressions in an ASPX page. Which of the following types of code blocks would you use to enclose the expression in an ASPX file?

- A. **<script runat="server">...</script>**
- B. **<script>...</script>**
- C. **<%=...%>**
- D. **<form>...</form>**

Answer C is correct. Only two of the given choices execute code on the server side: the `<script runat="server">...</script>` block and the `<%=...%>` block. Therefore, you should display the values of C# expressions in the `<%=...%>` block because the statement included in this block is executed while the page is rendered. Answer A is incorrect because code written in this block is compiled using a language compiler and writing an expression by itself will possibly raise a compilation error. Answers B and D are incorrect because these statements are executed on the client side instead of the Web server.

Question 9

> You have developed a timesheet entry application that will be used by all employees in your company. You have used ASP.NET to develop this application and have deployed it on the company's Web server. What should all the employees of the company install on their computers before accessing the timesheet entry application?
>
> ○ A. .NET Framework Redistributable
>
> ○ B. .NET Framework SDK
>
> ○ C. Visual Studio .NET
>
> ○ D. A Web browser

Answer D is correct. Users accessing an ASP.NET Web application need only to have a Web browser on their computers. Answer A is incorrect because the .NET Framework Redistributable is required only on the Web server that executes the server-side ASP.NET code. Answers B and C are incorrect because these tools are required only on the developer machine— not on the deployment server or the user's machine.

Question 10

> You have created a Web page that users will use to register with the Web site. Inside the event handler for the **Load** event of the **Page**, you want to access the data entered by the users on the Web page. Which of the following properties of the **Page** class can give you access to this data?
>
> ○ A. **ClientTarget**
>
> ○ B. **Request**
>
> ○ C. **Response**
>
> ○ D. **Trace**

Answer B is correct. The Request property contains information about the current HTTP request, which contains all the data entered by the users on a Web page. Answer A is incorrect because the ClientTarget property is used to detect the browser capabilities. Answer C is incorrect because the Response property contains the response of the Web server with respect to the current Web request. Answer D is incorrect because the Trace property is used to display the execution details of a Web page.

Need to Know More?

 Albahari, Ben, Peter Drayton, and Brad Merrill. *C# Essentials, Second Edition.* Sebastopol, CA: O'Reilly, 2002.

 Chappell, David. *Understanding .NET.* Reading, MA: Addison-Wesley, 2002.

 Visit the Official Microsoft ASP.NET site at www.asp.net.

 Visit the .NET Framework Community Web site at www. gotdotnet.com.

 ECMA C# and CLI Standards Specifications, msdn. microsoft.com/net/ecma.

 ASP.NET Roadmap, http://support.microsoft.com?scid=kb; EN-US;305140.

 ASP.NET Page Framework Overview, http://support.microsoft. com?scid=kb;EN-US;305141.

 ASP.NET Support Center, http://support.microsoft. com?scid=fh;en-us;aspnet.

 The .NET Show, The .NET Framework, http://msdn.microsoft. com/theshow/Episode007.

 The .NET Show, Programming in C#, http://msdn.microsoft. com/theshow/Episode008.

 MSDN C# Seminars, http://msdn.microsoft.com/seminar/ mmcfeed/mmcdisplayfeed.asp?Lang=en&Product=103363&Audience= 100402.

 MSDN Magazine's ".NET Column," http://msdn.microsoft.com/ msdnmag/find/default.aspx?type=Ti&phrase=.NET Column.

Controls

. . . .

Terms you'll need to understand:

✓ Cascading Style Sheets
✓ Client-side event handling
✓ HTML controls
✓ HTML server controls
✓ Server-side event handling
✓ Validation controls
✓ Web server controls

Techniques you'll need to master:

✓ Knowing how to use the common HTML and Web forms controls available in the Visual Studio .NET toolbox
✓ Understanding how to handle events for Web forms controls and getting comfortable with client-side and server-side event handling techniques
✓ Understanding how to create controls dynamically
✓ Working thoroughly with validation Web server controls and answering questions that ask you to choose the most appropriate validation control for a given scenario
✓ Knowing how to create and apply Cascading Style Sheets for consistent formatting of Web pages

Controls are the building blocks of a GUI. In this chapter, you'll work with HTML controls, HTML server controls, Web server controls, and validation controls to create the user interface for a Web application. You will also learn about user controls, composite controls, and custom controls, which enable you to extend the existing controls to achieve custom functionality.

HTML Controls

HTML controls represent common HTML elements and are available through the HTML tab of the Visual Studio .NET toolbox. You can drag these controls to a Web form and set their properties in the Properties window. An HTML control, such as Text Field or Label, is converted to its appropriate HTML equivalent, such as the <INPUT> and <DIV> element, respectively, in the source code of the ASPX file. All the HTML controls are automatically placed inside an HTML <FORM> element.

HTML controls are only of little use in ASP.NET programs because they can't be accessed from the server-side code. ASP.NET provides two other sets of controls that are much better suited for server-side programming: HTML server controls and Web server controls.

HTML Server Controls

HTML server controls are similar to HTML controls with the added feature of server-side availability. You can convert any HTML control to run as an HTML server control by adding a runat="server" attribute to its declaration. You can accomplish the same task visually by right-clicking an HTML control and selecting Run As Server Control from the shortcut menu.

Web Server Controls

Web server controls provide a higher level of abstraction than HTML server controls because their object model matches closely with the .NET Framework rather than matching with the requirements of HTML syntax.

The Web server controls have several advanced features, including

➤ Web server controls provide a rich object model that closely matches with the rest of the .NET Framework.

➤ Some Web server controls provide richer functionality, such as the Calendar control, AdRotator control, and so on, not available with HTML controls.

➤ Web server controls have advanced features such as automatic browser detection, automatic postback, and event bubbling.

 Because Web server controls are specifically designed to integrate well with the ASP.NET programming model, Exam 70-315 is likely to focus more on Web server controls than on HTML and HTML server controls.

Web server controls are declared in code explicitly by prefixing the class name of the Web server control with the namespace asp and separating both with a colon (:), as well as including the runat="server" attribute in its definition. For example, a Label Web server control can be declared in code as <asp:Label runat="server"/>.

Most Web server controls derive their functionality from the WebControl class of the System.Web.UI.WebControls namespace.

Table 3.1 lists some of the important properties inherited by Web server controls that derive from the WebControl class.

Table 3.1 Important Properties of the System.Web.UI.WebControls.WebControl Class	
Property	**Description**
AccessKey	Represents the single character keyboard shortcut key for quick navigation to the Web server control. The focus is moved to the Web server control when the Alt key and the key assigned to this property are pressed.
BackColor	Specifies the background color of the Web server control.
BorderColor	Specifies the border color of the Web server control.
BorderStyle	Specifies the border style of the Web server control. The possible values are defined in the **BorderStyle** enumeration values; they are **Dotted**, **Dashed**, **Double**, **Inset**, **NotSet**, **None**, **OutSet**, **Groove**, **Solid**, and **Ridge**.
BorderWidth	Specifies the border width of the Web server control.
Controls	Represents the collection of controls added to the Web server control as child controls. The **WebControl** class inherits this property from the **Control** class.
CssClass	Represents the CSS class in which the Web server control is rendered.
Enabled	Indicates whether the Web server control is enabled to receive focus.

(continued)

Table 3.1 Important Properties of the System.Web.UI.WebControls.WebControl Class (continued)	
Property	Description
EnableViewState	Indicates whether view state is enabled for the Web server control. The **WebControl** class inherits this property from the **Control** class.
Font	Specifies a **FontInfo** object that represents the font properties of a Web server control.
ForeColor	Specifies the color of text in the Web server control.
Height	Specifies the height of the Web server control.
ID	Specifies an identifier for the Web server control. The **WebControl** class inherits this property from the **Control** class.
Parent	Represents the parent control of the Web server control. The **WebControl** class inherits this property from the **Control** class.
Style	Specifies the collection of CSS properties applied to the Web server control.
TabIndex	Specifies the tab order of a Web server control. A negative value removes the control from the tab order.
ToolTip	Specifies the pop-up text displayed by the Web server control when the mouse hovers over it.
Visible	Indicates whether the Web server control is visible on the rendered page. The **WebControl** class inherits this property from the **Control** class.
Width	Specifies the width of the Web server control.

Common Web Server Controls

This section discusses some simple but commonly used controls available in the Visual Studio .NET toolbox. These controls are simple because they are usually rendered as single HTML elements and have only a few properties. Later in this chapter, you will learn about some advanced controls that provide myriad properties and render big chunks of HTML code.

Label Controls

A Label control is used to display read-only information to the user, label other controls, and provide the user with any useful messages or statistics. It exposes its text content through the Text property, which can be used to manipulate its text programmatically. The control is rendered as a <span> HTML element on the Web browser.

TextBox Controls

A TextBox control provides an area the user can use to input text. Depending on how you set the properties of this Web server control, you can either use it for multiline text input or use it like a password box that masks the characters entered by the user. Thus, this server control can be rendered as three types of HTML elements: <input type="text">, <input type="password">, and <textarea>. Table 3.2 summarizes the important members of the TextBox class.

Table 3.2 Important Members of the TextBox Class		
Member	**Type**	**Description**
AutoPostBack	Property	Indicates whether the Web form should be posted to the server automatically whenever the data in the text box is changed. It works only if the browser supports client-side scripting.
Columns	Property	Specifies the width, in characters, of the text box.
MaxLength	Property	Specifies the maximum number of characters allowed to be entered by the user. The default value is **0**. It works only if the **TextMode** property is not set to **MultiLine**.
ReadOnly	Property	Indicates whether the contents of the text box are read-only—that is, they cannot be modified. The default value is **false**.
Rows	Property	Specifies the height in characters of the multiline text box. The default value is **0**. It works only if the **TextMode** property is set to **MultiLine**.
Text	Property	Specifies the text contained in the text box.
TextChanged	Event	Occurs when the value of the **Text** property changes. **TextChanged** is the default event for the **TextBox** class.
TextMode	Property	Represents the type of the text box to be rendered in the Web page. It can be displayed in one of these **TextBoxMode** enumeration values: **MultiLine** (the text box can accept multiple lines of input), **Password** (a single-line text box with each character masked), and **SingleLine** (a single-line text box with normal text displayed).
Wrap	Property	Specifies whether the control can automatically wrap words to the next line. The default value is **true**. It works only if the **TextMode** property is set to **MultiLine**.

Image Controls

An Image Web server control displays images from bitmap, JPEG, PNG, and GIF files. The control is rendered as an `<img>` HTML element on the Web page. Table 3.3 summarizes the important properties of the Image class.

Table 3.3	Important Members of the **Image** Class
Property	**Description**
AlternateText	Specifies the text displayed in place of the **Image** Web server control when the image is being downloaded, the image is unavailable, or the browser doesn't support images. The specified text is also displayed as a ToolTip if the browser supports the ToolTip feature.
ImageAlign	Indicates the alignment of the **Image** Web server control relative to other elements on the Web page. It can be set to one of these **ImageAlign** enumeration values: **AbsBottom**, **AbsMiddle**, **Baseline**, **Bottom**, **Left**, **Middle**, **NotSet** (default value), **Right**, **TextTop**, and **Top**.
ImageUrl	Represents the URL (location) of the image the **Image** Web server control displays. The URL can be either relative or absolute.

Checkbox and RadioButton Controls

A CheckBox control enables the user to select one or more options from a group of options, and a group of RadioButton controls is used to select one out of several mutually exclusive options. If you want to place two groups of RadioButton controls on a form and have each group allow one selection, radio button controls of each group should individually set their GroupName property to indicate the group to which they belong. The check box and radio button Web server controls are rendered as `<input type="checkbox">` and `<input type="radio">` HTML elements on the Web page, respectively.

The RadioButton class inherits from the CheckBox class, and both of them share the same members—except the GroupName property available in the RadioButton class.

Table 3.4 summarizes the important members of the CheckBox and RadioButton classes.

Table 3.4	Important Members of the CheckBox and RadioButton Classes	
Member	**Type**	**Description**
AutoPostBack	Property	Indicates whether the Web form should be posted to the server automatically when the control is clicked. It works only if the browser supports client-side scripting.
Checked	Property	Returns **true** if the control has been checked. Otherwise, it returns **false**.
CheckedChanged	Event	Occurs every time a control is checked or unchecked. **CheckedChanged** is the default event for the **CheckBox** class.
Text	Property	Specifies the text displayed along with the control.
TextAlign	Property	Specifies the alignment of the text displayed along with the control. It can be one of the **TextAlign** enumeration values: **Left** (the text is displayed on the left of the control) or **Right** (by default, the text is displayed to the right of the control).

Button, LinkButton, and ImageButton Controls

A button is used to initiate a specific action when clicked by the user. Each of the three button controls is different in its appearance and therefore is rendered differently on the Web page. They include

➤ *Button*—This control is displayed as a push button on the Web page and is rendered as an `<input type="submit">` HTML element.

➤ *LinkButton*—This control is displayed as a hyperlink on the Web page and is rendered as an `<a>` HTML element.

➤ *ImageButton*—This control is displayed as an image button on the Web page and is rendered as an `<input type="image">` HTML element.

All three button Web server controls behave in the same way: They all post the form data to the Web server when they are clicked. However, the LinkButton control works only if client-side scripting is enabled in the Web browser.

Table 3.5 summarizes the important members that are applicable to the Button, LinkButton, and ImageButton classes.

Table 3.5 Important Members of the Button, LinkButton, and ImageButton Classes		
Member	**Type**	**Description**
CausesValidation	Property	Indicates whether the validation should be performed when the button control is clicked. Validation is discussed in detail later in this chapter.
Click	Event	Occurs when the button control is clicked. **Click** is the default event of all three classes. This event is mostly used for submit buttons.
Command	Event	Occurs when the button control is clicked. This event is mostly used for command buttons. The event handler receives an object of type **CommandEventArgs** that contains both the **CommandName** and **CommandArgument** properties containing event-related data.
CommandArgument	Property	Specifies the argument for a command. It works only if the **CommandName** property is set. The property is passed to the **Command** event when the button is clicked.
CommandName	Property	Specifies the command name for the button. The property is passed to the **Command** event when the button is clicked.
Text	Property	Specifies the text displayed on a button. The **ImageButton** class does not have this property.

By default, any type of button Web server control is a submit button. If you specify a command name via the CommandName property, the button control then becomes a command button.

A command button raises the Command event when it is clicked. The button passes the CommandName and CommandArgument properties encapsulated in a CommandEventArgs object to the event handlers. The Command button is useful when you want to pass some event-related information to the event handler.

The following example creates a Web form that uses some of the common Web server controls discussed in the previous sections. Do the following:

1. Launch Visual Studio .NET and create a new Visual C# Project based on the ASP.NET Web Application template. Specify the location of the project as `http://localhost/ExamCram/315C03`.

2. Add a new Web form to the project and name it `Example3_1.aspx`. Delete the default form, `WebForm1.aspx`, from the project.

3. Use the Web Forms controls to create a user interface similar to Figure 3.1.

Figure 3.1   **Example3_1.aspx** uses Web server controls to create the user interface.

4. Set the `ID` property of the Subscribe button to `btnSubscribe` and set the `ID` property of the Name text box to `txtName`.

5. Before the Name label and text box on the page, place a `Label` Web server control and set its `ID` property to `lblMessage`.

6. Double-click the Subscribe button. You are taken to Code view, where an event handler for the `btnSubscribe`'s `Click` event is added. Add the following code in the event handler:

```
private void btnSubscribe_Click(object sender, System.EventArgs e)
{
    // Display a personalized thank you message
    lblMessage.Text = txtName.Text +
        ", thank you for subscribing to \"" +
        ddlNewsletter.SelectedItem + "\".";
}
```

7. Run the project; then fill in details in the Web page and click the Subscribe button.

When you create a Web form, all the user interface elements are contained in the **<form runat="server">** control. The form, along with all its controls, is accessible to ASP.NET only when the **<form>** element has a **runat="server"** attribute attached to it. Only one **<form runat="server">** control can exist on a Web page.

You can note from the btnSubscribe_Click() method that Web server controls provide a very consistent model for programming. The text of the Label control can be accessed using the obvious Text property rather than the InnerText property, as is the case with HTML server controls.

Event Handling for Web Server Controls

The following list summarizes the features of event handling as it relates to Web server controls:

➤ *Intrinsic events*—Web server controls have a set of intrinsic events available to them. Some simple controls such as Button provide only two intrinsic events—Click and Command—whereas advanced controls such as DataGrid provide as many as nine intrinsic events.

➤ *Event arguments*—By convention, all events in the .NET Framework pass two arguments to event handlers—the object that raised the event and an object containing any event-specific information. Most events do not have any event-specific information; therefore, they just pass an object of type System.EventArgs as the second argument. Some Web server controls, however, pass event-specific data to their event handlers using a type extended from System.EventArgs. One such example is the ImageButton Web server control in which the second argument is of the type ImageClickEventArgs. The ImageClickEventArgs objects encapsulate information about the coordinates at which the user has clicked the ImageButton.

➤ *AutoPostBack*—Usually, the change events of server controls are cached and fired on the Web server at a later stage when the page is posted back as a result of a Click event of button controls. Some Web server controls, such as DropDownList, CheckBox, and so on, have a property named AutoPostBack. When this property is set to true, it causes an immediate postback of the page when the value of the control is changed. This enables the Web server to immediately respond to change events without waiting for a Click event to cause a page postback. In HTML, only a few controls inherently submit a form; to enable other controls to cause a postback, ASP.NET attaches a small client script with the control.

➤ *Bubbled events*—Some advanced Web server controls, such as DataGrid, can also contain other controls (such as a button). DataGrid controls usually display dynamically generated data, and if each row of the DataGrid contains a button, you might have a variable number of button controls. Writing an individual event handler for each button control in this case is a tedious process. To simplify event handling, controls such as DataGrid support *bubbling* of events. In bubbling, all events raised at the level of child control are bubbled up to the container control, where the container control can raise a generic event in response to the child events.

Client-side Event Handling for Web Server Controls

ASP.NET provides a set of validation controls that enable you to easily validate user input without manual client-side programming or frequent round trips to the server. However, you might still want to use some amount of client-side programming in your code, especially to handle frequently occurring events such as MouseMove or KeyPress.

ASP.NET already uses client-side event handling to perform automatic postback operations; therefore, the preferred way to add client-side event handling code for Web server controls is via the Attributes property of the Web server controls. For example, the following code fragment attaches the someClientCode() client-side method to the onMouseOver attribute of the btnSubmit button:

```
btnSubmit.Attributes.Add("onMouseOver", "someClientCode();")
```

The List Controls

The category of list controls includes the DropDownList, ListBox, CheckBoxList, and RadioButtonList controls. These controls display a list of items from which the user can select, and they inherit from the abstract base ListControl class. Table 3.6 summarizes the important members of the ListControl class with which you should be familiar.

Table 3.6	Important Members of the ListControl Class	
Member	**Type**	**Description**
AutoPostBack	Property	Indicates whether the Web form should be posted to the server automatically whenever the list selection is changed. It works only if the browser supports client-side scripting.
Items	Property	Specifies a collection of items in the list control.
SelectedIndex	Property	Specifies an index of the currently selected item. The default value is **–1**, which means that no item is selected in the list control.
SelectedIndexChanged	Event	Occurs when the **SelectedIndex** property changes. **SelectedIndexChanged** is the default event for the list controls.
SelectedItem	Property	Specifies the currently selected item.

Although these controls inherit their basic functionality from the ListControl class, they display lists of items in different styles and enable single or multiple modes of selection.

A DropDownList Web server control allows you to select only a single item from the drop-down list. This Web server control is rendered as a <select> HTML element, and its items are added as <option> elements in the <select> element.

 The default value of the **SelectedIndex** property of the **ListControl** object is **-1**, which indicates that no item is selected in the list control. However, the **DropDownList** control overrides this property and sets the default value to **0**, which indicates the first item in the list. This ensures that an item is always selected in the drop-down list.

A ListBox Web server control allows you to select single or multiple items from the list of items displayed in the list box. It is rendered as a <select> or <select multiple="multiple"> HTML element depending on whether single or multiple selection is allowed. The items are added as <option> elements in the <select> element. The ListBox class adds two more properties to enable it to select multiple items, as shown in Table 3.7.

Table 3.7   Important Members of the ListBox Class

Property	Description
Rows	Represents the number of rows to be displayed in the list box. The default value is **4**. The value of this property must be between **1** and **2000**.
SelectionMode	Indicates the mode of selection allowed in the list box. It can be one of the **ListSelectionMode** enumeration values: **Multiple** or **Single** (default).

The CheckBoxList and RadioButtonList Web server controls display lists of check boxes and radio buttons, respectively. The CheckBoxList and RadioButtonList controls render each list item as <input type="checkbox"> and <input type="radio"> HTML elements, respectively. The list items are displayed in a table or without a table structure, depending on the layout selected.

Table 3.8 summarizes the important properties of the CheckBoxList and RadioButtonList classes that relate to the formatting capabilities of these Web server controls.

Table 3.8 Important Formatting Properties of the CheckBoxList and RadioButtonList Classes	
Property	**Description**
CellPadding	Specifies the distance in pixels between the border and the contents (that is, check box or radio button) of the list control.
CellSpacing	Specifies the distance in pixels between the items (that is, check box or radio button) of the list control.
RepeatColumns	Specifies the number of columns to be displayed in the list control.
RepeatDirection	Specifies the direction of layout of the items in the list control. It can be one of the **RepeatDirection** enumeration values: **Horizontal** or **Vertical** (default).
RepeatLayout	Specifies the layout method of the items in the list control. It can be one of the **RepeatLayout** enumeration values: **Flow** (the items are not displayed in a table structure) or **Table** (default; the items are displayed in a table structure).
TextAlign	Specifies the alignment of the text displayed along with the individual items in the list control. It can be one of the **TextAlign** enumeration values: **Left** (the text is displayed on the left of the item control) and **Right** (default; the text is displayed on the right of the item control).

List controls such as **ListBox** and **CheckBoxList** enable you to make multiple selections from the list controls. When these controls allow multiple selections, the **SelectedIndex** and **SelectedItem** properties return the index of the first selected item and the first selected item, respectively. You must iterate through the **ListItemCollection** controls available via the **Items** property and check whether each item's **Selected** property is **true** to retrieve the items selected by the user.

This example shows how to use the list controls:

1. In the project 315C03, add a new Web form named `Example3_2.aspx`.

2. Add a `Label` control on the form and change its `Text` property to `Tourist Interests Survey`. Set the font size to `Large`. Then add another `Label` control and change its `Text` property to `Which national parks are you interested in visiting?`. Set the font size to `Medium`.

3. Drag a `ListBox` control onto the form and change its `ID` to `lbParks`. Using the Properties window, select the `Items` property and click the ellipse button (...). This opens the ListItem Collection Editor. Enter names for a few national parks. Set the `SelectionMode` property of the `lbParks` list box to `Multiple`.

4. Drag a CheckBoxList control (cblActivities) and a RadioButtonList control (rblVacation) to the form. Set the RepeatColumn property for both controls to 2. Add a couple of label controls and arrange the controls as shown in Figure 3.2.

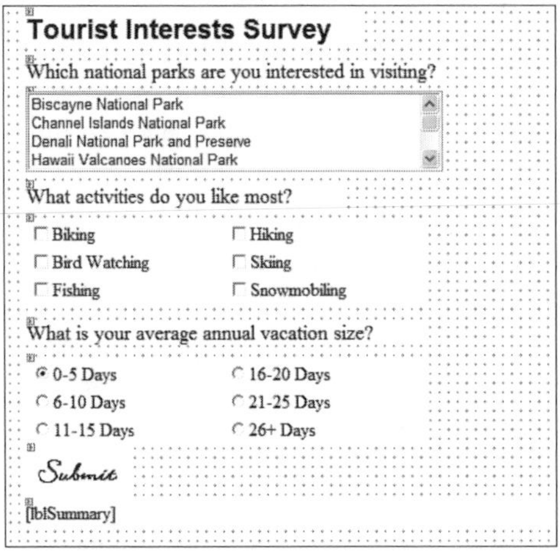

Tourist Interests Survey

Which national parks are you interested in visiting?

Biscayne National Park
Channel Islands National Park
Denali National Park and Preserve
Hawaii Valcanoes National Park

What activities do you like most?

☐ Biking   ☐ Hiking
☐ Bird Watching   ☐ Skiing
☐ Fishing   ☐ Snowmobiling

What is your average annual vacation size?

◉ 0-5 Days   ○ 16-20 Days
○ 6-10 Days   ○ 21-25 Days
○ 11-15 Days   ○ 26+ Days

Submit

[lblSummary]

Figure 3.2   **Example3_2.aspx** uses list controls to accept user input.

5. Place an ImageButton control (ibSubmit) on the Web form and set its ImageUrl property to a GIF file representing a button. Place a Label control (lblSummary) at the bottom of the form (refer to Figure 3.2).

6. Add the following using directive at the top of the code-behind file:

```
using System.Text;
```

7. Double-click the ibSubmit image button to attach an event handler with its Click event. Add the following code to the event handler:

```
private void ibSubmit_Click(object sender,
    System.Web.UI.ImageClickEventArgs e)
{
    // Create a StringBuilder object that you
    // will use to efficiently concatenate messages
    StringBuilder sb = new StringBuilder();
    sb.Append("<h3>Thank You! The following data ");
    sb.Append(" entered by you has been recorded</h3>");
    sb.Append("<h4>Selected Parks: </h4>");

    // Because the SelectionMode property of lbParks is Multiple,
    // you need to iterate through its Items collection to
    // individually gather the selected national parks
    foreach (ListItem li in lbParks.Items)
        if (li.Selected)
            sb.Append(String.Format("{0}<BR>", li.Text));
```

```
    sb.Append("<h4>Selected Activities: </h4>");
    // Multiple activities can be selected by the user. Therefore,
    // you need to iterate through the complete Items collection to
    // individually find the selected activities
    foreach (ListItem li in cblActivities.Items)
        if (li.Selected)
            sb.Append(String.Format("{0}<BR>", li.Text));

    sb.Append("<h4>Average Vacation Size: </h4>");
    // Only one item can be selected from a RadioButtonList
    sb.Append(rblVacation.SelectedItem.Text);

    // Copy the messages to the bottom label control
    lblSummary.Text = sb.ToString();
}
```

8. Set `Example3_2.aspx` as the start page of the project, build the project, and then run it. Fill the form and submit the details by clicking the Submit image button. You should see a summary message displaying all the selected items at the bottom of the form.

In the previous example, to find the selected items in the list controls in which multiple items can be selected, you must iterate through the `ListItemCollection` object corresponding to the list control. For those controls in which only single selection is allowed, you can simply use the `SelectedItem` property to find the selected item.

PlaceHolder and Panel Controls

A `PlaceHolder` Web server control enables you to reserve an area on a Web page. It also allows you to add controls dynamically in a Web page at the area it has reserved.

The `PlaceHolder` Web server control inherits from the `System.Web.UI.Control` class and does not share the common properties that Web server controls from the `WebControl` class do. The control also does not define any new properties, events, or methods and does not render any HTML element for itself.

A `Panel` Web server control acts as a container for other controls in the Web page and can be used to organize controls in the Web page. It can be used to hide or show controls contained in the panel in the Web page. Controls can also be added programmatically to the panel. The `Panel` Web server control is rendered as a `<div>` HTML element on the Web page.

This example shows how to use a `Panel` control to load controls dynamically on a form at runtime:

1. Add a new Web form (`Example3_3.aspx`) to the project.

2. Place a `Label` control on the form. Set its `Text` property to `Travel Expense Calculator` and set the font size to Medium. Place a horizontal rule after the label.

3. Place two more `Label` controls on the form, setting their `Text` properties to `Associate Name` and `Number of days`, respectively. Add a `TextBox` control and set its `ID` property to `txtName`.

4. Add a `DropDownList` control, setting its `ID` property to `ddlDays` and its `AutoPostBack` property to `true`. Use the ListItem Collection Editor to add values from `0` to `5` in the drop-down list.

5. At the bottom of the form, place a `Panel` control and set its `ID` property to `pnlDynamic`.

6. Switch to Code view and add the following code in the `Page_Load()` event handler:

```
// Use the Page_Load event to load the dynamically created controls
// so that they are available prior to rendering
private void Page_Load(object sender, System.EventArgs e)
{
    // Get the value selected by the user in the drop-down list
    int intDays = Convert.ToInt32(ddlDays.SelectedItem.Value);
    // Create text boxes to allow entering the travel expenses
    for (int i = 1; i <= intDays; i++)
    {
        LiteralControl lcExpenseCaption = new LiteralControl();
        lcExpenseCaption.Text =
          String.Format("Travel Expense for Day-{0} ", i);
        // Create a text box control
        TextBox txtExpense = new TextBox();
        // Set the ID property of the text box
        txtExpense.ID = String.Format("Expense{0}", i);
        HtmlControl lcBreak = new  HtmlGenericControl("br");
        pnlDynamic.Controls.Add(lcExpenseCaption);
        // Add the text box to the panel. if you omit this step,
        // the text box is created but not displayed
        pnlDynamic.Controls.Add(txtExpense);
        pnlDynamic.Controls.Add(lcBreak);
    }
    // Display a link button that allow users to post
    // the expenses after they have entered the data
    if(intDays>0)
    {
        LinkButton lbtnSubmit = new LinkButton();
        lbtnSubmit.Text = "Submit Expenses";
        // Add an event handler to the dynamically created link button
        lbtnSubmit.Click += new EventHandler(lbtnSubmit_Click);
        pnlDynamic.Controls.Add(lbtnSubmit);
        HtmlControl lcBreak = new HtmlGenericControl("br");
        pnlDynamic.Controls.Add(lcBreak);
    }
}
```

7. Add another method that handles the `Click` event for the dynamic link button:

```
// Handles the Click event for the dynamically created link button
private void lbtnSubmit_Click(object sender,  System.EventArgs e)
{
    double dblExpenses = 0;
    int intDays = Convert.ToInt32(ddlDays.SelectedItem.Value);
    // Find sum of all expenses
    for (int i = 1; i <= intDays; i++)
    {
        // Find control in the collection of controls
        TextBox txtExpense = (TextBox)
            pnlDynamic.FindControl(String.Format("Expense{0}", i));
        dblExpenses += Convert.ToDouble(txtExpense.Text);
    }
    // Display the results
    Label lblResults = new Label();
    lblResults.Text = String.Format("{0}, a sum of ${1} has been " +
        "credited to your account.", txtName.Text, dblExpenses);
    pnlDynamic.Controls.Add(lblResults);
}
```

8. Set `Example3_3.aspx` as the start page and run the project. Enter a name for the associate and select 3 from the drop-down list. You'll see that three text box controls have been created for you to enter travel expenses. A link button enables you to post the expenses to the Web server. Enter some values for the expenses and click the link button. Note that the expenses were all summed and a message is displayed.

Because the Web pages are re-created with each request, you should always use the **Load** event handler for loading the controls dynamically on the Web page. This event handler ensures that the controls are created each time the page is loaded. In addition, ASP.NET automatically maintains state for the controls that are loaded dynamically.

After you create a control, you must remember to add it to one of the container controls on the Web page. If you just create a control but forget to add it to the container control, your control will not be rendered in the page.

The **AdRotator** Control

The `AdRotator` Web server control provides a convenient mechanism for displaying advertisements randomly on a Web page. The advertisements are detailed in an Extensible Markup Language (XML) file. The following listing shows a partial sample advertisement file:

```
<?xml version="1.0" ?>
<Advertisements>
    <Ad>
        <ImageUrl>que.gif</ImageUrl>
        <NavigateUrl>http://www.quepublishing.com
        </NavigateUrl>
        <AlternateText>Que Publishing</AlternateText>
        <Impressions>40</Impressions>
        <Keyword>Books</Keyword>
        <Specialization>Certification Books</Specialization>
    </Ad>
    ...
</Advertisements>
```

The advertisements are individually stored in `<Ad>` elements, which specify the information for each advertisement by a collection of elements.

The `AdRotator` control is rendered as an `<a>` anchor HTML element with an embedded `<img>` image HTML element for displaying the image on the Web page. Table 3.9 summarizes the important members of the `AdRotator` class with which you should be familiar.

Table 3.9 Important Members of the AdRotator Class		
Member	**Type**	**Description**
AdCreated	Event	Occurs when the **AdRotator** control is created.
AdvertisementFile	Property	Specifies the location of an XML file that stores the advertisement information.
KeywordFilter	Property	Specifies the keyword (group name) on which the advertisements need to be filtered. The property relates to the **<Keyword>** element in an **<Ad>** element in the advertisement file.
Target	Property	Specifies the target window or frame in which the contents of the linked Web page will be displayed when the **AdRotator** control is clicked. Some of the possible values are **_blank** (new window), **_parent** (parent frame set), **_self** (current position in the window), and **_top** (current window).

When the **KeywordFilter** property of an **AdRotator** control is set to a keyword that does not correspond to any **<Keyword>** element in the XML advertisement file, **AdRotator** displays a blank image in place of the advertisement and a trace warning is generated.

The AdCreated event passes an object of type AdCreatedEventArgs that contains event-related data. The object consists of the following four properties: AdProperties, AlternateText, ImageUrl, and NavigateUrl. AdProperties contains a collection of key/value pairs representing all the elements (including custom) defined for the current <Ad> element.

The **Calendar** Control

The Calendar Web server control displays a calendar on the Web page and enables you to select a day, week, month, or range of days. You can customize the appearance of the control and even add custom content for each day. The control generates events when a selection changes or the visible month is changed in the Calendar control. The Calendar control is rendered as a <table> HTML element on the Web page. Please refer to the Microsoft .NET Framework documentation for the complete list of properties and events for the Calendar control.

User Input Validation

ASP.NET provides a set of Web server controls called *validation controls* that provide sophisticated validation on both the client side and the server side depending on the validation settings and the browser's capabilities.

ASP.NET ensures that validations are performed on the server side even if they were already performed on the client side. This ensures that validations are not bypassed if a malicious user circumvents client-side validation. If the client-side validation fails, the server-side validation is never performed.

ASP.NET validation controls derive their basic functionality from the BaseValidator abstract class available in the System.Web.UI.WebControls. Table 3.10 lists some of the important members of the BaseValidator class.

Table 3.10	Important Members of the BaseValidator Class	
Member	**Type**	**Description**
ControlToValidate	Property	Specifies the **ID** of the input server control that needs to be validated. This property should be passed a valid **ID**. However, it can be empty for a custom validation control.
Display	Property	Specifies how to display the inline error message contained in the **Text** property. It can be any of the **ValidatorDisplay** enumeration values, including **Dynamic** (the space is dynamically added), **None** (the message is never displayed), and **Static** (the space is occupied when the validation control is rendered).
EnableClientScript	Property	Indicates whether the client-side validation is enabled. The default is **true**.
Enabled	Property	Indicates whether the validation control is enabled. If **false**, the validation is never performed.
ErrorMessage	Property	Represents the error message to be displayed by the **ValidationSummary** control when the validation fails. If the **Text** property is not set, this message is displayed inline.
ForeColor	Property	Specifies the foreground color in which the message is displayed when the validation fails. The default value is **Color.Red**.
IsValid	Property	Indicates whether the input control passes the validation.
Text	Property	Specifies the text of the error message displayed by the validation control inline.
Validate()	Method	Performs the validation on the associated input control and then updates the **IsValid** property with the result of the validation.

When you set the **Enabled** property to **false** for a validation control, the validation on the control is performed neither at the client side nor at the server side. If you want to disable validation only at the client side, you should set the **EnableClientScript** property of the validation control to **false**.

When the **CausesValidation** property is set to **false**, it prevents client-side and server-side validations from occurring. This property is ideal for the Cancel and Reset buttons in a Web page. The **Button**, **LinkButton**, **ImageButton**, **HtmlButton**, **HtmlInputButton**, and **HtmlInputImage** controls contain this property.

Using the **Page.Validate()** Method and **Page.IsValid** Property

As you can see in Table 3.10, each validation control maintains an IsValid property that indicates the status of the validation test. The Page control that hosts the Web controls also contains a property called IsValid that indicates the status of the validation for the whole page. When all the validation controls on the Web form set their IsValid properties to true, Page.IsValid also becomes true. If the validation fails on any of the validation controls, Page.IsValid is false.

The Page class maintains a collection of the validation controls on a Web page that can be accessed through its Validators property. The Page class also contains a Validate() method that invokes the Validate() method of all the validation controls in the page. The Page.Validate() method is used to perform validation programmatically on all the validation controls of a Web page.

ASP.NET validation is performed after page initialization—that is, after the Load event of the Page is raised but before the event-handling code is called. Therefore, you cannot know the status of the validation test in the Page_Load() event handler, and the data posted from the client should not be accessed at this stage of page processing. You should always try to use data posted from the client in event-handling code such as the Click event of the Button control. However, if you need to access client-posted data in the Page_Load() event handler, you can do so by calling the Page.Validate() method.

Validation Web Server Controls

ASP.NET provides the following validation controls that derive their functionality from the BaseValidator class: RequiredFieldValidator, RegularExpressionValidator, RangeValidator, CompareValidator, and CustomValidator.

These validation controls are usually associated with the input server controls on which the validation needs to be performed. For validation to work properly, the validation control and the input server control should be placed in the same container control. The validation controls are usually placed next to the associated input control so that you can display error messages or indicators next to the input control. You can associate any number of validation controls with an input server control. For example, the Date of Hire input field in an Add Employee form cannot be left empty (validated through the RequiredFieldValidator control) and should be less than or equal to the current date (validated through the CompareValidator control). You'll learn more about the validation Web server controls in the following sections.

The RequiredFieldValidator Control

The RequiredFieldValidator control can be used to check whether the input control contains an entry. It makes the associated input control a required field in the Web page and ensures that some input data is passed to it. The control also trims whitespace prior to checking for the required field entry.

The RequiredFieldValidator control contains a special property called InitialValue that can be passed the initial value of the associated input control. During validation, if the input control's validation property contains the same initial value or is empty, it sets IsValid to false, indicating that the validation failed. For example, a drop-down list might allow users to select a state and when the page loads, its initial value could be Select a State. If a RequiredFieldValidator control is associated with the drop-down list control, its InitialValue property can be set to the same initial value of the drop-down list—Select a State. When the validation occurs, the validation control ensures that the item selected in the drop-down list is not the item set in the InitialValue property of the validation control.

 The **RequiredFieldValidator** control is the only validation control that ensures that the associated input control is a required field. Other validation controls assume the input control's data to be valid if it is left blank.

The RegularExpressionValidator Control

The RegularExpressionValidator control checks whether the associated input control's validation property matches a specified pattern. This pattern is specified by the ValidationExpression property using a regular expression. If you are not familiar with regular expressions, you can find more information in the Microsoft .NET Framework documentation.

The **RangeValidator** Control

The RangeValidator control is used to check whether the input control contains a value in the specified range. You can check the range of values against different data types such as String, Date, and Integer.

Table 3.11 shows the important properties of the RangeValidator class.

Table 3.11	Important Properties of the RangeValidator Class
Property	**Description**
MaximumValue	Specifies the upper value of the validation range.
MinimumValue	Specifies the lower value of the validation range.
Type	Specifies the data type to be used when comparing the data.

The **CompareValidator** Control

The CompareValidator control is used to compare the input server control's value against another value. The CompareValidator control can compare against a value specified to the validator control or against the value of another input control. The comparison can be made with different comparison operators such as equal, greater than, and so on. A special comparison operation can be used to verify that the associated input control's value is in the specified data type. You can make comparisons against various data types, such as String, Date, Integer, and so on.

Table 3.12 shows the important properties of the CompareValidator class.

Table 3.12	Important Properties of the CompareValidator Class
Property	**Description**
ControlToCompare	Specifies the input server control against whose value the associated input control is to be validated.
Operator	Specifies the comparison operation to be performed.
Type	Specifies the data type to be used when comparing the data.
ValueToCompare	Specifies the value against which the associated input control is to be validated.

If both the **ControlToCompare** and **ValueToCompare** properties are set for a CompareValidator control, the **ControlToCompare** property takes precedence.

If the **Operator** property of a **CompareValidator** is set to **DataTypeCheck**, the **ControlToCompare** and **ValueToCompare** properties are ignored. The validator control tries to convert the input control value to the data type specified by the **Type** property and sets the **IsValid** property with the result.

This example shows how to use the RangeValidator and CompareValidator controls on a Web form:

1. Add a new Web form (Example3_4.aspx) to the project.

2. Insert a table by selecting Table, Insert, Table. This opens the Insert Table dialog box. Create a table of two rows and two columns with a border size of 0 in the form. Add two Label controls and two TextBox controls (txtDate and txtTickets) to the table. Drag three Label controls and a Button control (btnSubmit) onto the Web form and arrange the controls.

3. Place one RangeValidator control (rvDate) on the table next to the txtDate control. Set its ControlToValidate property to txtDate, its Type property to Date, its MinimumValue property to 09/01/2003, its MaximumValue property to 09/30/2003, and its ErrorMessage property to an appropriate error message.

4. Place one CompareValidator control (cvTickets) on the table next to the txtTickets control. Set its ControlToValidate property to txtTickets, its Type property to Integer, its Operator property to GreaterThanEqual, its ValueToCompare property to 2, and its ErrorMessage property to an appropriate error message.

5. Set the ASPX page as the start page; then build and run the project. Enter an invalid date and an invalid number of tickets and click the Submit button. You will see the error messages from the RangeValidator and CompareValidator controls (see Figure 3.3). Enter valid values and click the Submit button. The form posts back successfully.

The **CustomValidator** Control

The CustomValidator control allows you to build a validation control for a custom specification. You can perform any custom validation both at the server side and at the client side with the help of this validation control.

This control exposes a property called ClientValidationFunction that specifies the name of the client script function to be executed for validation on the client side. This custom validation function is passed two arguments: The first one is the custom validator control, and the second argument is an object that contains two properties—IsValid and Value. The Value property contains the value that is to be validated, and the IsValid property is used to set the result of the validation.

Figure 3.3   Use the **RangeValidator** control to ensure that a control's value is in the specified range, and use the **CompareValidator** control to compare the control's value with a specified value.

At the server side, during the validation on the server, the validation control fires a ServerValidate event. An event handler containing the custom validation code is added to this event to perform validation on the server. The event sends a ServerValidateEventArgs object containing event-related data. This object contains two properties: The Value property contains the value of the control that is to be validated, and the IsValid property is used to set the result of the validation.

The **ValidationSummary** Control

The ValidationSummary control is used to display a summary of all the validation errors of a Web page. It displays the ErrorMessage property of the validation controls in the summary. If the ErrorMessage property is not set, the Text property is displayed as error messages for all the validation controls whose validations fail.

Table 3.13 shows the important properties of the ValidationSummary class.

Table 3.13 Important Properties of the ValidationSummary Class	
Property	**Description**
DisplayMode	Specifies the way in which the validation summary is displayed. Values are defined by the **ValidationSummaryDisplayMode** enumeration and include **BulletList** (default), **List**, and **SingleParagraph**.
EnableClientScript	Indicates whether the validation summary control should generate client-side script to update itself. The default is **true**.
ForeColor	Specifies the foreground color in which the error messages are displayed when the validation fails. The default value is **Color.Red**.
HeaderText	Specifies the header text of the validation summary control.
ShowMessageBox	Indicates whether the validation summary messages should be displayed in a message box. The default is **false**.
ShowSummary	Indicates whether the validation summary messages should be displayed inline in the validation summary control. The default is **true**.

Cascading Style Sheets

A *Cascading Style Sheet (CSS)* contains style definitions that are applied to elements in an HTML document. The information inside a CSS defines how HTML elements are displayed and where they are positioned on a Web page. With CSS, you can store all the formatting information for a Web application in a single CSS file and then instruct all the Web forms to use that file for formatting settings. This offers the following advantages:

➤ Uniform look and feel

➤ Ease of maintenance

You can use the GUI-based CSS designer available in Visual Studio .NET to easily create the CSS files and attach them to your Web application. The Web form does not automatically read the information in CSS files, though; you need to link a CSS file with the ASPX page using the HTML `<link>` element.

CSS also enables you to define custom style classes. A custom style class is applied to a Web server control using the `CssClass` property and to an HTML server control using the `class` property. For example, if you have the following definition in the CSS file associated with the ASPX page and you want to apply this style to a TextBox Web server control, you simply need to change the CssClass property of the TextBox Web server control to TextBoxStyle. Here's how you do so:

```
.TextBoxStyle
{
    border-right: blue double;
    border-top: blue double;
    font-size: medium;
    border-left: blue double;
    color: white;
    border-bottom: blue double;
    background-color: #6699cc;
}
```

Exam Prep Questions

Question 1

> Your company has recently decided to upgrade its supplier evaluation system from ASP to ASP.NET. You want to convert old ASP pages to Web forms as quickly as possible. You have noticed that you can keep the existing user interface but want to move the business logic to code-behind files. Which of the following approaches provides the smoothest migration path?
>
> ○ A. Continue to use HTML controls on ASP.NET Web forms. In the code-behind files, rewrite all business logic using C#.
>
> ○ B. Apply the **runat="server"** attribute to all HTML controls. In the code-behind files, rewrite all business logic using C#.
>
> ○ C. Use ASP.NET Web server controls instead of HTML controls. In the code-behind files, rewrite all business logic using C#.
>
> ○ D. Continue to use HTML controls for labels and text boxes but convert all **Button** controls to Web server controls. In the code-behind files, rewrite all business logic using C#.

Answer B is correct. Use of HTML server controls provides the easiest migration path for an existing HTML-based user interface. It does not take much effort to convert an HTML control to an HTML server control because you only need to add a `runat="server"` attribute to it. Answers A and D are incorrect because HTML controls are not directly available to the ASP.NET pages. Answer C is incorrect because ASP.NET Web server controls do not map one-to-one with HTML controls and will require additional conversion efforts.

Question 2

SurveyComm, Inc., is a marketing company that organizes surveys on behalf of large consumer goods companies. The surveys involve a large number of participants. SurveyComm recently decided to put its surveys online. You work as a Web developer for SurveyComm, and your responsibility is to design one of the online survey forms using ASP.NET. One of the questions in the survey form has a large number of options, and users can select multiple options as an answer to this question. You have used the **CheckBoxList** Web server control to display the options. In the code, you want to get all the options selected by the user so that you can store them in a database. Which of the following techniques should you use?

- ○ A. Use the **SelectedItem** property of the **CheckBoxList** control.
- ○ B. Use the **SelectedIndex** property of the **CheckBoxList** control.
- ○ C. Use the **DataValueField** property of the **CheckBoxList** control.
- ○ D. Use the **Items** property of the **CheckBoxList** control.

Answer D is correct. You should use the Items property of the CheckBoxList control to iterate through the list items and then use the Selected property of the ListItem object to find out whether the item has been selected. Answers A and B are incorrect because the SelectedIndex and SelectedItem properties return only the index of the first selected item and the first selected item, respectively. Answer C is incorrect because DataValueField is the data source that provides the item value and is used for populating the contents of CheckBoxList.

Question 3

You want to create a client-side event handler for the click event of a **Button** Web server control. The client-side event handler is written in JavaScript and is executed by the Web browser. The name of the **Button** control is **btnSubmit**, and the name of the JavaScript event handler is **GlowButton()**. How should you accomplish this in your Web form?

- ○ A.
```
<input id="btnSubmit" Type="Submit" Runat="Server"
       Value="Submit" onclick="GlowButton()"/>
```

- ○ B.
```
<input id="btnSubmit" Runat="Server"
       Value="Submit" onclick="GlowButton();"/>
```

```
○ C.
        <asp:Button id="btnSubmit" Runat="Server"
                    Value="Submit" onclick="GlowButton();"/>

○ D.
        btnSubmit.Attributes.Add("onclick", "GlowButton();")
```

Answer D is correct. The preferred way to add client-side event handling code for Web server controls is via the Attributes property of the Web server controls. Answers A, B, and C are incorrect because these techniques interfere with the client-side event handling code generated by ASP.NET to perform automatic postback operations.

Question 4

You are using a **DropDownList** Web server control on a Web page that allows users to select a country name. Based on the user's selection of country, you want to display the drop-down list showing states in the selected country and several other country-specific fields. You don't want users to click a button to submit country information to the Web server. All your users have JavaScript-enabled browsers. You want to write a minimum of code; which of the following techniques would you use?

○ A. Use an HTML server control instead of Web server controls.

○ B. Write client-side code in JavaScript to cause a postback when the user selects the country.

○ C. Set the **AutoPostBack** property to **true**.

○ D. Set the **AutoEventWireup** attribute to **true**.

Answer C is correct. You can specify a SelectedIndexChanged event to cause a form postback by setting the AutoPostBack property of the DropDownList Web server control to true. This technique automatically generates the required client-side code that causes the page postback when a user changes the selection. Answers A and B are incorrect because they require you to write additional code. Answer D is incorrect because the AutoEventWireup attribute is different from the AutoPostBack property and is used to specify whether ASP.NET will automatically call event handlers based on their names.

Question 5

You are creating a Web page that collects information about the various sports activities that interest your users. You want to display a sorted list of activities using a **CheckBoxList**, as shown in Figure 3.4. Which of the following ways should you choose to declare the **CheckBoxList** Web server control in your Web page?

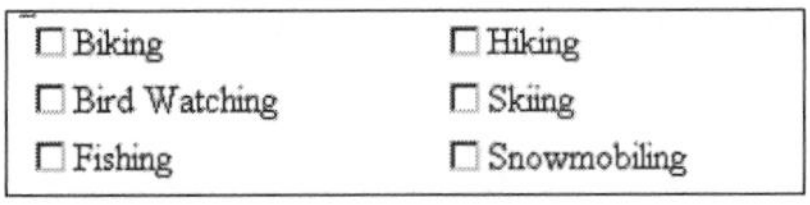

☐ Biking	☐ Hiking
☐ Bird Watching	☐ Skiing
☐ Fishing	☐ Snowmobiling

Figure 3.4   How should you declare the **CheckBoxList** to display its items in the way shown here?

○ A.

```
<asp:CheckBoxList id="cblActivities" runat="server"
     RepeatColumns="2" RepeatDirection="Vertical"
     RepeatLayout="Table">
...
</asp:CheckBoxList>
```

○ B.

```
<asp:CheckBoxList id="cblActivities" runat="server"
     RepeatColumns="2" RepeatDirection="Horizontal"
     RepeatLayout="Table">
...
</asp:CheckBoxList>
```

○ C.

```
<asp:CheckBoxList id="cblActivities" runat="server"
     RepeatColumns="2" RepeatDirection="Vertical"
     RepeatLayout="Flow">
...
</asp:CheckBoxList>
```

○ D.

```
<asp:CheckBoxList id="cblActivities" runat="server"
     RepeatColumns="2" RepeatDirection="Horizontal"
     RepeatLayout="Flow">
...
</asp:CheckBoxList>
```

Answer A is correct. The given list is sorted, and you want to organize the elements vertically in a table of two columns. To achieve this, you should set the RepeatColumns property to 2, the RepeatDirection property to Vertical, and the RepeatLayout property to Table. Answers B and D are incorrect because the value of the RepeatDirection attribute should be set to Vertical rather than Horizontal. Answer C is incorrect because the value of the RepeatLayout attribute should be set to "Table" instead of "Flow".

Question 6

> In a Web page, you are dynamically generating numerous **Button** controls. Each **Button** control is titled either **Add** or **Update**. You want to write a single event handler to handle events for all the **Button** controls. Which of the following options would you choose to ensure that you could take different actions when the Add or Update button is clicked?
>
> ○ A. Write an event handler for the **Click** event. Use the event arguments passed to the event handler to determine whether an Add button or Update button was clicked, and take appropriate actions in the event handler.
>
> ○ B. Write an event handler for the **Command** event. Use the event arguments passed to the event handler to determine whether an Add button or Update button was clicked, and take appropriate actions in the event handler.
>
> ○ C. Set the **CommandName** property for each button to either **Add** or **Update**. Write an event handler for the **Click** event. Use the event arguments passed to the event handler to determine whether an Add button or Update button was clicked, and take appropriate actions in the event handler.
>
> ○ D. Handle all the events in a page-level event handler such as the **Load** event.

Answer B is correct. The Command event is raised when the Button control is clicked. You can use the CommandEventArgs object to find the CommandName and CommandArguments associated with the button that initiated the event. Answers A and C are incorrect because the event arguments for the Click event do not give you enough information to determine the name of the button that was clicked. Answer D is incorrect because the Load event also does not have enough information available through its event arguments.

Question 7

You want to keep consistent formatting for all the Web forms in your application. To achieve this, you have created a CSS named **styles.css** and have linked it to all the Web pages. You have defined a style class named **TextBoxStyle** in **styles.css** to format text boxes onto the Web forms. Which of the following property settings would you use with the **TextBox** Web server control to use the **TextBoxStyle** style class?

- ○ A. **Class="TextBoxStyle"**
- ○ B. **CssClass="TextBoxStyle"**
- ○ C. **Class=".TextBoxStyle"**
- ○ D. **CssClass=".TextBoxStyle"**

Answer B is correct. When you want a Web server control to use a style class defined in a CSS file, you use the CssClass property of the Web server control. Answers A and C are incorrect because the Class property is used only with HTML server controls and not with Web server controls. Answer D is incorrect because, although the style itself might be defined as .TextBoxStyle, in the CSS file, you only need to specify the name (for example, TextBoxStyle) with the CssClass property.

Question 8

You are a Web developer working for a state-run agency and are creating a Web site for senior welfare programs. To register with the program, seniors must enter both their name and date of birth. The Web site should register a user only if her age is 65 years or more. You want to minimize the amount of validation code. How would you set up validation in the Web form to achieve this objective? (Select all that apply.)

- ❏ A. Use **RequiredFieldValidator** with the name.
- ❏ B. Use **RequiredFieldValidator** with the date of birth.
- ❏ C. Use **CompareValidator** with the date of birth.
- ❏ D. Use **RangeValidator** with the date of birth.
- ❏ E. Use **CustomValidator** with the date of birth.

Answers A, B, and C are correct. It is required that both the name and the date of birth be entered, so you must use the RequiredFieldValidator for both the fields. In addition to this, you need to compare the date of birth entered by the user with the current date to check whether she is 65 years or older.

This can be easily done using the CompareValidator control by programmatically setting its ValueToCompare property. Answer D is incorrect because no fixed range has been specified for the age. Answer E is incorrect because it requires you to write additional validation code.

Question 9

You are developing a scheduling application for your company's intranet. You are using a **Calendar** control to enable easy and correct selection of dates. You want to mark holidays on the calendar so that users are aware of them while creating a schedule. For example, January 1 should be marked as New Year's Day. You want to display the description of the holiday in the same cell that displays the date. Which of the following calendar events would you use to achieve this?

- ○ A. **DayRender**
- ○ B. **SelectionChanged**
- ○ C. **VisibleMonthChanged**
- ○ D. **Load**

Answer A is correct. The DayRender event is raised when the Calendar control is rendered. The DayRender event is therefore the preferred place for writing additional messages along with a day. Answers B and C are incorrect because these events are fired on a user action only after the Calendar control has been displayed. Answer D is incorrect because the Load event is fired prior to the actual rendering of the control.

Question 10

You are designing a Web site that allows users to file their taxes online. Users log on to the Web site using their tax identification number and a personal identification number. You want to ensure that users do not include spaces with the tax identification number. You want to achieve this by writing the minimum amount of code. Which of the following validation controls would you choose?

- ○ A. **RequiredFieldValidator**
- ○ B. **RangeValidator**
- ○ C. **RegularExpressionValidator**
- ○ D. **CustomValidator**

Answer C is correct. The RegularExpressionValidator control is the best choice for performing validations that require you to match the control's value against a specific pattern. Answer A is incorrect because the RequiredFieldValidator only ensures whether a value is entered. Answer B is incorrect because no specific range of values has been specified. Answer D is incorrect because the CustomValidator control requires you to write additional code.

Need to Know More?

 Kalani, Amit, et al. *ASP.NET 1.0 with C# Namespace Reference.* Hoboken, NJ: Wrox, 2002.

 Liberty, Jesse and Dan Hurwitz. *Programming ASP.NET.* Sebastopol, CA: O'Reilly, 2002.

 See the ASP.NET Server Controls Overview at http:// support.microsoft.com?scid=kb;en-us;Q306459.

 Visit the Microsoft Online Seminars on ASP.NET at www.microsoft.com/Seminar/MMCFeed/MMCDisplay.asp?Product= 103362.

 See The .NET Show: ASP.NET at www.msdn.com/theshow/ Episode009.

 See the MSDN TV: Client-Side Script in ASP.NET at www.msdn.com/msdntv/episode.aspx?xml=episodes/en/ 20030311ASPNETJC/manifest.xml.

 See the MSDN ASP.NET Seminars at www.msdn.com/seminar/ mmcfeed/mmcdisplayfeed.asp?Product=103362.

 Read *MSDN Magazine*'s "The ASP Column" at www.msdn.com/ msdnmag/find/default.aspx?phrase=The ASP Column.

 Read about the .NET Framework Regular Expressions at www.msdn.com/library/en-us/cpguide/html/ cpconcomregularexpressions.asp.

Implementing Navigation for the User Interface

Terms you'll need to understand:

✓ ASP.NET application
✓ Cookies
✓ HTTP request
✓ HTTP response
✓ Postback
✓ Session
✓ View state

Techniques you'll need to master:

✓ Understanding the differences, advantages, and disadvantages of the various state management techniques
✓ Using new features of ASP.NET, such as view state and smart navigation
✓ Knowing how to choose between the **Response.Redirect()**, **Server.Transfer()**, and **Server.Execute()** methods
✓ Knowing how to access and use the ASP.NET intrinsic objects

This chapter discusses various state management features provided by ASP.NET, including client-side techniques and server-side techniques. This chapter also discusses the ASP.NET intrinsic objects available via the Page class. Finally, this chapter demonstrates how various methods are used to navigate from one page to another and compares those methods.

Round Trip and Postback

A Web application has a distributed execution model. When a user interacts with a Web form, the browser might respond to some of the user actions by executing client-side scripts while sending some other actions that require server resources to the Web server for processing. When server-side processing is involved, a typical interactive user session with a Web form consists of the following steps:

1. The user requests a Web form from the Web server.

2. The Web server responds with the requested Web form.

3. The user enters the data and submits the form to the Web server.

4. The Web server processes the form and sends the result back to the user.

Step 3 is referred to as a *page postback*, whereas steps 3 and 4 are collectively referred to as a *round trip*. A round trip involves making a complete trip over the network to the Web server and getting the response back.

The Web applications use Hypertext Transmission Protocol (HTTP) to establish communication between the Web browser and Web server. HTTP is *disconnected* in nature, which means the life cycle of a Web page is just a single round trip. Between two page requests, the Web server and the clients are disconnected from each other and the values of page variables and controls are not preserved across the page requests.

This model of execution enables a Web server to support a large number of clients because each client request occupies the server resources only for a short duration. However, the disconnected nature of HTTP provides a major challenge to Web developers, who must implement the following functionality in their applications:

➤ Maintain values of controls and variables across page postbacks.

➤ Distinguish the initial request of a page from the page postback.

➤ Provide smart navigation features similar to those of desktop applications.

ASP.NET provides solutions to these problems built into the programming framework. From the discussion about server controls in Chapter 3, "Controls," you already know that server controls automatically retain their values across page postbacks. You will learn how ASP.NET actually retains the states for server controls later in this chapter in the section titled "State Management." For now, I'll talk about two properties of the Page class—IsPostBack and SmartNavigation—that provide the other two functionalities from the previous list.

The **IsPostBack** Property

The IsPostBack property of the Page class returns true when a page is being loaded in response to a client postback. If the page is being requested for the first time, the value of the IsPostBack property is false.

A typical case in which you would use this distinction is when you do not want the server to execute costly initialization operations for each page postback. Instead, the initializations are to be performed only with the first request to the page.

The following example helps you understand round trip and postback operations and demonstrates the use of the IsPostBack property:

1. Open Visual Studio .NET and create a new blank solution named 315C04 at c:\inetpub\wwwroot\ExamCram (you might need to change the directory based on your configuration).

2. Create a new Visual C# ASP.NET Web application project. Specify the location of the project as http://localhost/ExamCram/315C04/Example4_1.

3. Change the pageLayout property of the DOCUMENT element of the Web form to FlowLayout. Add a DropDownList Web server control (ddlCategories) to the form. Set its AutoPostBack property to true and the TabIndex property to 1.

4. Add a Label control (lblQuestion) to the Web form.

5. Add a TextBox control (txtTitle) and set its AutoPostBack to true and TabIndex to 2. Then, add another TextBox control (txtMessage) and set its TabIndex to 3 and TextMode to MultiLine (see Figure 4.1).

6. Add a Button control (btnPost) and set its Text to Post A Message. Place a Label control (lblWeblog) at the end of the form, as shown in Figure 4.1.

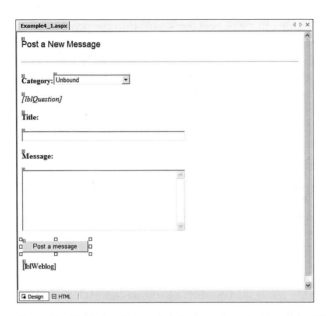

Figure 4.1 The design of a form that allows you to post messages to a Weblog.

7. Switch to the Code view of the Web form and add the following code to the `Page_Load()` event handler:

```csharp
private void Page_Load(object sender, System.EventArgs e)
{
    if (!Page.IsPostBack)
    {
        // If page is requested for the first time
        ddlCategories.Items.Add("Web development");
        ddlCategories.Items.Add("Programming Languages");
        ddlCategories.Items.Add("Certifications");
    }
    else
    {
        // On postback, change the case of the textbox's text
        txtTitle.Text = txtTitle.Text.ToUpper();
    }
    // Set the text of the label control on each page load
    lblQuestion.Text = "What do you want to write about "
        + ddlCategories.SelectedItem.Text + " today?";
}
```

8. Attach the following event handler to the `Click` event of the Post button:

```csharp
private void btnPost_Click(object sender, System.EventArgs e)
{
    // Format the data entered by the user and
    // append it to the existing contents of lblWeblog
    lblWeblog.Text = "<b>" + ddlCategories.SelectedItem.Text
            + " :: " + txtTitle.Text + "</b> ("
            + DateTime.Now.ToString() + ")<hr>"
            + txtMessage.Text + "<p>"
            + lblWeblog.Text + "</p>";
}
```

9. Run the project. Use the Tab key to navigate between various fields and publish a few entries to the Weblog, as shown in Figure 4.2.

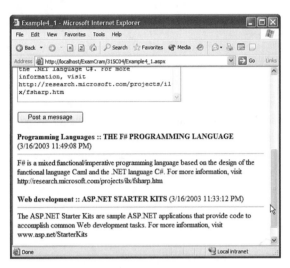

Figure 4.2   The Web form retains state for both postback and nonpostback controls.

The previous example uses the event handler for the Load event of the Page class to check whether the page is loaded by a postback operation. If that is the case, executing the code for adding items to the drop-down list is skipped.

Also note that the navigation between controls is not smooth. When the form returns after a postback, it does not remember the active control. However, the SmartNavigation property can solve this problem.

The **SmartNavigation** Property

ASP.NET has a feature called smart navigation that can greatly enhance the user experience of a Web page by

➤ Persisting element focus between postbacks

➤ Persisting scroll position between postbacks

➤ Eliminating page flash caused by page postback

➤ Preventing each postback from being saved in the browser history

NOTE

Smart navigation is supported only in Internet Explorer 5.0 or later browsers. Therefore, when you are targeting an application for a generic browser, this feature isn't very helpful.

Smart navigation is specified by the SmartNavigation attribute of the Page directive. To enhance the Web form created in the previous example to use the smart navigation feature, you need to modify its Page directive to the following:

```
<%@ Page language="c#"  Codebehind="WebForm1.aspx.cs"
        AutoEventWireup="false"
        Inherits="Example4_1.WebForm1"
        SmartNavigation="true"
%>
```

Smart navigation is very useful for intranet applications where you have more control over the browsers used by the users. For such applications, you might want to turn on smart navigation for the complete Web application instead of individual files. You can easily accomplish this by making the following changes to the web.config file of the Web application:

```
<configuration>
    <system.web>
        <pages smartNavigation="true"/>
    </system.web>
</configuration>
```

ASP.NET Intrinsic Objects

ASP.NET provides intrinsic objects to enable low-level access to the Web application framework. These objects allow you to work directly with the underlying HTTP streams and server, session, and application objects. The intrinsic objects can be accessed in a Web form through the properties of the Page class. Table 4.1 lists the important intrinsic objects and the properties of the Page class to which they are mapped.

Table 4.1 Intrinsic Objects and Their Mappings to the Page Class Properties

Intrinsic Object	Property of the Page Class
HttpRequest	Request
HttpResponse	Response
HttpServerUtility	Server
HttpApplicationState	Application
HttpSessionState	Session

The HttpRequest Object

The HttpRequest object represents the incoming request from the client to the Web server. The request from the client can come in two ways—GET or

POST. GET attaches the data with the URL, whereas POST embeds the data within the HTTP request body.

The HttpRequest intrinsic object can be accessed by the Request property of the Page class. Tables 4.2 and 4.3 list the properties and methods of the HttpRequest class, respectively. Note that all the properties except the Filter property of the HttpRequest class are read-only.

Table 4.2 Properties of the HttpRequest Class	
Property	**Description**
AcceptTypes	Specifies the MIME types that the client browser accepts
ApplicationPath	Represents the application's virtual application root path on the server
Browser	Provides access to the capabilities and characteristics of the requesting browser
ClientCertificate	Represents the certificate, if any, sent by the client for secure communications
ContentEncoding	Represents the character encoding (such as **UTF7**, **ASCII**, and so on) for the entity body
ContentLength	Specifies the length in bytes of the request
ContentType	Specifies the MIME type of the incoming request
Cookies	Represents the cookies collection that is sent by the client to the server
CurrentExecutionFilePath	Specifies the virtual path of the current executing page on the Web server
FilePath	Specifies the virtual path of the file on the Web server
Files	Represents the file collection that is posted by the client to the Web server
Filter	Represents a stream that is applied as a filter on the incoming request
Form	Specifies the contents of a form posted to the server
Headers	Represents the HTTP headers included with the incoming request
HttpMethod	Represents the method of the HTTP request (for example, **GET**, **POST**, or **HEAD**)
InputStream	Represents the stream that contains the incoming HTTP request body
IsAuthenticated	Indicates whether the client has been authenticated to the Web site

(continued)

Table 4.2 Properties of the HttpRequest Class *(continued)*	
Property	**Description**
IsSecureConnection	Indicates whether the client connection is over a secure HTTPS connection
Params	Represents the form, query string, cookies, and server variables collection of the current request
Path	Specifies the virtual path of the current request, along with additional path information
PathInfo	Specifies the additional path information of the current request
PhysicalApplicationPath	Specifies the physical file system path of the application's root directory
PhysicalPath	Specifies the physical file system path of the current request on the Web server
QueryString	Represents the query string collection sent by the client to the Web server through the URL
RawUrl	Specifies the URL portion of the current request, excluding the domain information
RequestType	Represents the type of request (**GET** or **POST**) made by the client
ServerVariables	Represents the collection of Web server variables
TotalBytes	Represents the total number of bytes posted to the server in the current request
Url	Specifies information about the current URL request
UrlReferrer	Specifies the URL of the client's previous request that linked to the current URL request
UserAgent	Represents the browser being used by the client
UserHostAddress	Represents the IP address of the requesting client's machine
UserHostName	Represents the domain name system (DNS) name of the requesting client's machine
UserLanguages	Specifies the languages preferred by the client's browser

Table 4.3 Methods of the HttpRequest Class	
Method	**Description**
BinaryRead()	Reads the specified number of bytes from the request stream. This method is provided for backward compatibility; you should use the **InputStream** property instead.

(continued)

Table 4.3 Methods of the HttpRequest Class *(continued)*	
Method	**Description**
MapImageCoordinates()	Returns the coordinates of a form image that is sent to the server in the current request.
MapPath()	Returns the physical file system path of the file for a specified virtual path of a Web server.
SaveAs()	Saves the current HTTP request into a disk file, with an option to include or exclude headers.

The following code segment displays the header information sent by the client to the server:

```
// Display the request header
System.Collections.Specialized.NameValueCollection
       nvcHeaders = Request.Headers;
String[] astrKeys = nvcHeaders.AllKeys;
// Iterate through all header keys and display their values
foreach (String strKey in astrKeys)
{
    Response.Write(strKey + ": " + nvcHeaders[strKey].ToString());
    Response.Write("<br>");
}
```

Some properties of the HttpRequest object—such as Form, QueryString, Headers, and so on—return a NameValueCollection containing a collection of key-value pairs of their contents. The previous code segment demonstrates how to iterate through this collection by iterating through the keys of the Headers collection and displaying the key and value of each header sent by the client.

The **HttpResponse** Object

The HttpResponse object represents the response sent back to the client from the Web server. It contains properties and methods that provide direct access to the response stream and enable you to set its behavior and operations. The Response property of the Page class provides access to the HttpResponse object. Tables 4.4 and 4.5 list the properties and methods of the HttpResponse class, respectively.

Table 4.4 Properties of the HttpResponse Class	
Property	**Description**
Buffer	Indicates whether output to the response stream needs to be buffered and sent to the client after the entire page is processed. This property is provided for backward compatibility; the **BufferOutput** property should be used instead.

(continued)

Table 4.4 Properties of the HttpResponse Class *(continued)*	
Property	**Description**
BufferOutput	Indicates whether the output to the response stream needs to be buffered and then sent to the client after the entire page is processed. The default is **true**.
Cache	Represents the caching policy of the page. The policy controls where caching can be done, the expiration time, and so on.
CacheControl	Specifies where the caching should be done. The possible values are **Public** and **Private**.
Charset	Represents the character set of the output stream. If set to **null**, the content-type header is suppressed.
ContentEncoding	Represents the character set of the response output stream.
ContentType	Represents the MIME type for the outgoing response stream, such as **text/html**, **text/xml**, and so on.
Cookies	Represents the cookies collection that is sent by the server to the client.
Expires	Indicates the number of minutes until the page is cached by the client browser.
ExpiresAbsolute	Indicates the specific date and time until the page is cached by the client browser.
Filter	Represents a stream that is applied as a filter to the outgoing response.
IsClientConnected	Indicates whether the client is connected to the server. This property is very helpful when running a lengthy request.
Output	Returns a **TextWriter** object that enables writing custom output to the outgoing response.
OutputStream	Allows writing binary output to the outgoing response.
Status	Specifies the status of the HTTP output that is sent to the client. This property returns both the status code and the text description of the status (for example, **200 OK**).
StatusCode	Specifies the numeric representation of the status of the HTTP output sent to the client (for example, **200**, **302**, and so on).
StatusDescription	Specifies the text representation of the status of the HTTP output sent to the client. (for example, **OK**, **Redirect**, and so on).
SupressContent	Indicates whether the content in the page should be suppressed and not sent to the client.

Table 4.5   Methods of the HttpResponse Class

Method	Description
AddCacheItemDependencies()	Specifies that the current cached response is dependent on the items specified in a given **ArrayList** object.
AddCacheItemDependency()	Specifies that the current cached response is dependant on the item specified in the given **String** object.
AddFileDependencies()	Adds a group of files to the collection on which the current response depends.
AddFileDependency()	Adds a file to the collection on which the current response depends.
AddHeader()	Adds an HTTP header to the outgoing response stream. This method is provided for backward compatibility with ASP.
AppendHeader()	Adds an HTTP header to the outgoing response stream.
AppendToLog()	Adds information to the IIS Web log file.
ApplyAppPathModifier()	In case of a cookieless session, it adds a session ID to the given virtual path.
BinaryWrite()	Allows writing binary data such as an image file or a PDF file to the response stream.
Clear()	Clears the entire response stream buffer, including its contents and headers.
ClearContent()	Clears the entire content portion of the response stream buffer.
ClearHeaders()	Clears the headers portion of the response stream buffer.
Close()	Closes the response object and the socket connection to the client.
End()	Stops the execution of the page after flushing the output buffer to the client.
Flush()	Flushes the currently buffered content out to the client.
Pics()	Adds a **PICS-label** HTTP header to the outgoing response.
Redirect()	Redirects the client browser to any URL. This method requires an additional round trip to the browser.
RemoveOutputCacheItem()	Removes all cache items for the path specified.
Write()	Writes output to the outgoing response.
WriteFile()	Writes a file to the outgoing response.

The following example shows the use of the HttpResponse object methods and properties to create a response that displays the File Download dialog box and allows the user to download a text file from the Web server to the client's machine:

1. Add a new Visual C# ASP.NET Web Application project to the solution, and name it **Example4_2**. Change the pageLayout property of the DOCUMENT element of the Web form to FlowLayout.

2. Add a text file to the project that contains some data that needs to be downloaded. Name it **Summary.txt**.

3. Add a LinkButton control (lbtnDownload) to the Web form with its Text property set to Download Summary.txt.

4. Double-click the lbtnDownload control and add the following code to the Click event handler:

```
private void lbtnDownload_Click(object sender, System.EventArgs e)
{
    // Force a download of Summary.txt as an attachment
    Response.AppendHeader("Content-Disposition",
        "Attachment;FileName=" + "Summary.txt");

    // The download file is a TXT file
    Response.ContentType = "text/plain";

    // Write the file to the Response
    Response.WriteFile("Summary.txt");

    // Stop further execution of the page
    Response.End();
}
```

5. Run the project. Click the link button; you should see a File Download dialog box that enables you to save the file locally.

The **HttpServerUtility** Object

The HttpServerUtility object contains utility methods and properties to work with the Web server. It also contains methods to enable HTML/URL encoding and decoding, execute or transfer to an ASPX page, create COM components, and so on. The Server property of the Page class provides access to the HttpServerUtility object. Tables 4.6 and 4.7 list the properties and methods of this class, respectively.

Table 4.6   Properties of the HttpServerUtility Class

Property	Description
MachineName	Returns the name of the server that hosts the Web application
ScriptTimeout	Indicates the number of seconds that are allowed to elapse when processing the request before a timeout error is sent to the client

Table 4.7   Methods of the HttpServerUtility Class

Method	Description
ClearError()	Clears the last exception from memory
CreateObject()	Creates a COM object on the server
CreateObjectFromClsid()	Creates a COM object on the server identified by a specified class identifier (CLSID)
Execute()	Executes an ASPX page within the current requested page
GetLastError()	Returns the last exception that occurred on the Web server
HtmlDecode()	Decodes a string that has been previously encoded to eliminate invalid HTML characters
HtmlEncode()	Encodes a string converting any characters that are illegal in HTML for transmission over HTTP
MapPath()	Returns the physical path for a specified virtual path on a Web server
Transfer()	Allows the transfer of ASPX page execution from the current page to another ASPX page on the same Web server
UrlDecode()	Decodes a string that has been previously encoded to eliminate invalid characters for transmission over HTTP in a URL
UrlEncode()	Encodes a given string for safe transmission over HTTP
UrlPathEncode()	Encodes the path portion of the URL string for safe transmission over HTTP

ASP.NET Applications

An ASP.NET application is made up of a collection of files including Web forms and assemblies that are stored in a virtual directory marked as an IIS application.

When a resource in an ASP.NET application is requested, ASP.NET instantiates an HttpApplication object that then takes over the processing of the incoming request. The HttpApplication class defines the methods, properties, and events common to all application objects in an ASP.NET application.

If you want to customize the behavior of an HttpApplication object, you can derive a class from the HttpApplication class and override the event handlers of the base class for various application-level events. An easy way to do this is by using the global.asax file.

The global.asax File

The global.asax file defines a class named Global that derives from the HttpApplication class. When ASP.NET notices that the global.asax file is present in the root directory of an application, rather than using the implicitly created HttpApplication object, ASP.NET creates instances of the class defined in the global.asax file to handle requests for an application.

For security reasons, ASP.NET restricts users of an application from downloading any file with the extension **.asax**.

Global Event Handlers

The global.asax file is an appropriate place to handle events that are not specific to a Web form, but rather apply to an application as a whole. I'll call these events *global* events and classify them in two categories— *application- and session-level events* and *per-request events*.

Application- and Session-level Events

Application- and session-level events are fired to signal the start and end of the application or user session. These events can be handled using the predefined event handlers in the global.asax file shown in Table 4.8.

Table 4.8 Application- and Session-level Event Handlers in the global.asax File	
Event Handler	**Purpose**
Application_Start()	Called when an application receives its first request. It's generally used to initialize data that is shared among all users of an application.
Application_End()	Called when an application shuts down. Here you can write code to persist the information stored in memory that you want to have reloaded when the application restarts.
Session_Start()	Called when an ASP.NET application creates a new session for a user of the application.
Session_End()	Called when the user's session expires. By default, this happens 20 minutes after the last request of a page from a user.

Per-request Events

The event handlers shown in Table 4.9 are invoked for each individual page request processed by the HttpApplication object.

Table 4.9 Per-request Event Handlers	
Event Handler	**Purpose**
Application_BeginRequest()	Called at the beginning of each request
Application_AuthenticateRequest()	Called when a security module has established the identity of the user
Application_AuthorizeRequest()	Called when a security module has verified user authorization
Application_ResolveRequestCache()	Called to resolve the current request by providing content from a cache
Application_AcquireRequestState()	Called to associate the current request with the session state
Application_PreRequestHandlerExecute()	Called when ASP.NET begins executing a page
Application_PostRequestHandlerExecute()	Called when ASP.NET finishes executing a page
Application_ReleaseRequestState()	Called to save the current state data
Application_UpdateRequestCache()	Called to update a cache with the responses
Application_EndRequest()	Called at the end of each request

As you can see from Table 4.9, you have complete control over how a request is processed. You can write code in any of these event handlers to modify the default behavior of ASP.NET. The following example uses the Application_BeginRequest() and Application_EndRequest() methods to determine the time it takes for each request to process and append this information with every response:

1. Open the global.asax file for the project Example4_2 and switch to Code view.

2. Add the following code to the Application_BeginRequest() event handler:

```
protected void Application_BeginRequest(Object sender, EventArgs e)
{
    // Store the begin time of the request in the HttpContext object
    this.Context.Items.Add("BeginTime", DateTime.Now);
}
```

3. Add the following code to the `Application_EndRequest()` event handler:

```
protected void Application_EndRequest(Object sender, EventArgs e)
{
    // Get the begin time from the HttpContext object
    DateTime dtBeginTime = (DateTime) this.Context.Items["BeginTime"];

    // Calculate the time span between the start and end of request
    TimeSpan tsProcessingTime = DateTime.Now-dtBeginTime;

    // Display the processing time taken by the response
    this.Context.Response.Output.Write("<hr>");
    this.Context.Response.Output.Write(
      "{0} took {1} milliseconds to execute.",
      this.Request.Url, tsProcessingTime.TotalMilliseconds);
}
```

4. Run the project. You should see that the page shows a message at the bottom indicating the processing time of the request.

We used the `Context` object in the preceding program to store the begin time. The `Context` object provides access to all the information about the current HTTP request. It also exposes a key-value collection via the `Items` property in which you can add values that will be available for the life of the current request.

State Management

The value of the variables and controls collectively make up the state of a Web page. *State management* is the process of maintaining state for a Web page across round trips.

State management is ubiquitous with desktop-based applications, and programmers need not even care about it while developing these applications. However, because of the disconnected nature of the HTTP, state management is an important issue for Web applications.

ASP.NET provides several techniques for preserving state information across page postbacks. I'll broadly categorize these techniques as either client-side or server-side, depending on where the resources are consumed for state management.

Client-side Techniques for State Management

Client-side techniques use the HTML code and capabilities of the Web browser to store state-related information. ASP.NET supports the following techniques for storing state information at the client side:

➤ Query strings

➤ Cookies

➤ Hidden fields

➤ View state

Query Strings

Query strings are used to maintain state by appending the state information to a page's URL. The state data is separated from the actual URL with a question mark (?). The data attached to the URL is usually a set of key-value pairs, in which each key-value pair is separated by an ampersand (&). For example, look at this URL that embeds two key-value pairs (name and city):

```
www.buddy.com/find.aspx?name=Bill+Gates&city=redmond
```

Because of their simplicity, query strings are widely used for passing a small amount of information to Web pages. However, query strings suffer the following limitations:

➤ Most browsers restrict the length of the query string; this reduces the amount of data you can embed in a URL.

➤ Query strings do not provide any support for structured data types.

➤ The information stored in a query string is not secure because it is directly visible to the user in the browser's address field.

Reading information from query strings in an ASP.NET program is easy using the `QueryString` property of the current `HttpRequest` object. The `QueryString` property returns a `NameValueCollection` object representing the key-value pairs stored in the query string. For example, the following expressions retrieve the value of the name and city, respectively, from the query string used in the previous URL:

```
Request.QueryString["name"]
Request.QueryString["city"]
```

Cookies

Cookies are small packets of information—each storing a key-value pair at the client side. These packets are associated with a specific domain and are sent along with each request to the associated Web server. Cookies are commonly used to store users' preferences and provide them with a personalized browsing experience on their subsequent visits to a Web page.

Use of cookies suffers from the following limitations:

➤ Most browsers limit the size of information you can store in a cookie. The typical size is 4,096 bytes with older browser versions and 8,192 bytes with newer browser versions.

➤ Some users configure their browsers to refuse cookies.

➤ When you request that the browser persist a cookie on a user's computer for a specified period, the browser might override that request by using its own rules for cookie expiration.

➤ Because cookies are stored at the client, they might be tampered with. You cannot trust data you receive from a cookie.

You can use the `Cookies` property of the `HttpRequest` object to get an `HttpCookieCollection` object that represents the cookies sent by the client for the current HTTP request. The following code segment shows how to set a cookie on a user's computer:

```
// Create a cookie called Name
HttpCookie cName = new HttpCookie("Name");
cName.Value = txtName.Text;
// Set the expiration time of the cookie
// to 15 minutes from the current time
cName.Expires = DateTime.Now + new TimeSpan(0,0,15,0);
// Add the cookie to the response cookies
// collection to send it to the client's machine
Response.Cookies.Add(cName);
```

To retrieve the value of a cookie, you just need to retrieve it from the HTTP request, as shown in the following code sample:

```
if(Request.Cookies["Name"] == null)
{
    // the Name cookie does not exist,
}
else
{
    // the Name cookie exists
    Response.Write(Request.Cookies["Name"].Value);
}
```

Hidden Fields

Hidden fields contain information that is not visible on the page but is posted to the server along with a page postback. All modern browsers support hidden fields on a Web page. However, hidden fields have the following limitations:

➤ Although information stored in a hidden field is not visible on the page, it is still part of the page's HTML code and users can see the value of a hidden field by viewing the HTML source of the page. Hidden fields are therefore not a good choice for storing information you want to keep secure.

➤ Hidden fields are part of the page HTML. If you store more information in hidden fields, it increases the size of the HTML page, making it slow for users to download.

➤ Hidden fields allow you to store only a single value in a field. If you want to store structured values such as those in a customer record, you must use several hidden fields.

ASP.NET provides an HTML server control, `HtmlInputHidden`, that maps to the `<input type="hidden">` HTML element. The `HtmlInputHidden` control is not available as a Web server control mainly because ASP.NET uses a similar, but more powerful, technique called *view state*.

View State

View state is the mechanism ASP.NET uses to maintain the state of controls across page postbacks. Just like hidden fields and cookies, you can also use view state to maintain state for noncontrol values in a page. However, it is important to note that view state works only when a page is posted back to itself.

The following sections explain how view state works in various scenarios.

View State for Postback Controls

Some server controls, such as `TextBox`, `CheckBox`, and so on, post their values as part of the postback operation. These types of controls are also known as *postback controls*. For postback controls, ASP.NET retrieves their values one by one from the HTTP request and copies them to the control values while creating the HTTP response. Traditionally, Web developers had to manually write this code for maintaining state for the postback controls, but now ASP.NET does this automatically.

View State for Nonpostback Controls

In addition to the postback controls, the view state mechanism of ASP.NET also retains values for nonpostback controls (that is, the controls that do not post their values as part of the postback operation, such as a `Label` control). You might wonder how ASP.NET manages to maintain values for a control even when the controls do not post their values. Actually, no magic is involved; ASP.NET extends the concept of hidden fields to accomplish this.

When ASP.NET executes a page, it collects the values of all nonpostback controls that are modified in the code and formats them into a single, base64-encoded string. This string is then stored in a hidden field in a control named __VIEWSTATE, as in this example:

```
<input type="hidden" name="__VIEWSTATE" value=
"dDwtMTg3NjA4ODA2MDs7PoYLsizcOhkv2XeRfSJNPt12o1HP" />
```

The hidden input field is a postback control, so in the next postback of the page, the encoded string stored in the __VIEWSTATE field is also posted. At the Web server, ASP.NET decodes the view state string at page initialization and restores the control's values in the page.

Maintaining state using this technique does not require many server resources, but it does increase the size of the HTML file, which therefore increases the amount of time it takes to load the page.

View State for Page-level Values

The ViewState property of the Page class is a great place to store page-level values. View state saves these values just prior to rendering the page and restores the values at the time of page initialization after the postback operation. This might sound like cookies or hidden fields, but a major improvement is that you are not just limited to storing simple values. You can use the ViewState to store any object as long as it is serializable.

The following example demonstrates how to use the view state to maintain state for page-level values, such as the number of posts on a Weblog:

1. Add a new Visual C# ASP.NET Web Application project to the solution; name it **Example4_3**.

2. Delete the WebForm1.aspx file. Copy WebForm1.aspx from the Example4_1 project to the current project. Then open the ASPX file and the CS file and replace all occurrences of Example4_1 with Example4_3. Place a Label control (lblPosts) next to the button control on the form.

3. Switch to Code view and add the following property to the class definition for WebForm1:

```
// get or set the number of posts in the Weblog
protected int NumberOfPosts
{
    get{
        if(ViewState["NumberOfPosts"] == null)
        {
            // The NumberOfPosts key is not present in the ViewState
            return 0;
        }
        else
        {
            // Retrieve the NumberOfPosts key from the ViewState
            return Convert.ToInt32(ViewState["NumberOfPosts"]);
        }
    }
    set{
        // Set the NumberOfPosts key in the ViewState
        ViewState["NumberOfPosts"] = value;
    }
}
```

4. Modify the event handler for the `Click` event of the `btnPost` control as shown here:

```
private void btnPost_Click(object sender, System.EventArgs e)
{
    // Format the data entered by the user and
    // append it to the existing contents of lblWeblog
    lblWeblog.Text = "<b>" + ddlCategories.SelectedItem.Text
        + " :: " + txtTitle.Text + "</b> (" + DateTime.Now.ToString()
        + ")<hr>" + txtMessage.Text + "<p>" + lblWeblog.Text + "</p>";
    // One more post is added, increment the value of NumberOfPosts
    // key in the Page's ViewState
    lblPosts.Text = "Total Posts : (" + ++NumberOfPosts + ")";
}
```

5. Run the project. Make a few entries in the Weblog; you should see that with each entry in the Weblog, the total posts value is increased by 1.

6. View the HTML code rendered in the Web browser. You'll note that the value associated with the __VIEWSTATE field increases as the size of the text in the `lblWeblog` control increases.

As you can see in the previous example, view state is internally maintained as a hidden field. However, view state provides a higher degree of customizability and other security features that you'll see shortly.

Disabling View State

By default, view state is enabled in an ASP.NET application. As you have observed in the previous example, the size of information stored in view state can increase the size of the HTML for a Web page. ASP.NET provides complete flexibility in disabling view state at various levels:

➤ *At the level of a control*—If you populate the control's state on each request, you can disable view state at the control level by setting the `EnableViewState` property of the control to `false`:

```
<asp:DataGrid EnableViewState="false" .../>
```

➤ *At the level of a page*—If the page doesn't post back to itself, you can disable view state at the page level by setting the `EnableViewState` attribute of the `Page` directive to `false` in the ASPX page:

```
<%@ Page EnableViewState="false" %>
```

➤ *At the level of an application*—If none of the pages in an application post back to themselves, you can disable view state at the application level by adding the following line to the `web.config` file:

```
<pages enableViewState="false"/>
```

➤ *At the level of the machine*—In the unlikely case in which you want to disable view state for all applications running on a Web server, you can do so by adding the following statement to the machine.config file:

```
<pages enableViewState="false"/>
```

Protecting View State

ASP.NET provides a way of knowing whether somebody has modified the contents of the view state to fool your application. With this technique, the view state is encoded using a hash code (using the SHA1 or MD5 algorithms) when it is sent to the browser. When the page is posted back, ASP.NET checks the encoded view state to verify that it has not been tampered with on the client. This type of check is called a *machine authentication check (MAC)*. By default, ASP.NET has the following entry in its machine.config file:

```
<pages enableViewStateMac="true" />
```

This enables tamper proofing for all applications running on a Web server. You can also manually enable or disable the tamper-proofing check at page level by setting the EnableViewStateMac attribute of the Page directive to true or false in the ASPX page:

```
<%@ Page EnableViewStateMac="false"%>
```

However, this scheme just makes the view state tamper proof; it does not restrict users from determining the contents of the view state. Although the values are not directly visible as in the cases of query strings or hidden variables, determined users can easily decode the view state.

With only a few configuration changes, you can instruct ASP.NET to encrypt the contents of the view state using the Triple DES symmetric algorithm (3DES), making it extremely difficult for the clients to decode the view state. This kind of encryption can be applied only at the machine level by specifying the following setting in the machine.config file:

```
<machineKey validation='3DES' />
```

When securing the view state for applications running on a Web farm configuration, you must use the same validation key for all the machines on the farm. To do this, use a manually assigned key instead of the default autogenerated key with the **<machineKey>** setting in the **machine.config** file.

Choosing a Client-side State Management Technique

Table 4.10 lists the advantages and disadvantages of the various client-side state management techniques. This table will help you make a quick decision about which client-side state management technique to choose in a given scenario.

Table 4.10 Comparing the Client-side State Management Techniques		
Technique	**Advantage**	**Disadvantage**
Query string	Requires no postback operation.	Most browsers limit the length of data that can be included in a query string. No security. No options for persistence. No support for storing structured values.
Cookies	State can be persisted on user's computer. Size restriction by browser operation.	Some users disable cookies in their browsers. Requires no postback (approx. 4KB–8KB). No support for storing structured values. No security.
Hidden fields	Can be used for pages that post to themselves or to other pages.	Increases HTML size. No support for storing structured values. No security. No options for persistence.
View state	Support for structured values. Involves less coding. Easy configuration options for security.	Increases HTML size. Works only when a page posts back to itself. No options for persistence.

Server-side Techniques for State Management

One of the advantages of using server-side techniques for state management is that the possibility of a user spoofing or reading the session data is eliminated. However, there is a disadvantage, too: These techniques use server resources, raising scalability issues.

ASP.NET supports server-side state management at two levels—at the level of the Web application using the application state and at the level of a user session using the session state.

Session State

An ASP.NET application creates a session for each user who sends a request to the application. ASP.NET distinctly identifies each of these sessions by sending a unique SessionID to the requesting browser. This SessionID is sent as a cookie or is embedded in the URL, depending on the application's configuration.

This mechanism of sending a SessionID ensures that when the next request is sent to the server, the server can use the unique SessionID to distinctly identify the repeat visit of the user. Both user visits are considered to belong to the same session.

The capability of uniquely identifying and relating requests can be used by Web developers to store session-specific data. A common example is storing shopping cart contents for users as they browse through the store. This session-specific information is collectively known as the session state of the Web application.

Comparing ASP.NET Session State with ASP

ASP.NET comes with a new implementation of session state that removes all the old problems associated with ASP. Table 4.11 compares these improvements.

Table 4.11 Managing the Session State	
The ASP Way	**The ASP.NET Way**
ASP maintains the state in the same process that hosts ASP. If the ASP process somehow fails, the session state is lost.	ASP.NET allows you to store session state out-of-process in a state service or database.
Each ASP Web server maintains its own session state. This creates a problem in the Web farm scenario, where the user's requests can be dynamically routed to different servers in the Web farm.	Because ASP.NET can store its session state out-of-process, several computers in a Web farm can use a common computer as their session state server.
ASP sessions do not work with browsers that don't support cookies or on which users have disabled cookies.	ASP.NET supports cookieless sessions by storing the **SessionID** in the URL itself by changing the application configuration.

Moreover, session state in ASP.NET is configurable. Depending on the requirements of your Web application, you can change the way the session state is maintained in your application by just changing a few lines in an XML-based configuration file (web.config). You learn about session state configuration in Chapter 16, "Configuring a Web Application."

Using Session State

ASP.NET uses an instance of the HttpSessionState class to provide access to the session data for the user who originated the request. In an ASPX page, this object is accessible through the Session property of the Page class. This property provides access to the HttpSessionState object that stores the session state as a collection of key-value pairs, in which the key is of string type while the value can be any type derived from System.Object. Tables 4.12 and 4.13 explain the properties and methods of the HttpSessionState class, respectively.

Table 4.12 Properties of the HttpSessionState Class	
Property	**Description**
CodePage	Specifies the codepage identifier for the current session. This provides compatibility with ASP. **Response.ContentEncoding.CodePage** should be used instead.
Contents	Gets a reference to the session state (**HttpSessionState**) object. This provides compatibility with ASP.
Count	Gets the number of objects in the session state.
IsCookieless	Indicates whether the session is managed using a cookieless session.
IsNewSession	Indicates whether the session has been created with the current request.
IsReadOnly	Indicates whether the session is read-only.
IsSynchronized	Indicates whether access to the session state is read-only (thread-safe).
Keys	Gets a collection of all session keys.
LCID	Specifies the locale identifier (LCID) of the current session.
Mode	Gets the current session state mode. The values are defined by the **SessionStateMode** enumeration: **Off** (disabled), **InProc** (default, session state is stored in process with **aspnet_wp.exe**), **SqlServer** (session state is stored in SQL Server), and **StateServer** (session state is stored in state service).
SessionID	Represents the unique session identifier used to identify a session.
StaticObjects	Returns an **HttpStaticObjectsCollection** object that contains the objects declared by **<object runat="server" scope="Session">** tags within the ASP.NET application file **global.asax**.
SyncRoot	Returns an object that can be used to synchronize access to the collection of session state values.
Timeout	Specifies the timeout period (in minutes) allowed between requests before the session state provider terminates the session.

Table 4.13	Methods of the HttpSessionState Class
Method	**Description**
Abandon()	Cancels the current session.
Add()	Adds the given object identified with the given name to the session state.
Clear()	Removes all objects from the session state.
CopyTo()	Copies the session state values to a one-dimensional array at the specified index.
GetEnumerator()	Returns an enumerator object for the session state values in the current session.
Remove()	Removes an object from the session state.
RemoveAll()	Removes all the objects from the session state. It calls the **Clear()** method internally.
RemoveAt()	Removes an object from the session state at a particular index.

The following example upgrades the Weblog example to maintain the session state at the server side:

1. Add a new Visual C# ASP.NET Web Application project to the solution and name it `Example4_4`.

2. Delete the `WebForm1.aspx` file; then copy `WebForm1.aspx` from the `Example4_1` project to the current project. Open the ASPX file and the CS file and change all occurrences of `Example4_1` to `Example4_4`. Place a new `Label` Web server control (`lblName`) just above the Category dropdown list.

3. Switch to Code view and add the following code above the existing code in the `Page_Load()` event handler:

```
private void Page_Load(object sender, System.EventArgs e)
{
    if(Session["Name"] == null)
    {
        // The Name key is not present in the session state,
        // navigate to WebForm2 to accept name of the user
        Response.Redirect("WebForm2.aspx");
    }
    else
    {
        // The Name key is present in the session state
        lblName.Text="Welcome " + Session["Name"].ToString();
    }
    ...
}
```

4. Double-click the Post button control and modify the `Click` event handler as shown here:

```csharp
private void btnPost_Click(object sender, System.EventArgs e)
{
    // Format the data entered by the user and
    // append it to the existing contents of lblWeblog
    lblWeblog.Text = "<b>" + ddlCategories.SelectedItem.Text
        + " :: " + txtTitle.Text + ":: by " + Session["Name"].ToString()
        + "</b> (" + DateTime.Now.ToString() + ")<hr>"
        + txtMessage.Text + "<p>"  + lblWeblog.Text + "</p>";
}
```

5. Add a new Web form to the project, and name it `WebForm2.aspx`. Change the `pageLayout` property of the DOCUMENT element to `FlowLayout`.

6. Add a `Label` control, `TextBox` control (`txtName`), and `Button` control (`btnSubmit`) to the Web form.

7. Double-click the Submit button control and add the following code in the `Click` event handler:

```csharp
private void btnSubmit_Click(object sender, System.EventArgs e)
{
    // Add the Name entered in the Session
    // Redirect the response to the Weblog page
    Session["Name"] = txtName.Text;
    Response.Redirect("WebForm1.aspx");
}
```

8. Set the project as the startup project for the solution. Set `WebForm1.aspx` as the start page in the project and run the project. You will see that you have been redirected to `WebForm2.aspx`. Enter a name and click the Submit button. You will now see the `WebForm1.aspx` page with a personalized greeting. If you post a message, you should see that your name is now posted along with the title of the message.

9. Close this browser window. Then, open another browser window and browse to `WebForm1.aspx`. You should see that you have again been redirected to `WebForm2.aspx` to enter your name.

The previous example demonstrates that session state is not persistently stored like cookies. The default technique of passing `SessionID` is with nonpersistent cookies, so this example works only if you are using a cookie-enabled browser. If element> element (web.config)> you want to use a cookieless session instead, you must modify the `web.config` file associated with this application to set the `cookieless` attribute to `true` in the `<sessionState>` element, like so:

```xml
<?xml version="1.0" encoding="utf-8" ?>
<configuration>
    <system.web>
        <sessionState mode="Inproc"
            cookieless="true" />
    ...
    </system.Web>
</configuration>
```

Application State

Application state is used to store data that is globally used throughout the application. The application state is stored in memory, and unlike the session state, application state can't be configured for storage on another server or a SQL database. This limits the usefulness of the application state for Web farm scenarios.

Application state can be easily accessed through the Application property of the Page class. This property provides access to the HttpApplicationState object that stores the application state as a collection of key-value pairs, in which the key is a string type and the value can be any type derived from System.Object. Tables 4.14 and 4.15 discuss the properties and methods of the HttpApplicationState class, respectively.

Table 4.14	Properties of the **HttpApplicationState** Class
Property	**Description**
AllKeys	Gets the collection of all key names in the application state as a string array.
Contents	Gets a reference to the application state (**HttpApplicationState**) object. This provides compatibility with ASP.
Count	Gets the number of objects in the application state.
Keys	Gets the **NameObjectCollectionBase.KeysCollection** collection of all the key names in the application state.
StaticObjects	Gets all objects declared via an **<object runat="server" scope="Application"></object>** tag in the ASP.NET application.

Table 4.15	Methods of the **HttpApplicationState** Class
Method	**Description**
Add	Adds a new object to the application state.
Clear	Removes all objects from the application state.
Get	Gets an object from the application state by key name or index.
GetKey	Gets an object from the application state by index.
Lock	Locks access to the application state object. This is used to prevent other clients from changing data stored in the application state.
Remove	Removes an object from the application state.
RemoveAll	Removes all the objects from the application state. Calls the **Clear()** method internally.
RemoveAt	Removes an object from the application state at a particular index.
Set	Updates the value of an object stored in the application state.
Unlock	Unlocks access to the application state.

The following example demonstrates the use of the `Application` property to store the applicationwide data:

1. Add a new Visual C# ASP.NET Web Application project to the solution, and name it **Example4_5**. Add a Label control (`lblInfo`) on the form.

2. Switch to Code view and add the following code in the `Page_Load()` event handler:

```
private void Page_Load(object sender, System.EventArgs e)
{
    // Lock the Application before modifying application state
    Application.Lock();
    if(Application["HitCount"] != null)
    {
        // Increment the HitCount variable in the application state
        Application["HitCount"] = (int) Application["HitCount"] + 1;
    }
    else
    {
        Application["HitCount"] = 1;
    }
    // Unlock the application as the changes are done
    Application.UnLock();
    // Fetch the value of HitCount from the application state
    lblInfo.Text = "This page has been accessed (" +
        Application["HitCount"].ToString() + ") times!";
}
```

3. Run the project. You should see that the page shows the number of times it has been accessed. Refresh the page, and you should see that the page access counter increments by 1.

4. Close this browser window. Run the project again; you should see that the page retains the value of the counter and increments it by 1.

Note that the technique used in the previous example is a volatile way to store the hit count (that is, users only see the total number of hits since the last time the application started). If you want the hit count to persist across application restarts, you should store the hit count periodically to a database.

In the example, you modified the contents of the application state using a pair of `Application.Lock()` and `Application.UnLock()` methods. Locking is important for keeping application state consistent when multiple users might want to modify the application object's content concurrently. While the application is locked, only the current user can change the contents of the application state. This locking mechanism can severely reduce the scalability of a Web application; therefore, you should usually not store any updatable data in the application state.

> You don't need to use the **Application.Lock()** and **Application.Unlock()** methods in the **Application_Start()** and **Application_End()** event handlers because these event handlers are called only once during the lifetime of an application.

> ASP.NET provides an alternative way of maintaining global state for an application using the application data cache. The application data cache should be your preferred choice for storing global data in an ASP.NET application. You'll learn more about this in Chapter 16.

Navigation Between Pages

A typical Web application is a collection of Web pages linked to each other. You can use the `HyperLink` control to navigate to a different Web page when the hyperlink is clicked. If you need to navigate to a Web page programmatically, you can use the following methods provided by ASP.NET:

➤ `Response.Redirect()`

➤ `Server.Transfer()`

➤ `Server.Execute()`

The `Response.Redirect()` Method

The `Response.Redirect()` method causes the browser to connect to the specified URL. When the `Response.Redirect()` method is called, it creates a response whose header contains a 302 (Object Moved) status code and the target URL. When the browser receives this response from the server, it uses the header information to generate another request to the specified URL. When using the `Response.Redirect()` method, the redirection occurs at the client side and involves two round trips to the server.

Using the `Response.Redirect()` method is recommended in the following cases:

➤ You want to connect to a resource on *any* Web server.

➤ You want to connect to a non-ASPX resource (such as an HTML file).

➤ You want to pass a query string as part of the URL.

The **Server.Transfer()** Method

The `Server.Transfer()` method transfers the execution from the current ASPX page to the specified ASPX page. The path specified to the ASPX page must be on the same Web server and must not contain a query string.

When this transfer occurs, execution of the current ASPX page terminates and control is transferred to another ASPX page. The new ASPX page still uses the response stream created by the prior ASPX page. The URL in the browser still shows the original page because the redirection occurs on the server side and the browser remains unaware of the transfer.

When you want to transfer control to an ASPX page residing on the same Web server, you should use `Server.Transfer()` instead of `Response.Redirect()` because `Server.Transfer()` avoids an unnecessary round trip and provides better performance and user experience.

The default use of the `Server.Transfer()` method does not pass the form data and the query string of the original page request to the page receiving the transfer. However, you can preserve the form data and query string of the original page by passing a `true` value to the optional second argument of the `Server.Transfer()` method. The second argument takes a Boolean value that indicates whether to preserve the form and query string collections.

In the **Server.Transfer()** method, when you choose to preserve the form and query string collections, you need to be aware of one thing: The destination page contains the form and query string collections that were created by the original page. As a result, the hidden **__VIEWSTATE** field of the original page is also preserved in the form collection. The view state is page scoped and is valid for a particular page only, which causes the ASP.NET MAC to announce that the view state of the new page has been tampered with. Therefore, when you choose to preserve the form and query string collections of the original page, you must set the **EnableViewStateMac** attribute of the **Page** directive to **false** for the destination page.

The **Server.Execute()** Method

The `Server.Execute()` method enables the current ASPX page to execute a specified ASPX page. However, the path to the specified ASPX page must be on the same Web server and must not contain a query string.

After the specified ASPX page is executed, control transfers back to the original page from which the `Server.Execute()` method was called. This technique of page navigation is analogous to making a method call to an ASPX page.

The called ASPX page has access to the form and query string collections of the calling page. Thus, for the reasons explained in the previous section, you must set the `EnableViewStateMac` attribute of the `Page` directive to `false` on the called ASPX page.

By default, the output of the executed page is added to the current response stream. This method also has an overloaded version in which the output of the redirected page can be fetched in a TextWriter object instead of adding the output to the response stream. This helps you control where the output is placed on the original page.

The output returned to the browser by **Server.Execute()** and **Server.Transfer()** might contain multiple **<html>** and **<body>** tags because the response stream remains the same while executing another ASPX page. Therefore, the output that results from calling these methods might contain invalid HTML code.

Exam Prep Questions

Question 1

> You are developing a Web form to display weather information. On the initial requests to the Web form, you need to do some initialization that will change the appearance of the form and assign values to some controls. However, this initialization should not be repeated again when the user submits the Web form. How should you write the code to accomplish this? (Select two.)
>
> ❑ A. Write the code inside the **Page_Init()** event handler.
> ❑ B. Write the code inside the **Page_Load()** event handler.
> ❑ C. Execute the initialization code only when the **Page.IsPostBack** property is **true**.
> ❑ D. Execute the initialization code only when the **Page.IsPostBack** property is **false**.

The correct answers are B and D. The code for the initialization of controls should be placed inside the Page_Load() event handler. If you want to execute the initialization code only when the page is first requested and do not want to run that code again at the time of the page postback, you must execute the code when the IsPostBack property of the Page class is false. Answer A is incorrect because during the Init event, server controls are not certain to be created and are not ready for access. Answer C is incorrect because, if you execute the code when the IsPostBack property of the Page class is true, the initialization code will be executed each time the page is submitted.

Question 2

> You have used ASP.NET to develop an inventory management system for your organization, and associates can access this application from the company's intranet. When analyzing users' feedback on the applications, you found that users complain that they receive an annoying flash when they submit forms. They also complain that the data entry form does not always remember the active controls and, because of this, users have to press the Tab key several times before they can focus again on the desired control. This makes the data entry inconvenient and time-consuming. On analyzing further usage data, you found that all the users in your company use Internet Explorer 5.0 or above to access your application. What should you do to eliminate the problems reported by the users?
>
> ○ A. Set the **SmartNavigation** attribute of the **Page** directive to **true**.
> ○ B. Set the **AutoEventWireup** attribute of the **Page** directive to **true**.
> ○ C. Set the **EnableViewState** attribute of the **Page** directive to **true**.
> ○ D. Set the **ClientTarget** attribute of the **Page** directive to **"ie5"**.

The correct answer is A. When all users are using Internet Explorer version 5.0 or later, you can set the SmartNavigation attribute to true. This eliminates the flash and causes Internet Explorer to focus active control. Answer B is incorrect because the AutoEventWireup attribute is useful only for deciding whether the event handlers (such as Page_Init() and Page_Load())for the page-level events will be automatically called. Answer C is incorrect because the EnableViewState attribute is used to enable or disable ViewState for a page; ViewState is only a state management technique and does not affect how the page is displayed. Answer D is incorrect because in this case, although the page is rendered for Internet Explorer version 5.0, the ClientTarget property will not eliminate the reported problem.

Question 3

You are developing an ASP.NET Web site for a popular Web development magazine. You want to keep track of how many times each page of your Web application is accessed. This data will help your company to analyze the application's usage patterns and develop appropriate Web content. You want to write minimum code to achieve this task; which of the following techniques will you use?

- ○ A. Use the **Page_Load()** event handler to increment the usage counter of the page.
- ○ B. Use the **Application_BeginRequest()** event handler to increment the usage counter of the page.
- ○ C. Use the **Session_Start()** event handler to increment the usage counter of the page.
- ○ D. Use the **Application_Start()** event handler to increment the usage counter of the page.

The correct answer is B. Answers C and D do not work with each page request, so only options A and B are viable choices. Between these two choices, you should choose to write the code in the Application_BeginRequest() event handler of the global.asax file because, if you use the Page_Load() event handler, you'll have to write code in each and every ASPX page in the application.

Question 4

Your ASP.NET page contains a page-level variable of **ArrayList** type. You want to preserve the value of this variable across page postbacks, but you do not need this variable in any other page in the application. Which of the following state management techniques provides the best way to achieve this?

○ A.   Query strings

○ B.   Cookies

○ C.   Session

○ D.   View state

The correct answer is D. In the given case, the variable is required on only a single page; therefore, it is most suitable to store its values in view state. Answers A and B are incorrect because client-side state management techniques such as cookies and query strings do not allow you to store structured data. Answer C is incorrect because storing values in the session involves consumption of server resources.

Question 5

You are developing a Web application for an online bank. Your application enables users to access their account information and transactions right from their desktops. When a user logs on to your application, you want to show the username and current balance on all the pages of the application until the user logs off. You also want your application to be safe from malicious users. Which of the following state management techniques should you use? (Select the best answer.)

○ A.   Cookies

○ B.   View state

○ C.   View state with encryption

○ D.   Session

The correct answer is D. Session data is stored at the server side and cannot be easily tampered with. Answer A is incorrect because cookies can be easily accessed and used by malicious users. Answer B is incorrect because view state information can be easily decoded. Answer C is incorrect because, although view state with encryption provides a high level of encryption, it is available only on the same page, and in the given scenario, you want the name and current balance to be displayed on all the pages.

Question 6

> You have developed and deployed a Web application for an online bank. This application enables users to access their account information and transactions right from their desktops. Because the application deals with financial data, you have enabled encryption for the view state of all the pages. The bank business has rapidly increased, and the management has decided to upgrade the single Web server to a Web farm of Web servers. When you were testing the application for the Web farm, sometimes the application worked fine but other times it generated a view state error. What should you do to resolve this problem?
>
> ○ A. Use the same validation key for all the Web servers in the Web farm.
>
> ○ B. Use different validation keys for all the Web servers in the Web farm.
>
> ○ C. Set the **EnableViewStateMac** attribute to **true** for all the pages in the application.
>
> ○ D. Set the **EnableViewStateMac** attribute to **false** for all the pages in the application.

The correct answer is A. If the validation keys don't match, an error will occur when the user is directed to a different server in the Web farm. Answer B is incorrect because, when you use view state encryption in a Web farm, you must use the same validation key for all the Web servers. Answer C is incorrect because the given scenario specifies that the encryption is already enabled on all the pages. Answer D is incorrect because setting the EnableViewStateMac attribute to false turns off the view state encryption and is not a desirable solution.

Question 7

> You have recently developed and deployed a Web application for a large automotive parts supplier. This application is used by users from the United States, Europe, and Asia. You have received complaints from several users that the Web pages take a very long time to download. You did some research and found that an HTML element named __VIEWSTATE in your pages is storing a large amount of data and is responsible for the bigger page sizes. Your manager recommended that you disable view state wherever it is unnecessary in the application. In which of the following cases would you want to disable view state in your application? (Select all that apply.)
>
> ❑ A. Those pages that do not postback
>
> ❑ B. Those pages that postback
>
> ❑ C. Those controls that are not dynamically changed
>
> ❑ D. Those controls that are dynamically changed
>
> ❑ E. Those controls that are modified at every page load
>
> ❑ F. Those controls that are not modified at every page load

The correct answers are A, C, and E. If the pages don't post back to themselves, they are not making use of view state; in that case, you should disable view state for the whole page. For all other pages, the controls that are not dynamically changed need not have their view states enabled. Also, the controls whose values are modified on every page load need not store their values in view state. Answers B, D, and F are incorrect because these cases require view state to be enabled in order to work.

Question 8

In a Web page of your application, you allow users to select a product and its quantity. When the user has made her selection, you want to transfer the user to another page named **ShoppingCart.aspx** with the **ProductId** and the **Quantity** as the query string parameters to the ASPX page. You want to write minimum code to accomplish this objective. Which of the following options should you select?

- ○ A. A **HyperLink** control
- ○ B. The **Response.Redirect()** method
- ○ C. The **Server.Transfer()** method
- ○ D. The **Server.Execute()** method

The correct answer is B. The Response.Redirect() method redirects the client to a new URL that might include query string parameters. Answer A is incorrect because, although the Hyperlink control supports query strings, the redirection needs to be performed within the code. Answers C and D are incorrect because you cannot use query strings with the Server.Transfer() and Server.Execute() methods.

Question 9

You are developing an online bill payment system using ASP.NET. When a user logs on to the application by entering her username and password, you want to programmatically redirect the user to a page named **accountdetails.aspx** in the same Web application. You want an application that responds quickly to your users. Which of the following methods would you use to accomplish this?

- ○ A. A **HyperLink** control
- ○ B. The **Response.Redirect()** method
- ○ C. The **Server.Transfer()** method
- ○ D. The **Server.Execute()** method

The correct answer is C. You should use the `Server.Transfer()` method to redirect users to another ASPX page on the same Web server. Answer A is incorrect because the `HyperLink` control requires additional action from the user. Answer B is incorrect because the `Response.Redirect()` method involves an additional round trip and is not a good option when you want the application to be faster. Answer D is incorrect because the `Server.Execute()` method is more like a procedure call and, after executing the specified page, the control comes back to the calling page.

Question 10

You are using a **DataGrid** control in an ASP.NET page (**ShowData.aspx**) of your Web application. You want to invoke another ASP.NET page (**GetData.aspx**) that returns the data to be displayed in the **DataGrid** control. You are using the **Server.Execute()** method to invoke **GetData.aspx** from the **ShowData.aspx** page. When you run the application, you get an **Invalid View** state error. Which of the following options would you choose to resolve this error?

- ○ A. Use the **Server.Transfer()** method instead of the **Server.Execute()** method.
- ○ B. Set the **EnableViewStateMac** attribute to **false** in the **Page** directive of **GetData.aspx**.
- ○ C. Set the **EnableViewStateMac** attribute to **false** in the **Page** directive of **ShowData.aspx**.
- ○ D. Set the **EnableViewState** attribute to **false** in the **Page** directive of **GetData.aspx**.

The correct answer is B. You get an error while executing the `Server.Execute()` method because the view state of the `ShowData.aspx` page is passed to the `GetData.aspx` page along with the form and query string collections, causing the ASP.NET machine authentication check to fail. You need to set the `EnableViewStateMac` attribute of the `Page` directive in the `GetData.aspx` page to `false` to resolve this error. Answer A is incorrect because you do not want to transfer the control to the `GetData.aspx` page. Answer C is incorrect because the view state of the `ShowData.aspx` page is mixing up the `GetData.aspx` page and not vice versa. Answer D is incorrect because disabling view state affects the functionality of Web server controls such as `DataGrid`.

Need to Know More?

 The Visual Studio .NET Combined Help Collection, including *Introduction to Web Forms State Management* and *Web Forms Page Processing*.

 Onion, Fritz. *Essential ASP.NET.* Reading, MA: Addison-Wesley, 2002.

 Watch the Visual Studio .NET Seminars at www.msdn.com/seminar/ mmcfeed/mmcdisplayfeed.asp?Lang=en&Product=103328&Audience= 100402.

 Read the How-To articles on Web Development at www. msdn.com/howto/webdev.asp#asp.

 Visit ASP.NET Forums at www.asp.net/forums.

 Download the ViewState Decoder utility from www.develop.com/ devresources/resourcedetail.aspx?type=t&id=827.

 Review the ASP.NET state management articles at http:// support.microsoft.com/common/canned.aspx?Sz=kbstate.

 Review the ASP.NET How-To articles at http://support. microsoft.com/common/canned.aspx?LL=kbaspnetSearch&Sz= kbhowtomaster.

Error Handling for the User Interface

Terms you'll need to understand:

✓ **Application.Error** event
✓ Custom error pages
✓ Custom exceptions
✓ Exception
✓ **Page.Error** event
✓ The **catch** block
✓ The **finally** block
✓ The **throw** statement
✓ The **try** block
✓ Unhandled exceptions

Techniques you'll need to master:

✓ Knowing how to handle exceptions using the **try-catch-finally** blocks
✓ Knowing how to create custom exception classes and custom error messages; learn to implement them in a program
✓ Knowing how to configure custom error pages in the **web.config** file
✓ Experimenting with code that performs error handling at the **Page_Error()** or **Application_Error()** event handlers

Exception handling helps you in creating robust applications. Fortunately, exception handling is an integral part of the .NET Framework. The framework classes, as well as user-defined classes, throw exception objects to indicate unexpected problems in the code. In this chapter, you will learn how to handle exceptions in ASP.NET Web applications.

Understanding Exceptions

An *exception* occurs when a program encounters any unexpected problem, such as running out of memory or attempting to read from a file that no longer exists.

An exception generally results in abruptly terminating the program after displaying an error message. Ideally, your program should be capable of handling these exceptional situations and, if possible, gracefully recover from them. This is called *exception handling*. Proper use of exception handling can make your programs robust, as well as easy to develop and maintain.

The Common Language Runtime (CLR) views an *exception* as any object that encapsulates any information about the problems that occurred during program execution. The FCL provides two categories of exceptions:

➤ ApplicationException—Represents exceptions thrown by applications

➤ SystemException—Represents exceptions thrown by the CLR

Both of these exception classes derive from the base Exception class. Table 5.1 lists the important properties of all three of these classes.

Table 5.1	Important Properties of the Exception Class
Property	**Description**
HelpLink	Specifies the uniform resource locator (URL) of the help file associated with this exception.
InnerException	Specifies an exception associated with this exception. This property is helpful when a series of exceptions is involved. Each new exception can preserve the information about the previous exception by storing it in the **InnerException** property.
Message	Specifies textual information that indicates the reason for the error and provides possible resolutions.
Source	Specifies the name of the application causing the error.

(continued)

Table 5.1	Important Properties of the Exception Class *(continued)*
Property	**Description**
StackTrace	Specifies where an error occurred. If the debugging information is available, the stack trace includes the name of the source file and the program line number.
TargetSite	Represents the method that throws the current exception.

Handling Exceptions

You can handle exceptions in Visual C# .NET programs by using a combination of these exception handling statements: try, catch, finally, and throw.

The try Block

You should place code that might cause exceptions in a try block. A typical try block looks similar to the following:

```
try
{
    // code that may cause exception
}
```

When an exception occurs at any point, rather than executing any further, the CLR searches for the nearest try block that encloses the exceptional code. The control is then passed to a matching catch block (if any) and then to the finally block (if any) associated with this try block.

A try block cannot exist on its own; it must be immediately followed either by one or more catch blocks or by a finally block.

The catch Block

You can have several catch blocks immediately following a try block. When an exception occurs in a statement placed inside the try block, the CLR looks for a matching catch block capable of handling that type of exception. A typical try-catch block looks like this:

```
try
{
    // code that may cause exception
}
catch(ExceptionTypeA)
{
```

```
    // Statements to handle errors
    // occurring in the associated try block
}
catch(ExceptionTypeB)
{
    // Statements to handle errors occurring
    // in the associated try block
}
```

The formula the CLR uses to match the exception is simple: It looks for the first `catch` block with either the same exception or any of the exception's base classes. For example, a `DivideByZeroException` exception would match with any of these exceptions: `DivideByZeroException`, `ArithmeticException`, `SystemException`, and `Exception`. In the case of multiple `catch` blocks, only the first matching `catch` block is executed and all other `catch` blocks are ignored.

 If no matching **catch** block exists, an unhandled exception occurs and is propagated back to its caller code (the code that called the current method). If the exception is not handled there, it propagates further up the hierarchy of method calls. If the exception is not handled anywhere, it goes to the CLR for processing. The CLR's default behavior is to immediately terminate the processing of the Web page and display error messages.

When you write multiple `catch` blocks, you need to arrange them from specific exception types to more general exception types. For example, the `catch` block for catching the `DivideByZeroException` exception should always precede the `catch` block for catching the `ArithmeticException` exception because the `DivideByZeroException` exception derives from the `ArithmeticException` exception and is therefore more specific than `ArithmeticException`. The compiler flags an error if you do not follow this rule.

A `try` block need not necessarily have a `catch` block associated with it; however, in that case, it must have a `finally` block associated with it.

The finally Block

You use the `finally` block to write cleanup code that maintains your application in a consistent state and preserves the external environment. For example, you can write code to close files, database connections, and related input/output (I/O) resources in a `finally` block.

A `try` block doesn't have to have an associated `finally` block. However, if you do write a `finally` block, you cannot have more than one, and the `finally` block must appear after all the `catch` blocks.

The `finally` block can be used in the form of a `try-finally` block without any `catch` block between them. Here's an example:

```
try
{
   // Write code to allocate some resources
}
finally
{
   // Write code to dispose all allocated resources
}
```

This use ensures that allocated resources are properly disposed of, no matter what happens in the `try` block. In fact, Visual C# .NET provides a `using` statement that does exactly the same job but with less code to write. A typical use of the `using` statement is as follows:

```
// Write code to allocate some resource list the allocated resources
in a comma-separated list inside the parentheses of the using block
using(...)
{
  // use the allocated resource
}
// Here, the Dispose() method is called automatically for all the
// objects referenced in the parentheses of the using statement
```

The following example shows you how to use a `try-catch-finally` block to handle exceptions:

1. Create a new Visual C# ASP.NET Web application project in the Visual Studio .NET IDE. Specify the location of the project as
   `http://localhost/ExamCram/315C05`.

2. Add a new Web form to the project, and name it `Example5_1.aspx`.

3. Place three `TextBox` controls (`txtMiles`, `txtGallons`, and `txtEfficiency`) and a `Button` (`btnCalculate`) on the Web form's surface and arrange them as shown in Figure 5.1. Add the `Label` controls as necessary.

4. Attach a `Click` event handler to the `btnCalculate` control and add the following code to it:

```
private void btnCalculate_Click(object sender, System.EventArgs e)
{
    try
    {
        decimal decMiles = Convert.ToDecimal(txtMiles.Text);
        decimal decGallons = Convert.ToDecimal(txtGallons.Text);
        decimal decEfficiency = decMiles/decGallons;
        txtEfficiency.Text = String.Format("{0:n}", decEfficiency);
    }
    catch (FormatException fe)
    {
        string msg = String.Format(
            "Message: {0}<br> Stack Trace:<br> {1}",
```

```
                    fe.Message, fe.StackTrace);
            lblMessage.Text = fe.GetType().ToString() +
                "<br>"  + msg + "<br>";
    }
    catch (DivideByZeroException dbze)
    {
        string msg = String.Format(
            "Message: {0}<br> Stack Trace:<br> {1}",
            dbze.Message, dbze.StackTrace);
        lblMessage.Text = dbze.GetType().ToString() +
            "<br>"  + msg + "<br>";
    }
    // Catches all CLS-compliant exceptions
    catch(Exception ex)
    {
        string msg = String.Format(
            "Message: {0}<br> Stack Trace:<br> {1}",
            ex.Message, ex.StackTrace);
        lblMessage.Text = ex.GetType().ToString() +
            "<br>"  + msg + "<br>";
    }
    // Catches all other exceptions including the
    // Non-CLS compliant exceptions
    catch
    {
        // Just rethrow the exception to the caller
        throw;
    }
    // Use finally block to perform cleanup operations
    finally
    {
        lblMessage.Text += "Finally block always executes " +
            " whether or not exception occurs" + "<br>";
    }
}
```

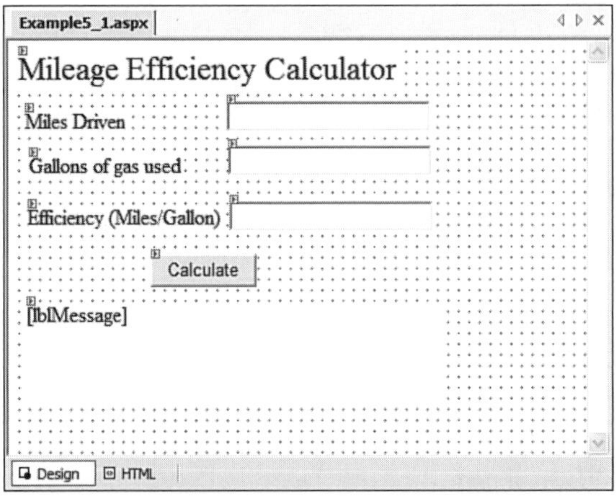

Figure 5.1 The Mileage Efficiency Calculator Web form implements exception handling for the user interface.

5. Set the Web form as the start page for the project and run the project. Enter values for miles and gallons and click the Calculate button. The program calculates the mileage efficiency, as expected. Now enter the value 0 in the Gallons of Gas Used field; the program shows a message about the DivideByZeroException exception (as shown in Figure 5.2) and continues running. Now enter some alphabetic characters in the fields and click the Calculate button. This time you get a FormatException message and the program continues to run. Now try entering a large value for both fields. If the values are large enough, the program encounters an OverflowException exception, but continues running.

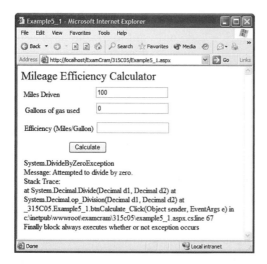

Figure 5.2 To get information about an exception, catch the exception object and access its **Message** property.

All languages that follow the Common Language Specification (CLS) throw exceptions of type **System.Exception** or a type that derives from **System.Exception**. A non-CLS-compliant language might throw exceptions of other types, too. You can catch those types of exceptions by placing a general **catch** block (one that does not specify any exception) with a **try** block. In fact, a general **catch** block can catch exceptions of all types, so it is the most generic of all **catch** blocks and should be the last **catch** block among the multiple **catch** blocks associated with a **try** block.

If you have a **finally** block associated with a **try** block, the code in the **finally** block always executes whether an exception occurs or not. In addition, if a transfer-control statement such as **goto**, **break**, or **continue** exists in either the **try** or the **catch** block, the control transfer happens only after the code in the **finally** block is executed. The Visual C# .NET compiler does not allow you to put a transfer-control statement such as **goto** inside a **finally** block.

The **throw** Statement

A `throw` statement explicitly generates an exception in code. You use `throw` when a particular path in code results in an anomalous situation.

There are two ways you can use the `throw` statement. In its simplest form, you can just rethrow the exception in a `catch` block:

```
catch(Exception e)
{
    //TODO: Add code to create an entry in event log
    throw;
}
```

This use of the `throw` statement rethrows the exception that was just caught. It can be useful in situations in which you do not want to handle the exception yourself but would like to take other actions (for example, recording the error in an event log or sending an email notification about the error) when an exception occurs. Then, you can pass the exception as is to its caller.

The second way of using a `throw` statement is to use it to throw explicitly created exceptions, as in this example:

```
string strMessage = "EndDate should be greater than the StartDate";
ArgumentOutOfRangeException newException =
    new ArgumentOutOfRangeException(strMessage);
throw newException;
```

In this example, you first create a new instance of the `ArgumentOutOfRangeException` object and associate a custom error message with it; then you throw the newly created exception.

You are not required to put this usage of the `throw` statement inside a `catch` block because you are just creating and throwing a new exception, rather than rethrowing an existing one. You typically use this technique to raise your own custom exceptions.

 When you create an exception object, you should use the constructor that allows you to associate a custom error message rather than use the default constructor. The custom error message can pass specific information about the cause of the error, as well as a possible way to resolve it.

 The **throw** statement is an expensive operation. Use of **throw** consumes significant system resources as compared to just returning a value from a method. You should therefore use the **throw** statement cautiously and only when necessary because it has the potential to make your programs slow.

An alternative way of rethrowing an exception is to throw it after wrapping it with additional useful information, like so:

```
catch(ArgumentNullException ane)
{
    // TODO: Add code to create an entry in the log file
    string strMessage = "CustomerID cannot be null";
    ArgumentNullException newException =
        new ArgumentNullException(strMessage, ane);
    throw newException;
}
```

You might need to catch an exception that you cannot handle completely. You would then perform any required processing and throw a more relevant and informative exception to the caller code so it can perform the rest of the processing. In this case, you can create a new exception whose constructor wraps the previously caught exception in the new exception's InnerException property. The caller code then has more information available to handle the exception appropriately.

Creating and Using Custom Exceptions

The .NET Framework enables you to define custom exception classes. To keep your custom-defined Exception class consistent with the .NET exception-handling framework, Microsoft recommends that you consider the following when you design a custom exception class:

➤ Create an exception class only if no exception class exists that satisfies your requirement.

➤ Derive all programmer-defined exception classes from the System.ApplicationException class.

➤ End the name of a custom exception class with the word Exception—for example, MyOwnCustomException.

➤ Implement three constructors with the signatures shown in the following code:

```
public class MyOwnCustomException : ApplicationException
{
    // Default constructor
    public MyOwnCustomException ()
    {
    }
```

```
        // Constructor accepting a string message
        public MyOwnCustomException (string message) : base(message)
        {
        }

        // Constructor accepting a string message and an inner exception
        // that will be wrapped by this custom exception class
        public MyOwnCustomException(string message,
            Exception inner) : base(message, inner)
        {
        }
    }
```

Managing Unhandled Exceptions

The unhandled exceptions are those exceptions that are not caught in a `try-catch` block (inline coding) in an application. Whenever an unhandled exception occurs, ASP.NET displays its default error page to the user. The default error page can provide error details, along with code that can be a major security concern. You're usually better off displaying your own custom error messages instead.

ASP.NET stops processing the Web page after it encounters an unhandled exception. However, you can trap an unhandled exception at an object level, such as `Page` or `Application`.

Using Custom Error Pages

ASP.NET provides full built-in support for configuring custom error pages in a Web application. This configuration information is stored in an XML-based configuration file (`web.config`) where you use the `<customErrors>` element to configure custom error pages. The `<customErrors>` element consists of two attributes—`mode` and `defaultRedirect`. The `mode` attribute specifies how the custom error pages should be displayed and can have one of the following three values:

➤ `On`—Displays custom error pages at both the local and remote clients.

➤ `Off`—Disables custom error pages at both the local and remote clients.

➤ `RemoteOnly`—Displays custom error pages only at remote clients. For the local machine, it displays the default ASP.NET error pages. This is the default setting in the `web.config` file.

The `defaultRedirect` attribute is an optional attribute that specifies the custom error page to be displayed when an error occurs. You can display either a static page, such as HTML, or a dynamic page, such as ASPX, as a custom error page. When the `defaultRedirect` attribute is not set to a custom error page, ASP.NET displays a generic error message in the browser.

A specific custom error page can be displayed for a specific HTTP error code by associating the error code with the Web page through the `<error>` element. Multiple `<error>` elements can be nested inside the `<customErrors>` element. The `<error>` element consist of the following two attributes:

➤ `statusCode`—HTTP error status code. For example: `403` (Forbidden), `404` (Not Found), `500` (Internal Server Error), and so on.

➤ `redirect`—The error page to which the browser should be redirected when the associated HTTP error occurs.

If an error occurs that has no specific page assigned through the `<error>` element, the custom error page specified by the `defaultRedirect` attribute of the `<customErrors>` element is displayed.

 An alternative way of configuring custom error pages is through Internet Information Services (IIS). When given a choice between IIS and ASP.NET custom error pages, you might prefer ASP.NET because in ASP.NET the custom pages are configured in an XML-based **web.config** (application configuration) file, resulting in easy (**xcopy**) deployment and management.

The following example shows how to set custom error pages for a Web application in the `web.config` file:

1. Open the `web.config` file of your project from the Solution Explorer. Search for the `<customErrors>` element in the file and modify it with the following code in the file:

```
<customErrors mode="On"
   defaultRedirect="ApplicationError.htm">
    <error statusCode="403" redirect="Forbidden.htm" />
    <error statusCode="404" redirect="NotFound.htm" />
</customErrors>
```

2. Add a new HTML page, called `ApplicationError.htm`, to your project. Switch to HTML view and modify it with the following HTML code:

```
<HTML>
    <HEAD>
        <TITLE>Application Error</TITLE>
    </HEAD>
    <BODY>
        <H1>Application Error</H1>
        <P>Sorry, there is a server application error.</P>
    </BODY>
</HTML>
```

3. Add a new HTML page, called Forbidden.htm, to your project. Switch to HTML view and modify it with the following HTML code:

```
<HTML>
    <HEAD><TITLE>Page Forbidden</TITLE></HEAD>
    <BODY>
        <H1>Page Forbidden</H1>
        <P>Sorry, this page is forbidden.</P>
    </BODY>
</HTML>
```

4. Add a new HTML page, called NotFound.htm, to your project. Switch to HTML view and modify it with the following HTML code:

```
<HTML>
    <HEAD><TITLE>Page Not Found</TITLE></HEAD>
    <BODY>
        <H1>Page Not Found</H1>
        <P>Sorry we don't have the page you requested.</P>
    </BODY>
</HTML>
```

5. Open the Example5_1.aspx file in code view. Comment the catch blocks in the btnCalculate_Click event handler so that exceptions are unhandled.

6. Set Example5_1.aspx as the start page for the project.

7. Run the project, enter invalid values for miles and gallons, and click the Calculate button. The Web page Example5_1.aspx comments the catch block and hence has no inline coding to handle exceptions. Therefore, it throws an unhandled exception and the ApplicationError.htm page is displayed.

8. Now try displaying the code-behind file of Example5_1.aspx by typing **http://localhost/ExamCram/315C05/Example5_1.aspx.cs**. You should see that the Forbidden.htm page is displayed.

9. Now, try displaying a nonexistent page in the Web application. Say that you make a mistake by typing a hyphen instead of an underscore symbol, such as **http://localhost/ExamCram/315C05/Example5-1.aspx**. Notice that the NotFound.htm page is displayed. The custom error page is displayed only if the not found page is one that would have been processed by ASP.NET. For example, if you tried to get to Example5-1.htm, you wouldn't see the custom error page because IIS would never call ASP.NET to process the request of the HTML page.

10. Repeat steps 7–9 after changing the value of the mode attribute (of the <customErrors> element in the web.config file) to Off (where no custom error pages will be displayed) and then RemoteOnly (where custom error

pages will be displayed on remote machines and default errors on the local machine).

> Sometimes a particular Web page in an application might want to display its own error page. This can be done by setting the **ErrorPage** attribute of the **Page** directive or the **ErrorPage** property of the **Page** class to the desired custom error page. You would use this code:
>
> **<%@ Page language="C#" ErrorPage="*SpecificErrorPage.htm*"%>**
>
> When the custom error page is set using this technique, it overwrites the settings that apply to this Web page via the **web.config** file.

Using Error Events

When an unhandled exception occurs in a Web application, the following events are fired in successive order:

1. Page.Error, which is a page-level event handled by the Page_Error() event handler

2. Application.Error, which is an application-level event handled by the Application_Error() event handler

Both of these event handlers can be used to trap and work with unhandled exceptions.

Using the **Page.Error** Event

The Page_Error() event handler can be used to trap unhandled exceptions at a page level, like so:

```
private void Page_Error(object sender, System.EventArgs e)
{
    Response.Write("Error Details: <br>");
    // Display error details. Get the last error on the Server
    Response.Write(Server.GetLastError().Message + "<br>");
    Response.Write(Server.GetLastError().StackTrace + "<br>");
    // Clear the error to flush the new response
    // and erase the default ASP.NET error page
    Server.ClearError();
}
```

The preceding Page_Error() event handler displays the details of the unhandled exception. This is achieved by calling the HttpServerUtility object's GetLastError() method via the Server property. The method returns an Exception object that provides a reference to the last exception that occurred on the server.

The ClearError() method of the HttpServerUtility object clears the last exception and does not fire subsequent error events (for example,

`Application.Error`) for the exception. For this reason, you will notice that the custom error page is not displayed even though an unhandled error exists. Also for the same reason, the default ASP.NET error page is not displayed if no custom error page is configured.

Using the **Application.Error** Event

You can also choose to trap unhandled exceptions of the entire application in the `Application.Error` event. This event is handled by the `Application_Error()` event handler available in the ASP.NET application file, `global.asax`. Handling exceptions at the application level can be helpful when you want to take custom actions, such as logging the exception-related information in the event log for all Web pages, like so:

```
protected void Application_Error(Object sender, EventArgs e)
{
   // Get the Exception object wrapped in the InnerException property
   Exception unhandledException =
     (Exception)Server.GetLastError().InnerException;

   //If no event source exists, create an event source
   if(!EventLog.SourceExists("Mileage Efficiency Calculator"))
      EventLog.CreateEventSource("Mileage Efficiency Calculator",
        "Mileage Efficiency Calculator Log");

   // Create an EventLog instance and assign its source.
   EventLog eventLog = new EventLog();
   eventLog.Source = "Mileage Efficiency Calculator";
   string type= unhandledException.Message;
   // Write an informational entry to the event log.
   eventLog.WriteEntry(unhandledException.Message);
   Response.Write("An exception occurred: " +
      "Created an entry in the event log.");
   Server.ClearError();
}
```

When ASP.NET propagates the unhandled exception to the `Application` object (the `Application.Error` event), the `Exception` object is wrapped in an `HttpUnhandledException` object. Therefore, to access the exception at the application level, you must access the `Exception` object's `InnerException` property.

If the `Page_Error()` event handler does not clear the unhandled exception through the `ClearError()` method, both the `Page.Error` and `Application.Error` events are fired. Further, if the `Application_Error()` event handler does not clear the exception, the error page (custom, if configured) is displayed in the browser. This happens because the error is not cleared although the event handlers for the `Page.Error` and `Application.Error` events are executed.

Exam Prep Questions

Question 1

> You are creating a data import utility for a personal information system you recently designed. When the record in the source data file is not in the required format, the application needs to throw a custom exception. You want to keep the name of this exception class as **InvalidRecordStructureException**. Which of the following classes would you choose as the base class for the custom exception class?
>
> ○ A. **ApplicationException**
>
> ○ B. **Exception**
>
> ○ C. **SystemException**
>
> ○ D. **InvalidFilterCriteriaException**

Answer A is correct. When you create a class for handling custom exceptions in your programs, the best practice is to derive it from the ApplicationException class. Answer B is incorrect because the Exception class is the base class for both the ApplicationException and SystemException classes and should not be derived from. Answer C is incorrect because the SystemException class represents the exceptions raised by the CLR and is used for system-defined exceptions. Answer D is incorrect because InvalidFilterCriteriaException is thrown when a filter criteria is not valid and it is not suitable as a base class for the exception defined in the question.

Question 2

> You are required to debug a program that contains exception-handling code. To understand the program better, you've created a stripped-down version of it and included some **Response.Write** statements to give you a clue about the flow of its execution. The program has the following code:
>
> ```
> try
> {
>     int num = 100;
>     int den = 0;
>     Response.Write("Message1" + "<br>");
>     try
>     {
>         int res = num/den;
>         Response.Write("Message2" + "<br>");
>     }
> ```

```
    catch(ArithmeticException ae)
    {
        Response.Write("Message3" + "<br>");
    }
}
catch(DivideByZeroException dbze)
{
    Response.Write("Message4" + "<br>");
}
finally
{
    Response.Write("Message5" + "<br>");
}
```

Which of the following options describes the correct order of displayed messages?

○ A.

```
Message1
Message2
Message3
Message4
Message5
```

○ B.

```
Message1
Message3
Message5
```

○ C.

```
Message1
Message4
Message5
```

○ D.

```
Message1
Message2
Message4
Message5
```

Answer B is correct. When an exception occurs in a try block, the program searches for a matching catch block associated with that try block. In all cases, the finally block is executed. Answers A and D are incorrect because, when an exception occurs, the control jumps from the try block to a matching catch block and the string Message2 never gets displayed. Answer C is incorrect because the ArithmeticException type is more general than the DivideByZeroException and therefore all DivideByZeroException exceptions are handled in the catch block that catches the ArithmeticException.

Question 3

What is the output displayed by the **Label lblResult** control in the following code segment?

```
try
{
    try
    {
        throw new ArgumentOutOfRangeException();
    }
    catch(ArgumentException ae)
    {
        throw new ArgumentException("Out of Range", ae);
    }
}
catch(Exception ex)
{
    lblResult.Text = ex.InnerException.GetType().ToString();
}
```

○ A. **System.Exception**

○ B. **System.ApplicationException**

○ C. **System.ArgumentException**

○ D. **System.ArgumentOutOfRangeException**

Answer D is correct. The label displays the System. ArgumentOutOfRangeException exception because the inner catch block caught this exception and wrapped it in the InnerException property of the newly thrown exception. Answers A and C are incorrect because, although these two types are the base types of the System.ArgumentOutOfRangeException type, the GetType() method returns the exact runtime type of the current instance. Answer B is incorrect because System.ArgumentOutOfRangeException is a system exception instead of an application exception.

Question 4

> You are designing a global time-entry system for a multinational company. It will be an ASP.NET application served over the Internet through the company's Web server. You are designing an error-handling mechanism for this application and want the application to show a customized error page for all HTTP errors. All unhandled exceptions caused by ASP.NET pages within your application should be logged in the Web server's event log; all other applications on the Web server should remain unaffected. You want a solution that requires minimum modifications. Which of the following places will be your preferred places to write this code? (Select two.)
>
> ❏ A. **web.config**
> ❏ B. **global.asax**
> ❏ C. In the ASPX page, using the **Page** directive
> ❏ D. **machine.config**

Answers A and B are correct. The customized error page for HTTP errors can be shown using the `<error>` element in the `web.config` file. To catch all unhandled exceptions in an application, the `Application_Error()` event handler in the `global.asax` file needs to be programmed. Answer C is incorrect because, if you use the `ErrorPage` attribute of the `Page` directive, you will have to modify (and in the future, maintain) all the pages within your ASP.NET application. Answer D is incorrect because, if you use the `<error>` element in the `machine.config` file, all the ASP.NET applications on the Web server will be affected.

Question 5

> You have developed a global time-entry system for a multinational company. The system is an ASP.NET application served over the Internet through the company's Web server in New York. The first phase of testing is being performed in the Los Angeles office, where it has been reported that users are getting default ASP.NET error pages instead of customized error pages. Which of the following actions do you need to take to enable custom error pages for those users? (Select two.)
>
> ❏ A. Set the **mode** attribute of the **<customErrors>** element in the **web.config** file to **On**.
> ❏ B. Set the **mode** attribute of the **<customErrors>** element in the **web.config** file to **Off**.
> ❏ C. Set the **mode** attribute of the **<customErrors>** element in the **web.config** file to **RemoteOnly**.
> ❏ D. Set the **defaultRedirect** attribute of the **<customErrors>** element in the **web.config** file to the location of the custom error page.

Answers C and D are correct. To set the custom error page, you need to set the `defaultRedirect` attribute to the location of the custom error page, and to enable custom error pages for the Los Angeles testing team, you must set the mode attribute to `RemoteOnly`. Answer A is incorrect because, when the `mode` attribute of the `<customErrors>` element is set to `On`, custom error pages are enabled for all the users. Answer B is incorrect because, when the `mode` attribute of the `<customErrors>` element is set to `Off`, custom error pages are disabled for all the users.

Question 6

You need to create a custom exception class in your Web application. You have written the following code for the exception class:

```
public class KeywordNotFound:
    ApplicationException
{
    public KeywordNotFoundException()
       {
       }
    public KeywordNotFoundException(
       string message, Exception inner)
       : base(message, inner)
       {
       }
}
```

Upon peer review of the code, it was found that you did not follow some of the best practices for creating a custom exception class. Which of the following suggestions do you need to incorporate? (Select all that apply.)

❑ A. Name the exception class **KeywordNotFoundException**.

❑ B. Derive the exception class from the base class **Exception** instead of **ApplicationException**.

❑ C. Add one more constructor to the class with the following signature:
```
public KeywordNotFoundException(
    string message) : base(message)
{
}
```

❑ D. Add one more constructor to the class with the following signature:
```
public KeywordNotFoundException(
    Exception inner) : base(inner)
{
}
```

❑ E. Derive the exception class from the base class **SystemException** instead of **ApplicationException**.

Answers A and C are correct. As a good exception handling practice, you should end the name of the exception class with the word Exception. In addition, an exception class must implement three standard constructors. The missing constructor is the one given in Answer C. Answers B and E are incorrect because, for custom exceptions, you should derive the custom exception class from the ApplicationException base class. Answer D is incorrect because the given constructor is not a standard constructor.

Question 7

> In your ASP.NET application, you are opening a file. You want to close the file regardless of an exception in the program. Which of the following code blocks can help you achieve this? (Select all that apply.)
>
> ❑ A. **try**
> ❑ B. **catch**
> ❑ C. **finally**
> ❑ D. **using**

Answers C and D are correct. You can use both finally and using for this purpose because the finally block is executed regardless of whether the exception occurs and the using statement ensures that the allocated resources in the statement are properly disposed. Answer A is incorrect because the try block is used to enclose those statements that might throw an exception. Answer B is incorrect because the catch block is used to write those statements that might handle an exception.

Question 8

> You want to capture all exceptions that escape from the exception-handling code in your application and log them to the system event log. You want a solution that requires minimum coding efforts. Which of the following techniques would you use?
>
> ○ A. Program the **Application_End()** event handler in the **global.asax** file.
> ○ B. Program the **Page_Unload()** event handler of the **Page** class.
> ○ C. Program the **Page_Error()** event handler of the **Page** class.
> ○ D. Program the **Application_Error()** event handler in the **global.asax** file.

Answer D is correct. You need to handle unhandled exceptions in the Error events. Because you need to trap exceptions for the complete application, the Application_Error() event handler is the best place to trap exceptions.

Answer A is incorrect because the `Application_End()` event handler is invoked only when the application quits. Answers B and C are incorrect because these event handlers need to be programmed for each page and require additional coding efforts.

Question 9

> The structured exception-handling mechanism of the .NET Framework allows you to handle which of the following types of exceptions? (Select all that apply.)
>
> ❑ A. Exceptions from all CLS-compliant languages
>
> ❑ B. Exceptions from non-CLS-compliant languages
>
> ❑ C. Exceptions from unmanaged COM code
>
> ❑ D. Exceptions from unmanaged non-COM code

Answers A, B, C, and D are correct. The .NET Framework allows you to handle all types of exceptions, including cross-language exceptions for both CLS- and non-CLS-compliant languages. It also allows you to handle exceptions from unmanaged code—both COM and non-COM.

Question 10

> Which of the following statements is true regarding the following code?
> ```
> const int someVal1 = Int32.MaxValue;
> const int someVal2 = Int32.MaxValue;
> int result;
> checked
> {
>     result = someVal1 * someVal2;
> }
> ```
>
> ○ A. The code generates an **OverflowException**.
>
> ○ B. The code executes successfully without any exceptions.
>
> ○ C. The code causes a compile-time error.
>
> ○ D. The code executes successfully, but the value of the variable result is truncated.

Answer C is correct. When constant values are inside the `checked` block, they are checked for overflow at compile time. Answers A, B, and D are incorrect because you are multiplying two maximum possible values for an integer and the result certainly could not be stored inside an integer. The compiler detects this and generates a compile-time error.

Need to Know More?

 Dietel, Harvey M., et al. *C# How to Program.* Upper Saddle River, NJ: Prentice Hall, 2001.

 Kalani, Amit. *MCAD/MCSD Developing and Implementing Web Applications with Visual C# .NET and Visual Studio .NET.* Indianapolis, IN: Que Certification, 2002.

 Ritcher, Jeffery. *Applied Microsoft .NET Framework Programming.* Redmond, WA: Microsoft Press, 2001.

 Visit the MSDN Library: Exception Management in .NET at http://msdn.microsoft.com/library/en-us/dnbda/html/exceptdotnet.asp.

 Visit the MSDN Library: Exception Handling Statements at http://msdn.microsoft.com/library/en-us/csref/html/vclrftrystatementss.asp.

 Visit the MSDN Library: Best Practices for Handling Exceptions at http://msdn.microsoft.com/library/en-us/cpguide/html/cpconbestpracticesforhandlingexceptions.asp.

 Visit the MSDN How-To Resources on Visual C# .NET at http://msdn.microsoft.com/howto/c.asp.

 Visit *MSDN Magazine*'s "Cutting Edge" Column at http://msdn.microsoft.com/msdnmag/find/default.aspx?type=Ti&phrase=Cutting Edge.

6

Data Binding

. . . .

Terms you'll need to understand:

✓ Data binding
✓ Foreign key
✓ Primary key
✓ Relation
✓ Relational database
✓ Table
✓ Templated control

Techniques you'll need to master:

✓ Understanding the difference between simple and complex data binding, as well as the syntax used for each
✓ Carefully reviewing the use of the **DataBind()** method and understanding how it provides control over data binding
✓ Knowing how to display the data you want to show to the end user
✓ Building several templated controls (**Repeater**, **DataList**, **DataGrid**) and knowing which one is appropriate for which situation

Data binding refers to the process of making a link between the user interface and data. As the user views and manipulates controls, the application takes care of translating the user's actions into reading and writing data from the data model. In this chapter, you'll learn about the data binding capabilities of ASP.NET.

Binding Data to the User Interface

ASP.NET includes extremely flexible data-binding capabilities, many of which are discussed in the following sections.

Simple Data Binding

Simple data binding means connecting a user interface element to a single value from the data model. ASP.NET supplies a special syntax for binding (<%# ... %>). You can write any valid expression within <%# ... %> and the expression is evaluated when the DataBind() method of a control is called.

For example, the following code binds a property of the Calendar control with the value of an expression:

```
<asp:Calendar id="calendar1" runat="server"
        SelectedDate="<%# DateTime.Today.AddDays(1) %>">
```

Note that if you call the DataBind() method of the Page class as shown here, only a single call to the DataBind() method is sufficient to bind all the user interface elements on that page:

```
private void Page_Load(object sender, System.EventArgs e)
{
    DataBind();
}
```

You can also bind a property of one server control directly to a property of another server control. This provides an easy method to transfer information from one part of a Web form to another. For example, you can bind a Label control with a date selected in a Calendar control as shown here:

```
<asp:Label id="lblInfo" runat="server" Visible="false"
Text = '<%# calendar1.SelectedDate.ToShortDateString() %>' >
</asp:Label>
```

You can then program the SelectionChanged event of the Calendar control to bind the Label control when the date selection changes, as shown here:

```
private void calendar1_SelectionChanged(object sender,
System.EventArgs e)
{
```

```
        lblInfo.Visible = true;
        lblInfo.DataBind();
}
```

Complex Data Binding

In complex data binding, you bind a user interface control to an entire collection of data, rather than to a single data item.

Binding to the List Controls

In this section, I discuss the data-binding capabilities of the controls derived from the System.Web.UI.WebControls.ListControls class, such as the CheckBoxList, DropDownList, ListBox, and RadioButtonList controls. These controls provide ways for the user to select one item from a list of data.

These controls can be bound to any collection that supports the IEnumerable, ICollection, or IListSource interface. This includes the ArrayList, HashTable, DataReader, and DataView classes.

In the following example, you'll use a complex data-bound ListBox in conjunction with a simple data-bound control such as a TextBox:

1. Open Visual Studio .NET and create a new blank solution named 315C06 at c:\inetpub\wwwroot\ExamCram (you might need to change the directory based on your configuration).

2. Add a new Visual C# ASP.NET Web application at the following location: http://localhost/ExamCram/315C06/Example6_1.

3. Place a ListBox control (lbExams) and a Label control (lblSelected) on the Web form. Set the AutoPostBack property of the ListBox control to true, and set the Text property of the Label control to the following code:

   ```
   <%# lbExams.SelectedItemValue %>
   ```

4. Add a new Visual C# .NET class file named Exam.cs to the project and add the following code:

   ```
   using System;
   using System.Data;
   using System.Collections;

   public class Exam
   {
       public ICollection DataLoad()
       {
           DataTable dtExam = new DataTable();
           DataView dvExam;
           DataRow drExam;
   ```

```
                  // Add two columns to the DataTable
                  dtExam.Columns.Add(new DataColumn("ExamNumber",
                      Type.GetType("System.String")));
                  dtExam.Columns.Add(new DataColumn("ExamName",
                      Type.GetType("System.String")));

                  // Put some data in
                  drExam = dtExam.NewRow();
                  drExam[0] = "70-315";
                  drExam[1] = "Developing Web Applications (Visual C# .NET)";
                  dtExam.Rows.Add(drExam);

                  drExam = dtExam.NewRow();
                  drExam[0] = "70-316";
                  drExam[1] = "Developing Windows Applications (Visual C# .NET)";
                  dtExam.Rows.Add(drExam);

                  drExam = dtExam.NewRow();
                  drExam[0] = "70-320";
                  drExam[1] =
            "Developing Web services and Server Components (Visual C# .NET)";
                  dtExam.Rows.Add(drExam);

                  drExam = dtExam.NewRow();
                  drExam[0] = "70-305";
                  drExam[1] = "Developing Web Applications (Visual Basic .NET)";
                  dtExam.Rows.Add(drExam);

                  drExam = dtExam.NewRow();
                  drExam[0] = "70-306";
                  drExam[1] = "Developing Windows Applications (Visual Basic
            .NET)";
                  dtExam.Rows.Add(drExam);

                  drExam = dtExam.NewRow();
                  drExam[0] = "70-310";
                  drExam[1] = "Developing Web Services and
                  ➥Server Components (Visual Basic .NET)";
                  dtExam.Rows.Add(drExam);

                  // And return the datatable wrapped in a dataview
                  dvExam = new DataView(dtExam);
                  return dvExam;
              }
          }
```

5. Double-click the Web form and add the following code in the
   Page_Load() event handler:

```
private void Page_Load(object sender, System.EventArgs e)
{
    if(!IsPostBack)
    {
        // Create an Exam class object and call the DataLoad()
        // method to assign it to the ListBox's DataSource
        Exam exam = new Exam();
        lbExams.DataSource = exam.DataLoad();
        lbExams.DataTextField = "ExamName";
        lbExams.DataValueField = "ExamNumber";
```

```
            DataBind();
        }
    }
```

6. Double-click the `ListBox` control and enter the following code in the `ListBox`'s `SelectedIndexChanged` event handler:

```
private void lbExams_SelectedIndexChanged(
    object sender, System.EventArgs e)
{
    lblSelected.DataBind();
}
```

7. Run the project. The `ListBox` control displays the `ExamName` property of every object in the `DataView`. Note that the `DataLoad()` method has a return value typed as `ICollection`, which is one of the types the `ListBox` can use as a `DataSource`. When you select an exam name, the corresponding `ExamNumber` value appears in the `Label` control.

Understanding the previous example is crucial for the effective use of the `DropDownList` and `ListBox` controls in applications. Using these controls can be a little tricky because the `ListBox` control is bound to two different things. Here's a review of how it all fits together:

➤ The `ListBox` control in the previous example draws the list of items to display from the `DataView` of exam information. The list portion of the list box is complex data bound to this object. The complex binding is managed by setting the `DataSource`, `DataTextField`, and `DataValueField` properties of the `ListBox` control.

➤ When you first load the form, the data is loaded by calling the `DataBind()` method of the `ListBox` control itself. The check of the `IsPostBack` property of the page ensures that this happens only once. If you neglect to check, the data is loaded when the form is posted back and you lose the information on which the `ListBox` item was selected.

➤ When you click an item in the `ListBox` control, it posts that information back to the server because the `AutoPostBack` property of the `ListBox` control is set to `true`.

➤ The `SelectedIndexChanged` event handles binding the currently selected row of the `ListBox` control to the `Label` control. The code for this calls the `DataBind()` method of the `Label` control itself.

➤ You can use the `DataTextField` and `DataValueField` properties of the `ListBox` control to cause it to show one value while binding another, as in the previous example.

Data binding works the same way for all the list controls, which means the code for data binding the CheckBoxList and RadioButtonList controls is similar.

Binding to a **DataGrid** Control

The DataGrid control is designed to let you see an entire collection of data (often called a *result set*) at one time. The following example shows how to bind a DataView object to a DataGrid control:

1. Add a new Visual C# ASP.NET Web Application project named Example6_2 to the solution.

2. Copy the Exam.cs class from the Example6_1 project to the current project.

3. Place a DataGrid control (dgExams) on the Web form. Double-click the Web form and add the following code in the Page_Load() event handler:

```
private void Page_Load(object sender, System.EventArgs e)
{
    // Create an Exam class object and call the DataLoad()
    method to assign it to the DataGrid's DataSource
    Exam exam = new Exam();
    dgExams.DataSource = exam.DataLoad();
    dgExams.DataBind();
}
```

4. Run the project. The DataGrid control displays all the information from the exam's DataView object.

The DataGrid control is extremely configurable. Visual Studio .NET includes two interfaces for setting the display properties of a DataGrid control. First, you can set individual properties to control the look of the DataGrid control in the Properties window. Second, you can right-click the DataGrid control and select AutoFormat. This invokes the AutoFormat dialog box that helps in changing the appearance of a DataGrid control.

The **DataBind()** Method

DataBind() is a method of the Page object (which, of course, represents the entire ASP.NET Web form) and of all the server controls. Data-binding expressions are not evaluated until you explicitly call the DataBind() method. This gives you flexibility to decide when to bind things and lets you run preliminary code to calculate values, if necessary.

The DataBind() method cascades from parent controls to their children. If you call the DataBind() method of the Page, all the data-binding expressions on the page are evaluated. Additionally, if you call the DataBind() method of a control that has constituent controls, all the data-binding expressions in any of those controls are evaluated.

In addition to the design-time data-binding expressions you've already seen, you can perform runtime data binding by responding to the DataBinding event of a control, as shown in the following example. This event is raised by each control when its DataBind() method is invoked:

1. Add a new Visual C# ASP.NET Web Application project named Example6_3 to the solution.

2. Place a Label control (lblRuntime) on the Web form.

3. Switch to Code view and add the following code to the Page_Load() event handler:

```
private void Page_Load(object sender, System.EventArgs e)
{
    lblRuntime.DataBind();
}
```

4. Attach an event handler to the DataBinding event of the Label control and add the following code to the event handler:

```
private void lblRuntime_DataBinding(object sender, System.EventArgs e)
{
    lblRuntime.Text = "Runtime data binding";
}
```

5. Set the project as the startup project for the solution and run the project. The user interface displays runtime data binding as the text of the Label control.

Using the Data Form Wizard

Visual Studio .NET offers a visual tool for automatic data binding: the Data Form Wizard. In the following example, you'll see how to use the wizard to quickly build a multiple-table form that displays data from the Customers and Orders tables in the Northwind sample database. Here's how:

1. Add a new Visual C# Empty Web Project (Example6_4) to the solution. Select Project, Add New Item. In the Add New Item dialog box, select the Data Form Wizard and click Open.

2. Read the Welcome screen of the wizard and click Next. The next screen helps you choose a DataSet object to use with the data form. A DataSet object is a .NET Framework object that you can think of as representing one or more tables from a database. (It's actually more

flexible than that, but that's enough for this example.) On this screen, choose to create a new `DataSet` object named `dsCustOrders`. Click Next.

3. The next screen helps you choose or build a data connection. A data connection tells Visual C# .NET which database contains the data you want to retrieve. You haven't set up any data connections yet, so click the New Connection button. This opens the Data Link Properties dialog box.

4. Click the Provider tab of the Data Link Properties dialog box and select Microsoft OLE DB Provider for SQL Server.

5. Click the Connection tab of the Data Link Properties dialog box and enter the information you need to use the Northwind database, as shown in Figure 6.1.

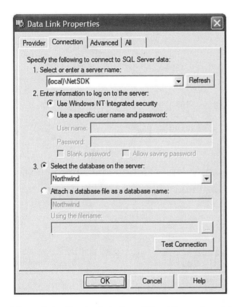

Figure 6.1 Use the Data Form Wizard to create a data connection to the Northwind sample database.

Whenever I use data from a database in this book, I use the Northwind sample database included with Microsoft .NET Framework Software Development Kit (SDK) QuickStart Samples. These samples use Microsoft Data Engine (MSDE), a stripped-down version of SQL Server. See the .NET Framework SDK readme file for information on installing MSDE. You can also download MSDE from **www.asp.net/msde**.

6. Click OK on the Data Link Properties dialog box to create the connection and return to the Data Form Wizard. Select the new connection in the combo box (it should have a name such as *MACHINENAME*.Northwind.dbo) and click Next.

7. On the Choose Tables or Views screen, select the Customers and the Orders table. Click Next.

8. The next screen helps you specify the relationship between the two tables, Customers and Orders. Name the new relationship relCustOrders. Then select Customers as the parent table, select Orders as the child table, and select CustomerID as the key field in each table. Figure 6.2 shows the wizard at this point. Click the > button to create the new relationship; then click Next.

9. On the Choose Tables and Columns to Display on the Form screen, leave all the columns in both tables selected; then click Finish.

10. Set Example6_4 as the startup project and set DataForm1 as the start page for the project. Run the project to experiment with the data form.

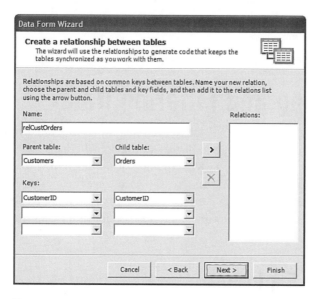

Figure 6.2   When you use the Data Form Wizard to create a relationship between tables, it automatically generates code to keep the tables synchronized.

The data form initially opens with only a Load button visible. Clicking the button loads all the rows from the Customers table. Each row has a Show Details link in the first column, and clicking this link loads the orders for that customer. The form knows which orders go with which customer thanks to the relationship you created between the two tables (see Figure 6.3).

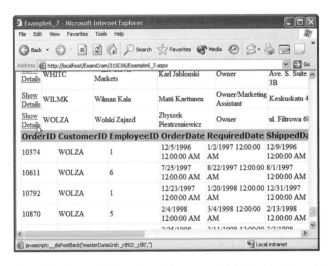

Figure 6.3 A two-table data form that uses one **DataGrid** control for each table and uses code to keep the two **DataGrid** controls synchronized.

Transforming and Filtering Data

When you're dealing with data from a database, you might find that the data is not in the exact form that you'd like to display to the user. Perhaps 5,000 rows are in the Customer table and you want to pull out the single row that interests your users. Or perhaps you want to show customer names with orders, but the Orders table stores only the CustomerID. In this section, you'll look at a few tools the .NET Framework offers for manipulating database data.

Using Server Explorer

You can invoke the Server Explorer window in Visual Studio .NET by selecting View, Server Explorer.

To work with bound data, you use the Data Connections node in Server Explorer and its children.

You've already seen that you can add a data connection to your project from within the Data Form Wizard. Those data connections are automatically available in Server Explorer as well. You can also add a data connection directly from Server Explorer by right-clicking the Data Connections node and then selecting Add Connection. This opens the Data Link Properties dialog box where you can fill in the connection information for your data source (refer to Figure 6.1).

Server Explorer can act as a source for drag-and-drop operations. Different visual data objects can be created, depending on which type of object you drag from Server Explorer:

➤ Dragging and dropping a database creates a SqlConnection object.

➤ Dragging and dropping a table, view, table column, or view column creates a SqlDataAdapter object (as well as a SqlConnection object if one does not exist already).

➤ Dragging and dropping a stored procedure or table-valued function creates a SqlCommand object (as well as a SqlConnection object if one does not exist already).

These three objects are members of the System.Data.SqlClient namespace; you'll learn more about this namespace in Chapter 7. This chapter concentrates more on what you can do with the objects than on the code that creates and supports them.

The following example demonstrates how to implement complex binding between a DataGrid control and a SQL Server table visually without writing much code:

1. Add a new Visual C# ASP.NET Web Application project named Example6_5 to the current solution.

2. Place a DataGrid control (dgCustomers) on the Web form.

3. Open Server Explorer. Expand the tree under Data Connections to show a SQL Server data connection that points to the Northwind sample database, then to the Tables node of the SQL Server, and then to individual tables.

4. Drag the Customers table from Server Explorer and drop it on the form. This creates two visual data objects: sqlConnecton1 and sqlDataAdapter1.

5. Select the sqlDataAdapter1 object. Then click the Generate Dataset link under the Properties window. In the Generate Dataset window, choose to create a new dataset named dsCustomers.

6. Set the DataSource property of the DataGrid control to dsCustomers1. Then set the DataMember property of the DataGrid control to Customers.

7. Switch to Code view and add the following code in the `Page_Load()` event handler:

```
private void Page_Load(object sender, System.EventArgs e)
{
    // Move the data from the database to the DataGrid
    sqlDataAdapter1.Fill(dsCustomers1, "Customers");
    dgCustomers.DataBind();
}
```

8. Set the project as the startup project and run the project. The `DataGrid` control displays all the data from the Customers table, and the code uses the visual data objects you created on the form to make the connection between the `DataGrid` control and the table.

Filtering Data

Filtering data refers to the process of selecting only some data from a larger body of data to appear on the user interface of a form. This can be a critical part of avoiding information overload for end users of an application. In most cases, users will need only a small subset of the larger data body. This section examines two ways to filter data in your applications.

Filtering with a **DataView** Object

To understand the `DataView` object, you need to know a little bit about the internal structure of the `DataSet` object. A `DataSet` object contains two collections. The `Tables` collection is made up of `DataTable` objects, each of which represents data from a single table in the data source. The `Relations` collection, on the other hand, is made up of `DataRelation` objects, each of which represents the relationship between two `DataTable` objects.

The `DataView` object supplies one more piece of this puzzle: It represents a bindable, customized view of a `DataTable` object. You can sort and filter the records from a `DataTable` object to build a `DataView` object.

If you want to modify `Example6_5` to display a sorted list of all customers from France, you need to modify the `Page_Load()` method, like so:

```
private void Page_Load(object sender, System.EventArgs e)
{
    // Move the data from the database to the DataSet
    sqlDataAdapter1.Fill(dsCustomers1, "Customers");
    // Create a dataview to filter the Customers table
    DataView dvCustomers = new DataView(dsCustomers1.Tables["Customers"]);
    // Apply a sort to the dataview
    dvCustomers.Sort = "ContactName";
    // Apply a filter to the dataview
    dvCustomers.RowFilter = "Country = 'France'";
    // and bind the results to the grid
```

```
    dgCustomers.DataSource = dvCustomers;
    dgCustomers.DataBind();
}
```

Filtering at the Database Server

The DataView class provides a useful way to filter data, but it's inefficient if you're working with large amounts of data. That's because all the data is first retrieved from the database server and stored on the Web server. Ideally, you should filter the data on the database server itself. One way to do this is by basing a SqlDataAdapter object on a view instead of a table, as described in the following example:

1. Add a new Visual C# ASP.NET Web Application project named Example6_6 to the current solution. Place a DataGrid control (dgCustomers) on the Web form.

2. Open Server Explorer and expand the tree under Data Connections to show a SQL Server data connection that points to the Northwind sample database; then expand the Views node of the SQL Server.

3. Right-click the Views node and select New View. In the Add Table dialog box, select the Customers table, click Add, and then click Close. This puts you in the view designer in Visual Studio .NET.

4. Click the check boxes for All Columns, ContactName, and Country in the column listing. Then fill in the details of the view as shown in Figure 6.4.

5. Click the Save button and save the view as **vwFranceCustomers**. Close the design window for the view.

6. Drag the vwFranceCustomers view from Server Explorer and drop it on the form. You get a configuration error because the view is read-only, but that's not a problem because you're not writing any data back to the database. Click OK to create objects. This creates two visual data objects: sqlConnection1 and sqlDataAdapter1.

7. Select the sqlDataAdapter1 object, and click the Generate Dataset link below the Properties window. In the Generate Dataset window, choose to create a new dataset named dsCustomers. Click OK.

8. Set the DataSource property of the DataGrid control to dsCustomers1. Set the DataMember property of the DataGrid control to vwFranceCustomers.

Figure 6.4 You can create a new SQL Server view by using the design tools in Visual Studio .NET.

9. Switch to Code view and add the following code in the `Page_Load()` event handler:

```
private void Page_Load(object sender, System.EventArgs e)
{
    // Move the data from the database to the DataGrid
    sqlDataAdapter1.Fill(dsCustomers1, "vwFranceCustomers");
    dgCustomers.DataBind();
}
```

10. Set the project as the startup project and run the project. The `DataGrid` control displays only the data from customers in France, sorted by the ContactName column. This time, the filtering and sorting is all done by the view you created on the SQL Server.

If you're operating over a slow network or Internet connection, this type of server-side filtering in the database server can save a lot of time.

Transforming Data

This section takes a brief look at transforming data by applying lookups. A *lookup* is a technique for replacing one column of data with another column from the same table. For example, given an order ID value, you could look up the corresponding company name that placed the order. The following example demonstrates how to accomplish this using server-side views:

1. Add a new Visual C# ASP.NET Web Application project named Example6_7 to the current solution. Place a DataGrid control (dgOrders) on the Web form.

2. Open Server Explorer and create a new view in the Northwind database. In the Add Table dialog box, add the Customers table and the Orders table.

3. In the View designer, click the check boxes for CompanyName in the Customers table and all columns except for CustomerID in the Orders table. Figure 6.5 shows the completed view.

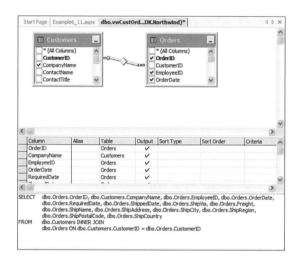

Figure 6.5 You can create a new SQL Server view that joins data from two tables together.

4. Save the view as **vwCustOrders**. Drag the **vwCustOrders** view from Server Explorer and drop it on the form. Ignore the configuration error and click OK to create objects. This creates two visual data objects, sqlConnection1 and sqlDataAdapter1.

5. Select the sqlDataAdapter1 object and click the Generate Dataset link below the Properties window. In the Generate Dataset window, create a new DataSet object named dsOrders. Click OK.

6. Set the DataSource property of the DataGrid control to dsOrders1. Set the DataMember property of the DataGrid control to vwCustOrders.

7. Switch to Code view and add the following code to the Page_Load() event handler:

```
private void Page_Load(object sender, System.EventArgs e)
{
    sqlDataAdapter1.Fill(dsOrders1, "vwCustOrders");
    dgOrders.DataBind();
}
```

8. Set the project as the startup project for the solution and run the project. The DataGrid control displays order data with full company names. The lookup operation is performed by the SQL Server view before the data is even sent to the application.

Using Templated Controls to Display Data

A *template* is a set of HTML elements and controls that collectively specify the layout for a control. A control that supports templates is known as a *templated* control. ASP.NET implements three templated controls: Repeater, DataList, and DataGrid.

The DataGrid control has a default look and feel that can be customized with the use of templates, but the Repeater and DataList controls have no default rendering, and their displays are entirely dictated by templates.

The Repeater Control

The Repeater control is a data-bound container control that produces a list of individual items. You use templates to define a customized layout of its items. The following example shows how:

1. Add a new Visual C# ASP.NET Web Application project named Example6_8 to the current solution. Place a Repeater control (rptOrders) on the Web form.

2. Drag the Orders table from the Northwind sample database and drop it on the form. This creates two visual data objects: sqlConnection1 and sqlDataAdapter1.

3. Select the sqlDataAdapter1 object and click the Generate Dataset link below the Properties window. Create a new dataset named dsOrders.

4. Set the DataSource property of the Repeater control to dsOrders1. Set the DataMember property of the Repeater control to Orders.

5. Switch to HTML view and enter the following code to customize the
   `Repeater` control:

```
<asp:Repeater id="rptOrders" runat="server"
 DataSource="<%# dsOrders1 %>" DataMember="Orders">
    <HeaderTemplate>
        <table>
            <thead bgcolor=#6699ff>
                <th>Order ID</th>
                <th>Customer ID</th>
                <th>Order Date</th>
                <th>Freight</th>
            </thead>
    </HeaderTemplate>
    <ItemTemplate>
      <tr bgcolor=#ccffff>
        <td><%# DataBinder.Eval(Container.DataItem, "OrderID") %></td>
        <td><%# DataBinder.Eval(Container.DataItem, "CustomerID")
            %></td>
        <td><%# DataBinder.Eval(
            Container.DataItem, "OrderDate", "{0:d}")%></td>
        <td><%# DataBinder.Eval(
            Container.DataItem, "Freight", "{0:c}")%></td>
      </tr>
    </ItemTemplate>
    <AlternatingItemTemplate>
      <tr bgcolor=#ffffff>
        <td><%# DataBinder.Eval(Container.DataItem, "OrderID") %></td>
        <td><%# DataBinder.Eval(
            Container.DataItem, "CustomerID")%></td>
        <td><%# DataBinder.Eval(
            Container.DataItem, "OrderDate", "{0:d}")%></td>
        <td><%# DataBinder.Eval(
            Container.DataItem, "Freight", "{0:c}")%></td>
      </tr>
    </AlternatingItemTemplate>
    <SeparatorTemplate>
        <tr height=4 bgcolor=#0000ff>
            <td></td><td></td><td></td><td></td>
        </tr>
    </SeparatorTemplate>
    <FooterTemplate>
        </table>
    </FooterTemplate>
</asp:Repeater>
```

6. Switch to Code view and add the following code to the `Page_Load()`
   event handler:

```
private void Page_Load(object sender, System.EventArgs e)
{
    sqlDataAdapter1.Fill(dsOrders1, "Orders");
    DataBind();
}
```

7. Set the project as the startup project and run the project. The `Repeater`
   control displays data from four columns of the Orders table, as shown
   in Figure 6.6.

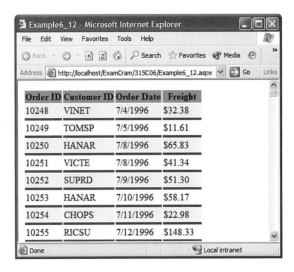

Figure 6.6 The **Repeater** control offers flexible formatting options for tabular data.

If you inspect the HTML, you'll see that the Repeater control allows you to specify five templates:

➤ The HeaderTemplate is rendered once at the start of the control.

➤ The ItemTemplate is rendered once for every row of data in the data source of the control.

➤ The AlternatingItemTemplate is used instead of the ItemTemplate for every other row of data. If you omit the AlternatingItemTemplate, the ItemTemplate is used for all rows.

➤ The SeparatorTemplate is rendered once between each row of data.

➤ The FooterTemplate is rendered once at the end of the control.

The only one of these templates that you're required to implement for a Repeater control is the ItemTemplate. You can perform data binding only in the ItemTemplate and AlternatingItemTemplate templates.

You'll also see a new object in the HTML code: the DataBinder. DataBinder exists to format data in templated controls (and other controls that contain subcontrols). The Eval() method of the DataBinder object takes three arguments:

➤ The first argument specifies the source of the data. The templates are contained in the Repeater control, and the Repeater control itself is bound to a collection of data. So in this case, the source of the data is Container.DataItem, a single item of data from the containing control.

➤ The second argument is the name of a column in the data to bind at this position.

➤ The third (optional) argument is a format string, of the type that could be supplied to the String.Format() method.

The DataBinder object handles all the necessary casting to make string formatting work properly with bound data, regardless of the data type of the underlying data.

The best thing about the **DataBinder.Eval()** method is that it saves you from writing complex expressions. However, using this method does impose a performance penalty on your code because all the work it does is late-bound. If you want the fastest possible code, you can replace calls to **DataBinder.Eval()** with explicit casts. For example, consider this binding expression:

<%# **DataBinder.Eval(Container.DataItem, "Freight", "{0:c}") %>**

An equivalent expression using casts would be this:

<%# **String.Format("{0:c}",**

    ((DataRowView) Container.DataItem)["Freight"]) %>

The DataList Control

The DataList control is similar to the Repeater control, but it provides more flexible formatting options. The control handles the layout of items in rows and columns, so you don't have to supply <table> tags in its templates. It also lets you build data-editing capabilities into the Web form.

In addition to the five templates supported by the Repeater control, DataList also allows you to set a SelectedItemTemplate to indicate a current row in the data and an EditItemTemplate that is used to render data being edited by the user. Unlike Repeater, however, DataList supports formatting templates directly in the Visual Studio .NET IDE. The following example shows how to apply templates on the DataList control to display data:

1. Add a new Visual C# ASP.NET Web Application project named Example6_9 to the current solution.

2. Place a DataList control (dlOrders) on the new Web form. Set the RepeatColumns property of the DataList control to 2 and the CellSpacing property of the control to 10.

3. Drag the Orders table from the Northwind sample database and drop it on the form. This creates two visual data objects: sqlConnection1 and sqlDataAdapter1.

4. Select the `sqlDataAdapter1` object and click the Generate Dataset link below the Properties window. In the Generate Dataset window, create a new dataset object named `dsOrders`.

5. Set the `DataSource` property of the `Repeater` control to `dsOrders1`. Set the `DataMember` property of the `Repeater` control to `Orders`.

6. Switch to HTML view and enter the following code to customize the `DataList` control. Note the `<DIV>` tags in the `ItemTemplate`, which are essential to preserve formatting:

```
<asp:DataList id="dlOrders" runat="server"
    DataSource="<%# dsOrders1 %>" DataMember="Orders"
    RepeatColumns="2" CellSpacing="10">
    <ItemTemplate><div>
        <b>Order ID: </b>
        <%# DataBinder.Eval(Container.DataItem, "OrderID") %>
        <br>
<b>Customer ID: </b>
        <%# DataBinder.Eval(Container.DataItem, "CustomerID") %>
        <br>
<b>Order Date: </b>
        <%# DataBinder.Eval(Container.DataItem, "OrderDate", "{0:d}") %>
        <br>
<b>Freight: </b>
        <%# DataBinder.Eval(Container.DataItem, "Freight", "{0:c}") %>
        <br></div>
    </ItemTemplate>
</asp:DataList>
```

7. Switch back to Design view. Right-click the `DataList` control and select Edit Template, Item Templates.

8. Click in the `ItemTemplate` area, below the text, so that you can see the properties for the `<DIV>` tag that wraps this template in the Properties window. Click in the Style property and click the builder (...) button to open the Style Builder dialog box. Use the Style Builder to set the font and color properties as you like; then click OK.

9. Select all the text in the `ItemTemplate`, copy it, and paste a copy into the `AlternatingItemTemplate`. Use the Style Builder to set the properties for the `AlternatingItemTemplate`.

10. Switch to Code view and add the following code to the `Page_Load()` event handler:

```
private void Page_Load(object sender, System.EventArgs e)
{
    sqlDataAdapter1.Fill(dsOrders1, "Orders");
    dlOrders.DataBind();
}
```

11. Set the project as the startup project for the solution and run the project. The DataList control displays data in two columns. The number of columns is controlled by the RepeatColumns property of DataList. Also, each item is rendered according to the formatting you specified in the Style Builder.

Editing Data with a **DataList** Control

The DataList control also offers support for editing data. To enable this support, you need to supply an EditItemTemplate and respond properly to several events as demonstrated in the following example:

1. Add a new Visual C# ASP.NET Web Application project named Example6_10 to the current solution. Place a DataList control (dlOrders) on the Web form. Set the RepeatColumns property of the control to 1 and the CellSpacing property of the control to 10.

2. Bind dlOrders to the dsOrders DataSet object.

3. Switch to HTML view and enter the following code to customize the DataList control. This code includes an EditItemTemplate with a control to edit the freight charge for a row:

```
<asp:DataList id="dlOrders" runat="server" DataSource="<%# dsOrders1%>"
    DataMember="Orders" RepeatColumns="1"  CellSpacing="10">
    <ItemTemplate>
      <b>Order ID: </b>
      <%# DataBinder.Eval(Container.DataItem, "OrderID") %>
      <br><b>Customer ID: </b>
      <%# DataBinder.Eval(Container.DataItem, "CustomerID") %>
      <br><b>Order Date: </b>
      <%# DataBinder.Eval(Container.DataItem, "OrderDate", "{0:d}") %>
      <br><b>Freight: </b>
      <%# DataBinder.Eval(Container.DataItem, "Freight", "{0:c}") %>
      <br><asp:Button id="btnEdit" runat="server"
         Text="Edit" CommandName="Edit"></asp:Button>
    </ItemTemplate>
    <EditItemTemplate>
       <b>Order ID: </b>
       <%# DataBinder.Eval(Container.DataItem, "OrderID") %>
       <br><b>Customer ID: </b>
       <%# DataBinder.Eval(Container.DataItem, "CustomerID") %>
       <br><b>Order Date: </b>
       <%# DataBinder.Eval(Container.DataItem, "OrderDate", "{0:d}") %>
       <br><b>Freight: </b><input id=freight type=text
         runat="server" value='<%# DataBinder.Eval(
            Container.DataItem, "Freight") %>' >
       <br><asp:Button id="btnUpdate" runat="server"
        Text="Update" CommandName="Update"></asp:Button>
       <asp:Button id="btnCancel" runat="server"
         Text="Cancel" CommandName="Cancel"></asp:Button>
    </EditItemTemplate>
  </asp:DataList>
```

4. Switch to Code view and add the following code to the `Page_Load()` event handler:

```
private void Page_Load(object sender, System.EventArgs e)
{
    // Load the data
    if(!IsPostBack)
    {
        sqlDataAdapter1.Fill(dsOrders1, "Orders");
        DataBind();
    }
}
```

5. Attach event handlers for the `CancelCommand`, `EditCommand`, `UpdateCommand`, events of the `DataList` control, and add the following code to the event handlers:

```
private void dlOrders_CancelCommand(object source,
System.Web.UI.WebControls.DataListCommandEventArgs e)
{
    // Turn off the editing controls
    dlOrders.EditItemIndex = -1;
    // Re-bind the data
    sqlDataAdapter1.Fill(dsOrders1, "Orders");
    DataBind();
}

private void dlOrders_EditCommand(object source,
System.Web.UI.WebControls.DataListCommandEventArgs e)
{
    // Turn on the editing controls
    dlOrders.EditItemIndex = e.Item.ItemIndex;
    // Re-bind the data
    sqlDataAdapter1.Fill(dsOrders1, "Orders");
    DataBind();
}

private void dlOrders_UpdateCommand(object source,
System.Web.UI.WebControls.DataListCommandEventArgs e)
{
    HtmlInputText htEdit;
    // Get the existing data
    sqlDataAdapter1.Fill(dsOrders1, "Orders");
    // Get the changed data and put it in the database
    htEdit = (HtmlInputText)e.Item.FindControl("freight");
    dsOrders1.Tables["Orders"].Rows[
        e.Item.ItemIndex][7] = htEdit.Value;
    // Turn off editing
    dlOrders.EditItemIndex = -1;
    // re-bind the data
    DataBind();
}
```

6. Set the project as the startup project for the solution and run the project. The `DataList` control displays data from four columns of the Orders table. Click the Edit button for any row, and you'll be able to edit the Freight value.

After you've created a DataList with an EditItemTemplate, you can tell the control to use that template for a specific row by supplying the (zero-based) index of that row. The CommandName tags in the HTML code correspond to the events that DataList raises in the C# code. When you raise an EditCommand event, the parameters passed to the event include the data item in which the event was raised. The code uses the index of this item to determine which row to show in the edited state (using the Item.ItemIndex property of the DataListCommandEventArgs object). Note that you need to rebind the data when you do this because in reality, you're rebuilding the entire page from scratch.

To cancel an edit, set the EditItemIndex property back to -1 and rebind the control.

To update the data, the code uses the FindControl() method of the data item to find the input control where the freight value was edited. This control can be represented by an HtmlInputText object in the code. The code then uses the Value property of that object to update the corresponding row in the DataSet object.

The **DataList** control also has a **SelectedIndex** property that can be used to highlight a particular row in the **DataList** control. Similar to the **EditItemIndex** property, the **SelectedIndex** property is zero based. If you set **SelectedItemIndex** to **3**, for example, the fourth row in the **DataList** control is displayed using **SelectedItemTemplate**.

Exam Prep Questions

Question 1

The data model for your application includes an array of **Product** objects named **Products**. Each **Product** object exposes public properties named **ProductNumber** and **ProductName**. You want to provide an interface that allows users to select the **ProductNumber** and see the corresponding **ProductName**. What should you do?

○ A. Create two **TextBox** controls. Bind the **ProductNumber** property to one **TextBox** control and the **ProductName** property to the other **TextBox** control. Provide navigation buttons to allow users to scroll through the data.

○ B. Create a **DataGrid** control and bind the **Products** array to the **DataGrid** control.

○ C. Create a **DropDownList** control. Set the **Products** array as the **DataSource** of the control. Bind the **DataTextField** property to the **ProductNumber** property, and bind the **DataValueField** property to the **ProductName** property. Bind a **TextBox** on the form to the **SelectedItem.Value** property of the **DropDownList** control. Add code to the **SelectedIndexChanged** property of the **DropDownList** control to invoke the **DataBind()** method of the **TextBox** control.

○ D. Create a **TextBox** control and a **Label** control. Bind the **ProductNumber** property to the **TextBox** control and the **ProductName** property to the **Label** control.

The correct answer is C. Binding the DropDownList control to the data source and responding to its SelectedIndexChanged event lets the DropDownList control transfer data from the source to the TextBox control. Answer A is incorrect because it requires searching for the data rather than choosing it. Answer B is incorrect because it displays all the data at once. Answer D is incorrect because it does not have any provision for choosing a ProductNumber.

Question 2

> You have designed a Web form that will use a **Repeater** control with the ID of
> **rptEmployees** to display employee information. The form includes a
> **SqlDataAdapter** object, named **sqlDataAdapter1**, that draws data from the
> Employees table and a **DataSet** object, named **dsEmployees1**, that will contain
> the data. What code should you add to initialize the display when the page is
> loaded?
>
> O A.
>
> ```
> if(!IsPostBack)
> {
>     sqlDataAdapter1.Fill(dsEmployees1, "Employees");
>     rptEmployees.DataSource = dsEmployees1;
>     rptEmployees.DataMember = "Employees";
>     DataBind();
> }
> ```
>
> O B.
>
> ```
> if(IsPostBack)
> {
>     sqlDataAdapter1.Fill(dsEmployees1, "Employees");
>     rptEmployees.DataSource = dsEmployees1;
>     rptEmployees.DataMember = "Employees";
>     DataBind();
> }
> ```
>
> O C.
>
> ```
> if(!IsPostBack)
> {
>     sqlDataAdapter1.Fill(dsEmployees1, "Employees");
>     rptEmployees.DataSource = dsEmployees1;
>     rptEmployees.DataTextField = "Employees";
>     DataBind();
> }
> ```
>
> O D.
>
> ```
> if(IsPostBack)
> {
>     sqlDataAdapter1.Fill(dsEmployees1, "Employees");
>     rptEmployees.DataSource = dsEmployees1;
>     rptEmployees.DataTextField = "Employees";
>     DataBind();
> }
> ```

The correct answer is A. To initialize data when the page is loaded, you want
to check that you're not in a postback. Answers B and D are incorrect because
you need to execute the code when the page is being loaded for the first time.
Answer C is incorrect because loading data requires a four-step process: Fill
the DataSet, set the DataSource property of the Repeater, set the DataMember property of the Repeater, and call the DataBind() method to bind the data.

Question 3

Your application includes a database table that contains a list of course numbers and course names. You've used Server Explorer to create a **SqlConnection** object and a **SqlDataAdapter** object to access this data. You've also created a **DataSet** object named **dsCourses1** to hold this data. Your form includes code to fill the **DataSet** object when it's loaded.

Now you want to display the list of courses in a **ListBox** control named **lbCourses** on your form. The **ListBox** control should show the course names and return the course numbers. Which of these code snippets should you use?

○ A.
```
lbCourses.DataSource = dsCourses1;
lbCourses.DataTextField = "CourseName";
lbCourses.DataValueField = "CourseNumber";
lbCourses.DataBind();
```

○ B.
```
lbCourses.DataSource = dsCourses1.Tables["Courses"];
lbCourses.DataTextField = "CourseName";
lbCourses.DataValueField = "CourseNumber";
lbCourses.DataBind();
```

○ C.
```
lbCourses.DataSource = dsCourses1.Tables["Courses"];
lbCourses.DataTextField = "CourseName";
lbCourses.SelectedItem = "CourseNumber";
lbCourses.DataBind();
```

○ D.
```
lbCourses.DataTextField = "CourseName";
lbCourses.DataValueField = "CourseNumber";
lbCourses.DataBind();
```

The correct answer is B. The code in answer B performs the required task. Answer A is incorrect because it does not properly specify which data from the DataSet object to use. Answer C is incorrect because it neglects to bind the DataValueField property, which controls the value of the ListBox control. Answer D is incorrect because it neglects to set the DataSource property, without which there is no data to bind.

Question 4

> Your application includes a **SqlDataAdapter** object named **sqlDataAdapter1** that was created by dragging and dropping the **Physicians** table from a database to your form. Your application also includes a **DataSet** object named **dsPhysicians1** that is based on this **SqlDataAdapter** object. Which line of code should you use to load the data from the database into the **DataSet** object?
>
> ○ A. **dsPhysicians = sqlDataAdapter1.Fill("Physicians");**
>
> ○ B. **sqlDataAdapter1.Fill("dsPhysicians1", "Physicians");**
>
> ○ C. **sqlDataAdapter1.Fill("dsPhysicians1");**
>
> ○ D. **sqlDataAdapter1.Fill(dsPhysicians1, "Physicians");**

The correct answer is D. This answer uses the correct syntax for the `SqlDataAdapter.Fill()` method. Answers A and C are incorrect because in a call to the `Fill()` method of a `SqlDataAdapter` object, you must specify the `DataSet` object to fill as an object and the table to fill as a string. Answer B is incorrect because `dsPhysicians1` should not be within quotation marks.

Question 5

> The application you're designing should display employee information on a **DataGrid** control using complex data binding. Your database contains a table of departments and a table of employees. The employees table has a foreign key that points back to the departments table. The application will communicate with the database via a slow WAN link. The list of departments changes approximately once every two months.
>
> The form should display all the employees from a single department. Although users will view only one department at a time, they will frequently need to view several departments during the course of a session with the application.
>
> How should you design the filtering for this form?
>
> ○ A. Build one view on the server for each department. At runtime, have the program use the appropriate view to retrieve the requested department.
>
> ○ B. Each time the user requests a department, retrieve all the data into a **DataSet** object. Then delete all the rows from the **DataSet** object that do not apply to this department.
>
> ○ C. Retrieve all the data into a **DataSet** object. Then use a **DataView** object with its **RowFilter** property set at runtime to retrieve individual departments as needed.
>
> ○ D. Build one form for each department. Each form should be based on a view that returns only the employees for that department. At runtime, open the appropriate form. Hide the form when the user is done so that it can be opened more quickly if it's needed a second time.

The correct answer is C. By setting the `DataView.RowFilter` at runtime, you can programmatically filter the data without having additional overhead or need for program modification. Answers A and D are incorrect because they require maintenance programming every time the list of departments changes. Answer B is incorrect because it retrieves more data than necessary over the slow WAN link.

Question 6

Your application is connected to a SQL Server database that contains customer and order information. You have a form in your application that fills a **DataSet** object with information from the Orders table that includes the **CustomerID**. The **DataSet** object is displayed on the form by using complex data binding to a **DataGrid** control.

Now you've been asked to display the **CustomerName** column from the Customers table in the **DataGrid** control, instead of the **CustomerID** column. How should you proceed?

- O A. Create a view in the SQL Server database that combines the Customers and Orders tables. Replace the **DataSet** object on the form with a new **DataSet** object based on this new view; then bind the new **DataSet** object to the **DataGrid** control.

- O B. Add a second **DataSet** object to the form, and base it on the Customers table from the database. Use each **DataSet** object to fill the appropriate columns of the **DataGrid** control.

- O C. Create a **DataView** object in code from the existing **DataSet** object. Filter the **DataView** object to remove the **CustomerID** column.

- O D. Add an array of **Customer** objects to your application and initialize it in code with customer names and IDs. Use a view to join this array to the existing **DataSet** object.

The correct answer is A. This answer lets you set up the `DataGrid` control so that it's automatically kept up-to-date. Answers B and C are incorrect because they provide no way to establish a relationship between the Customers and the Orders tables. Answer D is incorrect because it requires you to maintain the code to synchronize the array with the actual data in the database.

Question 7

Your application uses a **DataList** control to display course information. The information is supplied by a **DataSet** object named **dsCourses1**. You want users to be able to edit the **CourseName** field, so you've created a **Button** control in the **ItemTemplate** with this code:

```
<asp:Button id="btnEdit" runat=
    "server" Text="Edit"
    CommandName="Edit" />
```

You've also created an **EditItemTemplate** that includes a **TextBox** control with an ID of **txtCourseName** for editing the **CourseName** field. Which code should your application run when a user clicks the **btnEdit** button?

○ A.
```
private void dlCourses_EditCommand(
  Object sender, DataListCommandEventArgs e)
  {
      dlCourses.EditItemIndex = e.Item.ItemIndex;
  }
```

○ B.
```
private void dlCourses_EditCommand(
  Object sender, DataListCommandEventArgs e)
  {
      dlCourses.EditItemIndex = e.Item.ItemIndex;
      sqlDataAdapter1.Fill(dsCourses1, "Courses");
      DataBind();
  }
```

○ C.
```
private void dlCourses_EditCommand(
        Object sender, DataListCommandEventArgs e)
  {
      dlCourses.EditItemIndex = -1;
      sqlDataAdapter1.Fill(dsCourses1, "Courses");
      DataBind();
  }
```

○ D.
```
private void dlCourses_EditCommand(
  Object sender, DataListCommandEventArgs e)
  {
      dlCourses.EditItemIndex = -1;
  }
```

The correct answer is B. This answer follows the correct steps to place the selected row into edit mode, including setting the EditItemIndex property to the row number and then rebinding the data so that the edit controls are initialized. Answer A is incorrect because it doesn't rebind the data. Answers C and D are incorrect because they set the EditItemIndex property to -1, which is how you end an edit, not how you begin one.

Question 8

You have developed a form with a **DataList** control that displays order information. One of the database columns you want to display on this form is named
Tax. This column contains a currency value. Which binding expression should
you use to display this value on the user interface, formatted as currency?

○ A.

```
<%# DataBinder.Eval(Container.DataItem, "Tax") %>
```

○ B.

```
<%# "Tax" %>
```

○ C.

```
<%# "Tax", "{0:c}" %>
```

○ D.

```
<%# DataBinder.Eval(Container.DataItem, "Tax", "{0:c}") %>
```

The correct answer is D. This answer correctly uses the DataBinder object's
Eval() method to format the data. Answer A is incorrect because it won't
apply any format. Answers B and C are incorrect because they fail to retrieve
the correct information.

Question 9

The data model of your application includes a task list that might have from one
to eight items in it. Each item is characterized by five pieces of information. You
need to display the entire task list on a single form, and your users want to be
able to see all the tasks at one time. What should you do?

○ A. Use simple data binding to display a single task in individual **TextBox**
controls. Provide a **DropDownList** control to allow users to select the
task to display.

○ B. Use the **System.Reflection.Emit** namespace to create the appropriate
number of **TextBox** controls at runtime. Then use simple data binding
to bind each task to a different set of controls.

○ C. Use complex data binding to display the task list in a **DropDownList**
control.

○ D. Use complex data binding to display the task list in a **DataGrid** control.

The correct answer is D. The DataGrid control allows users to see all the tasks
at the same time. Answers A and C are incorrect because they result in only
one task being visible at a time. Answer B is incorrect because it uses a lot of
complicated programming where a complex data binding call will suffice.

Question 10

You have an XML file containing information on customers. You plan to make this information available to your users by using simple data binding controls on the user interface. What must you do?

○ A. Transfer the data from the XML file to a data structure that implements the **ICollection** interface.

○ B. Create an XML Web Service to retrieve information from the file.

○ C. Store the XML file in a SQL Server database.

○ D. Set the **Tag** property of each control that you will use for data binding to **XML**.

The correct answer is A. You should import the data from the XML file to a data structure that implements the ICollection interface. Answers B, C, and D are incorrect because these options do not produce data that can be bound.

Need to Know More?

 Mitchell, Scott. *ASP.NET Data Web Controls Kick Start.* Indianapolis, IN: Sams Publishing, 2003.

 See the ASP.NET QuickStart Tutorial: Databinding Server Controls at `http://samples.gotdotnet.com/quickstart/aspplus/doc/webdatabinding.aspx`.

 See the ASP.NET QuickStart Tutorial: Server-Side Data Access at `http://samples.gotdotnet.com/quickstart/aspplus/doc/webdataaccess.aspx`.

 See the ASP.NET QuickStart Tutorial: WebForms Controls Reference at `http://samples.gotdotnet.com/quickstart/aspplus/doc/webcontrolsref.aspx`.

 Visit the MSDN Library: Accessing Data with ADO.NET at `www.msdn.com/library/en-us/cpguide/html/cpconaccessingdatawithadonet.asp`.

 The .NET Show: Visual Studio .NET, at `www.msdn.com/theshow/Episode015`, has good information.

 Visit the MSDN How-To Resources on Visual Studio .NET at `www.msdn.com/howto/visualstudio.asp`.

 See *MSDN Magazine*'s "Web Q&A" column at `www.msdn.com/msdnmag/find/default.aspx?type=Ti&phrase=Web Q%26A`.

Consuming and Manipulating Data

Terms you'll need to understand:

✓ Concurrency control
✓ Dataset
✓ DOM (Document Object Model)
✓ Extensible Markup Language (XML)
✓ Namespace
✓ Schema

Techniques you'll need to master:

✓ Accessing and manipulating data from a Microsoft SQL Server database by creating and using ad hoc queries and stored procedures
✓ Knowing how to work with a dataset object
✓ Knowing how to read and write XML data using the classes from the **System.Xml** namespace
✓ Knowing how to handle database-related errors in your code
✓ Practicing reading and writing file-based data with the **FileStream**, **StreamReader**, and **StreamWriter** objects

In this chapter, you learn how to access and manipulate data in relational databases such as Microsoft SQL Server, data in XML format, and the data stored in disk files.

The ADO.NET Object Model

ADO.NET is the overall name for the set of classes the .NET Framework provides under the System.Data namespace for working with data from multiple sources.

ADO.NET provides two distinct sets of classes: the data provider classes that enable you to directly work with a data source and the dataset-related classes that provide a memory-resident, disconnected cache of data retrieved from a data source. The data provider also serves as a conduit between the data source and the disconnected dataset.

Data Provider Classes

A *data provider* is a collection of classes used to access a data source. ADO.NET provides various sets of classes for working with each data source. For example, the classes for interacting with Microsoft SQL Server are organized in the System.Data.SqlClient namespace, the classes for interacting with Oracle are organized in the System.Data.OracleClient namspace, the classes for interacting with OLEDB data sources are organized in the System.Data.OleDb namespace, and the classes for interacting with Open Database Connectivity (ODBC) are organized in the System.Data.Odbc namespace.

 The exam focuses on the use of the Microsoft SQL Server database. However, you should expect common functionality among data provider classes because they all implement the common interfaces defined in the **System.Data** namespace. For example, the **SqlConnection** class in the **System.Data.SqlClient** namespace provides the functionality for connecting to a SQL Server database—the same functionality that is provided by the **OracleConnection** class in the **System.Data.OracleClient** namespace.

The SqlConnection Class

SqlConnection represents a single persistent connection to a SQL Server data source. Table 7.1 shows the most important members of the SqlConnection class.

Table 7.1	Important Members of the SqlConnection Class	
Member	**Type**	**Description**
BeginTransaction()	Method	Starts a new transaction on this **SqlConnection** object
Close()	Method	Returns the **SqlConnection** object to the connection pool
ConnectionString	Property	Specifies the server to be used by this **SqlConnection** object
CreateCommand()	Method	Returns a new **SqlCommand** object that executes via this **SqlConnection** object
Open()	Method	Opens the **connection** to the database

The following code segment shows how to create a SqlConnection object:

```
SqlConnection cnn = new SqlConnection();
cnn.ConnectionString = @"Data Source=(local)\NetSDK;"
    + "Initial Catalog=Northwind;Integrated Security=SSPI";
cnn.Open();
```

You should know how to construct a SQL Server connection string for use with the SqlConnection object. There are three parts to the string. First is the data source, which is the name of the server to which you want to connect. (local)\NetSDK is the name for the SQL Server instance installed with the .NET Framework QuickStart samples. Second is the initial catalog, which is the name of the database on the server to use. Third is authentication information. This can be either Integrated Security=SSPI for use with Windows authentication or User ID=*username*;Password=*password* (this can be abbreviated as UID=*username*;PWD=*password*) for use with SQL Server authentication. Other optional parameters exist, but these three are the most important.

Establishing database connection is one of the slowest database operations. Therefore, ADO.NET supports automatic connection pooling to increase performance. When you call the **Close()** method of a **SqlConnection** object, the connection is returned to a connection pool. Connections in a pool are not immediately destroyed by ADO.NET. Instead, they're available for reuse if another part of an application requests a **SqlConnection** object that has the exact same connection string as a previously closed **SqlConnection** object.

The **SqlCommand** and **SqlParameter** Classes

The SqlCommand class represents something that can be executed, such as an ad hoc query string or a stored procedure name. The SqlParameter class, on the other hand, represents a single parameter to a stored procedure. Table 7.2 details the most important members of the SqlCommand class.

Table 7.2	Important Members of the SqlCommand Class	
Member	**Type**	**Description**
CommandText	Property	Specifies the statement to be executed by the **SqlCommand** object
CommandType	Property	Indicates which type of command this **SqlCommand** object represents
Connection	Property	Represents the **SqlConnection** object through which this **SqlCommand** object executes
CreateParameter()	Method	Creates a new **SqlParameter** object for this **SqlCommand** object
ExecuteNonQuery()	Method	Executes a **SqlCommand** object that does not return a result set
ExecuteReader()	Method	Executes a **SqlCommand** object and places the results in a **SqlDataReader** object
ExecuteScalar()	Method	Executes a **SqlCommand** object and returns the first column of the first row of the result set
ExecuteXmlReader()	Method	Executes a **SqlCommand** object and places the results in an **XmlReader** object
Parameters	Property	Contains a collection of **SqlParameter** objects for this **SqlCommand** object

The **SqlDataReader** Class

The SqlDataReader class is designed to be the fastest possible way to retrieve a result set from a database. SqlDataReader objects can be constructed by calling the ExecuteReader() method of a SqlCommand object. The result set contained in a SqlDataReader object is forward-only and read-only. That is, you can only read the rows in the result set sequentially from start to finish, and you can't modify any of the data:

```
// Connect to the database
SqlConnection cnn = new SqlConnection();
cnn.ConnectionString = @"Data Source=(local)\NetSDK;"
    + "Initial Catalog=Northwind;Integrated Security=SSPI";
// Create a new ad hoc query to retrieve customer names
SqlCommand cmd = cnn.CreateCommand();
cmd.CommandType = CommandType.Text;
cmd.CommandText = "SELECT CompanyName FROM Customers ORDER BY CompanyName";
// Dump the data to the user interface
cnn.Open();
SqlDataReader dr = cmd.ExecuteReader();
```

```
while (dr.Read())
    lbCustomers.Items.Add(dr.GetString(0));
// Clean up
dr.Close();
cnn.Close();
```

 The **SqlDataReader** object makes exclusive use of its **SqlConnection** object as long as it is open. You can't execute any other **SqlCommand** objects on that connection as long as the **SqlDataReader** object is open. Therefore, you should always call the **SqlDataReader.Close()** method as soon as you're finished retrieving data.

 You can improve the code's performance even more by using a stored procedure instead of an ad hoc query to retrieve the data.

Table 7.3 shows the most important members of the SqlDataReader class. There's no need to memorize all the members (and the others that aren't shown in this table), but you should understand the patterns they represent.

Table 7.3 Important Members of the SqlDataReader Class		
Member	**Type**	**Description**
Close()	Method	Closes the **SqlDataReader** object
GetBoolean()	Method	Gets a Boolean value from the specified column
GetByte()	Method	Gets a byte value from the specified column
GetChar()	Method	Gets a character value from the specified column
GetDateTime()	Method	Gets a date/time value from the specified column
GetDecimal()	Method	Gets a decimal value from the specified column
GetDouble()	Method	Gets a double value from the specified column
GetFloat()	Method	Gets a float value from the specified column
GetGuid()	Method	Gets a global unique identifier (GUID) value from the specified column
GetInt16()	Method	Gets a 16-bit integer value from the specified column
GetInt32()	Method	Gets a 32-bit integer value from the specified column
GetInt64()	Method	Gets a 64-bit integer value from the specified column
GetName()	Method	Gets the column name for the specified zero-based column ordinal
GetOrdinal()	Method	Gets the column ordinal for the specified column name
GetString()	Method	Gets a string value from the specified column

(continued)

Table 7.3 Important Members of the SqlDataReader Class *(continued)*		
Member	Type	Description
GetValue()	Method	Gets a value from the specified column
GetValues()	Method	Gets an entire row of data and places it in an array of objects
IsDbNull()	Method	Indicates whether a specified column contains a null value
Read()	Method	Loads the next row of data into the **SqlDataReader** object

The SqlDataAdapter Class

The SqlDataAdapter class provides a bridge between the data provider and the dataset. You can think of the SqlDataAdapter object as a two-way pipeline between the data in its native storage format and the data in a more abstract representation (the DataSet object) that's designed for manipulation in an application. Table 7.4 details the most important members of the SqlDataAdapter class.

Table 7.4 Important Members of the SqlDataAdapter Class		
Member	Type	Description
DeleteCommand	Property	Specifies the **SqlCommand** object used to delete rows from the data source
Fill()	Method	Transfers data from the data source to a **DataSet** object
InsertCommand	Property	Specifies the **SqlCommand** object used to insert rows into the data source
SelectCommand	Property	Specifies the **SqlCommand** object used to retrieve rows from the data source
Update()	Method	Transfers data from a **DataSet** object to the data source
UpdateCommand	Property	Specifies the **SqlCommand** object used to update rows in the data source

The DataSet Classes

Unlike the data provider classes, only one set of DataSet classes exists. The DataSet classes are all contained in the System.Data namespace, and they represent data in an abstract form that's not tied to any particular database implementation. This section introduces you to the DataSet class and the other objects it contains, including

➤ DataTable

➤ DataRelation

➤ DataRow

➤ DataColumn

➤ DataView

The DataSet class itself is a self-contained, memory-resident representation of relational data. A DataSet object contains other objects, such as DataTable and DataRelation objects, that hold the actual data and information about the design of the data. Table 7.5 shows the most important members of the DataSet class.

Table 7.5	Important Members of the DataSet Class	
Member	**Type**	**Description**
AcceptChanges()	Method	Marks all changes in the dataset as having been accepted
Clear()	Method	Removes all data from the dataset
GetChanges()	Method	Gets a **DataSet** object that contains only the changed data in the dataset
GetXml()	Method	Gets an XML representation of the dataset
GetXmlSchema()	Method	Gets an XML Schema Definition (XSD) representation of the dataset schema
Merge()	Method	Merges two datasets
ReadXml()	Method	Loads the dataset from an XML file
ReadXmlSchema()	Method	Loads the dataset schema from an XSD file
Relations	Property	Specifies a collection of **DataRelation** objects
Tables	Property	Specifies a collection of **DataTable** objects
WriteXml()	Method	Writes the dataset to an XML file
WriteXmlSchema()	Method	Writes the dataset schema to an XSD file

The **DataTable** Class

The DataTable class represents a single table within the DataSet object. A single DataSet object can contain many DataTable objects. Table 7.6 shows the most important members of the DataTable class.

Table 7.6	Important Members of the DataTable Class	
Member	Type	Description
ChildRelations	Property	Specifies a collection of **DataRelation** objects that refer to children of the **DataTable** class
Clear()	Method	Removes all data from the **DataTable** class
ColumnChanged	Event	Occurs when the data in any row of a specified column has been changed
ColumnChanging	Event	Occurs when the data in any row of a specified column is about to be changed
Columns	Property	Specifies a collection of **DataColumn** objects
Constraints	Property	Specifies a collection of **Constraint** objects
DataSet	Property	Retrieves the **DataSet** object to which the **DataTable** object belongs
NewRow()	Method	Creates a new, blank row in the data table
ParentRelations	Property	Specifies a collection of **DataRelation** objects that refer to parents of the **DataTable**
PrimaryKey	Property	Specifies an array of **DataColumn** objects that provide the primary key for the **DataTable**
RowChanged	Event	Occurs when any data in a **DataRow** has been changed
RowChanging	Event	Occurs when any data in a **DataRow** is about to be changed
RowDeleted	Event	Occurs when a row has been deleted
RowDeleting	Event	Occurs when a row is about to be deleted
Rows	Property	Specifies a collection of **DataRow** objects
Select()	Method	Selects an array of **DataRow** objects that meet specified criteria
TableName	Property	Specifies the name of the **DataTable**

As you can see, you can manipulate a DataTable as either a collection of DataColumn objects or a collection of DataRow objects. The DataTable class also provides events that you can use to monitor data changes. For example, you might bind a DataTable to a DataGrid control and use these events to track the user's operations on the data in the DataGrid control.

The **DataRelation** Class

The DataRelation object stores information on the relationships between DataTable objects in a DataSet object. The most important members of the DataRelation class are listed in Table 7.7.

Table 7.7 Important Members of the DataRelation Class		
Member	**Type**	**Description**
ChildColumns	Property	Specifies a collection of **DataColumn** objects that defines the foreign key side of the relationship
ChildKeyConstraint	Property	Returns a **ForeignKeyConstraint** object for the relationship
ChildTable	Property	Specifies a **DataTable** object from the foreign key side of the relationship
DataSet	Property	Retrieves the **DataSet** object to which the **DataRelation** object belongs
ParentColumns	Property	Specifies a collection of **DataColumn** objects that defines the primary key side of the relationship
ParentKeyConstraint	Property	Returns a **PrimaryKeyConstraint** object for the relationship
ParentTable	Property	Specifies a **DataTable** from the primary key side of the relationship
RelationName	Property	Specifies the name of the **DataRelation**

The DataRow Class

A DataRow object represents a single row of data. When you're selecting, inserting, updating, or deleting data in a DataSet object, you're normally working with DataRow objects. Table 7.8 shows the most important members of the DataRow class.

Table 7.8 Important Members of the DataRow Class		
Member	**Type**	**Description**
BeginEdit()	Method	Starts editing the **DataRow** object
CancelEdit()	Method	Discards an edit in progress
Delete()	Method	Deletes the **DataRow** object from its parent **DataTable** object
EndEdit()	Method	Ends an edit in progress, saving the changes
IsNull()	Method	Returns **true** if a specified column contains a null value
ItemArray	Property	Allows the manipulation of a **DataRow** object through an array of values
RowState	Property	Returns information on the current state of a **DataRow** object (for example, whether it has been changed since it was last saved to the database)
Table	Property	Retrieves the **DataTable** object to which the **DataRow** object belongs

The **DataColumn** Class

A DataColumn object represents a single column in a DataTable object. By manipulating the DataColumn objects, you can determine and even change, the structure of the DataTable object. Table 7.9 lists the most important members of the DataColumn class.

Table 7.9	Important Members of the DataColumn Class	
Member	**Type**	**Description**
AllowDbNull	Property	Indicates whether the **DataColumn** object can contain **null** values
AutoIncrement	Property	Indicates whether the **DataColumn** object is an identity column
ColumnName	Property	Specifies the name of the **DataColumn** object
DataType	Property	Specifies the data type of the **DataColumn** object
DefaultValue	Property	Specifies the default value of this **DataColumn** object for new rows of data
Expression	Property	Specifies an expression that can be used to filter rows, calculate the values in a column, or create an aggregate column
MaxLength	Property	Specifies the maximum length of a text **DataColumn** object
Unique	Property	Indicates whether values in the **DataColumn** object must be unique across all rows in the **DataTable** object

The **DataView** Class

The DataView object represents a view of the data contained in a DataTable object. A DataView object might contain every DataRow object from the DataTable object, or it might be filtered to contain only specific rows. That filtering can be done by SQL expressions (for example, returning only rows for customers in France) or by row state (for example, returning only rows that have been modified). The most important members of the DataView class are detailed in Table 7.10.

Table 7.10	Important Members of the DataView Class	
Member	**Type**	**Description**
AddNew()	Method	Adds a new row to the **DataView** object
AllowDelete	Property	Indicates whether deletions can be performed through this **DataView** object
AllowEdit	Property	Indicates whether updates can be performed through this **DataView** object
AllowNew	Property	Indicates whether insertions can be performed through this **DataView** object
Count	Property	Returns the number of rows in this **DataView** object
Delete()	Method	Deletes a row from this **DataView** object
Find()	Method	Searches for a row in the **DataView** object
FindRows()	Method	Returns an array of rows matching a filter expression
RowFilter	Property	A string expression that specifies how the rows are filtered
RowStateFilter	Property	One of the values from the **DataViewRowState** enumeration that specifies how the rows are filtered
Sort()	Method	Sorts the data in a **DataView** object

Using **DataSet** Objects

Before you can do anything with data in a DataSet object, you have to get that data into the DataSet object somehow. In general, you can follow this four-step process to move data from the database to a DataSet object:

1. Create a SqlConnection object to connect to the database.

2. Create a SqlCommand object to retrieve the desired data.

3. Assign the SqlCommand object to the SelectCommand property of a SqlDataAdapter object.

4. Call the Fill() method of the SqlDataAdapter object to retrieve data from the database and populate the DataSet object with the data.

Here, you don't have to explicitly call the Open() and Close() methods of the SqlConnection object. Instead, the Fill() method makes those calls when it needs the data. Doing this not only cuts down the amount of code you need to write, but also improves the scalability of your application by keeping the SqlConnection object open for the shortest possible period of time.

A variety of syntaxes exists that you can use to retrieve data. Given a `DataTable` variable named `dt` that refers to the data from the `Customers` table, for example, either of these statements would retrieve the value in the first column of the first row of data in the `DataTable` object:

```
dt.Rows[0][0]
dt.Rows[0]["CustomerID"]
```

Strongly Typed **DataSet** Objects

The sytaxes used for retrieving data in the previous section were all late bound. That is, the .NET Framework doesn't know until runtime that a column name (such as `CustomerID`) is valid. ADO.NET also facilitates the creation of strongly typed `DataSet` objects. In a strongly typed `DataSet` object, columns actually become properties of the row, enabling you to write an early-bound version of the data-retrieval expression:

```
dt.Rows[0].CustomerID
```

In addition to being faster than the late-bound syntaxes, the early-bound syntax has the added advantage of making column names show up in IntelliSense tips as you type code.

Anytime you use the Generate DataSet link in the Properties window for a `SqlDataAdapter` object, Visual Studio .NET builds a strongly typed `DataSet` object. You can also build strongly typed `DataSet` objects using the XSD designer.

Using **DataSet** Objects with Multiple Tables

By using `DataAdapter` objects, you can connect a single `DataSet` object to more than one table in the SQL Server database. You can also define `DataRelation` objects to represent the relationships between the `DataTable` objects in the `DataSet` object. Take the following steps to learn how to build a `DataSet` object that contains multiple `DataTable` objects:

1. Open Visual Studio .NET and create a new blank solution named `315C07` at `c:\inetpub\wwwroot\ExamCram`. (You might need to change the directory based on your configuration.)

2. Add a new Visual C# ASP.NET Web Application project at the following location: `http://localhost/ExamCram/315C07/Example7_1`.

3. Use the Properties window to change the `pageLayout` property of the `DOCUMENT` object from `GridLayout` to `FlowLayout` for the Web form.

4. Place two `DataGrid` controls (`dgCustomers` and `dgOrders`) on the form. Set the `DataKeyField` property of the `dgCustomers` control to `CustomerID`.

5. Click the Property Builder hyperlink beneath the Properties window for the `dgCustomers` control. Select the Columns section of the dgCustomers Properties dialog box. In the Available Columns list, expand the node for Button Column. Select the Select item and then click the > button to move this item to the Selected Columns list. Click OK.

6. Switch to Code view and add the following `using` directive:

```
using System.Data.SqlClient;
```

7. Attach an event handler to the `ItemCommand` event of the `dgCustomers` control and enter the following code in the class definition:

```
DataSet ds = new DataSet();
private void Page_Load(object sender, System.EventArgs e)
{
    // Initialize the DataSet
    LoadData();
    // And show the data on the user interface
    dgCustomers.DataSource = ds;
    dgCustomers.DataMember = "Customers";
    dgCustomers.DataBind();
}
private void dgCustomers_ItemCommand(object source,
system.Web.UI.WebControls.DataGridCommandEventArgs e)
{
    // Create a DataView showing orders for the selected customer
    DataView dv = new DataView(ds.Tables["Orders"]);
    dv.RowFilter = "CustomerID = '" +
        dgCustomers.DataKeys[e.Item.ItemIndex] + "'";
    // And show the data on the user interface
    dgOrders.DataSource = dv;
    dgOrders.DataBind();
    // shift the focus to the dgOrders control
    RegisterStartupScript("select",
    "<script language = 'JavaScript'>dgOrders.focus();</script>");
}

private void LoadData()
{
    // Create a SqlConnection and a DataSet
    SqlConnection cnn = new SqlConnection(@"Data Source=(local)\NetSDK;"
        + "Initial Catalog=Northwind; Integrated Security=SSPI");
    // Add the customers data to the DataSet
    SqlCommand cmdCustomers= cnn.CreateCommand();
    cmdCustomers.CommandType = CommandType.Text;
    cmdCustomers.CommandText = "SELECT * FROM Customers";
    SqlDataAdapter daCustomers = new SqlDataAdapter();
    daCustomers.SelectCommand = cmdCustomers;
    daCustomers.Fill(ds, "Customers");
    // Add the Orders data to the DataSet
    SqlCommand cmdOrders = cnn.CreateCommand();
    cmdOrders.CommandType = CommandType.Text;
```

```
cmdOrders.CommandText = "SELECT * FROM Orders";
SqlDataAdapter daOrders = new SqlDataAdapter();
daOrders.SelectCommand = cmdOrders;
daOrders.Fill(ds, "Orders");
// Add Relation
DataRelation relCustOrder = ds.Relations.Add("CustOrder",
    ds.Tables["Customers"].Columns["CustomerID"],
    ds.Tables["Orders"].Columns["CustomerID"]);
}
```

8. Set the project as the startup project and run the application. The program loads both database tables into the DataSet object and then displays the customer information on the DataGrid control.

9. Click the Select hyperlink for one of the rows; this posts the form back to the server. First, the Load event of the page fires, loading the DataSet object and initializing the dgCustomers control. Then the ItemCommand event of the DataGrid fires. In the handler for this event, the code retrieves the key from the selected row and uses this key to build a DataView object containing orders for the selected customer.

Finding and Sorting Data in **DataSet** Objects

Using the Select() method of the DataTable object is a convenient way to find particular DataRow objects in the DataTable object. For example, the following code returns all customers in Brazil:

```
DataRow[] adr = ds.Tables["Customers"].Select("Country = 'Brazil'");
```

The Select() method of the DataTable object constructs an array of DataRow objects based on up to three factors: a filter expression, sort expression, and state constant.

Filter expressions are essentially SQL WHERE clauses constructed according to these rules:

➤ Column names containing special characters (such as space) should be enclosed in square brackets.

➤ String constants should be enclosed in single quotation marks.

➤ Date constants should be enclosed in pound signs.

➤ Numeric expressions can be specified in decimal or scientific notation.

➤ Expressions can be created using AND, OR, NOT, parentheses, IN, LIKE, comparison operators, and arithmetic operators.

➤ The + operator is used to concatenate strings.

➤ Either * or % can be used as a wild card to match any number of characters. Wild cards can be used only at the start or end of strings.

➤ Columns in a child table can be referenced with the expression *Child.Column*. If the table has more than one child table, you use the expression *Child(RelationName).Column* to choose a particular child table.

➤ The Sum, Avg, Min, Max, Count, StDev, and Var aggregates can be used with child tables.

➤ Supported functions include CONVERT, LEN, ISNULL, IIF, and SUBSTRING.

If you don't specify a sort order in the Select() method, the rows are returned in primary key order or in the order of addition if the table doesn't have a primary key. You can also specify a sort expression that consists of one or more column names and the keyword ASC or DESC to specify an ascending or descending sort. For example, this is a valid sort expression:

```
Country ASC, CompanyName DESC
```

This expression sorts first by country, in ascending order, and then by company name within each country, in descending order.

Finally, you can also select DataRow objects according to their current states by supplying one of the DataViewRowState constants. Table 7.11 lists these constants.

Table 7.11 DataViewRowState Constants	
Constant	**Meaning**
Added	Specifies new rows that have not yet been committed
CurrentRows	Specifies all current rows, whether they are unchanged, modified, or new
Deleted	Specifies deleted rows
ModifiedCurrent	Specifies modified rows
ModifiedOriginal	Specifies original data from modified rows
None	Specifies no rows
OriginalRows	Specifies original data, including rows that have been modified or deleted
Unchanged	Specifies rows that have not been changed

You can also sort and filter data using a `DataView` object. The `DataView` object has the same structure of rows and columns as a `DataTable` object, but it also lets you specify sorting and filtering options. Typically, you create a `DataView` object by starting with a `DataTable` object and specifying options to include a subset of the rows in the `DataTable` object as shown in the following code segment:

```
DataView dv = new DataView(ds.Tables["Customers"]);
dv.RowFilter = "Country = 'France'";
dv.Sort = "CompanyName ASC";
dgCustomers.DataSource = dv;
dgCustomers.DataBind();
```

By setting the `RowFilter`, `Sort`, and `RowStateFilter` properties of the `DataView` object, you can control which rows are available in the `DataView` object and the order in which they are presented. I didn't use the `RowStateFilter` property in the previous code segment. `RowStateFilter` allows you to select, for example, only rows that have been changed since the `DataTable` object was loaded. The `RowStateFilter` property can be set to any one of the `DataViewRowState` constants listed previously in Table 7.11.

Editing Data with ADO.NET

ADO.NET supports all the normal database operations of updating existing data, adding new data, and deleting existing data.

Updating Data

Updating data is easy: You simply assign a new value to the item in the `DataRow` object that you want to change. But there's more to finishing the job. For the `Update()` method of the `SqlDataAdapter` object to write changes back to the database, you need to set its `UpdateCommand` property to an appropriate `SqlCommand` object. Follow these steps to see how to use a `SqlDataAdapter` object to update data in a database:

1. Add a new Visual C# ASP.NET Web Application project (`Example7_2`) to the existing solution.

2. Place three `Label` controls (name one of them `lblResults`), two `TextBox` controls (`txtCustomerID` and `txtContactName`), and a `Button` control (`btnUpdate`) on the form. Figure 7.1 shows the layout of this form.

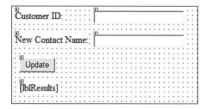

Figure 7.1   You can update the data in a database using a **SqlDataAdapter** object.

3. Switch to Code view and add the following `using` directive:

```
using System.Data.SqlClient;
```

4. Double-click the `Button` control and enter this code to handle its `Click` event:

```
private void btnUpdate_Click(object sender, System.EventArgs e)
{
    // Create some ADO.NET objects
    SqlConnection cnn = new SqlConnection(@"Data Source=(local)\NetSDK;"
        + "Initial Catalog=Northwind;Integrated Security=SSPI");
    DataSet ds = new DataSet();
    SqlDataAdapter da = new SqlDataAdapter();
    // Create a SqlCommand to select data
    SqlCommand cmdSelect = cnn.CreateCommand();
    cmdSelect.CommandType = CommandType.Text;
    cmdSelect.CommandText =
        "SELECT CustomerID, ContactName FROM Customers";
    // Create a SqlCommand to update data
    SqlCommand cmdUpdate = cnn.CreateCommand();
    cmdUpdate.CommandType = CommandType.Text;
    cmdUpdate.CommandText = "UPDATE Customers SET " +
        "ContactName = @ContactName WHERE CustomerID = @CustomerID";
    cmdUpdate.Parameters.Add("@ContactName",
        SqlDbType.NVarChar,30, "ContactName");
    cmdUpdate.Parameters.Add("@CustomerID",
        SqlDbType.NChar,5, "CustomerID");
    cmdUpdate.Parameters["@CustomerID"].SourceVersion
        = DataRowVersion.Original;
    // Set up the DataAdapter and fill the DataSet
    da.UpdateCommand = cmdUpdate;
    da.SelectCommand = cmdSelect;
    da.Fill(ds, "Customers");

    // Get the DataRow to edit
    DataRow[] adrEdit = ds.Tables["Customers"].Select("CustomerID = '"
        + txtCustomerID.Text + "'");
    // Make sure there's some data
    if(adrEdit.Length > 0)
    {
        adrEdit[0]["ContactName"] = txtContactName.Text;
        // Save the changes
        da.Update(ds, "Customers");
        // And make a note on the UI
        lblResults.Text = "Row has been updated";
    }
}
```

5. Set the project as the startup project for the solution and run the application. Enter a customer ID (such as ALFKI) and a new contact name; then click OK. The code writes the change back to the database and shows the Row has been updated text on the form.

The Update() method of the SqlDataAdapter object is syntactically similar to the Fill() method. It takes as its parameters the DataSet object to be reconciled with the database and the name of the DataTable object to be saved. You don't have to worry about which rows or columns of data are changed because the SqlDataAdapter object automatically locates the changed rows. It then executes the SqlCommand object specified in its UpdateCommand property for each of those rows.

In the previous example, the UpdateCommand property has two parameters. The SqlParameter objects are created using a version of the constructor that takes four parameters rather than the three you saw earlier in the chapter. The fourth parameter is the name of a DataColumn that contains the data to be used in this particular parameter. Note also that you can specify whether a parameter should be filled in from the current data in the DataSet object (the default) or the original version of the data, before any edits were made. In this case, the @CustomerID parameter is being used to locate the row to edit in the database, so the code uses the original value of the column as the value for the parameter.

Adding Data

To add data to the database, you must supply a SqlCommand object for the InsertCommand property of the SqlDataAdapter object, as shown in the following code segment:

```
SqlDataAdapter da = new SqlDataAdapter();
// Create a SqlCommand to insert data
SqlCommand cmdIns = cnn.CreateCommand();
cmdIns.CommandType = CommandType.Text;
cmdIns.CommandText = "INSERT INTO Customers(CustomerID, CompanyName, " +
    "ContactName) " + "VALUES(@CustomerID, @CompanyName, @ContactName)";
cmdIns.Parameters.Add("@CustomerID", SqlDbType.NChar,5, "CustomerID");
cmdIns.Parameters.Add("@CompanyName", SqlDbType.NVarChar,40, "CompanyName");
cmdIns.Parameters.Add("@ContactName", SqlDbType.NVarChar,30, "ContactName");
cmdIns.Parameters["@CustomerID"].SourceVersion = DataRowVersion.Original;
// Set up the DataAdapter and fill the DataSet
da.InsertCommand = cmdIns;
```

The process of adding a new DataRow object to a DataTable object has several steps. First, you call the NewRow() method of the DataTable object, which returns a DataRow object that has the proper schema for that particular

DataTable object. Then you can set the values of the individual items in the DataRow object. Finally, you call the Add() method of the DataTable object to actually append this DataRow object to the DataTable object, as shown in the following code segment:

```
// Create a new DataRow
DataRow dr = ds.Tables["Customers"].NewRow();
// Set values
dr[0] = txtCustomerID.Text;
dr[1] = txtCompanyName.Text;
dr[2] = txtContactName.Text;
// And append the new row to the DataTable
ds.Tables["Customers"].Rows.Add(dr);
// Now save back to the database
da.Update(ds, "Customers");
```

Of course, appending the DataRow object to the DataTable object doesn't make any changes to the database. For that, you need to call the Update() method of the SqlDataAdapter object again. If the SqlDataAdapter object finds any new rows in its scan of the database, it calls the SqlCommand object specified by its InsertCommand property once for each new row. This SqlCommand object is the one that does the actual work of permanently saving the data.

Deleting Data

To delete a row from the database, you must supply a SqlCommand object for the DeleteCommand property of the SqlDataAdapter object, as shown in the following code segment:

```
// Create a SqlCommand to delete data
SqlCommand cmdDelete = cnn.CreateCommand();
cmdDelete.CommandType = CommandType.Text;
cmdDelete.CommandText = "DELETE FROM Customers " +
    "WHERE CustomerID = @CustomerID";
cmdDelete.Parameters.Add("@CustomerID",
    SqlDbType.NChar,5, "CustomerID");
cmdDelete.Parameters["@CustomerID"].SourceVersion
    = DataRowVersion.Original;
// Set up the DataAdapter and fill the DataSet
da.SelectCommand = cmdSelect;
da.DeleteCommand = cmdDelete;
```

The DataRow object supports a Delete() method that deletes an entire DataRow object from the DataTable object, as in the following code:

```
dr.Delete();
```

To cause the changes to the database to persist, you need to call the Update() method of the SqlDataAdapter object, as in the following code:

```
da.Update(ds, "Customers");
```

Handling Data Errors

You should always check for errors in any production code so that you can take corrective action if something goes wrong. The following sections show you how to do this.

Handling Database Errors

The `System.Data.SqlClient` namespace includes two objects to help you handle SQL Server–specific errors. These are the `SqlException` class, which inherits from `System.Exception`, and the `SqlError` class, which represents a single SQL Server error.

The following code segment shows how to trap SQL Server errors:

```
try
{
    // Create a SqlConnection
    SqlConnection cnn = new SqlConnection(
        @"Data Source=(local)\NetSDK;Initial Catalog=Northwind;" +
        "Integrated Security=SSPI");
    // Create a SqlCommand
    SqlCommand cmd = cnn.CreateCommand();
    cmd.CommandType = CommandType.Text;
    cmd.CommandText = "INSERT INTO Customers (CompanyName) " +
            "VALUES ('New Company')";
    // And execute it
    cnn.Open();
    cmd.ExecuteNonQuery();
    cnn.Close();
}
catch(SqlException sqlEx)
{
    // Handle SQL Server specific errors
    foreach (SqlError err in sqlEx.Errors)
    {
        lbErrors.Items.Add("SQL Error " + err.Number + ": " + err.Message);
    }
}
catch(Exception ex)
{
    // Handle general errors
    lbErrors.Items.Add("Non-SQL Exception " + ex.Message);
}
```

Here, the `SqlException` object exposes an `Errors` property. This property is a collection of `SqlError` objects—each of which contains a SQL Server error.

Handling Multiuser Errors

Whenever you have more than one user updating the same data, concurrency issues can arise. The basic question is, "Who wins in case of multiple updates?"

"It depends." When you're creating the sqlCommand object that is used for the UpdateCommand property of a sqlDataAdapter object, it's up to you to choose between two strategies for dealing with such conflicts:

➤ With optimistic concurrency control, an update to a row succeeds only if no one else has changed that row after it was loaded into the DataSet object.

➤ With last-one-wins concurrency control, an update to a row always succeeds, whether another user has edited the row (as long as the row still exists).

Consider the following SQL statement that is used to update the database:

```
UPDATE Customers SET ContactName = @ContactName
WHERE CustomerID = @CustomerID
```

The key thing to look at here is the WHERE clause. The only column it looks at is the CustomerID column. CustomerID is the primary key of this table, a value that should never change. As long as that one column has not been changed, the UPDATE statement succeeds, no matter what might have changed about other columns in the same table.

You can modify the previous SQL statement project to implement optimistic concurrency control, like so:

```
UPDATE Customers SET ContactName = @ContactName
WHERE CustomerID = @CustomerID AND ContactName = @ContactNameOrig
```

The new WHERE clause finds a row to update only if both the CustomerID and ContactName fields are unchanged from what they were when the row was originally loaded.

In adition, you need to include a try-catch block to handle exceptions during the update operation, as shown in the following code segment:

```
try
{
    // Save the changes
    da.Update(ds, "Customers");
    // And make a note on the UI
    lblResults.Text = "Row has been updated";
}
catch(SqlException sqlEx)
{
```

```
    // Handle SQL Server specific errors
    foreach (SqlError err in sqlEx.Errors)
    {
        lblResults.Text += "SQL Error " + err.Number + ": " + err.Message;
    }
}
catch(Exception ex)
{
    // Handle general errors
    lblResults.Text += "Non-SQL Exception " + ex.Message;
}
```

 Strictly speaking, you can enforce optimistic concurrency control only if you check every column of the table in the **WHERE** clause. If you retrieve only a few columns, you can miss a change in a column you didn't retrieve.

Using XML Data

The following sections introduce you to the basic terminology and format of Extensible Markup Language (XML) files, including a discussion of the XmlDocument and XmlNode classes, which are part of the System.Xml namespace. You will also learn how you can synchronize data in a DataSet object with data in an XmlDocument object.

Using the XmlNode, XmlDocument, XmlTextReader, and XmlTextWriter Classes

To understand the .NET Framework representation of an XML document, let's start with the concept of a node. A *node* is one item in an XML document—it might be an attribute, a comment, an element, or something else. In the System.Xml namespace, nodes are represented by XmlNode objects. Table 7.12 shows the most important members of the XmlNode class.

Table 7.12	Important Members of the XmlNode Class	
Member	**Type**	**Description**
AppendChild()	Method	Adds a new child node to the end of this node's list of children.
Attributes	Property	Specifies a collection of the attributes of this node.
ChildNodes	Property	Specifies a collection of child nodes of this node.
FirstChild	Property	Specifies the first child node of this node.
InnerText	Property	Specifies the value of this node and all its children.

(continued)

Table 7.12   Important Members of the XmlNode Class *(continued)*

Member	Type	Description
InnerXml	Property	Specifies the XML code representing just the children of this node.
InsertAfter()	Method	Inserts a new node after this node.
InsertBefore()	Method	Inserts a new node before this node.
LastChild	Property	Specifies the last child node of this node.
Name	Property	Specifies the name of the node.
NextSibling	Property	Specifies the next child node of this node's parent node.
NodeType	Property	Specifies the type of this node. The **XmlNodeType** enumeration includes values for all possible node types.
OuterXml	Property	Specifies the XML code representing this node and all its children.
ParentNode	Property	Specifies the parent of this node.
PrependChild()	Method	Adds a new child node to the start of this node's list of children.
PreviousSibling()	Method	Specifies the previous child node of this node's parent node.
RemoveAll()	Method	Removes all children of this node.
RemoveChild()	Method	Removes a specified child of this node.
ReplaceChild()	Method	Replaces a child node with a new node.
Value	Property	Specifies the value of the node.

XmlNode objects are collected into an XmlDocument object. The XmlDocument class provides an in-memory representation of an XML document. Table 7.13 lists the most important members of the XmlDocument class.

Table 7.13   Important Members of the XmlDocument Class

Member	Type	Description
CreateAttribute()	Method	Creates a new attribute node
CreateElement()	Method	Creates a new element node
CreateNode()	Method	Creates a new **XmlNode** object
DocumentElement	Property	Returns the **XmlNode** object that represents the root node of this document
GetElementsByTagName()	Method	Returns a list of all elements with the specified tag name

(continued)

Table 7.13	Important Members of the XmlDocument Class *(continued)*	
Member	**Type**	**Description**
Load()	Method	Loads an XML document into an **XmlDocument** object
LoadXml()	Method	Loads a string of XML data into an **XmlDocument** object
Save()	Method	Saves the **XmlDocument** object as a file or stream
WriteTo()	Method	Saves the **XmlDocument** object to an **XmlWriter** object

Follow these steps to learn how to read the contents of an XML document:

1. Add a new Visual C# ASP.NET Web Application project (Example7_3) to the current solution.

2. Add a new XML file (BobsTractors.xml). Enter this text in the new file and then save the file:

```
<?xml version="1.0" encoding="UTF-8"?>
<!-- Customer list for Bob's Tractor Parts -->
<Customers>
    <Customer CustomerNumber="1">
        <CustomerName>Lambert Tractor Works
            </CustomerName>
        <CustomerCity>Millbank</CustomerCity>
        <CustomerState>WA</CustomerState>
    </Customer>
    <Customer CustomerNumber="2">
        <CustomerName><![CDATA[Joe's Garage]]>
            </CustomerName>
        <CustomerCity>Doppel</CustomerCity>
        <CustomerState>OR</CustomerState>
    </Customer>
</Customers>
```

3. Place a Button control (btnLoadXml) and a ListBox control (lbNodes) on the form.

4. Switch to Code view and add the following using directives:

```
using System.Xml;
using System.IO;
```

5. Double-click the Button control and enter this code to load data when the button is clicked:

```
private void btnLoadXml_Click(object sender, System.EventArgs e)
{
    // Hook up to the disk file
    XmlTextReader xtr = new XmlTextReader(
        Server.MapPath("BobsTractors.xml"));
```

```
    xtr.WhitespaceHandling = WhitespaceHandling.None;
    XmlDocument xd = new XmlDocument();
    // Load the file into the XmlDocument
    xd.Load(xtr);
    // Add an item representing the document to the ListBox
    lbNodes.Items.Add("XML Document");
    // Find the root node, and add it together with its children
    XmlNode xnod = xd.DocumentElement;
    AddWithChildren(xnod, 1);
}

private void AddWithChildren(XmlNode xnod, Int32 intLevel)
{
    // Adds a node to the ListBox, together with its children.
    // intLevel controls the depth of indenting
    XmlNode xnodWorking;
    string strIndent = "";
    for (int i=0; i< 2*intLevel; i++)
        strIndent += " ";

    // Get the value of the node (if any)
    String strValue= (String) xnod.Value;
    if(strValue != null)
        strValue = " : " + strValue;

    // Add the node details to the ListBox
    string str = strIndent + xnod.Name + strValue;
    StringWriter writer = new StringWriter();
    Server.HtmlDecode(str, writer);
    lbNodes.Items.Add(writer.ToString());

    // For an element node, retrieve the attributes
    if(xnod.NodeType == XmlNodeType.Element)
    {
        XmlNamedNodeMap mapAttributes= xnod.Attributes;
        // Add the attributes to the ListBox
        foreach(XmlNode xnodAttribute in mapAttributes)
        {
            str = strIndent + "  " +
                xnodAttribute.Name + " :  " +
                xnodAttribute.Value;
            writer = new StringWriter();
            Server.HtmlDecode(str, writer);
            lbNodes.Items.Add(writer.ToString());
        }
    // If there are any child nodes, call this procedure recursively
    if(xnod.HasChildNodes)
    {
        xnodWorking = xnod.FirstChild;
        while (xnodWorking != null)
        {
            AddWithChildren(xnodWorking, intLevel + 1);
            xnodWorking = xnodWorking.NextSibling;
        }
    }
  }
}
```

6. Set the Web project as the startup project for the solution and run the application. Click the button. The contents of the XML file will be dumped to the ListBox control.

> The **Server.MapPath()** method takes a relative virtual path for a file and returns its physical path. Remember, all the ASP.NET code is running on the server, so any file paths must make sense in the context of the server's file system.

The code in the previous example uses an XmlTextReader object to read the disk file into the XmlDocument object.

The code uses the DocumentElement property of the XmlDocument object to find the node at the root of the tree representation of the XML document. After that, it's just a matter of recursively calling a procedure that adds information about the node to the ListBox control.

One bit of added complexity in the code is necessary to deal with attributes. Attribute nodes are not included in the ChildNodes collection of a node in the XmlDocument object. Instead, you can use the Attributes property of the XmlNode object to get a collection of attribute nodes only. The code uses an XmlNamedNodeMap object to hold this collection; this object can hold an arbitrary collection of XmlNode objects of any type.

You can also modify an XML document through the XmlDocument object. To do so, you need to modify the individual XmlNode objects and then write the file back to disk as shown in the following code segment:

```
// Write the modified file to disk
XmlTextWriter xtw = new XmlTextWriter(
Server.MapPath("BobsTractors.new.xml"), System.Text.Encoding.UTF8);
xd.WriteTo(xtw);
xtw.Flush();
xtw.Close();
```

> When you have to read data fast in a forward-only manner and memory is a constraint, you should use **XmlTextReader**.
>
> When memory is not a constraint and you want flexibility for inserting, deleting, and updating data in any direction, you should use **XmlDocument**.

Treating XML As Relational Data

You can treat an XML document as relational data. To do this, you can use the XmlDataDocument class, which inherits from XmlDocument. The key feature of the XmlDataDocument class is that it can be synchronized with a DataSet object.

For example, consider the following code segment that reads the BobsTractor.xml file and populates a DataGrid control:

```
// Create an XmlTextReader object to read the file
XmlTextReader xtr = new XmlTextReader(Server.MapPath("BobsTractors.xml"));
XmlDataDocument xdd = new XmlDataDocument();
// Get the DataSet
DataSet ds = xdd.DataSet;
// Read the schema of the file to initialize the DataSet
ds.ReadXmlSchema(xtr);
xtr.Close();
xtr = new XmlTextReader(Server.MapPath("BobsTractors.xml"));
xtr.WhitespaceHandling = WhitespaceHandling.None;
// Load the file into the XmlDataDocument
xdd.Load(xtr);
xtr.Close();
// And display it on the DataGrid
dgXml.DataSource = ds;
dgXml.DataBind();
```

For the DataSet object to properly represent the XML, it must have the same schema (structure) as the XML file. In the previous code segment, I've ensured this by using the ReadXmlSchema() method of the DataSet object to load the schema from the same XML file the XmlDataDocument object holds. The XmlTextReader object has to be closed and reopened after the schema is read because it's a forward-only object.

The synchronization between the XmlDataDocument object and the DataSet object is two way. If you derive a dataset object from an XmlDataDocument object, modify the dataset object, and then write the XmlDataDocument object back to disk, the changes you made in the DataSet object are reflected in the XML file.

If you already have a **DataSet** object in your code, you can create the equivalent XML document by calling an overloaded constructor of the **XmlDataDocument** class, like so:

```
XmlDataDocument xdd = new XmlDataDocument(ds);
```

Working with Disk Files

The classes from the System.IO namespace enable you to manipulate the data stored in disk files.

Using the File Class

The File class represents a disk file and contains static methods that enable you to create, open, move, copy, and delete files. It also contains a set of methods that provide access to information about the files.

The .NET Framework also provides the **FileInfo** class for working with files. You can do almost everything with the **FileInfo** class that you can do with the **File** class. Use the following facts to choose one over another in a given situation:

➤ Unlike the **File** class, the **FileInfo** class does not contain any static methods; therefore, you need to create an instance of the **FileInfo** class before using it.

➤ The **File** class performs security checks whenever a static method is called. However, in the case of the **FileInfo** class, security checks are performed only once when the object is created.

In most cases, you should use the **FileInfo** class instead of the **File** class if you are going to reuse an object several times in your program.

Using the **FileStream** Class

The FileStream class treats a file as a stream of bytes.

Consider the following code segment that uses a FileStream object to create a backup copy of a file:

```
// Get the physical path of the file
String strFileName = Server.MapPath("XMLFile1.xml");
// Open the file for reading as a stream
FileStream fsIn = File.OpenRead(strFileName);
// Open the file for writing as a stream
FileStream fsOut = File.OpenWrite(strFileName + ".bak");
// Copy all data from in to out, using a 4K buffer
Byte[] buf = new Byte[4096];
int intBytesRead;
while((intBytesRead = fsIn.Read(buf, 0, 4096)) > 0)
    fsOut.Write(buf, 0, intBytesRead);
// Clean up
fsOut.Flush();
fsOut.Close();
fsIn.Close();
```

This code creates two FileStream objects, one each for the input and output files, by using static methods of the File object (which represents a disk file). The FileStream.Read() method takes three parameters:

➤ A buffer to hold the data being read

➤ An offset in the buffer where newly read bytes should be placed

➤ The maximum number of bytes to read

The Read() method returns the number of bytes that were actually read. Similarly, the Write() method takes three parameters:

➤ A buffer to hold the data being written

➤ An offset in the buffer where the writing of bytes should begin

➤ The number of bytes to write

Using the **StreamReader** and **StreamWriter** Classes

The FileStream class is your best option when you don't care (or don't know) about the internal structure of the files with which you're working. But in many cases, you have additional knowledge that lets you use other objects. Text files, for example, are often organized as lines of text separated by end-of-line characters. The StreamReader and StreamWriter classes provide tools for manipulating such files as shown in the following code segment:

```
// Create a new file to work with
FileStream fsOut = File.Create(Server.MapPath("test.txt"));
// Create a StreamWriter to handle writing
StreamWriter sw = new StreamWriter(fsOut);
// And write some data
sw.WriteLine("Test Data Line 1");
sw.WriteLine("Test Data Line 2");
sw.Flush();
sw.Close();

// Now open the file for reading
FileStream fsIn = File.OpenRead(Server.MapPath("test.txt"));
// Create a StreamReader to handle reading
StreamReader sr = new StreamReader(fsIn);
// And read the data
while (sr.Peek() > -1)
   Response.Write(sr.ReadLine());
sr.Close();
fsIn.Close();
fsOut.Close();
```

You can think of the StreamWriter and StreamReader classes as forming an additional layer of functionality on top of the FileStream class. The FileStream object handles opening a particular disk file; then it serves as a parameter to the constructor of the StreamWriter or StreamReader object. The code in the previous example first opens a StreamWriter object and calls its WriteLine() method multiple times to write lines of text to the file. It then creates a StreamReader object that uses the same text file. The code uses the Peek() method of the StreamReader object to watch for the end of the file. This method returns the next byte in the file without actually reading it, or it returns -1 if no more data is to be read. As long as there is data to read, the ReadLine() method of the StreamReader object can read it to place in the list box.

In addition to the methods in the previous example, the StreamWriter has a Write() method that writes output without adding a newline character. The StreamReader class implements the Read() and ReadToEnd() methods, which offer additional functionality for reading data. The Read() method reads a specified number of characters, and the ReadToEnd() method reads all the remaining characters to the end of the stream.

Using the **BinaryReader** and **BinaryWriter** Classes

For files with known internal structures, the BinaryReader and BinaryWriter classes offer streaming functionality that's oriented toward particular data types. The following code segment demonstrates how to use the BinaryWriter and BinaryReader objects:

```
// Create a new file to work with
FileStream fsOut = File.Create(Server.MapPath("test.dat"));
// Create a BinaryWriter to handle writing
BinaryWriter bw = new BinaryWriter(fsOut);
// And write some data
Int32 intData1 = 7;
Decimal dblData2 = 3.14159M;
String strData3 = "Pi in the Sky";
bw.Write(intData1);
bw.Write(dblData2);
bw.Write(strData3);
bw.Flush();
bw.Close();
fsOut.Close();

// Now open the file for reading
FileStream fsIn = File.OpenRead(Server.MapPath("test.dat"));
// Create a BinaryReader to handle reading
BinaryReader br = new BinaryReader(fsIn);
// And read the data
lbData.Items.Add("Int32: " + br.ReadInt32());
lbData.Items.Add("Decimal: " + br.ReadDecimal());
lbData.Items.Add("String: " + br.ReadString());
br.Close();
fsIn.Close();
```

Like the StreamWriter and StreamReader classes, the BinaryWriter and BinaryReader classes provide a layer on top of the basic FileStream class. BinaryWriter and BinaryReader classes are oriented toward writing and reading particular types of data. The BinaryWriter.Write() method has overloads for many data types, so it can handle writing almost anything to a file.

Exam Prep Questions

Question 1

Your SQL Server database contains a table called Sales with these columns:

SalesID (int, identity)

StoreNumber (int)

Sales (int)

You want to create a stored procedure that accepts as inputs the store number and sales, inserts a new row in the table with this information, and returns the new identity value. Which SQL statement should you use?

○ A.
```
CREATE PROCEDURE procInsertSales
 @StoreNumber int, @Sales int, @SalesID int
AS
 INSERT INTO Sales (StoreNumber, Sales)
    VALUES (@StoreNumber, @Sales)
  SELECT @SalesID = @@IDENTITY
```

○ B.
```
CREATE PROCEDURE procInsertSales
  @StoreNumber int, @Sales int,
  @SalesID int OUTPUT
AS
  INSERT INTO Sales (SalesID,
    StoreNumber, Sales)
  VALUES (@SalesID, @StoreNumber, @Sales)
```

○ C.
```
CREATE PROCEDURE procInsertSales
  @StoreNumber int, @Sales int,
  @SalesID int OUTPUT
AS
  INSERT INTO Sales (SalesID,
   StoreNumber, Sales)
  VALUES (0, @StoreNumber, @Sales)
  SELECT @SalesID = @@IDENTITY
```

○ D.
```
CREATE PROCEDURE procInsertSales
  @StoreNumber int, @Sales int,
  @SalesID int OUTPUT
AS
  INSERT INTO Sales (StoreNumber, Sales)
  VALUES (@StoreNumber, @Sales)
  SELECT @SalesID = @@IDENTITY
```

Answer D is correct. It correctly inserts the values and returns the identity value. Answer A is incorrect because it does not indicate that @SalesID is an output parameter. Answers B and C attempt to insert values into the identity column, rather than letting SQL Server assign the new value, so they are incorrect.

Question 2

Your application includes 15 double-precision, floating-point numbers you want to write out to a disk file. You'd like to minimize the size of the disk file. Which object should you use to write the file?

○ A. **FileStream**

○ B. **StreamWriter**

○ C. **BinaryWriter**

○ D. **XmlTextWriter**

Answer C is correct. The BinaryWriter object provides a compact format for data storage on disk, as long as you don't need the data to be human readable. Answers A, B, and D are incorrect because these objects store the data as ASCII text, which takes more space.

Question 3

Your application includes a **DataSet** object that contains a **DataTable** object named **Suppliers**. This **DataTable** object contains all the rows from the **Suppliers** table in your database. You want to bind an object to a **DataGrid** control on a form such that the **DataGrid** control displays only the suppliers from Pennsylvania. What should you do?

○ A. Create a filtered array by calling the **DataTable.Select()** method on the suppliers **DataTable** object and bind the array to the **DataGrid** control.

○ B. Create a new **SqlCommand** object to retrieve only suppliers from Pennsylvania. Use a new **SqlDataAdapter** object to fill a new **DataSet** object with these suppliers. Then bind the new **DataSet** object to the **DataGrid** control.

○ C. Use a **foreach** loop to move through the entire suppliers **DataTable** object. Each time you find a **DataRow** object representing a supplier from Pennsylvania, bind that **DataRow** object to the **DataGrid** control.

○ D. Create a filtered **DataView** object from the suppliers **DataTable** object and bind the **DataView** object to the **DataGrid** control.

Answer D is correct. The DataView class provides a data-bindable and customized view of a DataTable suitable for sorting, filtering, searching, editing, and navigation. Answers A and C are incorrect because these answers do not give you objects that can be bound to the DataGrid control. Answer B is incorrect because retrieving the data from the database a second time will be slower than filtering it from the existing DataTable object.

Question 4

Your application needs to return the total number of customers in a database. What is the fastest way to do this?

- O A. Write ad hoc SQL queries to return the total number of customers. Use the **SqlCommand.ExecuteScalar()** method to execute the SQL statement.

- O B. Write ad hoc SQL queries to return the total number of customers. Use the **SqlDataAdapter.Fill()** method to execute the SQL statement.

- O C. Create a stored procedure to return the total number of customers. Use the **SqlCommand.ExecuteScalar()** method to execute the stored procedure.

- O D. Create a stored procedure to return the total number of customers. Use the **SqlDataAdapter.Fill()** method to execute the stored procedure.

Answer C is correct. Stored procedures execute more quickly than the corresponding ad hoc SQL statements because stored procedures are stored in the database in compiled form. Answers A and B are incorrect because they use ad hoc SQL queries that can be slower than stored procedures. Answer D is incorrect because using the ExecuteScalar() method is faster than filling a dataset object for returning a single value.

Question 5

Your application needs to retrieve a list of customer balances from a SQL Server database. The application should move through the list once, processing each balance in turn. The application does not need to write to the database. Your solution should process the data as quickly as possible. Which object should you use to hold the list in the data model?

- O A. **DataSet**
- O B. **SqlDataReader**
- O C. **DataTable**
- O D. **DataView**

The correct answer is B. The SqlDataReader object gives you a fast, forward-only, read-only view of the data. Answers A, C, and D are incorrect because these objects have significant overhead when compared to SqlDataReader.

Question 6

Your application uses a **SqlDataReader** object to retrieve information about customer balances. When you find a past-due balance, you want to write a new entry to a billing table by executing a stored procedure in the same database. You have used a **SqlCommand** object to represent the stored procedure. Calling the **ExecuteNonQuery()** method of the **SqlCommand** object is causing an error. What is the most likely cause of this error?

- ○ A. You must use a **SqlDataAdapter** object to execute the stored procedure.

- ○ B. You must use an ad hoc SQL statement rather than a stored procedure to insert new rows in a database.

- ○ C. You are using the **ExecuteNonQuery()** method of the **SqlCommand** object, and you should be using the **ExecuteScalar()** method instead.

- ○ D. You are using the same **SqlConnection** object for both the **SqlDataReader** object and the **SqlCommand** object, and the **SqlDataReader** object is still open when you try to execute the **SqlCommand** object.

The correct answer is D. While a SqlDataReader object is open, you cannot execute other commands on the SqlConnection object the SqlDataReader object is using. Answer A is incorrect because the SqlCommand object can be used to execute the stored procedure. Answer B is incorrect because stored procedures can be used to insert new rows in a database. Answer C is incorrect because the ExecuteScalar() method is used to return just a single value; however, the insert operation does not return any rows, so using the ExecuteNonQuery() method is correct.

Question 7

Your application has two **FileStream** objects. The **fsIn** object is open for reading, and the **fsOut** object is open for writing. Which code snippet would copy the contents of **fsIn** to **fsOut** using a 2KB buffer?

○ A.

```
Int32[] buf = new  Int32[2048];
Int32 intBytesRead;
while((intBytesRead =
        fsIn.Read(buf, 0, 2048)) > 0)
    fsOut.Write(buf, 0, intBytesRead);
fsOut.Flush();
fsOut.Close();
fsIn.Close();
```

○ B.

```
Int32[] buf = new  Int32[2048];
Int32 intBytesRead;
while((intBytesRead =
        fsIn.Read(buf, 0, 2048)) > 1)
    fsOut.Write(buf, 0, intBytesRead);
fsOut.Flush();
fsOut.Close();
fsIn.Close();
```

○ C.

```
Byte[] buf = new  Byte[2048];
Int32 intBytesRead;
while((intBytesRead =
        fsIn.Read(buf, 0, 2048)) > 0)
    fsOut.Write(buf, 0, intBytesRead);
fsOut.Flush();
fsOut.Close();
fsIn.Close();
```

○ D.

```
Byte[] buf = new  Byte[2048];
Int32 intBytesRead;
while((intBytesRead =
    fsIn.Read(buf, 0, 2048)) > 1)
    fsOut.Write(buf, 0, intBytesRead);
fsOut.Flush();
fsOut.Close();
fsIn.Close();
```

The correct answer is C. This answer correctly uses the Read() and Write() methods of the FileStream class to copy the contents of a file using a 2KB buffer. The Read() method returns the number of bytes read, so answers B and D fail when there is 1 byte in the file. The Read() method reads to a byte array, so answers A and B will fail because the buffer has the wrong data type.

Question 8

Your application allows the user to edit product data on a **DataGrid** control, which is bound to a **DataSet** object. The **DataSet** object is filled through a **SqlDataAdapter** object. The **InsertCommand**, **UpdateCommand**, and **DeleteCommand** properties of the **SqlDataAdapter** object are set to **SqlCommand** objects, and you have tested the SQL in those **SqlCommand** objects.

When users submit the page, none of their changes are saved to the database, and they do not receive any errors. What could be the problem?

○ A. You have neglected to call the **SqlDataAdapter.Update()** method in your code.

○ B. The users do not have permission to write to the database.

○ C. You have neglected to fill the **DataSet** object from the **DataGrid** control after the users finish editing the data.

○ D. The **DataSet** object is a read-only object.

The correct answer is A. If you do not call the `SqlDataAdapter.Update()` method, all changes to the data model are lost. Answer B is incorrect because it returns an error to the users. Answer C is incorrect because a bound `DataSet` object automatically reflects changes to the `DataGrid` control. Answer D is incorrect because `DataSet` objects are designed to be edited.

Question 9

Your application reads an XML file from disk into an **XmlDocument** object; then it modifies some of the nodes in the document. Which of the following classes should you use to write the modified **XmlDocument** object back to disk?

○ A. **XmlTextWriter**

○ B. **FileStream**

○ C. **StreamWriter**

○ D. **BinaryWriter**

○ E. **TextWriter**

The correct answer is A. The `XmlTextWriter` class is designed to write XML files, preserving the proper XML structure. Answers B, C, D, and E are incorrect because, although these classes can process an XML file as a set a characters or bytes, these classes have no knowledge of the XML structure of the file.

Question 10

You allow users to edit product information on a **DataGrid** control bound to a **DataSet** object. When a user clicks the Update button on the form, you call the **SqlDataAdapter.Update()** method to cause the changes from the **DataSet** object to persist to the underlying database.

Users reports that new records and updated rows are saved properly but deleted rows are reappearing the next time they run the application. What could be the problem?

○ A. The users do not have permission to update the underlying table.

○ B. The **Update()** method does not delete rows.

○ C. Someone is restoring an old version of the database between the two executions of the program.

○ D. The **DeleteCommand** property of the **SqlDataAdapter** object points to a **SqlCommand** object that does not properly delete rows.

The correct answer is D. Answers A and C are incorrect because, if this would have been the case, none of the changes would have been saved. Answer B is incorrect because the Update() method can delete rows from the data source if the corresponding row has been deleted from the DataSet object.

Need to Know More?

 Beauchemin, Bob. *Essential ADO.NET.* Reading, MA: Addison-Wesley, 2002.

 Delaney, Kalen. *Inside SQL Server 2000.* Redmond, WA: Microsoft Press, 2000.

 Sceppa, David. *Microsoft ADO.NET (Core Reference).* Redmond, WA: Microsoft Press, 2002.

 See the .NET Show: ADO.NET at www.msdn.com/theshow/Episode017.

 Read *MSDN Magazine*'s "Data Point" column at www.msdn.com/msdnmag/find/default.aspx?type=Ti&phrase=Data Points.

 See the .NET Show: SQL Server at www.msdn.com/theshow/Episode004.

 Read the MSDN How-TO Resources on XML at www.msdn.com/howto/webdev.asp#xml.

 Read *MSDN Magazine*'s "XML Files" column at www.msdn.com/msdnmag/find/default.aspx?type=Ti&phrase=XML Files.

Creating and Managing .NET Components and Assemblies

Terms you'll need to understand:

✓ Assembly

✓ Custom control

✓ Global assembly cache (GAC)

✓ Resource-only assembly

✓ Satellite assembly

✓ User control

Techniques you'll need to master:

✓ Knowing how to create and use a user control

✓ Knowing how to create and use a custom control

✓ Understanding the concept of assemblies

✓ Creating and implementing a resource-only assembly

This chapter discusses several types of components supported by .NET. I first discuss Web user controls and Web custom controls, which provide two reuse models for ASP.NET applications. Finally, I discuss assemblies, which can be used to package components for security, deployment, and versioning.

Creating and Using Web User Controls

You can think of a Web user control as a chunk of your application's user interface with the processing logic packaged in such a way that it can be used as a pluggable component for easy reuse.

A Web user control, similar to an ASP.NET Web form, can be encapsulated in text files (with the file extension .ascx) and can optionally include the programming logic in the code-behind file. Visual Studio .NET creates a Web user control (.ascx) with a code-behind file (.ascx.cs) that is precompiled. Just like ASPX files, ASCX files are also compiled when they are first requested.

Web user controls inherit from the System.Web.UI.UserControl class, which inherits from the System.Web.UI.TemplateControl and System.Web.UI.Control base classes.

Creating a Web User Control

The process of creating a Web user control is very similar to the process of creating a Web form. Follow these steps to create a Web user control:

1. Open Visual Studio .NET and create a new blank solution named 315C08 at c:\inetpub\wwwroot\ExamCram. (You might need to change the directory based on your configuration.)

2. Add a new Visual C# ASP.NET Web Application project at the following location: http://localhost/ExamCram/315C08/Example8_1.

3. Select Project, Add Web User Control; then name the new Web user control SearchControl.ascx.

4. Add a Panel control (pnlSearch), a Label control, a Textbox control (txtSearch), a Button control (btnSearch), and two RadioButton controls (rbSite and rbWWW) to the Web user control. Set the Visible property of the radio button controls to false and the GroupName property to SearchOption. Arrange the controls as shown in Figure 8.1.

Figure 8.1   Similar to a Web form, you can design a Web user control by dragging and dropping controls from the Visual Studio .NET toolbox.

5. Switch to Code view for the `SearchControl.ascx` Web user control and add the following code to the class definition:

```
// indicate whether the radio buttons should be displayed.
private bool showSearchOption=false;

// Web site name to be displayed in the rbSite radio button
public string WebSite
{
    get{
        return rbSite.Text;
    }
    set{
        rbSite.Text = value;
    }
}

// Back color of the search control
public Color BackColor
{
    get{
        return pnlSearch.BackColor;
    }
    set{
        pnlSearch.BackColor = value;
    }
}

// Whether the search option radio buttons should be displayed
public bool ShowSearchOption
{
    get{
        return showSearchOption;
    }
    set{
        showSearchOption = value;
        rbSite.Visible = showSearchOption;
        rbWWW.Visible = showSearchOption;
    }
}
```

6. Add the following code to the `Click` event handler of the `btnSearch` control:

```
private void btnGo_Click(object sender, System.EventArgs e)
{
    if(!showSearchOption || rbWWW.Checked)
    {
```

```
                // Use Google to search the Web
                Response.Redirect("http://www.google.com/search?q="
                    + txtSearch.Text);
        }
        else
        {
                // Use Google to search a Web site
                Response.Redirect("http://www.google.com/search?q="
                    + txtSearch.Text + " site:" + rbSite.Text);
        }
}
```

7. Drag `SearchControl.ascx` from Solution Explorer and drop it on the Web form.

8. Switch to the HTML view of the Web form. Alter the tag for `SearchControl1` as follows:

```
<uc1:SearchControl id="SearchControl1" BackColor="Beige"
    ShowSearchOption="true" WebSite="www.TechContent.com"
    runat="server"></uc1:SearchControl>
```

9. Run the project, enter a string to search, and click the Go button. The code in the button's `Click` event handler is executed and the browser is redirected to the Google Web site with the search mentioned.

When you switch to the HTML view of the Web form after dragging the Web user control, notice that a `Register` directive is added to the Web form:

```
<%@ Register TagPrefix="uc1" TagName="SearchControl"
    Src="SearchControl.ascx" %>
```

The `Register` directive registers a Web user control within an ASP.NET Web form and adds the following three attributes:

➤ *TagPrefix*—This attribute provides an alias to a namespace to which the user control belongs.

➤ *TagName*—This attribute provides an alias to the user control.

➤ *Src*—This attribute specifies the path to the user control (the `.ascx` file).

The user control is then added to the Web form using the `TagPrefix:TagName` element.

The following are a few points you should be aware of when creating Web user controls:

➤ Web user controls should be created with the file extension `.ascx`, and they inherit directly or indirectly from the `System.Web.UI.UserControl` class.

➤ Web user controls can specify user control–related attributes in the Control directive, which can then be used by the ASP.NET compiler when the user control (ASCX file) is compiled.

➤ Web user controls cannot be independently requested from a Web server; they need to be hosted on a Web form.

➤ The Web user control's Load and PreRender events are fired only after the Web form's Load and PreRender events are fired, respectively.

➤ You should not use elements such as <html>, <body>, and <form> in a user control because these elements are already present in the Web form and can cause nesting problems.

➤ Every application that wants to use a user control should have its own copy of that user control.

➤ User controls can be dragged and dropped into a Web form of the same application from Solution Explorer, but they cannot be added in the Visual C# .NET toolbox.

➤ Web user controls do not expose their properties through the Properties window.

Loading Web User Controls Programmatically

Web user controls can be loaded programmatically in a Web form using the Page.LoadControl() method. The following steps show you how to load a user control programmatically and set its properties:

1. Open the SearchControl.ascx Web user control in the HTML view and add a ClassName="SearchControl" attribute to the Control directive, as shown here:

```
<%@ Control ClassName="SearchControl" Language="c#"
    AutoEventWireup="false" Codebehind="SearchControl.ascx.cs"
    Inherits="Example8_1.SearchControl"
    TargetSchema= "http://schemas.microsoft.com/intellisense/ie5"%>
```

2. Add a Web form (WebForm2) to the project. Switch to the HTML view of the Web form and add a Reference directive to indicate that ASP.NET should dynamically compile and link the user control with the current page, like so:

```
<%@ Reference Control = "SearchControl.ascx" %>
```

3. Add a `PlaceHolder` control (`phSearch`) to the Web form.

4. Add the following code in the `Page_Load()` event handler:

```
private void Page_Load(object sender, System.EventArgs e)
{
    // Load the user control
    Control c = Page.LoadControl("SearchControl.ascx");
    // Typecast the user control and set its properties
    ((SearchControl)c).BackColor = Color.Beige;
    ((SearchControl)c).ShowSearchOption = false;
    // Add the user control to the placeholder
    phSearch.Controls.Add(c);
}
```

5. Set the Web form as the start page for the project and run the project. The page displays the user control without search options and with a beige background color. Enter a string for which to search and click the Go button. The code in the button's `Click` event handler will run and redirect your browser to the Google Web site with the search mentioned.

 A Web user control is available only to the project in which it is contained. To reuse a Web user control in another project, you must copy the ASCX and associated CS files to the new project.

Creating and Using Web Custom Controls

Web custom controls provide a more flexible (and more complex) alternative to Web user controls for reusing user interface functionality on Web forms. The following sections show you three basic ways to create a Web custom control.

Creating a Composite Control

A *composite* control is a Web custom control composed of two or more standard Web server controls. Take the following steps to create a new composite control consisting of a `TextBox` control and a `Button` control:

1. Add a new project to the solution. Select the Visual C# Projects project type and create a new Web Control Library project named `Example8_2`.

2. Add a new class, `CompositeControl.cs`, to the project. Then delete the `WebCustomControl1.cs` file.

3. Enter the following code for the CompositeControl.cs class:

```
using System;
using System.Web.UI;
using System.Web.UI.WebControls;
using System.ComponentModel;

namespace Example8_2
{
    public class CompositeControl : Control, INamingContainer
    {
        public CompositeControl()
        {
            // Set default values for persisted properties
            ViewState["MinValue"] = 0;
            ViewState["MaxValue"] = 1000;
        }
        protected override void CreateChildControls()
        {
            // Create the constituent controls
            Label lbl = new Label();
            Button btn = new Button();
            // Set initial properties
            lbl.Height = Unit.Pixel(25);
            lbl.Width = Unit.Pixel(75);
            lbl.Text = "0";
            btn.Height = Unit.Pixel(25);
            btn.Width = Unit.Pixel(75);
            btn.Text = "Go";
            // Add them to the controls to be rendered
            Controls.Add(lbl);
            Controls.Add(btn);
            // Attach an event handler
            btn.Click += new EventHandler(btnClick);
        }

        // Public properties to display in the Properties window
        [Category("Behavior"), Description("Minimum value")]
        public int MinValue
        {
            get{
                return Convert.ToInt32(ViewState["MinValue"]);
            }
            set{
                ViewState["MinValue"] = value;
            }
        }
        [Category("Behavior"), Description("Maximum value")]
        public int MaxValue
        {
            get{
                return Convert.ToInt32(ViewState["MaxValue"]);
            }
            set{
                ViewState["MaxValue"] = value;
            }
        }

        // Handle the constituent control event
        public void btnClick(Object sender, EventArgs e)
```

```
{
    System.Random r = new System.Random();
    int intValue;
    // Generate a new random value
    intValue = r.Next(Convert.ToInt32(ViewState["MinValue"]),
        Convert.ToInt32(ViewState["MaxValue"]));
    // Find the constituent label control
    Label lbl = (Label) Controls[0];
    // Make sure the controls really exist
    this.EnsureChildControls();
    // And set the text to display
    lbl.Text = intValue.ToString();
}
    }
}
```

4. Open the `AssemblyInfo.cs` file. Scroll down in the file and change the `AssemblyVersion` attribute as shown here:

   ```
   [assembly: AssemblyVersion("1.0")]
   ```

5. Build the `Example8_2` project.

6. Add a new Visual C# ASP.NET Web Application project named `Example8_2Test`.

7. Select the Components tab in the toolbox. Right-click the tab and select Add/Remove Items. Then click the Browse button and browse to the `Example8_2.dll` file. Click Open and then click OK. This adds the `CompositeControl` control to the toolbox.

8. Drag `CompositeControl` from the toolbox and drop it on the Web form. Access the Properties window for the control and set the `MinValue` property to `500` and the `MaxValue` property to `1500`.

9. Set the `Example8_2Test` project as the startup project for the solution and run the project. The composite control will render as a label and a button in the browser. Click the button to display a random number between 500 and 1,500.

The `CompositeControl` control in the previous steps uses the `ViewState` container to store property values that need to be persisted across round trips to the browser. `ViewState` enables you to automatically read existing values from a hidden value that is sent as part of a postback. Using `ViewState` is a necessity for values that are required for postback processing (such as the minimum and maximum values, in this case).

ASP.NET automatically calls the `CreateChildControls()` method when it's time to render the control. In this procedure, the composite control creates new instances of the server controls it will contain, sets their properties, and adds them to its own `Controls` collection. This is also the point at which any event handlers can be attached.

Finally, the event handler in the previous steps demonstrates how you can retrieve a control from the collection of constituent controls to continue working with it. Controls in the collection are numbered, starting at zero, in the order in which they were added to the collection. Note also the call to the `EnsureChildControls()` method. This method should be used to protect any access to properties of the child controls; it causes the code to exit if the control does not exist for some reason.

Creating a Derived Control

Another way to create a Web custom control is to derive the control from an existing Web server control. For example, the following code segment creates a new custom control, `CustomTextBox`, which is derived from the `TextBox` control:

```
public class CustomTextBox : TextBox
{
    public CustomTextBox()
    {
        // Change the BorderColor and BorderStyle
        this.BorderColor = System.Drawing.Color.Red;
        this.BorderStyle = BorderStyle.Dashed;
    }
}
```

Derived custom controls are useful in situations in which you want behavior very much like that of a built-in server control. In the previous example, the only behavior added by the `CustomTextBox` control is the specific default display of the control's border style and color; all the other methods, properties, and events are inherited directly from the original `TextBox` control.

Creating a Control from Scratch

The third way to create a Web custom control is to create the control from scratch by deriving it from the `WebControl` class and writing code to handle the rendering and other tasks, rather than depending on existing controls. Follow these steps to create a control from scratch:

1. Add a new Visual C# Web Control Library project named `Example8_3` to the solution.

2. Rename the `WebCustomControl1.cs` class `CustomWebControl.cs`. Open the CS file and change all occurrences of `WebCustomControl1.cs` to `CustomWebControl.cs` instead.

3. Open the `CustomWebControl` class and add the following code to it:

```
private bool bold;
[Category("Appearance")]
public bool Bold
{
    get{
          return bold;
    }
    set{
          bold = value;
    }
}
```

4. Modify the render method as shown here:

```
protected override void Render(HtmlTextWriter output)
{
    //Preserve grid positioning information
    System.Collections.IEnumerator enumerator =
        this.Style.Keys.GetEnumerator();
    while(enumerator.MoveNext())
        output.AddStyleAttribute((string)enumerator.Current,
            this.Style[(string)enumerator.Current]);
    //Render the control
    output.RenderBeginTag(HtmlTextWriterTag.Div);
    if (bold)
    {
        output.RenderBeginTag(HtmlTextWriterTag.B);
        output.Write(Text);
        output.RenderEndTag();
    }
    else
        output.Write(Text);
    output.RenderEndTag();
}
```

5. Open the `AssemblyInfo.cs` file. Scroll down the file and change the `AssemblyVersion` attribute as shown here:

```
[assembly: AssemblyVersion("1.0")]
```

6. Build the `Example8_3` project.

7. Add a new Visual C# ASP.NET Web Application project named `Example8_3Test`.

8. Customize the Components tab in the toolbox to add the `CustomWebControl` control (present in `Example8_3.dll`).

9. Drag the `CustomWebControl` control from the toolbox and drop it on the Web form.

10. Invoke the Properties window and set the `Bold` property of the control to `true`. Then set the `Text` property of the control to `This is my custom control`.

11. Set the project as the startup project for the solution and run the project. You should see the text from the control displayed in bold on the resulting HTML page.

The previous steps demonstrate the Render() method, which is called to draw text in both design and run modes. Because this control implements its own version of the Render() method, it can display text easily in either mode. Note also the use of the RenderBeginTag() and RenderEndTag() methods to add HTML markup to the control's output.

You can also see some new attributes at both the class and the property level, including the following:

➤ DefaultProperty—Specifies the name of a property that is the default property for the control

➤ ToolboxData—Provides the default HTML the control will generate when it is dropped on a form

➤ Bindable—Specifies whether the property can participate in data binding

➤ DefaultValue—Specifies the default value for the property on a new instance of the control

Custom Control Choices

The following are some points to consider as you decide which architecture to implement for a particular control:

➤ Web user controls can be used only in the same project that contains their ASCX file, so they're not well suited for controls that need to be used across many projects.

➤ Web user controls are much easier to create than Web custom controls.

➤ Web user controls don't support a good representation at design time. Web custom controls can be represented with high fidelity at design time, although you might need to write additional code to do so.

➤ Web user controls cannot be added to the Visual Studio .NET toolbox, whereas Web custom controls can be added to the toolbox.

➤ Web custom controls are better suited than Web user controls to dynamic layout tasks in which constituent controls must be created at runtime.

➤ Composite custom controls are a good choice when you have a group of controls that must be repeated consistently on the user interface of an application.

➤ Derived custom controls are a good choice when you want most of the functionality of an existing server control with only a few changes.

➤ Writing a Web custom control from scratch provides the most flexibility and control over the generated HTML.

Creating and Managing .NET Assemblies

An *assembly* is the unit of deployment, scoping, versioning, and security in the .NET Framework. Microsoft uses assemblies to deliver these benefits to .NET:

➤ *Each assembly has a version number*—All the types and resources in an assembly share the same version number so applications can easily refer to the correct version of files and avoid problems such as the infamous "DLL Hell," in which installing a new version of a shared library breaks older applications.

➤ *The self-describing nature of assemblies enables you to deploy applications using the zero-impact XCOPY installation*—There's nothing to register and no system files to change.

➤ *Assemblies define a security boundary*—This enables the CLR to restrict a set of operations to be executed depending on the identity and origin of the assembly.

All .NET code executes as part of an assembly. When a user browses to a page on your ASP.NET Web site, the compiled class for the page is part of an assembly.

One of the files in the assembly contains a special piece of information called the *assembly manifest*. The manifest contains the metadata for the assembly, which includes information such as the name and version of the assembly, the files that make up the assembly (including their names and hash values), the compile-time dependency of this assembly on other assemblies, the culture or language an assembly supports, and the set of permissions required for the assembly to run properly.

Single-File and Multifile Assemblies

A *single-file assembly* consists of a single EXE or DLL file. This file consists of code, any embedded resources, and the assembly manifest of the assembly. All the assemblies created so far in the examples in this book have been single-file assemblies.

A *multifile assembly* is an assembly that can include multiple files. At least one of the files in a multifile assembly should be a DLL or EXE file. You can either attach the assembly manifest with any of the assembly files or create a separate file containing just the manifest. Unfortunately, Visual Studio .NET does not support the creation of multifile assemblies, so you must use command-line tools to create them. The following steps describe this process:

1. Create a new project based on the Empty Project template; name it Example8_4. Select the project and then select Project, Properties. On the project's property page, select the Configuration Properties and then click the Configuration Manager button. In the Configuration Manager dialog box, uncheck the Build option for the Example8_4 project. With this setting, Visual Studio .NET will not automatically attempt to build the project files.

2. Add a new class named MathLib in the project, and add the following method to the class:

```
public static int Add (int first, int second)
{
    return first + second;
}
```

3. Add another class to the project and name this class StringLib. Add the following method to it:

```
public static string Concat(string firstHalf, string secondHalf)
{
    return firstHalf + secondHalf;
}
```

4. Open Visual Studio .NET's command prompt and change the current working directory to the directory of project Example8_4. Issue the following command to compile StringLib.cs as a module that is not yet part of any assembly:

```
csc /t:module StringLib.cs
```

A file named StringLib.netModule is generated.

5. Type the following command to open `StringLib.netModule` in the MSIL Disassembler:

```
ildasm StringLib.netModule
```

Open its manifest. You'll note that this manifest is not an assembly manifest because it has no `.assembly` directive.

 NOTE

The MSIL Disassembler (**ildasm.exe**) can be used to view the metadata and disassembled code for .NET libraries, modules, and executables in a hierarchical tree view format.

6. Now compile the `MathLib.cs` file into a module. When you inspect the `MathLib.netModule` file through the MSIL Disassembler, you should again note that this file is just a module and not an assembly.

7. Type the following command to read module files and create an assembly:

```
csc /t:library /out:Utils.dll /addmodule:MathLib.netModule,
➥StringLib.netModule
```

8. Open the `Utils.dll` file in the MSIL Disassembler. Note that `Utils.dll` contains just the manifest and no code. Examine the manifest and note that it has an `.assembly Utils` directive that identifies it as an assembly manifest for an assembly named `Utils`. The assembly directive is followed by two `.file` directives that identify other files in the assembly.

The `Utils.dll` file created in the previous steps just specifies the assembly manifest. The assembly actually consists of three files: `Utils.dll`, `MathLib.netModule`, and `StringLib.netModule`. So you can see that the concept of an assembly is logical and not physical. Although `Utils.dll`, `MathLib.netModule`, and `StringLib.netModule` are three distinct files physically, logically they belong to the same assembly: `Utils`.

Take the following steps to see how you can use a multifile assembly from an application:

1. Add a new Visual C# ASP.NET Web Application project named `Example8_5`.

2. Add a reference for the file `Utils.dll`. (It should be in the folder of project `Example8_4`.)

3. Switch to Code view and add the following using directive at the top of the code:

```
using Example8_4;
```

4. In Design view, arrange the controls on the form (see Figure 8.2). Name the top two TextBox controls txtFirst and txtSecond; name the Button control on the top btnAdd; and name the Label control below them lblAddResult. Name the bottom two TextBox controls txtFirstHalf and txtSecondHalf; name the Button control btnConcat; and name the Label control at the bottom lblConcatResult.

5. Add the following event handling code to the Click event of btnAdd:

```
private void btnAdd_Click(object sender, System.EventArgs e)
{
    int intAddResult = MathLib.Add(Convert.ToInt32(txtFirst.Text),
        Convert.ToInt32(txtSecond.Text));
    lblAddResult.Text = String.Format(
        "The Result of Addition is: {0}", intAddResult);
}
```

6. Add the following event handling code to the Click event of btnConcat:

```
private void btnConcat_Click(object sender, System.EventArgs e)
{
    lblConcatResult.Text = "The Result of concatenation is: " +
        StringLib.Concat(txtFirstHalf.Text, txtSecondHalf.Text);
}
```

7. Set the project as the startup project and run the project. Enter two integer values in the text boxes at the top and click the Add button. This invokes the MathLib.Add() method from the MathLib.netModule file. Enter two string values in the text boxes at the bottom and click the Concat button. This invokes the StringLib.Concat() method from the StringLib.netModule file. You should see output similar to that shown in Figure 8.2.

Static and Dynamic Assemblies

When you compile programs using Visual Studio .NET or through the command-line compiler, they emit the files that make up an assembly. These files are physically stored on disk. Such an assembly is called a *static assembly*.

However, you can also create and execute assemblies on-the-fly (while a program is still under execution). Such assemblies are called *dynamic assemblies*. In fact, dynamic assemblies are used extensively by ASP.NET. While executing ASPX pages, the ASP.NET process creates the corresponding assemblies at runtime. If needed, dynamic assemblies can be saved to disk to be loaded again later. The classes used to create dynamic assemblies are available in the `System.Reflection.Emit` namespace.

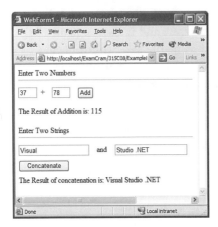

Figure 8.2 A Web application can use classes from a multifile assembly.

Private and Shared Assemblies

Assemblies can be deployed using two approaches:

➤ You can deploy an assembly for use with a single application. When an assembly is deployed this way, it is called a *private assembly*.

➤ You can deploy an assembly for use with several applications. When an assembly is deployed in the shared mode, it is called a *shared assembly*.

Here are some fast facts about private assemblies:

➤ Private assemblies are intended to be used only by the application with which they are deployed.

➤ Private assemblies are deployed in the directory (or a subdirectory) where the main application is installed.

➤ The CLR does not impose a strict versioning policy for the private assembly and instead leaves the versioning to the developer.

Here are some fast facts about shared assemblies:

➤ All the shared assemblies on a computer are installed in a special place called the global assembly cache (GAC). Because of the shared nature of the GAC, the CLR imposes special security and versioning requirements on any assembly installed in the GAC.

➤ All assemblies installed in the GAC must have a strong name. A strong name consists of an assembly's name, a version number, a culture, a public key, and an optional digital signature. Having a strong name ensures an assembly's identity.

➤ The CLR checks for the assembly's integrity before installing it in the GAC and ensures that an assembly has not been tampered with by checking the strong name of the assembly.

➤ The GAC is capable of maintaining multiple copies of an assembly with the same name but different versions.

➤ The runtime can determine which version of an assembly to load based on the information in an application's configuration file or the machinewide configuration file (`machine.config`).

Satellite and Resource-only Assemblies

A Web application typically contains resources, such as images and strings, in addition to code. When you add these resources to a Visual Studio .NET project, their default build type is `Content`. When you compile the project, the assemblies contain just code, metadata, and links to files that exist externally. This means that the resource files are distributed with the application as separate files, and all these files must be available at runtime for the application to function correctly.

If you set the build type of a project to `Embedded Resources` instead of `Content`, the contents of the resource file are included in the assembly itself at compile time. Visual Studio .NET does this in the following three steps:

1. It creates an XML resource file with an extension of `.resx`. This file stores the resources as key/value pairs—for example, the name of a resource file and its location.

2. At the time of compilation, all resources referenced by the `.resx` file are embedded into a binary file with the extension `.resources`.

3. The binary resource file is embedded into the code assembly.

Of course, all these steps can be done manually. The `.resx` file is an XML file, so you can create it using any text editor. It can be compiled into a `.resources` file using the Resource File Generator tool (`resgen.exe`). A `.resources` file can be embedded in an assembly using the `csc.exe` compiler's `/resource` option.

These steps create an assembly that contains both code and resources. Assemblies created in such a way are not dependent on external resource files but have all the necessary information.

Another way to attach resources to an application is by creating resource-only assemblies. These assemblies just contain resources without any code.

Visual Studio .NET does not allow you to create a resource-only assembly. However, you can use the command-line tools provided by the .NET Framework to create such assemblies.

The .NET Framework provides various classes in the System.Resources namespace that can be used to work with resource files. Some important classes of this namespace are listed in Table 8.1.

Table 8.1 Some Important Classes That Deal with Resources	
Class	**Explanation**
ResourceManager	Provides access to resources at runtime. You can use this class to read information from resource-only assemblies.
ResourceReader	Enables you to read resources from a binary resource file (**.resources**).
ResourceWriter	Enables you to write resources to a binary resource file (**.resources**).
ResXResourceReader	Enables you to read resource information from an XML-based **.resx** file.
ResXResourceWriter	Enables you to write resource information to an XML-based **.resx** file.

The following example uses some of these classes to write an application that shows how to programatically generate .resx and .resources files from given resources. The objective is to create resource files for storing the flags of various countries. You can get these graphics from the common7\ graphics\icons\flag folder from your Visual Studio .NET installation. For this example, I renamed those files with their corresponding two-letter International Standards Organization (ISO) country codes. Perform the following steps to learn how to work with resources:

1. Add a new Windows Application project to your solution and name it Example8_6.

2. In Solution Explorer, right-click the project and select Add, New Folder. Name the folder Flags. Right-click the Flags folder and select Add, Add Existing Item; then add all the icon files of the country flags to this folder.

3. Place two `Button` controls on the form and name them `btnGenerateResX` and `btnGenerateResources`.

4. Place the following `using` directive at the top of the code:

```
using System.Resources;
using System.IO;
```

5. Add an event handler for the `Click` event of `btnGenerateResX` and add the following code to it:

```
private void btnGenerateResX_Click(object sender, System.EventArgs e)
{
    ResXResourceWriter rsxw = new ResXResourceWriter("Flags.resx");
    //the EXE will be placed in bin\debug folder so
    // refer to Flags folder from there
    foreach (string file in Directory.GetFiles(
        @"..\..\Flags", "*.ico"))
    {
        string countryCode = file.Substring(file.Length-6, 2);
        Image img = Image.FromFile(file);
        //store the Key-Value pair.
        rsxw.AddResource(countryCode,img);
    }
    rsxw.Close();
    MessageBox.Show("Flags.resx file generated");
}
```

6. Add an event handler for the `Click` event of `btnGenerateResources` and add the following code to it:

```
private void btnGenerateResources_Click
            (object sender, System.EventArgs e)
{
    ResourceWriter rw = new ResourceWriter("Flags.resources");
    //the EXE will be placed in bin\debug folder so
    // refer to Flags folder from there
    foreach (string file in Directory.GetFiles(
        @"..\..\Flags", "*.ico"))
    {
        string countryCode = file.Substring(file.Length-6, 2);
        Image img = Image.FromFile(file);
        //store the Key-Value pair.
        rw.AddResource(countryCode,img);
    }
    rw.Close();
    MessageBox.Show("Flags.resources file generated");
}
```

7. Set the project as the startup project and run the project. Click each of the buttons to create both a `Flags.resx` file and a `Flags.resources` file. The location of these files is the same as the location of the project's EXE file.

Note that the `Flags.resources` file is not generated by compiling the `Flags.resx` file; rather, it is directly created using the `ResourceWriter` class. If you chose to create a `.resources` file from a `.resx` file, you could use the following command:

```
resgen Flags.resx
```

Although the `Flags.resources` file has resources embedded in binary format, it is not an assembly. To create an assembly from this file, you can use the command-line Assembly Linker tool (`al.exe`) as shown here:

```
al /embed:Flags.resources /out:Flags.Resources.dll
```

Now that you know how to create a resource-only assembly, let's see how to use it from a Web application. I'll demonstrate this in the following example. In this example you should especially focus on the use of the `ResourceManager` class to load the resources from resource-only assemblies. Do the following:

1. Create a new Visual C# ASP.NET Web Application project and name it `Example8_7`.

2. Add a `TextBox` control (`txtCountryCode`), an `Image` control (`imgFlag`), a `Button` control (`btnGetFlag`), and a `Label` control to the Web form. Arrange the controls on the form (see Figure 8.3). Set the `ImageUrl` property of `imgFlag` to `WebForm2.aspx`.

3. Add the following code to the page's `Load` event handler:

```
private void Page_Load(object sender, System.EventArgs e)
{
    if (! Page.IsPostBack)
        Session["Country"] = "US";
    else
        Session["Country"] = txtCountryCode.Text.ToUpper();
}
```

4. Add another Web form (`WebForm2.aspx`) to the project. Switch to Code view and add the following `using` directives:

```
using System.Reflection;
using System.Resources;
```

5. Add an event handler for the `Load` event of the `WebForm2.aspx` Web form, like so:

```
private void Page_Load(object sender, System.EventArgs e)
{
    // Build a new resource manager on the resource-only assembly
    ResourceManager rm = new ResourceManager("Flags",
        System.Reflection.Assembly.LoadFrom(
        Server.MapPath("Flags.resources.dll")));
    // Use the session variable to retrieve the appropriate bitmap
    Bitmap bmp = (Bitmap) rm.GetObject(Session["Country"].ToString());
    // And stream it back as the result of this page
    Response.ContentType = "image/gif";
    bmp.Save(Response.OutputStream,
```

```
                    System.Drawing.Imaging.ImageFormat.Gif);
             // Cleanup
             bmp.Dispose();
                    }
```

6. Copy the `Flags.resources.dll` file to the folder for this project where the `WebForm2.aspx` page is stored.

7. Set the project as the startup project for the solution and run the project. It will default to displaying the U.S. flag. Enter another country code in the text box and click the Get Flag button. The appropriate flag will be loaded into the `Image` control from the resource assembly, as shown in Figure 8.3.

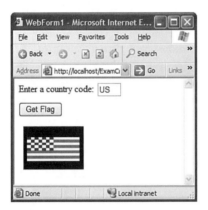

Figure 8.3 The **ResourceManager** class enables you to load the resources from resource-only assemblies.

A common use of resource-only assemblies is to store language and culture-specific information. A Web application designed for international usage might package resource information for each locale in a separate assembly file. When a user downloads the application, she can ignore the assemblies for other cultures. Skipping the unnecessary files can significantly reduce the user's download time for the application.

Resource-only assemblies that store culture-specific information are also known as *satellite assemblies*. Visual Studio .NET offers user interface support for creating and using satellite assemblies for Windows forms but not for Web forms. To use a satellite assembly for a Web form, you need to build your own resource-only assembly and use custom code to retrieve the resources, as shown in the previous example.

Exam Prep Questions

Question 1

You are building a new control that will track Quality of Service (QoS) by issuing pings from the browser and uploading the results. The control will not have a runtime user interface. What type of control should you create?

- ○ A. Composite Web custom control
- ○ B. Web custom control that inherits directly from **Label**
- ○ C. Web custom control that inherits directly from **WebControl**
- ○ D. Web user control

Answer C is correct. The control in question doesn't require a user interface, so you can build it simply by deriving it directly from the WebControl class. Answers A, B, and D are incorrect because a composite Web custom control, a control derived from the Label control, and a Web user control are useful only when providing a runtime user interface.

Question 2

You are developing a component that needs to expose a property named **Count** to its container. The **Count** property should be read-only. How should you implement the property?

- ○ A.

```
private int count;
public int Count
{
    get {return count;}
}
```

- ○ B.

```
private int count;
public int Count
{
    get {count = value;}
}
```

O C.

```
    private int Count;
```

O D.

```
    private int count;
    public int Count
    {
        get {return count;}
        set {count = value;}
    }
```

Answer A is correct. To create a read-only property, you simply need to define a get accessor for the property. Answer B is incorrect because the get accessor is not returning any value. Answer C is incorrect because it declares a private variable called count, which will not be accessible from the container control. Answer D is incorrect because the set accessor allows you to perform a write operation on the property.

Question 3

You have created a custom component that reads configuration information from a database. Because many instances of this component might be in operation at any given time, you decide to implement a **Dispose()** method in the component to close the database connection. The database connection is represented by a class-level member variable called **mcnn**. How should you implement the **Dispose()** method?

O A.

```
    protected override void Dispose
                        (bool disposing)
    {
        if (!disposing)
            if(components == null)
                components.Dispose();
        base.Dispose(disposing);
        mcnn.Close();
        mcnn = null;
    }
```

O B.

```
    protected override void Dispose
                        (bool disposing)
    {
        if (disposing)
            if(components != null)
                components.Dispose();
        base.Dispose(disposing);
        mcnn.Close();
        mcnn = null;
    }
```

○ C.

```
protected override void Dispose
                    (bool disposing)
{
    if (!disposing)
        base.Dispose(disposing);
        mcnn.Close();
        mcnn = null;
}
```

○ D.

```
protected override void Dispose
                    (bool disposing)
{
    if (disposing)
    {
        components.Dispose();
    }
    base.Dispose(disposing);
    mcnn.Close();
    mcnn = null;
}
```

Answer B is correct. The Dispose() method should call Dispose() on its own Components collection, but only if the disposing parameter is set to true (because you want to dispose of managed resources) and if the collection actually exists. Answers A and C are incorrect because the disposing parameter is set to false for releasing unmanaged resources only. Answer D is incorrect because it does not check whether the Components collection already exists before calling the Dispose() method.

Question 4

You have created a Web user control named **menu.ascx** that encapsulates the standard navigation menu to be used on your company's Web sites. You now want to use this control in Web applications other than the one in which you built the control. What should you do?

○ A. Install the control in the GAC.

○ B. Include the control's project in the solution containing each application.

○ C. Copy the control's files into each application.

○ D. Compile the control and copy the compiled assembly into each application's bin folder.

Answer C is correct. A Web user control can be used only by a project containing the control's files. Answer A is incorrect because only assemblies and not source files (such as menu.ascx) can be installed in the GAC. Answer B is incorrect because there is no need to include the whole project when all you need is the .ascx file. Answer D is incorrect because, although you can compile the code-behind file, the .ascx file must still be copied to every application.

Question 5

You have created a Web custom control named **menu.cs** that encapsulates the standard navigation menu to be used on your company's Web sites. You now want to use this control in Web applications other than the one in which you built the control. What should you do?

- ○ A. Install the control in the GAC.
- ○ B. Include the control's project in the solution containing each application.
- ○ C. Copy the control's files into each application.
- ○ D. Compile the control and copy the compiled assembly into each application's bin folder.

Answer A is correct. A Web custom control can be used by any application that can set a reference to the compiled version of the control. If you install a Web custom control in the GAC, it can be used by any application on the computer. Answers B, C, and D are incorrect because when an assembly is used by multiple applications, the best choice is to install the assembly to the GAC.

Question 6

You are creating a Web custom control by inheriting directly from the **System.Web.UI.WebControls.WebControl** class. What can you do to provide a design-time representation of your control? (Select two.)

- ❑ A. Implement an **Init()** method that returns HTML text.
- ❑ B. Implement a **Render()** method that returns HTML text.
- ❑ C. Create a control designer class and specify it using attributes of the control class.
- ❑ D. Include a bitmap of the control in the assembly with the control's code.

Answers B and C are correct. The design-time representation of a control is composed of HTML code representing the control. This HTML code can come from the control's Render() method or from the GetDesignTimeHtml() method of a control designer class. Answer A is incorrect because you should only write the code to initialize a server control inside the Init() method. All rendering code must be part of the Render() method. Answer D is incorrect because including a bitmap of the control in the assembly is just a mechanism for packaging the resources and will not help you provide a design-time interface for the control.

Question 7

> You are creating an ASP.NET Web application to serve as the Web site for a small business client. Each page in the site will have the same controls functioning as a menu. You won't need to reuse these controls for any other project. What type of control should you create to represent the menu?
>
> ○ A. Composite Web custom control
>
> ○ B. Web custom control that inherits directly from **Label**
>
> ○ C. Web custom control that inherits directly from **WebControl**
>
> ○ D. Web user control

Answer D is correct. For reuse in a single project, a Web user control is the quickest and easiest choice. Answers A, B, and C are incorrect because custom controls require additional programming efforts and are mostly suitable when they are reused across multiple projects.

Question 8

> You are creating a specialized control that will manage image uploads for your company. This control must be installed into the Visual Studio toolbox so that it can be used in many projects. The control's user interface will be a single button that can be used to browse for a file. Which type of control should you create?
>
> ○ A. Composite Web custom control
>
> ○ B. Web custom control that inherits directly from **Button**
>
> ○ C. Web custom control that inherits directly from **WebControl**
>
> ○ D. Web user control

Answer B is correct. For toolbox support, you need to use a Web custom control. Answers A, C, and D are incorrect because, when the user interface is similar to an existing control, you should derive your new control directly from that control.

Question 9

You have a standard set of controls you use to implement menus in Web applications for a wide variety of customers. These controls include a series of **LinkButtons**, **Images**, and **Labels**. You've decided that you want to encapsulate these controls for easy reuse. Which type of control should you create?

○ A. Composite Web custom control

○ B. Web custom control that inherits directly from **Label**

○ C. Web custom control that inherits directly from **WebControl**

○ D. Web user control

Answer A is correct. You can encapsulate multiple controls in either a Web user control or a composite Web custom control. The composite control is a much better choice for use in multiple projects because it can be added to the GAC and the toolbox. Answers B and C are incorrect because, when you inherit directly from the Label or WebControl class, you inherit the functionality of just one control. Answer D is incorrect because a Web user control cannot be added to the GAC and toolbox.

Question 10

You have created a Web custom control you will be using in numerous ASP.NET applications on multiple servers. You are considering installing the control in the GAC. What is a potential drawback of this action?

○ A. Controls in the GAC cannot be used by ASP.NET applications.

○ B. Controls in the GAC cannot be signed to ensure their security.

○ C. You cannot deploy a control to the GAC via FTP or XCOPY.

○ D. The GAC can contain only one version of any particular control.

Answer C is correct. To deploy a control to the GAC, you must use a setup program, which can be a problem if you're managing multiple remote Web servers. Answer A is incorrect because ASP.NET applications can use controls from the GAC without problems. Answer B is incorrect because the controls in the GAC must be signed. Answer D is incorrect because the GAC can host more than one version of the same control without conflicts.

Need to Know More?

Kalani, Amit. *MCAD/MCSD Training Guide (70-315): Developing and Implementing Web Applications with Visual C# .NET and Visual Studio .NET.* Indianapolis, IN: Que Certification, 2003.

Kothari, Nikhil, and Vandana Datye. *Developing Microsoft ASP.NET Server Controls and Components.* Redmond, WA: Microsoft Press, 2002.

Leinecker, Richard. *Special Edition Using ASP.NET.* Indianapolis, IN: Que Publishing, 2002.

Web Services

Terms you'll need to understand:

✓ Disco
✓ Simple Object Access Protocol (SOAP)
✓ Universal Description, Discovery, and Integration (UDDI)
✓ Web method
✓ Web reference
✓ Web Services Description Language (WSDL)

Techniques you'll need to master:

✓ Knowing how to create a Web service
✓ Using the Web reference feature of Visual Studio .NET to locate Web services and automatically generate proxy classes for them
✓ Knowing how to instantiate and invoke a Web service

In this chapter, you'll see how to build and use Web services in your .NET applications and learn about the major protocols used when you communicate with a Web service.

Understanding Web Services

The key to understanding Web services is knowing something about the protocols that make them possible, which are as follows:

➤ Simple Object Access Protocol (SOAP)

➤ Disco and Universal Description, Discovery, and Integration (UDDI)

➤ Web Services Description Language (WSDL)

SOAP

For Web services to manipulate objects through XML messages, there has to be a way to translate objects (as well as their methods and properties) into XML. SOAP is a way to encapsulate method calls as XML sent via HTTP.

Using SOAP to communicate with Web services has two major advantages. First, because HTTP is so pervasive, it can travel to any point on the Internet, regardless of intervening hardware or firewalls. Second, because SOAP is XML based, it can be interpreted by a wide variety of software on many operating systems.

Disco and UDDI

Before you can use a Web service, you need to know where to find it. Protocols such as Disco and UDDI enable you to communicate with a Web server to discover the details of the Web services available at that server.

WSDL

Another prerequisite for using a Web service is knowledge of the SOAP messages it can receive and send. You can obtain this knowledge by parsing WSDL files. WSDL is a standard by which a Web service can tell clients what messages it accepts and which results it will return.

WSDL files define everything about the public interface of a Web service, including the following:

➤ The data types it can process

➤ The methods it exposes

➤ The URLs through which those methods can be accessed

 Although the WSDL files enable interaction with Web services without any prior knowledge, these files are not required for a Web service to function. You can make a Web service available on the Internet without any WSDL files. In that case, only clients who already know the expected message formats and the location of the Web service are capable of using it.

Invoking a Web Service

Now that you know the basics, it's time to see a Web service in action. The following steps show how you can use a Web service—in this case, one that supplies the weather at any airport worldwide:

1. Create a blank solution using Visual Studio .NET. Name the solution `315C09` and specify its location as `C:\Inetpub\wwwroot\ExamCram`. (You can modify the location to match your configuration.)

2. Add a new Visual C# ASP.NET Web application project to the solution. Specify `http://localhost/ExamCram/315C09/Example9_1` as the location of the project.

3. Right-click the References folder in Solution Explorer and select Add Web Reference. This opens the Add Web Reference dialog box. Type `http://live.capescience.com/wsdl/AirportWeather.wsdl` in the Address bar of the Add Web Reference dialog box and press Enter. This connects to the Airport Weather Web service and downloads the information shown in Figure 9.1.

4. Click the Add Reference button to add a reference to the Airport Weather Service in your project.

5. Open the Web form and place a `Label` control, `TextBox` control (txtCode), `Button` control (btnGetWeather), and `Listbox` control (lbResults) on the form. Change the `Text` property of the `Label` control to `Airport Code:`.

6. Double-click the `Button` control and enter the following code to invoke the Web service when the user clicks the Get Weather button:

```
private void btnGetWeather_Click(object sender,
    System.EventArgs e)
{
    // Declare the Web service main object
    com.capescience.live.AirportWeather aw =
        new com.capescience.live.AirportWeather();
```

```
        // Invoke the service to get a summary object
        com.capescience.live.WeatherSummary ws =
            aw.getSummary(txtCode.Text);

        // And display the results
        lbResults.Items.Clear();
        lbResults.Items.Add(ws.location);
        lbResults.Items.Add("Wind " + ws.wind);
        lbResults.Items.Add("Sky " + ws.sky);
        lbResults.Items.Add("Temperature " + ws.temp);
        lbResults.Items.Add("Humidity " + ws.humidity);
        lbResults.Items.Add("Barometer " + ws.pressure);
        lbResults.Items.Add("Visibility " + ws.visibility);
    }
```

Figure 9.1   The Add Web Reference dialog box enables you to connect to a Web service over the Internet.

7. Select Debug, Start to execute the Web form and enter a four-digit ICAO airport code (such as **KDTW** for Detroit). Then click the Get Weather button. After a brief pause while the Web service is invoked, you'll see the current weather at that airport in the list box, as shown in Figure 9.2.

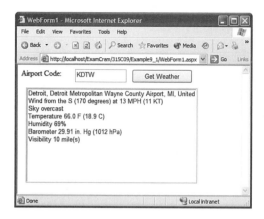

Figure 9.2   You can invoke a remote Web service and access the objects returned by it.

You can find a list of four-letter ICAO airport codes to use with this Web service at **www.ar-group.com/icaoiata.htm**. Codes for airports in the United States all start with K; codes for Canadian airports all start with C.

When you create the Web reference, for example, Visual Studio .NET reads the appropriate WSDL file to determine which classes and methods are available from the remote server. When you call a method on an object from that server, the .NET infrastructure translates your call and the results into SOAP messages and transmits them without any intervention on your part.

When you invoke a Web service, by default the client uses synchronous methods to communicate with the Web service. This means that the client waits for the SOAP response before allowing any other code to execute. This can result in slow performance of the application. To increase the responsiveness of the client program, you can call the Web service asynchronously, as shown in the following code segment:

```
private void btnGetWeather_Click(object sender, System.EventArgs e)
{
  // Declare the Web service main object
  com.capescience.live.AirportWeather aw =
    new com.capescience.live.AirportWeather();

  // Invoke the Web service asynchronously.
  // First, create a callback method
  AsyncCallback wcb = new AsyncCallback(WebServiceCallback);
  // And then initiate the asynchronous call
  IAsyncResult ar = aw.BegingetSummary(txtCode.Text, wcb, aw);
```

```
  // Process other code and then wait
  // for the asynchronous request to complete
  ar.AsyncWaitHandle.WaitOne();
}

// This method will get called when the Web service call is done
public void WebServiceCallback(IAsyncResult ar)
{
  // Retrieve the state of the proxy object
  com.capescience.live.AirportWeather aw =
    (com.capescience.live.AirportWeather) ar.AsyncState;

  // Call the End method to finish processing
  com.capescience.live.WeatherSummary ws = aw.EndgetSummary(ar);

  // And display the results
  lbResults.Items.Clear();
  lbResults.Items.Add(ws.location);
  lbResults.Items.Add("Wind " + ws.wind);
  lbResults.Items.Add("Sky " + ws.sky);
  lbResults.Items.Add("Temperature " +  ws.temp);
  lbResults.Items.Add("Humidity " +  ws.humidity);
  lbResults.Items.Add("Barometer " + ws.pressure);
  lbResults.Items.Add("Visibility " + ws.visibility);
}
```

If you compare the previous code with the synchronous calling code, you should find some significant changes. When you add a Web reference, the proxy class includes Begin and End methods for each Web method. In this case, those are the BegingetSummary() and EndgetSummary() methods.

The Begin method takes all the same parameters as the underlying Web method, plus two others. The first is the address of a callback method, and the second is an object whose properties should be available in the callback method. When you call the Begin method, the .NET Framework launches the call to the Web service in the background and returns an IAsyncResult object that represents the status of the asynchronous operation. After the call to the Begin method, you can add any code you want to run parallel to the asynchronous operation. To wait for the asynchronous operation to complete before the Web response is completed, you can call the WaitHandle.WaitOne() method of the IAsyncResult object. When the Web method call completes, the Callback() method is invoked. You then retrieve the original object and use its End method to finish the work of using the Web service.

When a client program calls a Web service asynchronously, the execution control returns to the client program without waiting for the complete execution of the Web service. This approach of invoking Web services helps make the user interface responsive.

If you have multiple outstanding asynchronous Web method calls, you can wait for them all to come back by using the static **WaitHandle.WaitAll()** method. Or you can wait for any first one to return by using the static **WaitHandle.WaitAny()** method.

Creating Web Services

To better understand Web services, you should be familiar with both sides of the conversation.

Creating a Web Service Project

In this section you learn how to create a Web service of your own. Take the following steps to create a simple string manipulation Web service:

1. Create a new Visual C# project based on the ASP.NET Web Service template. Name the project `Example9_2`.

2. Right-click the `Service1.asmx` file in Solution Explorer and rename it `Strings.asmx`.

3. Click the hyperlink on the `Strings.asmx` design surface to switch to Code view. Then add the following attribute definition before the `Strings` class declaration:

```
[WebService(Namespace="http://techcontent.com/315C09/Example9_2")]
public class Strings : System.Web.Services.WebService
```

4. Modify the name of the constructor from `Service1` to `Strings`.

5. Enter the following methods in the class definition:

```
[WebMethod()]
public String ToUpper(String inputString)
{
    return inputString.ToUpper();
}
[WebMethod()]
public String ToLower(String inputString)
{
    return inputString.ToLower();
}
```

6. Select Build, Build Solution to create the Web service on the server.

You now have a functioning Web service on your Web server. Although a lot is involved in properly hooking up a Web service, Visual Studio .NET protects you from having to set up any of it. Instead, you only have to do three things:

1. Build the project from the ASP.NET Web Service template.

2. Mark the classes that should be available via the Web service with the WebService attribute.

3. Mark the methods that should be available via the Web service with the WebMethod attribute. The methods marked with the WebMethod attributes are also known as *Web methods*.

NOTE   The **WebService** attribute requires you to supply a value for the **Namespace** property. This is just a unique identifier for your Web service.

Testing the Web Service Project

ASP.NET enables you to test a Web service project without building any client applications for the Web service. This can save a lot of time when you're debugging a Web service. Here's how:

1. Set Example9_2 as the startup project for the solution and select Debug, Start to start the project. A browser window is launched, showing the test page.

2. Click the ToUpper link on the test page. A page for testing the ToUpper() method appears, as shown in Figure 9.3.

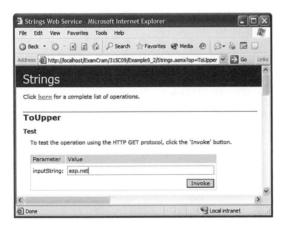

Figure 9.3   The Web method test page enables you to test the Web method using the HTTP **GET** protocol.

3. Enter a string with mixed upper- and lowercase characters at the inputString prompt and click the Invoke button. A second browser

window opens with the XML message that the Web service sends back when you call the ToUpper() method on the test string.

4. Experiment with the ToLower() method in the same way you experimented with the ToUpper() method. When you click the Invoke button, the test page constructs the appropriate XML message and passes it to the Web service, which returns the results.

Discovering Web Services

One of the problems with Web services is simply finding them. Even if you find them, you need some way to determine which messages they accept and which services they provide. The usual term for this process is *discovery*, which encompasses both finding Web services and determining their interfaces.

Disco and UDDI

Disco is a Microsoft standard for the creation of discovery documents. A Disco document is kept at a standard location on a Web services server and contains paths and information for retrieving other useful information, such as the WSDL file that describes a service. Disco is generally not used outside the .NET world.

UDDI is a method for finding services by referring to a central directory. These can be Web services, URLs for information, or any other online resource. UDDI registries are sites that contain information that is available via UDDI; you can search such a registry to find information about Web services.

UDDI registries come in two forms: public and private. A *public* UDDI registry is available to everyone via the Internet, and it serves as a central repository of information about Web and other services for businesses. A *private* UDDI registry follows the same specifications as a public UDDI registry, but it is located on an intranet for the use of workers at one particular enterprise.

The UDDI specification is being developed jointly by several industry partners, including Microsoft and IBM. For more information and a public directory, visit **www.uddi.org**.

Using the Web Services Discovery Tool (disco.exe)

When you set a Web reference in Visual Studio .NET, the software automatically handles the details of discovery for you. But you can also get into the details of the process yourself. One of the tools included in the .NET Framework SDK (and also in Visual Studio .NET) is the Web Services Discovery tool, `disco.exe`. For example, when you issue the `disco http://live.capescience.com/wsdl/AirportWeather.wsdl` command, the tool contacts the CapeScience Airport Web service to create these: `AirportWeather.wsdl` and `results.discomap`.

 NOTE The Web Services Discovery tool (**disco.exe**) retrieves the discovery document if the Web service includes a static discovery document (**.disco** file). The **.disco** file is an XML file containing useful URLs, including the URL for the WSDL file describing the service, the URL for the documentation of the service, and the URL to which SOAP messages should be sent.

Instantiating and Invoking Web Services

After you have discovered a Web service and retrieved information about its interface, you can instantiate an object representing that Web service and then invoke its methods.

Creating Proxy Classes with the Web Services Description Language Tool (wsdl.exe)

The .NET Framework SDK includes the Web Services Description Language tool, `wsdl.exe`. This tool can take a WSDL file and generate a corresponding proxy class you can use to invoke the Web service. This tool does not require the Web service client to use Visual Studio .NET. The following steps show how to use `wsdl.exe`:

1. Select Start, Programs, Microsoft Visual Studio, Visual Studio .NET Tools, Visual Studio .NET Command Prompt. A command prompt window opens and the environment is set so that you can use any of the command-line tools from the .NET Framework SDK.

2. Navigate to the folder that contains the WSDL file you created using `disco.exe`.

3. Enter the following command to create a proxy class to call the AirportWeather Web service: `wsdl /language:CS`
`/out:AirportWeatherProxy.cs AirportWeather.wsdl`.

The tool reads the WSDL file and creates a new file, named `AirportWeatherProxy.cs`.

4. Create a new Visual C# ASP.NET Web application in the current solution and name it `Example9_3`. Select Project, Add Reference to add a reference to `System.Web.Services.dll`.

5. Add the `AirportWeatherProxy.cs` file to the project by selecting File, Add Existing Item.

6. Place a `Label` control, `TextBox` control (`txtCode`), `Button` control (`btnGetWeather`), and `Listbox` control (`lbResults`) on the Web form. Change the `Text` property of the label to `Airport Code:`.

7. Double-click the `Button` control and enter the following code to invoke the Web service when the user clicks the Get Weather button:

```
private void btnGetWeather_Click(object sender,
    System.EventArgs e)
{
    // Connect to the Web service by declaring
    // a variable of the appropriate type
    // available in the proxy
    AirportWeather aw = new AirportWeather();

    // Invoke the service to get a summary object
    WeatherSummary ws = aw.getSummary(txtCode.Text);

    // And display the results
    lbResults.Items.Clear();
    lbResults.Items.Add(ws.location);
    lbResults.Items.Add("Wind " + ws.wind);
    lbResults.Items.Add("Sky " + ws.sky);
    lbResults.Items.Add("Temperature " + ws.temp);
    lbResults.Items.Add("Humidity " + ws.humidity);
    lbResults.Items.Add("Barometer " + ws.pressure);
    lbResults.Items.Add("Visibility " + ws.visibility);
}
```

8. Set the project as the start page for the solution. Select Debug, Start to execute the project.

9. Use the Web form to invoke the Web service. The difference between this project and `Example9_1` is that this code explicitly defines the objects it uses rather than discovering them at runtime. The `AirportWeather` and `WeatherSummary` objects are proxy objects that pass calls to the Web service and return results from the Web service.

Table 9.1 shows some of the command-line options you can use with wsdl.exe. You don't need to memorize this material, but you should be familiar with the overall capabilities of the tool. You can use either the path to a local WSDL or Disco file or the URL of a remote WSDL or Disco file with this tool.

Table 9.1	Command-line Options for wsdl.exe
Option	**Meaning**
/domain:*DomainName* /d:*DomainName*	Specifies the domain name to use when connecting to a server that requires authentication.
/language:*LanguageCode* /l:*LanguageCode*	Specifies the language for the generated class. The **LanguageCode** parameter can be **CS** (for C#, which is the default), **VB** (for Visual Basic .NET), or **JS** (for JScript).
/namespace:*Namespace* /n:*Namespace*	Specifies a namespace for the generated class.
/out:*Filename* /o:*FileName*	Specifies the filename for the generated output. If it's not specified, the filename is derived from the Web service name.
/password:*Password* /p:*Password*	Specifies the password to use when connecting to a server that requires authentication.
/server	Generates a class to create a server based on the input file. By default, the tool generates a client proxy object.
/username:*Username* /u:*Username*	Specifies the username to use when connecting to a server that requires authentication.
/?	Displays full help on the tool.

Using Web References

As an alternative to using the Web Services Discovery and Web Services Description Language tools to create explicit proxy classes, you can simply add a Web reference to your project to enable the project to use the Web service. This is the same technique you used in the Example9_1 project.

In fact, there's no difference in the end result between using the tools to create a proxy class and adding a Web reference because, behind the scenes, the Web reference creates its own proxy class. To see this, click the Show All Files toolbar button in Solution Explorer and then expand the Solution Explorer node for a Web reference. You'll see a set of files similar to that shown in Figure 9.4.

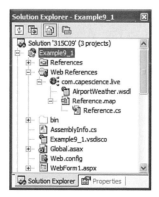

Figure 9.4 When you add a Web reference, the proxy file is automatically generated.

The .wsdl file is the same file that is generated by running the Web Services Discovery tool on the URL of the Web reference, and the .map file is the same as the .discomap file generated by the Web Services Discovery tool. The .cs file defines the proxy objects to be used with the Web service represented by this Web reference, as you can see by opening this file. The major difference between this file and the proxy you generated with the Web Services Description Language tool is that the autogenerated file uses a namespace based on the name of the Web reference.

 Why use a Web reference? The major benefit of using a Web reference (as compared to constructing proxy classes with the command-line tools) is that updating the proxy classes is easier if the Web service changes. All you need to do in that case is right-click the Web Reference node in Solution Explorer and select Update Web Reference.

Testing a Web Service

If you want to test a Web service without building an entire client application, you can use a testing tool. Several of these tools are easily available:

➤ *NetTool*—A free Web services proxy tool from CapeClear. You can get a copy from http://capescience.capeclear.com/articles/using_nettool.

➤ *.NET Webservice Studio*—This tool comes from Microsoft. You can download a free copy from www.gotdotnet.com/team/tools/web_svc.

➤ *XML Spy*—Includes a SOAP debugger that can be used to test Web services. You can download a trial copy of this XML editor and toolkit from www.xmlspy.com.

All three of these tools work in the same basic way: They intercept SOAP messages between Web service clients and servers so that you can inspect and, if you like, alter the results.

Exam Prep Questions

Question 1

> You have used the Web Services Discovery tool to retrieve information about a Web service named **ZipcodeService**. Which file would contain the URL for any documentation of the **ZipcodeService** Web service?
>
> ○ A. **disco.exe**
>
> ○ B. **results.discomap**
>
> ○ C. **ZipcodeService.wsdl**
>
> ○ D. **ZipcodeService.disco**

Answer D is correct. The .disco file is the only one that contains documentation URLs. Answer A is incorrect because disco.exe is the Web services discovery tool that discovers the URLs of XML Web services. Answers B and C are incorrect because the .discomap and .wsdl files are XML files that do not contain any documentation URLs.

Question 2

> You have created a Web service to return financial information using ASP.NET. One of the methods in your Web service is defined with this code:
> ```
> public double Cash()
> {
>     // Calculations omitted
> }
> ```
>
> Potential consumers of your Web service report that, although they can set a reference to the Web Service, the **Cash()** method is not available. What could be the problem?
>
> ○ A. The **.asmx** file for the Web service is not available on your Web server.
>
> ○ B. The Web service class is not marked with the **[WebService]** attribute.
>
> ○ C. The **Cash()** method is not marked with the **[WebMethod]** attribute.
>
> ○ D. Web service methods can return only string values.

Answer C is correct. All exposed methods of a Web service must be marked with the [WebMethod] attribute. Answer A is incorrect because consumers of the Web service can set a reference to the Web service and the .asmx file must be available on the server. Answer B is incorrect because the [WebService] attribute is used only to set a namespace for the Web service. Answer D is incorrect because Web service methods can be of any serializable type, including string and double.

Question 3

Your application invokes a Web service named **Northwind** that includes a Web method named **GetOrders()**. **GetOrders()** returns a **DataSet** object containing order information. What must you do to use this **DataSet** object in your client application?

- ○ A. Create a new **DataSet** object and use the **ReadXml()** method of **DataSet** to initialize it from the returning SOAP message.
- ○ B. Obtain an XSD file that specifies the schema of the **DataSet** object. Then use this XSD file to instantiate a **DataSet** object from the returned data from the **GetOrders()** method.
- ○ C. Assign the return value from the **GetOrders()** method to an array of **DataRow** variables. Then loop through the array to build the **DataSet** object.
- ○ D. Assign the return value from the **GetOrders()** method to a **DataSet** variable.

Answer D is correct. The only thing you need to do to use a complex variable returned by the Web service is to declare an instance of the same data type in the client application. Answers A and B are incorrect because they involve additional efforts. Answer C is incorrect because a DataSet object cannot be mapped to an array of DataRow objects.

Question 4

You are using the Web Services Description Language tool to create a proxy class for a Web service. The Web service exposes a class named **Customer**, but you already have a **Customer** class in your application. What is the best way to allow both classes to coexist in the same application?

- ○ A. Use the **/namespace** option of the Web Services Description Language tool to specify a unique namespace for the new class.
- ○ B. Rename the existing class.
- ○ C. Use the **/out** option of the Web Services Description Language tool to specify a unique output filename for the new class.
- ○ D. Manually edit the generated proxy class to change the class name it contains.

Answer A is correct. Specifying a unique namespace for the new object eliminates the possibility that it could clash with a preexisting object name. Answer B is incorrect because renaming a class can break other applications that depend on it. Answer C is incorrect because the /out option of the

WSDL tool specifies only the file in which to save the generated proxy code and doing so does not help in the coexistence of the given classes. Answer D is incorrect because it requires additional coding efforts.

Question 5

> You want to use a Web service that supplies inventory-level information in your application. You know the URL of the **.asmx** file published by the Web service. Which step should you take first?
>
> ○ A. Open the **.asmx** file in a Web browser.
>
> ○ B. Run the XML Schema Definition tool.
>
> ○ C. Run the Web Services Discovery tool.
>
> ○ D. Copy the **.asmx** file to your client project.

Answer C is correct. The Web Services Discovery tool retrieves copies of the files you need to proceed with this project. Answer A is incorrect because opening the .asmx file in the Web browser will not help you create client projects to invoke the Web service. Answer B is incorrect because the XML Schema Definition tool will not help you locate WSDL and other files needed to invoke the Web service. Answer D is incorrect because you should not copy the .asmx file to the client project—you might not always have access to the .asmx file.

Question 6

> One of your business partners has informed you that he's making his inventory information available via a Web service. You do not know the URL of the Web service, so you want to discover the URL of the Web service with the least amount of effort. Which of the following actions should you take?
>
> ○ A. Use the Web Services Discovery tool to download the information.
>
> ○ B. Use the Web Services Description Language tool to create a proxy class.
>
> ○ C. Use a UDDI registry to locate the Web service.
>
> ○ D. Use a search engine to explore your partner's Web site.

Answer C is correct. UDDI registries exist so that you can find business services by browsing or searching. Answers A and B are incorrect because the Web Services Discovery tool requires you to know the URL of the WSDL contract file (.wsdl), the XSD schema file (.xsd), or the discovery document (.disco) of the Web service. Answer D is incorrect because typical search

engines do not provide a direct facility for searching or browsing Web services and can require additional efforts to discover the URL of the Web service.

Question 7

> Your application includes a Web reference to a Web service that delivers cus-
> tomer information as an object with multiple properties. The developer of the
> Web service has added a new property named **CreditRating** to the object. You
> want to use the **CreditRating** property in your code with the least amount of
> effort. Which of the following actions should you take?
>
> ○ A. Create an entirely new client application, and then add to the new
> application a Web reference for the Web service.
>
> ○ B. Delete and re-create the Web reference in the existing application.
>
> ○ C. Update the Web reference in the existing application.
>
> ○ D. Use a generic **Object** variable to hold customer information so that you
> can call any property you want.

Answer C is correct. The Update Web Reference menu item for a Web reference refreshes local configuration information from the server that hosts
the Web service. Answers A, B, and D are incorrect because these actions
require additional efforts to complete.

Question 8

> Your application calls a Web service that performs complex, time-consuming
> calculations. Users complain that the user interface of the application freezes
> while it's recalculating. Which approach below is guaranteed to solve this
> problem?
>
> ○ A. Move the application to a faster computer.
>
> ○ B. Install a faster link to the Internet.
>
> ○ C. Install more memory in the computer.
>
> ○ D. Use asynchronous calls to invoke the Web service.

Answer D is correct. An asynchronous call to invoke the Web service returns
the control to the user without waiting for the complete execution of the
Web service. This approach of invoking Web services assists in making the
user interface responsive. Answers A, B, and C are incorrect because speed-
ing up the client computer does nothing to speed up the Web service, which
runs on the server computer.

Need to Know More?

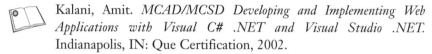 Cerami, Ethan. *Web Services Essentials.* Sebastopol, CA: O'Reilly, 2002.

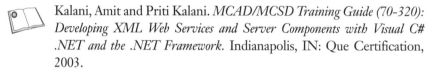 Kalani, Amit. *MCAD/MCSD Developing and Implementing Web Applications with Visual C# .NET and Visual Studio .NET.* Indianapolis, IN: Que Certification, 2002.

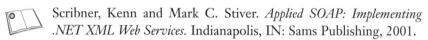 Kalani, Amit and Priti Kalani. *MCAD/MCSD Training Guide (70-320): Developing XML Web Services and Server Components with Visual C# .NET and the .NET Framework.* Indianapolis, IN: Que Certification, 2003.

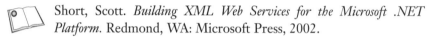 Scribner, Kenn and Mark C. Stiver. *Applied SOAP: Implementing .NET XML Web Services.* Indianapolis, IN: Sams Publishing, 2001.

 Short, Scott. *Building XML Web Services for the Microsoft .NET Platform.* Redmond, WA: Microsoft Press, 2002.

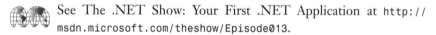 See the MSDN Web Services How-To Resources at http:// msdn.microsoft.com/howto/webservices.asp.

 See The .NET Show: Your First .NET Application at http:// msdn.microsoft.com/theshow/Episode013.

 See The .NET Show: The .NET Architecture Overview at http:// msdn.microsoft.com/theshow/Episode006.

Read *MSDN Magazine*'s "House of Web Services" column at http://msdn.microsoft.com/msdnmag/find/default.aspx?type= Ti&phrase=House+of+Web+Services.

Globalization

· ·

Terms you'll need to understand:

✓ Culture
✓ Culture code
✓ Encoding
✓ Globalization
✓ Localizability
✓ Localization
✓ Resource file
✓ Unicode

Techniques you'll need to master:

✓ Knowing how to implement localizability for the user interface and understanding how to handle culture-specific issues such as different date/time formats, currency formats, and left-to-right text mirroring

✓ Experimenting with code that uses the **CurrentCulture** and **CurrentUICulture** properties, setting these properties to several different values, and inspecting the differences in your code's output

✓ Changing the mirroring of a complex form from one of your own applications and watching how its properties change at runtime

In this chapter, you learn about the concepts and techniques the .NET Framework makes available for developing world-ready applications. You'll need a basic understanding of these concepts and techniques to pass the "Implement Globalization" section of the certification exam.

Understanding Localization and Globalization

People around the world use different languages and different conventions for writing the date, time, and currencies. If you want to target all those people as potential users of your application, you need to customize your application to different cultures. One approach to doing this is to create a separate version of the application for each culture. However, this approach is likely to be prohibitively expensive.

Not surprisingly, the .NET Framework encourages you to take a different approach for developing such applications: writing one set of source code and then customizing only culture-specific resources for different locations around the world.

The Localization Process

The technical term for the process of preparing an application for shipment in a new location-specific version is *localization*. Microsoft divides this process of preparing a world-ready application into three phases:

➤ *Globalization*—In the globalization stage, you identify all the localizable resources in the application and separate them from the executable code so they can be modified easily. Ideally, you perform the globalization step during the design phase so the resources always remain separate from the code.

➤ *Localizability*—In the localizability stage, you ensure that translating the application for a new location won't require design changes. If you've planned for localization from the beginning, localizability will typically be part of your quality assurance (QA) process.

➤ *Localization*—In the localization phase, you customize the application for new locales. This consists primarily of translating resources that you identified during the globalization phase.

Although in theory the terms *globalization*, *localizability*, and *localization* are precise and distinct, in practice they tend to be used interchangeably. Indeed, even the objectives for the certification exam are not careful in the way they use these terms. In this chapter, I often use the terms *globalization* and *localization* to mean the same thing—developing world-ready applications.

What Should Be Localized?

Obviously, you must modify text that shows on the user interface when you're localizing an application. This includes text on Web forms, text in error messages, and any other text shown to the user. But there are many other things you might need to localize in any given application. Here's a list of items that are commonly localized, depending on the target locale:

➤ Menu item text.

➤ Form layouts. Text in German, for example, averages nearly twice as long as the same text in English. You might need to move and resize controls to accommodate this.

➤ The display format for dates and times.

➤ The display format for currency.

➤ The display format for numbers. For example, some countries use commas as the thousands separator in long numbers.

➤ Data input fields. (What if you're asking for a ZIP Code in a country other than the United States?)

➤ Maps, road signs, photos, or other graphics with local content.

➤ Shortcut keys. Not every character you know appears on every keyboard.

➤ Calendars. Countries such as Korea and Saudi Arabia use completely different calendars from each other.

➤ Alphabetical order for the items in a list.

You'll need to use some judgment in deciding which of these things really need to be localized in an application. You might decide, for example, that a set of general-purpose data entry fields can serve your needs for collecting addresses, rather than try to research address formats worldwide.

Implementing Localization for the User Interface

The two key pieces to keep in mind when implementing localization for the user interface are cultures and resource files. A *culture*, as you'll see, is an identifier for a particular locale. A *resource file* is a place where you can store some culture-dependent resources such as strings and bitmaps. (The .NET Framework handles translating other resources, such as date formats, automatically.)

Understanding Cultures

A *culture*, in .NET terms, is a more precise identifier than a location or language. A culture identifies all the things that might need to be localized in an application, which requires you to know more than just the language. For example, just knowing that an application uses English as its user interface language doesn't give you enough information to completely localize it: Should you format dates and currency amounts in that application in a way appropriate to the United States, the United Kingdom, Canada, Australia, or New Zealand (among other possibilities)?

About Culture Codes

The .NET Framework follows the IETF Standard RFC 1766 to identify cultures, meaning cultures are identified by abbreviations called *culture codes*. A full culture code consists of a neutral culture code (written in lowercase) followed by one or more subculture codes (written in mixed case or uppercase). Here are a few culture codes as examples:

➤ de—Identifies the German clture. This is a *neutral* culture, a culture that does not specify a subculture code. Neutral cultures generally do not provide sufficient information to localize an application.

➤ en-GB—Identifies the English (United Kingdom) culture. This is a *specific* culture, a culture that provides enough information to localize an application (in this case, for English speakers in Great Britain).

➤ az-AZ-Cyrl—An example of a specific culture with two subculture codes. This particular culture refers to the Azeri language in Azerbaijan, written with Cyrillic characters.

The **CultureInfo** Class

The .NET Framework represents cultures with the System.Globalization. CultureInfo class. This class lets you retrieve a wide variety of information about any particular culture, as shown in the following steps:

1. Open Visual Studio .NET and create a new blank solution named 315C10 at c:\inetpub\wwwroot\ExamCram (you might need to change the directory based on your configuration).

2. Add a new Visual C# ASP.NET Web application at the following location: http://localhost/ExamCram/315C10/Example10_1.

3. On the Web form, place a Button control with an ID of btnGetInfo, a TextBox control with an ID of txtCulture, and a ListBox control with an ID of lbInfo on the form. Set the Text property of the Button control to Get Info.

4. Switch to Code view and add the following using directive:

```
using System.Globalization;
```

5. Double-click the Button control and enter the following code to handle the button's Click event:

```
private void btnGetInfo_Click(object sender, System.EventArgs e)
{
    // Create a CultureInfo object for the specified culture
    CultureInfo ci = new CultureInfo(txtCulture.Text);
    // Dump information about the culture
    lbInfo.Items.Clear();
    lbInfo.Items.Add("Display Name: " + ci.DisplayName);
    lbInfo.Items.Add("English Name: " + ci.EnglishName);
    lbInfo.Items.Add("Native Name: " + ci.NativeName);
    // Get day names
    lbInfo.Items.Add("Day Names:");
    String[] strDayNames = ci.DateTimeFormat.DayNames;
    foreach(String strDay in strDayNames)
    {
        lbInfo.Items.Add("  " + strDay);
    }
    // Get the current year
    lbInfo.Items.Add("Current year: " +
        ci.Calendar.GetYear(DateTime.Today));
    // And the currency symbol
    lbInfo.Items.Add("Currency symbol: " +
        ci.NumberFormat.CurrencySymbol);
}
```

6. Select Debug, Start to execute the project. Enter the name of a culture in the text box and click the Get Info button. The form retrieves and displays some of the information the CultureInfo object can return, as shown in Figure 10.1.

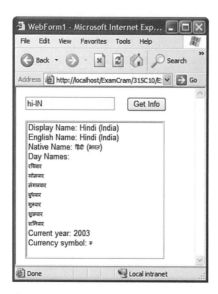

Figure 10.1   You can retrieve information about a culture using the **CultureInfo** class.

This program works by creating a CultureInfo object to represent the specified culture. It then uses properties of the CultureInfo object (and of the objects the CultureInfo contains, such as the DateTimeFormat, NumberFormat, and Calendar objects) to retrieve information about that culture. This information is useful in localizing applications, and it's all built right in to the .NET Framework.

You might want a list of all the supported cultures. The static **CultureInfo.GetCultures()** method returns an array of **CultureInfo** objects you can enumerate to get that list.

The CultureInfo class is the key to localizing applications. After you've retrieved the proper CultureInfo object, you can derive a wide variety of information from it.

The **CurrentCulture** and **CurrentUICulture** Properties

The .NET Framework handles localization on a thread-by-thread basis. Each thread has two properties used for determining the culture to use: CurrentCulture and CurrentUICulture. You can set or view these properties on the Thread.CurrentThread object.

The CurrentUICulture property tells the Common Language Runtime (CLR) which culture to use when choosing resources for the user interface.

The CurrentCulture property is also used by the CLR to manage localization, but it's used in a different way. The CurrentCulture property dictates the format for dates, times, currency, numbers, and other culture-specific functionality such as string comparison rules and casing rules.

The Invariant Culture

One more culture that you should know about is the invariant culture, a special culture that doesn't have an abbreviation. It has two purposes:

➤ To interact with other software, such as system services, where no user is directly involved

➤ To store data in a culture-independent format that is not displayed directly to end users

There are two ways to create a CultureInfo object that represents the invariant culture as shown in the following code:

```
CultureInfo ciInv = new CultureInfo("");
CultureInfo ciInv = CultureInfo.InvariantCulture;
```

Displaying Localized Information

Now that you know how culture information is stored in the .NET Framework, you're ready to see its use in code. Take the following steps to learn how to display localized information in a Web form:

1. Create a new Visual C# ASP.NET Web Application project to the existing solution. Name the project **Example10_2**.

2. Place a Label control (set its Text property to Select a Culture:), a DropDownList control (ddlSelectCulture), and four TextBox controls (txtCulture, txtDate, txtCurrency, and txtNumber) on the form. Set the AutoPostBack property of the DropDownList control to true.

3. Switch to Code view and enter the following using directives:

```
using System.Globalization;
using System.Threading;
```

4. Attach an event handler to the SelectedIndexChanged event of the drop-down list. Enter the following code in the class definition:

```
private void Page_Load(object sender,
    System.EventArgs e)
{
    // Stock the Dropdownlist
    if (!IsPostBack)
```

```
      {
        foreach(CultureInfo ci in CultureInfo.GetCultures(
           CultureTypes.SpecificCultures))
        {
             ddlSelectCulture.Items.Add(ci.Name);
        }
      }
  }

  private void ddlSelectCulture_SelectedIndexChanged(
      object sender, System.EventArgs e)
  {
    // Create an appropriate CultureInfo object for the thread
    Thread.CurrentThread.CurrentCulture = new CultureInfo(
      ddlSelectCulture.SelectedItem.Text);
    // Display the name of the culture
    txtCulture.Text =
        Thread.CurrentThread.CurrentCulture.EnglishName;
    // Refresh the display of the data
    DisplayData();
  }

  private void DisplayData()
  {
      DateTime dtNow = DateTime.Now;
      Double dblcurrency = 13472.85;
      Double dblnumber = 1409872.3502;

      txtDate.Text = dtNow.ToLongDateString();
      txtCurrency.Text = dblcurrency.ToString("c");
      txtNumber.Text = dblnumber.ToString("n");
  }
```

5. Set the project as the start project for the solution and select Debug, Start to execute the project.

6. Select a culture from the drop-down list. The form refreshes to display localized information, as shown in Figure 10.2.

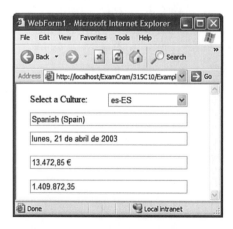

Figure 10.2   You can set the culture for the currently running thread using the **Thread.CurrentThread.CurrentCulture** property.

When you select a culture from the drop-down list, the code uses that information to create a `CultureInfo` object assigned to the `CurrentCulture` property of the `CurrentThread`. It then calls a method to display some data on the form. Note that the `DisplayData()` method simply uses the `ToLongDateString()` and `ToString()` methods to format the data it displays. You don't have to do anything special to tell these methods which culture to use—they automatically use the culture specified by the `CurrentCulture` property.

Setting Culture Properties

When you set the `CurrentCulture` and `CurrentUICulture` properties, you have two choices:

➤ You can set them based on information stored in the user's operating system.

➤ You can provide a user interface to let the user choose a culture for formatting.

To use the culture of the operating system, you don't have to do anything because the .NET Framework chooses the appropriate culture automatically. However, this strategy does not work well in ASP.NET applications because the culture the .NET Framework detects is the culture on the Web server, not the culture on the user's computer.

You can also code your ASP.NET application to sense the culture from the user's browser. The ASP.NET `Request` object returns an array of strings specifying the language preferences the user's browser has set. The first member of this array is the default language of the browser, in the standard culture code format. You can use this value to create an appropriate `CultureInfo` object for the current thread. For example, you could use this code:

```
Thread.CurrentThread.CurrentCulture = _
  new CultureInfo(Request.UserLanguages[0])
```

Attractive though this strategy sounds, it doesn't work well in practice for several reasons:

➤ Web browsers aren't required to specify a user language when sending an HTTP request for a Web page.

➤ Even if a Web browser specifies one or more acceptable languages, there's no guarantee that any of those languages will exactly match a culture the .NET Framework makes available.

➤ The user might be using a Web browser whose language doesn't match the user's own preferred language.

Generally, you should let the user choose the culture the application should use. If you want to let the user choose the culture to use, you can follow a strategy similar to the one you just saw: Provide a control to select a culture and update the CurrentCulture and CurrentUICulture properties when the user makes a selection from this control.

Working with Resource Files

So far, you've seen how to use the CurrentCulture property to handle localized formatting of things such as currency, dates, and numbers. But localizing the text displayed on the user interface is perhaps even more important. The .NET Framework offers support for user interface localization through its capability to select a set of user interface resources at runtime.

The resources you select at runtime are contained in assembly resource files, which are specially formatted XML files that contain localized text. Visual Studio .NET enables you to work directly with assembly resource files.

The following example demonstrates how to use Visual Studio .NET to localize the user interface of a simple application:

1. Add a new Visual C# ASP.NET Web Application project to the current solution and name it **Example10_3**.

2. Place a Label control with an ID of lblFolder, three RadioButton controls (rbMyDocuments, rbDesktop, and rbNewFolder), a DropDownList control with an ID of ddlCulture, and a Button control with an ID of btnSave on the form. Set the AutoPostBack property of the DropDownList control to true.

3. Select Project, Add New Item; then select the Assembly Resource File template. Name the new item **AppStrings.resx** and click Open to create the file. The new file opens in the Visual Studio .NET IDE with a grid-based editing interface.

4. Enter names and values to identify all the text strings on the user interface, as shown in Figure 10.3. You can optionally enter a comment for each string. The type and mimetype columns are not used for localizing strings.

| Data for data | | | | |
name	value	comment	type	mimetype
Folder	Folder	(null)	(null)	(null)
My_Document	My Documents	(null)	(null)	(null)
Desktop	Desktop	(null)	(null)	(null)
New_Folder	New Folder	(null)	(null)	(null)
Save	Save	(null)	(null)	(null)

Figure 10.3 You can enter invariant resources with the help of a grid-based editing interface provided by the Assembly Resource File template.

5. Add two more assembly resource files to the project. The first, named AppStrings.en-US.resx, should contain another copy of the strings in English. The second, named AppStrings.fr-FR.resx, should contain the strings in French, as shown in Figure 10.4. Note that the Name column is the same in the English and French versions; only the Value column changes.

Data for data				
name	value	comment	type	mimetype
Folder	Dossier	(null)	(null)	(null)
My_Documents	Mes Documents	(null)	(null)	(null)
Desktop	Bureau	(null)	(null)	(null)
New_Folder	Nouveau Dossier	(null)	(null)	(null)
Save	Enregister	(null)	(null)	(null)

Figure 10.4 You can enter culture-specific resources with the help of the grid-based editing interface provided by the Assembly Resource File template.

6. Switch to Code view and enter the following using directives:

```
using System.Globalization;
using System.Resources;
using System.Threading;
```

7. Attach an event handler to the drop-down list's SelectedIndexChanged event. Enter the following code in the class definition:

```
private void Page_Load(object sender,
    System.EventArgs e)
{
    if (!IsPostBack)
    {
        // Put language choices in the DropDownList
        ddlCulture.Items.Add("English");
        ddlCulture.Items.Add("French");
        // Initialize the UI text
        SetUIText();
    }
}

private void ddlCulture_SelectedIndexChanged(object
    sender, System.EventArgs e)
{
    // When the user selects a language
    // change the UI culture
    switch (ddlCulture.SelectedItem.Text)
    {
        case "English":
            Thread.CurrentThread.CurrentUICulture =
                new CultureInfo("en-US");
            break;
        case "French":
            Thread.CurrentThread.CurrentUICulture =
                new CultureInfo("fr-FR");
            break;
```

```
        }
        // Initialize the UI text
        SetUIText();
    }

    private void SetUIText()
    {
        // Create a ResourceManager object
        // by passing the fully qualified base name
        // and the resource assembly to its constructor
        ResourceManager rm = new ResourceManager(
            "Example10_3.AppStrings", Type.GetType(
                "Example10_3.WebForm1").Assembly);
        lblFolder.Text = rm.GetString("Folder");
        rbMyDocuments.Text = rm.GetString("My_Documents");
        rbDesktop.Text = rm.GetString("Desktop");
        rbNewFolder.Text = rm.GetString("New_Folder");
        btnSave.Text = rm.GetString("Save");
    }
```

8. Set the project as the start page for the solution. Select Debug, Start to execute the application. As you select languages in the drop-down list, the user interface is refreshed with the appropriate resources.

The naming of resource files follows a required pattern. The .NET Framework looks for several specific files when it's loading resources, depending on the base name of the resources and the selected culture. The base name is the second part of the first parameter to the ResourceManager constructor—in this case AppStrings. When the CurrentUICulture is set to a CultureInfo object representing the fr-FR (French in France) culture, the .NET Framework checks for resources in three possible files, in this order:

1. A specific culture file, in this case AppStrings.fr-FR.resx

2. A neutral culture file, in this case AppStrings.fr.resx

3. An invariant culture file, in this case AppStrings.resx

In other words, the .NET Framework falls back on increasingly more general resources when trying to load resources for a form.

Runtime user interface resources are actually loaded by an instance of the System.Resources.ResourceManager class. After you have initialized a ResourceManager object by calling one of the class's constructors, you can use these two methods to retrieve localized resources:

➤ GetObject()—Returns an object from the appropriate resource file

➤ GetString()—Returns a string from the appropriate resource file

Converting Existing Encodings

Many different schemes have been developed for representing the characters in a language as numeric codes within a computer. These schemes are referred to as *encodings*. The .NET Framework provides support for encodings through the System.Text.Encoding class.

Internally, preferred encoding for characters is 16-bit Unicode, commonly known as UTF-16. This encoding represents characters as 16-bit numbers, giving the .NET Framework the capability to represent approximately 65,000 distinct characters.

The System.Text namespace contains classes designed to let you convert characters from the UTF-16 Unicode encoding to other encodings, and vice versa. You might need to use these classes for compatibility or communication with older applications. Table 10.1 lists these classes.

Table 10.1 Encoding Classes in the System.Text Namespace	
Class	**Use**
ASCIIEncoding	Converts characters between Unicode and ASCII.
Encoding	Functions as a general-purpose class. The **Encoding.GetEncoding()** static method returns encodings that can be used for legacy code page compatibility.
UnicodeEncoding	Converts characters to and from Unicode-encoded text as consecutive bytes in either big-endian or little-endian order.
UTF7Encoding	Converts characters to and from 7-bit Unicode encoding.
UTF8Encoding	Converts characters to and from 8-bit Unicode encoding.

Implementing Mirroring

The process of switching a user interface between a left-to-right language, such as German or English, and a right-to-left language, such as Hebrew or Arabic, is called *mirroring*.

The .NET Framework offers support for mirroring in Web forms through the HTML dir attribute, as shown in the following code sample:

```
<HTML dir="rtl">
```

Setting the HTML dir attribute (which can also be set on individual controls) handles most of the facets of the mirroring process automatically. Controls fill from right to left as you enter text, and the DropDownList, RadioButton, and CheckBox controls reverse their appearances.

If you want to mirror part of a form, you can set the **dir** property to **rtl** on individual controls instead of on the entire form.

Validating Non-Latin User Input

Another area in which world-ready applications might require code changes is in handling character strings. Two areas in which different alphabets might require you to implement code changes are string indexing and data sorting. These areas require the most coding attention for non-Latin characters (such as Arabic, Hebrew, or Cyrillic characters), but they can be important when dealing with Latin characters as well.

String Indexing

String indexing refers to the process of extracting single characters from a text string. You might think you could simply iterate through the data that makes up the string 16 bits at a time, treating each 16 bits as a separate character. However, things aren't that simple in the Unicode world.

Unicode supports surrogate pairs and combining character sequences. A *surrogate pair* is a set of two 16-bit codes that represents a single character from the extended 32-bit Unicode character space. A *combining character sequence*, on the other hand, is a set of 16-bit codes that represents a single character. Combining character sequences are often used to combine diacritical marks, such as accents, with base characters.

This presents a problem: If characters in a string aren't all the same length, how can you move smoothly from one character to the next? The answer, of course, is to use the System.Globalization.StringInfo class, which is specially designed for this purpose. The static GetTextElementEnumerator() method of the StringInfo class returns an iterator you can use to move through the string one character at a time, properly handling surrogate pairs and combining characters. The iterator has a MoveNext() method that returns either true when more characters are to be read or false when it has exhausted the characters in the string. The Current property of the iterator returns a single character from the current position of the iterator.

Comparing and Sorting Data

Another area in which you might need to alter code to produce a world-ready application is in working with strings. Different cultures use different alphabetical orders to sort strings, and different cultures compare strings differently. For example, the single-character ligature "Æ" is considered to match the two characters *AE* in some cultures but not in others.

For the most part, you don't have to do any special programming to account for these factors in the .NET Framework. To make your application world ready, you're more likely to need to remove old code—for example, code that assumes that characters are properly sorted if you sort their ASCII character numbers. Specifically, the .NET Framwork provides the following culture-aware features:

➤ `String.Compare()`—This method compares strings according to the rules of the `CultureInfo` class referenced by the `CurrentCulture` property.

➤ `CultureInfo.CompareInfo`—This object can search for substrings according to the comparison rules of the current culture.

➤ `Array.Sort()`—This method sorts the members of an array by the alphabetic order rules of the current culture.

➤ `SortKey.Compare()`—This method compares strings according to the rules of the current culture.

Exam Prep Questions

Question 1

Your application allows users to select a culture, such as English, French, or Spanish, from an options drop-down list. Users complain that some information is not displayed correctly, even after they select the proper culture. What could be the problem?

○ A. The users are running your application on an English-only version of Windows.

○ B. You're using a neutral **CultureInfo** object to retrieve information instead of a specific **CultureInfo** object.

○ C. The users have not yet installed .NET Framework Service Pack 1.

○ D. Your application is constructed as an executable file rather than a satellite library.

Answer B is correct. Neutral cultures do not contain enough information to properly localize an application. You should be using the appropriate specific culture instead. Answer A is incorrect because you can display culture-specific information on an English-only version of Windows. Answer C is incorrect because the use of .NET Framework Service Pack 1 is not related to the given problem. Answer D is incorrect because the fact that the application is an executable file cannot be the reason for the given problem.

Question 2

Your application needs to search for substrings in longer strings, and this searching should be culture aware. What should you use to perform these searches?

○ A. **CultureInfo.CompareInfo**

○ B. **Array.Sort()**

○ C. **String.IndexOf()**

○ D. **String.IndexOfAny()**

Answer A is correct. The CultureInfo.CompareInfo property returns an object of the CompareInfo type. The CompareInfo type implements a set of methods for culture-sensitive string comparisons. Answer B is incorrect because the Array.Sort() method does not locate substrings. Answers C and D are incorrect because the String.IndexOf() and String.IndexOfAny() methods can find substrings but are not culture aware.

Question 3

Your application allows users to select a culture from the Culture drop-down list in the Welcome page. Users want to include the day of the week when your application displays dates. They want this to be in the culture selected by them. What can you do to address this need? (Select the two best answers.)

- ❑ A. Use the **DateTime.ToLongDateString()** method to format dates.
- ❑ B. Use the **CultureInfo.DateTimeFormat** property to retrieve the names of the weekdays, and select the proper name from that array.
- ❑ C. Force the user to enter the day of the week whenever he enters a date in the system.
- ❑ D. Use the **RegionInfo** object to retrieve the names of the weekdays, and select the proper name from that array.

Answers A and B are correct. Both the DateTime class and the CultureInfo class can supply the information you need here. Answer C is incorrect because there's no point in forcing the user to enter days when they're already available. Answer D is incorrect because the RegionInfo object does not expose weekday names.

Question 4

A user wants to see French dates and currencies displayed in an application but wants the user interface to remain in English. How can you accomplish this?

- ○ A. Set the **CurrentCulture** property to a **CultureInfo** object that represents the **fr-FR** culture, and set the **CurrentUICulture** property to a **CultureInfo** object that represents the **en-US** culture.
- ○ B. Set the **CurrentCulture** property to a **CultureInfo** object that represents the **en-US** culture, and set the **CurrentUICulture** property to a **CultureInfo** object that represents the **fr-FR** culture.
- ○ C. Set the **CurrentCulture** property to a **CultureInfo** object that represents the **fr-FR** culture, and set the **CurrentUICulture** property to a **CultureInfo** object that represents the **fr-FR** culture.
- ○ D. Set the **CurrentCulture** property to a **CultureInfo** object representing the **en-US** culture, and set the **CurrentUICulture** property to a **CultureInfo** object representing the **en-US** culture.

Answer A is correct. The CurrentCulture property controls formatting, and the CurrentUICulture property controls user interface resource loading. Answers B and C are incorrect because, if the CurrentUICulture property is set to a CultureInfo object that represents the fr-FR culture, the user interface will be displayed in French. Answer D is incorrect because in this case currencies and dates as well as the user interface will be displayed in English.

Question 5

Your application displays order information including the total cost of each order. You are beginning to sell this application in multiple countries. How should you ensure that the correct currency symbol is used in all cases?

○ A. Allow the user to select a culture from a list. Then create a **CultureInfo** object based on the user's selection and assign it to the **Thread.CurrentThread.CurrentCulture** property. Use the **ToString()** method to format currency amounts.

○ B. Accept the **Thread.CurrentThread.CurrentCulture** property as it is set when you run your application; then use the **ToString()** method to format currency amounts.

○ C. Prompt the user for a currency symbol and store it in the Registry.

○ D. Allow the user to select a currency symbol from a list of supported symbols.

Answer A is correct. Allowing the user to choose a culture is the best option in the given scenario. Answer B is incorrect because the user might be running a version of Windows that's not appropriate for her culture. Answers C and D are incorrect because there's no need to prompt or store a currency symbol when all the necessary currency symbols are stored in the .NET Framework.

Question 6

Your Web application includes three assembly resource files: **Strings.resx** contains the default (English) resources; **Strings.en-US.resx** contains the English resources; and **Strings.France.resx** contains the French resources. Users report that they are getting the default English user interface when they've selected the option for a French user interface. What should you do?

○ A. Instruct users to close and reopen the application after selecting a new user interface language.

○ B. Add French resources to the **Strings.resx** file.

○ C. Rename the French resource file **Strings.fr-FR.resx**.

○ D. Delete the **Strings.en-US.resx** file from the project.

Answer C is correct. Naming for assembly resource files must follow the scheme the .NET Framework expects. Otherwise, the .NET Framework won't be able to find the resource file. Answer A is incorrect because resources can be dynamically loaded and there is no need to restart the application.

Answer B is incorrect because, in the .NET Framework, localized resources are stored in separate files (that are identified with a culture code) and loaded according to the UI culture setting. Answer D is incorrect because, if you delete the `strings.en-US.resx` file from the project, searches for the requested resource will fall back on the default resource file `string.resx`, which again has English resources.

Question 7

> You are writing an application on a system that uses U.S. English Windows (culture code **en-US**). The application will run on a system that uses Japanese Windows (culture code **jp-JP**) and will send information to Windows services on the target computer. Which culture should you use to format your application's output?
>
> ○ A. **en-US**
> ○ B. **jp-JP**
> ○ C. **jp**
> ○ D. The invariant culture

Answer D is correct. You should always use the invariant culture for communication with Windows services. Answers A, B, and C are incorrect because even the localized Windows version should communicate with the Windows service in invariant format.

Question 8

> Your Web application contains Unicode strings encoded in UTF-16 format. You want to save a copy of those strings to disk in UTF-8 format. What should you do?
>
> ○ A. Use the **UnicodeEncoding.GetBytes()** method to perform the conversion.
> ○ B. Use the **UnicodeEncoding.GetChars()** method to perform the conversion.
> ○ C. Use the **UTF8Encoding.GetBytes()** method to perform the conversion.
> ○ D. Use the **UTF8Encoding.GetChars()** method to perform the conversion.

Answer C is correct. The `UTF8Encoding.GetBytes()` method encodes Unicode characters into bytes that are appropriate for storing to disk. Answers A and B are incorrect because the methods of the `UnicodeEncoding` class do not support encoding to the UTF-8 format. Answer D is incorrect because the `UTF8Encoding.GetChars()` method does the reverse job—that is, it decodes an array of bytes to Unicode characters.

Question 9

A Web page in your application reports the number of characters in a particular data entry form. You're dividing the number of bits taken up by the data by 16 to arrive at this figure. Users of the localized version in Saudi Arabia complain that the number of characters is persistently overestimated. What should you do?

- ○ A. Divide the number of bits by 32 to arrive at a more accurate figure.
- ○ B. Use the **String.Length()** method to retrieve the actual length of the string.
- ○ C. Divide the number of bits by 8 to arrive at a more accurate figure.
- ○ D. Use a **GetTextElementEnumerator** object to enumerate the characters.

Answer D is correct. The problem is that the algorithm for simple division by 16 does not take into account composed characters. The `GetTextElementEnumerator` object correctly enumerates all the characters in a Unicode string. Answers A and C are incorrect because a simple division by 32 or 8 will not account for the composed characters in a Unicode string. Answer B is incorrect because `String.Length()` method does not take the combined characters into account.

Question 10

You are shipping an application to France and Russia and are using assembly resource files to hold localization resources. Now you need to start shipping to Spain. If the application is running on the Spanish version of Windows, you want to show the user interface in Spanish. What should you do? (Select two.)

- ❏ A. Create an assembly resource file to hold the user interface text translated into Spanish.
- ❏ B. Build a new project that contains only the Spanish version of the form, and then build this new project to sell in Spain.
- ❏ C. Use a **ResourceManager** object to assign resources from the new assembly resource file at runtime.
- ❏ D. Create a new **CultureInfo** object for the Spanish (Spain) culture. Assign this object to the **Thread.CurrentThread.CurrentUICulture** property.

Answers A and C are correct. To display a translated user interface on a form, you must supply a translated resource file and use code to move the resources to the form at runtime. Answer B is incorrect because creating a completely different project for the Spanish version requires additional coding efforts. Answer D is incorrect because, if the application is running on the Spanish version of Windows, the value of the `Thread.CurrentThread.CurrentUICulture` property is already set for the Spanish culture.

Need to Know More?

 Symmonds, Nick. *Internationalization and Localization Using Microsoft .NET.* Berkeley, CA: Apress, 2002.

 Visit the Localization section of the ASP.NET QuickStart tutorial at `http://samples.gotdotnet.com/quickstart/aspplus`.

 Visit the Microsoft Global Development and Computing Portal at `www.microsoft.com/globaldev`.

 See "Globalization Step-By-Step" at `www.microsoft.com/globaldev/getwr/steps/wrguide.mspx`.

 Visit the Developing World-Ready Applications page at `http://msdn.microsoft.com/library/en-us/cpguide/html/cpcondesigningglobalapplications.asp`.

 See the Globalization Support in Microsoft .NET Framework presentation from the 20th International Unicode Conference at `www.microsoft.com/globaldev/reference/presentations/unicode20/20-dotNetFr-Globaliz.pdf`.

 Visit the Unicode Web site at `www.unicode.org`.

Working with Legacy Code

Terms you'll need to understand:

✓ Managed code
✓ Platform invoke
✓ Runtime callable wrapper (RCW)
✓ Unmanaged code

Techniques you'll need to master:

✓ Incorporating existing ASP code into ASP.NET applications
✓ Instantiating and invoking existing COM/COM+ components by creating a runtime callable wrapper (RCW)
✓ Using platform invoke (PInvoke) to invoke some common Windows API calls

In this chapter, you learn about the tools and techniques necessary to call ActiveX controls, COM components, and Windows API code from the .NET Framework. You also learn how you can migrate an existing ASP application to ASP.NET.

Incorporating Existing Code

You can continue to run existing ASP pages on your ASP.NET servers, convert the pages to the new format, or move COM components from ASP pages to ASP.NET pages. In this section, you learn about this level of interoperability.

Running ASP and ASP.NET Together

ASP and ASP.NET run well together on the same server—that's a fundamental consequence of the architecture of the two systems. Internet Information Services (IIS) forwards the requests for ASP pages to `asp.dll` (usually present in the `System32\inetsrv` folder of the Windows installation directory), whereas ASP.NET pages are handled by `aspnet_isapi.dll` (usually present in the Microsoft .NET Framework installation directory). Thus, there's no confusion on the part of the server between the two file types, and you don't need to worry that old pages will be executed incorrectly after you install ASP.NET.

 The Session state and the Application state are not shared between the ASP and ASP.NET pages. If you set a session or application variable in ASP.NET code, you can't retrieve it from ASP code, and vice versa.

Converting ASP Pages to ASP.NET

The syntax of ASP.NET pages is very close to the syntax of ASP pages, but it's not identical. Here's a partial list of things you might need to change if you want to convert an existing ASP page to run as an ASP.NET page:

➤ In ASP, you can declare global variables and procedures in `<%...%>` blocks, and they will be visible to all code on the page. In ASP.NET, such variables and procedures should be declared inside a `<script runat="server">` block. ASP.NET still executes code inside `<%...%>` blocks, but such code is executed at render time after all the code behind the page is already finished executing.

➤ In ASP, you can mix programming languages within a single page. ASP.NET, however, requires each page to use a single programming language.

➤ ASP uses scripting languages such as VBScript. ASP.NET uses object-oriented programming languages, such as C# and Visual Basic .NET.

➤ ASP defaults to passing parameters by reference, and ASP.NET defaults to passing parameters by value.

➤ The set keyword, the Let keyword, and default properties have been removed from ASP.NET.

➤ ASP allows you to use nondeclared variables. ASP.NET, on the other hand, requires you to declare all variables by default.

Using Late-bound COM Components

ASP.NET still supports the Server.CreateObject() method for creating late-bound COM components. For example, you can create an ADO Connection object in either an ASP page or an ASP.NET page with this line of code:

```
cnn = Server.CreateObject("ADODB.Connection");
```

Not all COM components can be instantiated in ASP.NET this way, however. In particular, components that use the Single-Threaded Apartment (STA) threading model do not function properly in ASP.NET pages unless you add a compatibility directive to the page, like so:

```
<%@Page aspcompat="true"%>
```

You should note that C# is a strongly typed language and does not allow specific operations on generic objects whose type is unknown at compile time. A solution is to invoke the methods of the generic object dynamically by calling the Type.InvokeMember() method. The InvokeMember() method uses the following five parameters:

➤ The name of the constructor, method, field, or property to invoke.

➤ The type of the member to be invoked as specified by the System.Reflection.BindingFlags enumeration, such as InvokeMethod, SetProperty, GetProperty, and so on.

➤ The binder object (a null value specifies that the default binder should be used).

➤ The object on which this method needs to be invoked.

➤ An array of objects to pass as the parameters to the method to be invoked. If no parameters are required to be passed, you can pass null. If the parameters are optional, you need to pass the Type.Missing field.

You should consider using late-bound COM objects as only a temporary measure. Although the ASP.NET engine will execute the new page, it won't benefit from any of the new capabilities of the .NET Framework.

Using ActiveX Controls

ActiveX controls are a client-side technology, not a server-side technology. It doesn't matter whether the controls are hosted on an HTML, ASP, or ASP.NET page; in every case, it's up to the browser to handle the ActiveX control.

To drag and drop ActiveX controls on your Web form just like an ASP.NET Web control, you need to take the following steps in Visual Studio .NET:

1. Create a new Visual C# ASP.NET Web Application project.

2. Select Tools, Customize Toolbox to invoke the Customize Toolbox dialog box.

3. Select the COM Components tab in the Customize Toolbox dialog box.

4. Scroll down the list of components, which includes all the ActiveX controls registered on your computer, until you find the control you want to add to your project. Click the check box for the control, and then click OK to add the control to the Toolbox.

5. The new control shows up at the bottom of the Toolbox. You can click and drag the control to a form just like any native .NET control.

 Remember, any ActiveX control that you use on a Web form must be present on (or downloaded to) the client's computer to function. You can include a **codebase** tag that specifies a download location for the control, if necessary.

You should consider the following issues before you use ActiveX controls in your .NET applications:

➤ If the ActiveX control isn't already present on the client, it needs to be downloaded when your page is sent to the client, potentially involving a long delay.

> Because ActiveX controls are not managed code, they don't get any of the protection the Common Language Runtime (CLR) brings to your .NET applications.

> In the .NET Framework, a native Windows forms control can be hosted in Internet Explorer, eliminating the need for ActiveX controls. Before importing an ActiveX control into your project, you should consider whether a native .NET control could fulfill your requirements.

Using COM Components

In this section of the chapter, you learn to encapsulate COM components for use with .NET applications. Both command-line and GUI tools are available for working with COM components. Before working with those tools, though, you should know a bit about wrapper classes.

Understanding Runtime Callable Wrappers

Code that operates within the CLR is called *managed code*. Managed code benefits from various services the CLR offers, such as garbage collection, memory management, and support for versioning and security.

COM components are unmanaged code because COM was designed before the CLR existed, and COM components don't use any of the services of the CLR.

How can you take a component developed before the advent of .NET and make it look like a .NET component to other .NET components? The answer is to use a *proxy*. In general terms, a proxy accepts commands and messages from one component, modifies them, and passes them to another component. The particular type of proxy that enables you to use COM components in a .NET application is called a *runtime callable wrapper (RCW)*. That is, it's a proxy that can be called by the CLR. Figure 11.1 shows how the pieces fit together.

To see how COM interoperability works, you need a COM library. Follow these steps to build a simple one:

1. Launch Visual Basic 6.0 and create a new ActiveX DLL project.

2. Select the Project1 node in the Project Explorer window and rename it `MyCustomer`.

3. Select the Class1 node in the Project Explorer window and rename it `Balances`.

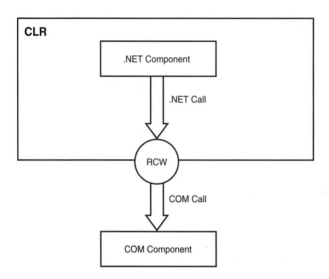

Figure 11.1 RCWs enable you to use COM components in the .NET Framework.

4. Add this code to the `Balances` class:

```
Option Explicit

Private mintCustomerCount As Integer
Private macurBalances(1 To 10) As Currency

' Create a read-only CustomerCount property
Public Property Get CustomerCount() As Integer
    CustomerCount = mintCustomerCount
End Property

' Create a GetBalance method
Public Function GetBalance(CustomerNumber As Integer)_
    As Currency
    GetBalance = macurBalances(CustomerNumber)
End Function

' Initialize the data
Private Sub Class_Initialize()
    Dim intI As Integer
    mintCustomerCount = 10
    For intI = 1 To 10
      macurBalances(intI) = Int(Rnd(1) * 100000) / 100
    Next intI
End Sub
```

5. Save the Visual Basic project. Then select File, Make MyCustomer.dll to create the COM component. This step also registers the COM component on your computer.

Using the Type Library Importer Tool (tlbimp.exe)

The task of using COM components from .NET is made substantially easier by the fact that COM components, like .NET components, have metadata that describe their interfaces. For .NET components, this metadata is embedded in the assembly manifest, whereas for COM components, the metadata is stored in a type library. A type library can be either a separate file or (as with Visual Basic 6 class libraries) embedded within another file.

The .NET Framework includes a tool, called the Type Library Importer (tlbimp.exe), that can create an RCW from COM metadata contained in a type library. Take the following steps to see how to work with the Type Library Importer:

1. Launch a .NET command prompt by selecting Start, Programs, Microsoft Visual Studio .NET, Visual Studio .NET Tools, Visual Studio .NET Command Prompt.

2. Inside the command prompt window, navigate to the folder that contains the MyCustomers.dll COM library and enter this command to run the Type Library Importer: **tlbimp MyCustomer.dll /out:NETMyCustomer.dll.**

3. Open Visual Studio .NET and create a new blank solution named 315C11 at c:\inetpub\wwwroot\ExamCram. (You might need to change the directory based on your configuration.)

4. Add a new Visual C# ASP.NET Web Application project at the following location: http://localhost/ExamCram/315C11/Example11_1.

5. Place three Label controls (name one of then lblBalance), one TextBox control (txtCustomerNumber), and a Button control (btnGetBalance) on the form.

6. Right-click the References node in the Solution Explorer and select Add Reference.

7. Click the Browse button in the Add Reference dialog box. Select the NETMyCustomer.dll file you created in step 2. Click OK to add the reference to the project.

8. Switch to the form's Code view and add the following using directive:
   using NETMyCustomer;

9. Double-click the Button control and enter the following code in the Click and Page_Load() event handlers:

```
Balances b;

private void Page_Load(object sender, System.EventArgs e)
{
    b = new Balances();
    txtCustomerNumber.Text = b.CustomerCount.ToString();
}

private void btnGetBalance_Click(object sender, System.EventArgs e)
{
    Int16 custNumber = Int16.Parse(txtCustomerNumber.Text);
    lblBalance.Text = b.GetBalance(ref custNumber).ToString();
}
```

10. Run the project. Enter a number between 1 and 10 in the Customer Number TextBox control and click the Get Balance button to see that customer's balance.

When you build the DLL using Visual Basic 6.0, it automatically registers the DLL in the Windows Registry. If you are using the code files from the CD, you must register **MyCustomer.dll** using **regsvr32.exe**, as shown here:

regsvr32 MyCustomer.dll

The Type Library Importer creates an RCW for the COM type library. This RCW is a library you can add to your .NET project as a reference. After you do that, the classes in the COM component can be used just like native .NET classes. When you use a class from the COM component, .NET makes the call to the RCW, which in turn forwards the call to the original COM component and returns the results to your .NET managed code.

Using COM Components Directly

As with ActiveX controls, the Visual Studio .NET interface provides a streamlined way to use a COM component from your .NET code. Complete the following steps to work with Direct Reference:

1. Add a new Visual C# .NET Web Application project in the existing solution, and name it Example11_2.

2. Create a user interface similar to that of Example11_1.

3. Right-click the References node in Solution Explorer and select Add Reference. Select the COM tab in the Add Reference dialog box. Then scroll down the list of COM components until you come to the MyCustomer library. Select the MyCustomer library, click Select, and then click OK.

4. Switch to Code view and enter this code in the class definition; be sure to attach the event handlers to their respective events:

```
MyCustomer.Balances b;

private void Page_Load(object sender, System.EventArgs e)
{
   b = new MyCustomer.Balances();
   txtCustomerNumber.Text = b.CustomerCount.ToString();
}

private void btnGetBalance_Click(object sender, System.EventArgs e)
{
    Int16 custNumber = Int16.Parse(txtCustomerNumber.Text);
    lblBalance.Text = b.GetBalance(ref custNumber).ToString();
}
```

5. Set the project as the startup project for the solution and run the project. Enter a number between 1 and 10 in the Customer Number TextBox control and click the Get Balance button to see that customer's balance.

When you directly reference a COM library from the Visual Studio .NET Integrated Development Environment (IDE), the effect is almost the same as if you used the Type Library Importer to import the same library. Visual Studio .NET creates a new namespace with the name of the original library and then exposes the classes from the library in that namespace.

Although you can use either of the two methods you've seen to call a COM component from a .NET component, the following are some reasons to prefer one method over the other:

➤ For a COM component that will be used in only a single Visual C# .NET project, and that you wrote yourself, use the easiest method: a direct reference from the .NET project. This method is suitable only for a truly private component that does not need to be shared by other projects.

➤ If a COM component is shared among multiple projects, use the Type Library Importer so you can sign the resulting assembly and place it in the global assembly cache (GAC). Shared code must be signed.

➤ If you need to control details of the created assembly, such as its name, namespace, or version number, you must use the Type Library Importer. The direct reference method gives you no control over the details of the created assembly.

You should not import methods on code that is written by another developer because you are not allowed to sign code that is written by someone else. If you need to use a COM component from another developer, you should obtain a *primary interop assembly (PIA)* from the original developer of the component. Microsoft supplies PIAs for all its own common libraries.

Using COM+ Components

COM+ is the Component Services layer in Windows 2000 and later operating systems. It supplies a number of services to components running under Windows, such as

➤ Role-based security

➤ Object pooling and just-in-time activation

➤ Queued components for asynchronous calls

➤ Transactional processing

➤ A publish-and-subscribe events model

The Type Library Importer tool and Visual Studio .NET can both create wrappers for COM+ components using the same procedures they use for COM components.

Using Platform Invoke

The *platform invoke* (often abbreviated as PInvoke) feature of .NET enables .NET code to call functions from unmanaged libraries such as the Win32 API. The following example lets you see this in detail:

1. Add a new Visual C# ASP.NET Web Application project to the existing solution, and name it `Example11_3`.

2. Place a `Label` control named `lblComputerName` on the form.

3. Switch to Code view and add the following `using` directives to the top of your code:

```
using System.Text;
using System.Runtime.InteropServices;
```

4. Add the following lines of code in the class definition, which indicates that the `GetComputerName()` method is implemented in `kernel32.dll`:

```
[DllImport("kernel32.dll", CharSet=CharSet.Auto)]
public static extern int GetComputerName
        (StringBuilder buffer, ref uint size);
```

5. Add this code to the `Page_Load()` event handler:

```
private void Page_Load(object sender, System.EventArgs e)
{
    StringBuilder sbBuf = new StringBuilder(128);
    UInt32 intLen = (uint) sbBuf.Capacity;
    Int32 intRet=0;
```

```
    // Call the Win API method
    intRet = GetComputerName(sbBuf, ref intLen);

    lblComputerName.Text = "This computer is named " +
        sbBuf.ToString();
}
```

6. Set the project as the startup project for the solution and run it. The form displays the name of the computer on which the code is run. Remember, if you're using a client on one computer and a server on another, the ASP.NET code executes on the server. In that case, the browser displays the name of the server, not the name of the client.

Note the use of the `CharSet.Auto` parameter in the `DllImport` attribute of the `GetComputerName()` method declaration. You might know that many Windows API calls come in two versions, depending on the character set you're using. For example, `GetComputerName` really exists as `GetComputerNameA` (for ANSI characters) and `GetComputerNameW` (for Unicode characters). The `Auto` modifier instructs the .NET Framework to use the appropriate version of the API call for the platform on which the code is running.

You should use the **StringBuilder** object for a Windows API call that expects a string buffer.

PInvoke can also handle API calls that require structures as parameters. For example, many API calls require a `Rect` structure, which consists of four members filled in with the coordinates of a rectangle. In Visual C# .NET, you can declare a structure with explicit byte offsets for each member, which lets you define any structure the Windows API requires, like so:

```
[StructLayout(LayoutKind.Explicit)]
public struct Rect
{
    [FieldOffset(0)] public Int32 left;
    [FieldOffset(4)] public Int32 top;
    [FieldOffset(8)] public Int32 right;
    [FieldOffset(12)] public Int32 bottom;
}
```

The `StructLayout` attribute tells the Visual C# .NET compiler that you'll explicitly specify the location of the individual fields in the structure. The `FieldOffset` attribute specifies the starting byte of each field in the structure. By using these attributes, you can ensure that the .NET Framework constructs the same structure the API function is expecting to receive.

Exam Prep Questions

Question 1

> Your application uses a communications library from a third-party developer, and this library is implemented as a COM component. You are migrating your application to .NET. What should you do to continue to use the classes and methods in the communications library?
>
> ○ A. Obtain a primary interop assembly from the developer of the library, and install the PIA in the GAC.
>
> ○ B. Use the Type Library Importer to create a signed RCW for the library, and install the RCW in the GAC.
>
> ○ C. Use the Type Library Importer to create an unsigned RCW for the library, and install the RCW in the GAC.
>
> ○ D. Create wrapper code that uses PInvoke to call functions from the library, and import this wrapper code into your application.

Answer A is correct. The proper way to proceed is to obtain a PIA from the original author. Answer B is incorrect because you did not write the code for the communications library and therefore cannot sign it. Answer C is incorrect because only signed assemblies can be installed in the GAC. Answer D is incorrect because PInvoke is not used for invoking COM components.

Question 2

> You have an existing COM component that contains shared classes, which encapsulate functionality you want to use in your ASP.NET application. How can you use these classes while maintaining the benefits of managed code, such as type safety and automatic garbage collection?
>
> ○ A. Use the Type Library Importer with the **/strictref** option to create an RCW for the COM component.
>
> ○ B. Call the methods from the COM component directly via PInvoke.
>
> ○ C. Add a direct reference to the COM component.
>
> ○ D. Rewrite the COM component as a .NET component.

Answer D is correct. Only managed code benefits from the features of the CLR, and the only way to turn the component into managed code is to rewrite it in .NET. Answers A and C are incorrect because these techniques just create a wrapper over the existing COM code. The COM code is not converted to the managed code. Answer B is incorrect because PInvoke is not for used for invoking COM components.

Question 3

Your application uses the **GetComputerName()** API function. This function exists in **kernel32.dll** in both ANSI and Unicode versions. Your declaration is as follows:

```
[DllImport("kernel32.dll")]
public static extern int GetComputerName(
    StringBuilder buffer, ref uint size);
```

Your code is failing with a **System.EntryPointNotFoundException** exception when you call this function. What should you do to fix this failure?

- ○ A. Supply the full path for **kernel32.dll**.
- ○ B. Add the **CharSet.Auto** parameter to the declaration.
- ○ C. Declare the function as **GetComputerNameA()** instead of **GetComputerName()**.
- ○ D. Declare the function as **GetComputerNameW()** instead of **GetComputerName()**.

Answer B is correct. The `CharSet.Auto` parameter is necessary to tell the CLR to use the ANSI or Unicode version of the function as appropriate to the operating system. Answer A is incorrect because the program automatically searches for the DLL file in the Windows system directory. Answers C and D are incorrect because the `GetComputerName` function exists as `GetComputerNameA` (for ANSI characters) and `GetComputerNameW` (for Unicode characters) and the system cannot determine which one to invoke.

Question 4

You are responsible for migrating an existing ASP application to ASP.NET. The existing application consists of eight COM server components and a single client user interface component (written as a set of ASP pages) that instantiates and invokes objects from the server components. You want to give the user interface of the application an overhaul and migrate to ASP.NET with low risk and minimal downtime. How should you proceed?

- ○ A. Completely rewrite the entire application using Visual C# .NET.
- ○ B. Convert the user interface component from ASP to ASP.NET. Use a COM interop to call the existing COM servers from the .NET user interface code, and then migrate the servers one by one.
- ○ C. Convert all the server components into Visual C# .NET. Use a COM interop to call the converted server components from the existing ASP pages.
- ○ D. Cut and paste all the existing code into a Visual C# ASP.NET project.

Answer B is correct. Converting the user interface component from ASP to ASP.NET and then migrating the servers one by one provides the most effective solution. Answers A and D are incorrect because moving all the code takes longer than moving part of the code, and doing so introduces additional risk. Answer C is incorrect because, if you want to rewrite the user interface, you should move that component to .NET before moving the server components.

Question 5

You wrote a COM component to supply random numbers in a specific distribution to a simple statistical client program. Now you're moving that client program to .NET. The COM component is used nowhere else, and you have not shipped copies to anyone else. You want to call the objects in the COM server from your new .NET client. How should you proceed?

- O A. Set a direct reference from your .NET client to the COM server.
- O B. Use the Type Library Importer to create an unsigned RCW for the COM component.
- O C. Use the Type Library Importer to create a signed RCW for the COM component.
- O D. Use PInvoke to instantiate classes from the COM component.

Answer A is correct. For components used in a single project, and that you've written, the simple method of creating the RCW is best. Answer B is incorrect because only signed assemblies can be installed in the GAC. Answer C is incorrect because you are not distributing the code to other developers and therefore signing is not required. Answer D is incorrect because PInvoke is not used for invoking COM components.

Question 6

You're moving a legacy ASP application to ASP.NET. Some of the pages use ADO to load data. You use the **Server.CreateObject()** method to create the ADO connection. Other parts of the application work fine, but those pages that call **Server.CreateObject()** will not load. What must you do to use the ADO objects in your ASP.NET application?

- O A. Use a **Page** directive to set the ASP compatibility mode.
- O B. Build an RCW for the ADO objects.
- O C. Convert the ADO objects to ADO.NET.
- O D. Use a **Page** directive to set the page language to VBScript.

Answer A is correct. The ADO library uses STA as its threading model, and the .NET Framework allows only STA components on a page that's set to ASP compatibility mode. Answer B is incorrect because you can use the `Server.CreateObject()` method to create late-bound calls to ADO without the need to build an RCW. Answer C is incorrect because this requires you to write more code. Answer D is incorrect because VBScript is not supported in .NET Framework programs.

Question 7

Your project contains the following API declaration:

```
[DllImport("kernel32.dll", CharSet=CharSet.Auto)]
public static extern int GetComputerName(String buffer, ref
  unit size);
```

The project also contains the following code to use this API to display the computer name:

```
public static void ShowName()
{
    String buf = "";
    UInt32 intLen=128;
    Int32 intRet;

    // Call the Win API method
    intRet = GetComputerName(buf, ref intLen);

    Console.WriteLine("This computer is named " +
    buf.ToString());
}
```

Users report that no computer name is displayed. What should you do?

- O A. Use **ref** with the variable **buf** in the call to the **GetComputerName()** function.
- O B. Tell the users that their computers have no names set in their network properties.
- O C. Replace the use of **String** with **StringBuilder** in the code.
- O D. Use **out** with the variable **buf** in the call to the **GetComputerName()** function.

Answer C is correct. In the PInvoke calls, you should use `StringBuilder` instead of the `string` data type to hold the return value. Answers A and D are incorrect because using `ref` or `out` with the variable `buf` will not match the methods prototype in the declaration. Answer B is incorrect because all computers do have some name associated with them.

Question 8

Your application will use functions from a COM+ component that uses COM+ for publish-and-subscribe events and object pooling. Which of these methods can you use to access the classes in the COM+ component? (Select two.)

❏ A.   Use PInvoke to declare the functions in the COM+ component.

❏ B.   Add the COM+ component directly to the Visual C# .NET Toolbox.

❏ C.   Set a direct reference to the COM+ component.

❏ D.   Use the Type Library Importer to create an RCW for the COM+ component.

Answers C and D are correct. You can use COM+ components through the same techniques you use with COM components. Answer A is incorrect because PInvoke cannot be used to invoke COM+ components. Answer B is incorrect because COM+ components are not controls and cannot be added to the Visual C# .NET Toolbox.

Need to Know More?

Kalani, Amit and Priti Kalani. *MCAD/MCSD Training Guide: Developing XML Web Services and Server Components with Microsoft Visual C# .NET and the Microsoft .NET Framework (Exam 70-320).* Indianapolis, IN: Que Certification, 2003.

Nathan, Adam. *.NET and COM: The Complete Interoperability Guide.* Indianapolis, IN: Sams Publishing, 2002.

Troelsen, Andrew. *COM and .NET Interoperability.* Berkeley, CA: Apress, 2002.

See .NET Interop: Get Ready for Microsoft .NET by Using Wrappers to Interact with COM-based Applications at www.msdn.com/msdnmag/issues/01/08/Interop/Interop.asp.

See Troubleshooting .NET Interoperability at www.msdn.com/library/en-us/dv_vstechart/html/vbtchTroubleshooting NETInteroperability.asp.

See the MSDN Online Seminar: Using COM Objects from .NET Framework Applications at www.microsoft.com/seminar/shared/asp/view.asp?url=/seminar/en/20020121cominterop1/manifest.xml.

User Assistance and Accessibility

Terms you'll need to understand:

✓ Accessibility

✓ User assistance

Techniques you'll need to master:

✓ Knowing how to implement user assistance for a Web application

✓ Following the accessibility guidelines to make a Web application accessible

✓ Using the testing strategies described in this chapter to evaluate a Web application for accessibility

This chapter examines two of the necessary parts of shipping any complex application:

➤ *User assistance*—User assistance refers to the process of providing help within an application through a variety of means.

➤ *Accessibility*—Accessibility refers to the coding you must do to make your application usable for everyone regardless of disability.

Implementing User Assistance

Several alternatives are available for delivering user assistance with Web applications, including

➤ Help in a separate browser window

➤ Help in a browser pane

➤ Embedding Help

Using a Second Browser Window

The simplest way to provide user assistance on Web pages is by opening a second browser window. To do this, you add a HyperLink control on the Web page where you want to provide assistance. Then you set the Text property of the HyperLink control to an intuitive string such as Help, set the NavigateUrl property to the URL of the help file, and set the Target property to _blank. When a user clicks the Help hyperlink, it opens the corresponding link in another browser window.

This method of displaying user assistance uses the target="_blank" attribute to open help pages in a second browser window. Another method of displaying a second window is by writing JavaScript client-side code. However, users might become confused with multiple browser windows open, and it can be annoying to have the help window overlap the window in which you are trying to do work.

Using the Search Pane

One way to address the problems of using a separate browser window for user assistance is to use the Internet Explorer search pane instead. To use the search pane, you set the Target property of the HyperLink control to _search. The following example shows you how:

1. Open Visual Studio .NET and create a new blank solution named 315C12 at `c:\inetpub\wwwroot\ExamCram`. (You might need to change the directory based on your configuration.)

2. Add a new Visual C# ASP.NET Web Application project at the following location: `http://localhost/ExamCram/315C12/Example12_1`.

3. Set the `pageLayout` property of the Web form to `FlowLayout`. Arrange two `Label` controls (`lblHeadLine` and `lblInstructions`), an `Image` control (`imgDecor`), a `TextBox` control (`txtRandomNumber`), a `Button` control (`btnGetRandom`), and a `Hyperlink` control (`hlHelp`) on the Web form. Set the `Text` property of the `HyperLink` control to `Help`, set its `NavigateUrl` property to `Help.aspx`, and set its `Target` property to `_search`.

4. Add code to handle the `Button` control's `Click` event, like so:

```
private void btnGetRandom_Click(object sender, System.EventArgs e)
{
    Random r = new Random();
    txtRandomNumber.Text = r.Next(1000).ToString();
}
```

5. Add a new Web form to your application and name it `Help.aspx`. Switch to HTML view and modify `Help.aspx` as follows:

```
<%@ Page language="c#" Codebehind="Help.aspx.cs"
    AutoEventWireup="false" Inherits="Example12_1.Help" %>
<html>
    <head><title>Help</title></head>
    <body>
    <form id="Help" method="post" runat="server">
    <h2>Random Number Help</h2>
    <p>The Random number application is designed to generate
    random numbers between 0 and 999. Just run the program
    and click to get as many random numbers as you would
    like. Randomness guaranteed or your money back
    (this application is 100% free)!</p>
    </form>
    </body>
</html>
```

6. Build the project and view the results in an external Internet Explorer window. When you click the Help hyperlink on the form, it will open the corresponding link in the search companion window, as shown in Figure 12.1.

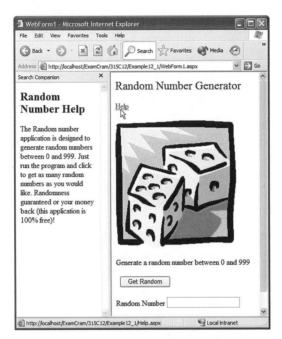

Figure 12.1 You can keep the help text with the application by using the Internet Explorer search pane.

Although using the search pane does address the problem of keeping the help with the application, it raises other issues. If your users are sophisticated enough to actually use the search pane (for search, history, or favorites, for example), they might not be pleased at having it hijacked by your application's help pages. Worse, though, is the fact that the _search target is specific to Internet Explorer.

Embedding Help

To avoid the problems with extra browser windows or with the search pane, you might choose to embed the user assistance directly in your Web pages.

To do this, you can use controls such as the Label control and set its text property to the help text that you want to display. You can also programmatically set the Visible property of the control to ensure that users see help only when they want.

This approach for providing user assistance is compatible with all browsers (because the .NET Framework is delivering pure HTML when you show the Label control).

The **ToolTip** property of the server controls can be used to display brief help strings to the user when he hovers his mouse pointer over a control. ASP.NET renders ToolTips by using the **TITLE** attribute of HTML control tags.

Implementing Accessibility Features

Although software developers have long ignored accessibility features, modern software takes accessibility into account from both ethical and economic standpoints, as well as to comply with the law. In fact, Microsoft has made accessibility a key feature of the Windows logo certification program.

The following are the five basic principles to accessible design:

> *Flexibility*—The user interface should be flexibile and customizable so that users can adjust it to their own individual needs and preferences.

> *Choice of input methods*—All operations in your application should be accessible to the keyboard, and basic operations should be available via the mouse as well. In the future, voice and other types of input might also be considered here.

> *Choice of output methods*—You should not depend on a single method of output (such as sound, color, or text) for important information.

> *Consistency*—Your application should be consistent with the Windows operating system and other applications to minimize difficulties in learning and using new interfaces.

> *Compatibility with accessibility aids*—Windows includes several accessibility aids such as the Magnifier (which can blow up text or graphics to a larger size) and the On-Screen Keyboard (which enables keyboard input via the mouse). Your application should not circumvent these accessibility aids.

Understanding Accessible Design Guidelines

Table 12.1 lays out some of the important accessibility guidelines you should consider for any application.

Table 12.1 Accessibility Guidelines for Web Application Design	
Area	**Guidelines**
ALT text	Every graphic should have ALT text, and the ALT text should convey the important information about an image.
Imagemaps	Do not depend on imagemaps for navigation; also include a set of text links for those who cannot use the images.
Link text	Link text should be useful in isolation because some accessible browsers present a list of links with no context for fast navigation. If this isn't possible, use the **TITLE** attribute of the link to provide a more descriptive string.
Keyboard navigation	The Tab key will move between all links and imagemap areas in the order in which they're defined in the HTML. Use the **TABINDEX** attribute where appropriate to override this.
Access keys	All controls and links that act as controls should have an **ACCESSKEY** attribute. Underline the access key in the control's label.
Control identification	Use the **TITLE** attribute or **LABEL** tags to associate a name with every control.
Frames and tables	Provide alternative pages that do not use frames or tables.
Support formatting options	Do not assume that text will be in a specific font, color, or size. Do not assume that things will line up because the width might change. Use heading tags such as **<TH>** rather than specially formatted text.
Style sheets	Make sure that the page works even if the style sheet is turned off. Otherwise, offer an alternative page that is designed to work without a style sheet.
Audio and video	Provide captions or transcripts for audio and video content.

The W3C Guidelines

The World Wide Web Consortium (W3C) is the body that governs standards for the Internet. The W3C has invested considerable effort in defining accessibility guidelines. More information about the W3C Web Accessibility Initiative is available at www.w3.org/WAI.

The Section 508 Guidelines

Section 508 of the Rehabilitative Act sets standards for all U.S. federal agencies that maintain Web sites. This gives accessibility the force of law for federal Web sites (and serves to emphasize that it's a good idea for all Web sites).

There's an excellent discussion of the Section 508 standards at `www.access-board.gov/sec508/guide/1194.22.htm`.

Making a Web Application Accessible

If at all possible, you should plan to make your Web applications accessible from the start. Sometimes, though, you won't have any choice except to add accessibility features after the fact. In the following example, you'll modify the random number application for accessibility.

1. Open the `Example12_1` project.

2. Set the `TabIndex` property of `lblHeadLine` to `0`.

3. Set the `TabIndex` property of `hlHelp` to `1`, and set its `AccessKey` property to `H`.

4. Set the `TabIndex` property of `imgDecor` to `2`, and set its `AlternateText` property to `[Dice Image]`.

5. Set the `TabIndex` property of `lblInstructions` to `3`.

6. Set the `TabIndex` property of `btnGetRandom` to `4`, and set its `AccessKey` property to `G`.

7. Set the `Text` property of the `Label` control before the `txtRandomNumber` control to `<u>R</u>andom Number`. Set its `TabIndex` property to `5`.

8. Set the `TabIndex` property of `txtRandomNumber` to `6`, and set its `AccessKey` property to `R`.

9. Run the project. Verify that the tab order and access keys work as designed.

The Button Web server control does not support underlined text. If you want to show underlined text on a button, you can use an HTML **Button** control. In that case, though, you'll need to move any processing from the button's click event to the **Postback** portion of the page's **Load** event.

Testing Application Accessibility

Before shipping an application, you should test its accessibility features. Here are some tests you should perform:

➤ Make sure that all functionality is accessible by using the keyboard alone. Test all access keys. Press Enter to follow a selected link.

➤ View the page with graphics turned off to ensure that the ALT attributes are a good substitute. In Internet Explorer, you can turn off graphics from Tools, Internet Options, Advanced.

➤ Use the application with sound turned off to ensure that that no important information is lost.

➤ Turn on the High Contrast option under Control Panel. Display the page and ensure that it is still readable.

➤ Alter the page's font size (you can do this with View, Text Size in Internet Explorer) and ensure that the page is still readable.

➤ Resize the browser window and check for readability.

One of the accessibility guidelines states that you should supply row and column headers for data tables. This facilitates specialized browsers designed to help users understand the structure of tabular information.

You can use the scope attribute to associate the row and column headers explicitly with the data in the rows and columns. This enables screen reader software to more easily tell a visually impaired user which row and column are associated with a particular data value.

Exam Prep Questions

Question 1

You are deploying a Web application on your company's intranet. Your company has selected Internet Explorer 5.5 as its standard Web browser. Users would like to have online help available for your application with minimal overhead and without needing to manage additional windows. How should you implement user assistance for this application?

○ A. Display help in a second browser window.

○ B. Display help by using control properties to hide and show **Label** controls.

○ C. Display help in the Internet Explorer search pane.

○ D. Display help using DHTML to hide and show controls.

Answer C is correct. With Internet Explorer as a standard browser, you can use the IE search pane to display help. Answer A is incorrect because a second browser window can be difficult to manage for end users. Answer B is incorrect because this solution requires an additional round trip to the server. Answer D is incorrect because downloading the help and hiding it until it is needed can require users to download larger Web pages.

Question 2

Users with certain browsers report that they are having difficulty using your Web application because they are browsing without graphics. What should you do to make your application more accessible in this situation?

○ A. Ensure that the graphics are saved in GIF format so that they will quickly download.

○ B. Add ALT text to all graphics to indicate their purpose.

○ C. Use the **AccessKey** property to associate access keys with all graphics.

○ D. Provide an alternative version of the page with no graphics.

Answer B is correct. All graphics should have an ALT attribute that conveys the important information about the image. Answer A is incorrect because download speed alone does not improve the accessibility of the application. Answer C is incorrect because only the controls and links that act as controls should have an `AccessKey` property. Answer D is incorrect because providing an entirely separate page should be viewed as a last resort because keeping the modifications to the regular and alternative pages synchronized can be difficult.

Question 3

Which of these Web pages violates common accessibility guidelines? (Select two.)

❑ A. A page that supplies a link to a transcript in addition to an audio file

❑ B. A page that beeps and waits for a correction when the user enters an invalid date on a form

❑ C. A page that uses the **<H1>** and **<H2>** tags for two levels of outlining

❑ D. A page that shows a red bullet for bad values and a green bullet for good values in a complex table

Answer B and D are correct. Accessibility guidelines specify that you should not use only sound or only color to convey information. Answers A and C are incorrect because they both follow the guidelines for making the application more accessible.

Question 4

Your Web application allows data entry through a form. The form uses the browser's default colors and fonts throughout. When the user makes a data entry mistake, the computer beeps and the cursor remains in place. When the user saves a record, the entry colors are cleared and the cursor is returned to the first control on the form.

What should you do to make this form more accessible?

○ A. Prompt the user before clearing the form.

○ B. Set the form's **bgColor** to **white** instead of depending on the system properties.

○ C. Provide audio notification of saves.

○ D. Provide an additional, non-audio means of notification for data entry errors.

Answer D is correct. Providing an additional non-audio notification as a means of feedback will increase the accessibility of the application. Answer A is incorrect because it is more of a usability issue rather than an accessibility issue. Answer B is incorrect because using a specific background color can interfere with the user's system settings. Answer C is incorrect because accessible applications should not depend on sound as the sole means of feedback.

Question 5

Your application will be used by people who depend on accessibility aids such as screen readers. Which properties should you explicitly set for controls in this application? (Select two.)

- ❑ A. The **bgColor** property of the **Document** object
- ❑ B. ALT text for **Image** controls
- ❑ C. The **scope** attribute for Table Header cells
- ❑ D. **AccessKey** properties for **Label** controls

Answer B and C are correct. All graphics require ALT text to be accessible to those who are browsing with graphics turned off. Table header cells should have a scope attribute to indicate that their contents apply to the entire column in the table. Answers A and D are incorrect because these properties do not assist accessibility aids such as screen readers.

Question 6

Your group is designing a new Web application to be deployed on your company's Internet site. The project lead proposes using Microsoft's new HTML Help 2.0 for user assistance in this application. Should you endorse this proposal?

- ○ A. Yes, because HTML Help is the standard help for Visual Studio .NET applications.
- ○ B. Yes, because HTML Help can be viewed in any Web browser.
- ○ C. No, because HTML Help cannot use the full range of standard HTML 4.01 tags.
- ○ D. No, because HTML Help is available only on the Microsoft Windows operating system.

Answer D is correct because the HTML Help viewer is a Windows-only technology and might not be appropriate for use on an Internet Web site where users might use different operating systems. Answers A and B are incorrect because these reasons are not enough if the help cannot be displayed successfully across the operating systems. Answer C is incorrect because an HTML Help file can use any valid HTML markup.

Question 7

Your Web application includes a **Label** control with an ID of **lblCaption** and a **TextBox** control with an ID of **txtData**. The **Text** property of the **Label** control is set to **Enter Data**. Which two properties of the **TextBox** control should you set to ensure that it can be accessed by the expected keyboard actions? (Select all that apply.)

❑ A. **TabIndex**

❑ B. **AccessKey**

❑ C. **CssClass**

❑ D. **TextMode**

Answers A and B are correct. The TabIndex property is important to ensure that the control can be accessed by the Tab key, and the AccessKey property is important to ensure that the control can be accessed by an accelerator key. Answers C and D are incorrect because these properties do not impact the keyboard actions.

Question 8

You are developing an online checkbook application. Currently, the application plays a music file when the checkbook is in balance. Which of these modifications would make the application more accessible? (Select two.)

❑ A. Add a message box that is also displayed when the checkbook is in balance.

❑ B. Allow the user to select a custom music file to play when the checkbook is in balance.

❑ C. Allow the user to set the volume of the music played when the checkbook is in balance.

❑ D. Display a check mark graphic when the checkbook is in balance.

Answers A and D are correct. To make an application that depends on sound for notification more accessible, you must add a non-audio means of notification. Answers B and C are incorrect because these modifications do not increase accessibility of the application.

Question 9

Your Web application uses a frame set to organize information. What must you do to comply with the Section 508 accessibility guidelines?

❍ A. Provide title text for each frame.

❍ B. Provide a link to an alternative, non-framed page.

❍ C. Replace the frame set with a table.

❍ D. Add an **ALT** text tag to the **FRAMESET** tag.

Answer A is correct. You should provide a title text for each frame. Answers B and C are incorrect because frames can be used in accessible sites as long as frames are titled with text that makes identifying and navigating between frames easy. Answer D is incorrect because the ALT text applies to images rather than the FRAMESET tag.

Need to Know More?

 Kalani, Amit. *MCAD/MCSD Developing and Implementing Web Applications with Visual C# .NET and Visual Studio .NET.* Indianapolis, IN: Que Certification, 2002.

 Visit the MSDN Library: Designing Accessible Applications at `http://msdn.com/library/en-us/vsent7/html/vxconDesigningAccessibleApplications.asp`.

 Visit the W3C WAI Web site at `www.w3.org/WAI`.

 See the Section 508 Web site at `www.section508.gov`.

 See the Microsoft Accessibility Web site at `www.microsoft.com/enable/dev`.

Testing and Debugging a Web Application

Terms you'll need to understand:

✓ Debugging

✓ Testing

✓ Tracing

Techniques you'll need to master:

✓ Understanding how to use the **web.config** file to enable tracing for an application and also learning to enable tracing at the page level

✓ Knowing how to call different methods of the **Trace** and **Debug** classes and noting the differences in the output when you run a program using the Debug and Release configurations

✓ Experimenting with attaching predefined and custom-made listeners to **Trace** objects

✓ Knowing how to implement trace switches and conditional compilation in a Web application

✓ Gaining experience with various types of debugging windows available in Visual C# .NET, understanding their advantages, and learning to use them effectively

✓ Understanding how to perform local and remote debugging, debugging client-side scripting, and debugging SQL Server stored procedures

In this chapter, you'll learn about the various testing, tracing, and debugging capabilities of Visual Studio .NET.

Testing

Testing is the process of executing a program with the intention of finding errors, or *bugs*. By *errors*, I mean any case in which a program's actual results fail to match the expected results. The criteria of the expected results might not include just the correctness of the program; they might also include other attributes such as usability, reliability, and robustness. The process of testing can be manual, automated, or a mixture of both techniques.

Unit testing involves performing basic tests at the component level to ensure that each unique path in the component behaves exactly as documented in its specifications.

Tracing

Tracing is a process for collecting information about program execution. Information revealed through tracing can help you resolve errors and issues with an application.

Using the **TraceContext** Class

The `TraceContext` class of the `System.Web` namespace is responsible for gathering execution details of a Web request. You can access the `TraceContext` object for the current request through the `Trace` property of the `Page` class. After you have the `TraceContext` object, you can invoke its member methods to write trace messages to the trace log. Table 13.1 lists some of the important members of the `TraceContext` class with which you should be familiar.

Table 13.1	Important Members of the TraceContext Class	
Member	**Type**	**Description**
IsEnabled	Property	Specifies whether tracing is enabled for a request.
TraceMode	Property	Indicates the sort order in which the messages should be displayed. It can have one of three values—**Default**, **SortByCategory**, or **SortByTime**.
Warn()	Method	Writes the messages to the trace log in red, which indicates that they are warnings.
Write()	Method	Writes the messages in the trace log.

The **IsEnabled** property can be dynamically assigned to turn tracing for a page on or off. It can also be used to include or exclude code based on the trace setting for a page.

You can enable tracing for a Page using the Trace attribute of the Page directive. When the Trace attribute is set to true in the Page directive, the page appends the tracing information of the current Web request with its output.

Take the following steps to enable tracing in a page and display debugging information:

1. Open Visual Studio .NET and create a new blank solution named 315C13 at c:\inetpub\wwwroot\ExamCram. (You might need to change the directory based on your configuration.)

2. Add a new Visual C# ASP.NET Web Application project at the following location: http://localhost/ExamCram/315C13/Example13_1.

3. Change the pageLayout property of the DOCUMENT object to FlowLayout. Place one TextBox control (txtNumber), two Label controls (name one of them lblResult), and a Button control (btnCalculate) on the Web form.

4. Switch to the HTML view of the form in the designer. Add the trace="true" attribute to the Page directive, like so:

```
<%@ Page language="c#" Codebehind="WebForm1.aspx.cs"
AutoEventWireup="false" Inherits="Example13_1.WebForm1" Trace="true"%>
```

5. Double-click the Button control and add the following code to the event handler to handle the Click event:

```
private void btnCalculate_Click(object sender, System.EventArgs e)
{
    // write a trace message
    Trace.Write("Factorial", "Inside Button Click event handler");
    int intNumber;
    try
    {
        intNumber = Convert.ToInt32(txtNumber.Text);
    }
    catch (Exception ex)
    {
        Trace.Warn("Factorial", "Invalid value", ex);
        return;
    }
    if(intNumber < 0)
    {
        Trace.Warn("Factorial", "Invalid negative value");
    }
    int intFac = 1;
    for (int i = 2; i <= intNumber; i++)
    {
```

```
            intFac = intFac * i;
            Trace.Write("Factorial", "Value of i: " + i);
        }
    if(intFac < 1)
        Trace.Warn("Factorial" , "There was an overflow");
    lblResult.Text = String.Format(
        "The factorial of {0} is {1}", intNumber, intFac);
    Trace.Write("Factorial" , "Done with computations.");
}
```

6. Run the project. Enter a small value, such as 5 into the number text box and click the Calculate Factorial button. You will see the factorial value displayed in the factorial text box, along with some trace messages in the Trace Information section.

7. Try entering a negative value, or a larger value such as 100, and notice the trace messages displayed in the trace log. You should see warning messages displayed in red.

You can enable tracing for an entire Web application using the application configuration file (web.config). The <trace> element is used to configure tracing for an application; its attributes are as follows:

➤ *enabled*—Indicates whether tracing is enabled for an application. If enabled, trace information can be viewed using the trace viewer.

➤ *localOnly*—Indicates whether the trace viewer can be viewed by only the local client (running on the Web server itself) or by any client.

➤ *pageOutput*—Indicates whether the trace information should be displayed along with the page output.

➤ *requestLimit*—Indicates the number of requests whose trace information should be stored on the server. Tracing is disabled when the request limit is reached.

➤ *traceMode*—Indicates the order in which the trace messages should be displayed in the Trace Information section of the trace log. It can be either SortByCategory (sorted by the Category column) or SortByTime (sorted by the First(s) column).

The page-level trace setting overrides the trace setting for the application. For example, if **pageOutput** is set to **false** in the **web.config** file and the **trace** attribute is enabled at page level, the trace information is still displayed along with the page output.

Enabling tracing through the web.config file enables you to view the trace information using the trace viewer in a separate page (trace.axd) instead of displaying it with the page output. The following code segment shows how to modify the <trace> element defined in the <system.web> element of the web.config file:

```
<trace enabled="true" requestLimit="10"
    pageOutput="false" traceMode="SortByTime"
    localOnly="true" />
```

Conditional Compilation

The C# programming language provides a set of preprocessing directives (as listed in Table 13.2). You can use these directives to skip sections of source files for compilation, report errors and warnings, or mark distinct regions of source code.

Table 13.2 C# Preprocessing Directives	
Directives	**Description**
#if, **#else**, **#elif**, and **#endif**	These directives conditionally skip sections of code. The skipped sections are not part of the compiled code.
#define and **#undef**	These directives define or undefine symbols in the code.
#warning and **#error**	These directives explicitly generate error or warning messages.
#line	This directive alters the line numbers and source file-names reported by the compiler in warning and error messages.
#region and **#endregion**	These directives mark sections of code. Visual Studio .NET uses these directives to show, hide, and format code.

The following example shows how to define a symbol named in your program:

```
#define MYSYMBOL
```

The following example shows how to use a preprocessor directive to include or exclude code from compilation:

```
#if MYSYMBOL
    // call ThisMethod() only when MYSYMBOL is defined
    ThisMethod();
#else
    // call ThisMethod() only when MYSYMBOL is NOT defined
    InitializeReleaseMode();
#endif
```

Another option for the conditional compilation is the Conditional attribute, which can be used to mark a method for conditional compilation. The Conditional attribute takes one argument that specifies a symbol. If the symbol definition is available, the code of the method is included; otherwise, the code of the method is excluded from the compiled code. For example, the call to the following method executes only if the DEBUG symbol is defined:

```
[Conditional("DEBUG")]
public void DebugMethod()
{
    // Method code goes here
}
```

 A method must have its return type set to void to have the **Conditional** attribute applied to it.

Visual Studio .NET provides two compilation configurations already set up for you: the Debug configuration and the Release configuration. The Debug configuration defines the DEBUG and the TRACE symbols, whereas the Release configuration defines only the TRACE symbol. You can define additional symbols and compilation configurations using the project's Property Pages dialog box in Visual Studio .NET.

Using the Trace and Debug Classes

Tracing in Visual C# .NET can also be done by generating messages about a program's execution with the use of the Debug and Trace classes.

The Debug and Trace classes both belong to the System.Diagnostics namespace and have members with the same names. The members of the Debug class are conditionally compiled only when the DEBUG symbol is defined. On the other hand, members of the Trace class are conditionally compiled only when the TRACE symbol is defined.

Table 13.3 summarizes the members of both the Debug and Trace classes.

Table 13.3	Members of the Debug and Trace Classes	
Member	**Type**	**Description**
Assert()	Method	Checks for a condition and displays a message if the condition is **false**.
AutoFlush	Property	Specifies whether the **Flush()** method should be called on the listeners after every write.
Close()	Method	Flushes the output buffer and then closes the listeners.
Fail()	Method	Displays an error message.
Flush()	Method	Flushes the output buffer and causes the buffered data to be written to the listeners.
Listeners	Property	Specifies the collection of listeners that is monitoring the output generated by the **Trace** and **Debug** classes.
Write()	Method	Writes the given information to the trace listeners in the **Listeners** collection.
WriteIf()	Method	Writes the given information to the trace listeners in the **Listeners** collection only if a condition is **true**.
WriteLine()	Method	Acts the same as the **Write()** method but appends the information with a newline character.
WriteLineIf()	Method	Acts the same as the **WriteIf()** method but appends the information with a newline character.

For example, the following code segment displays the message only when the TRACE symbol is defined and when the expression intFac < 1 evaluates to true:

```
Trace.WriteLineIf(intFac < 1, "There was an overflow");
```

Trace Listeners

Listeners are the classes responsible for forwarding, recording, and displaying the messages generated by the Trace and Debug classes. You can have multiple listeners associated with Trace and Debug classes by adding Listener objects to their Listeners properties.

Both the **Debug** and **Trace** classes share their **Listeners** collections, so an object added to the **Listeners** collection of the **Debug** class is automatically available in the **Trace** class and vice versa.

The `TraceListener` class is an abstract class that belongs to the `System.Diagnostics` namespace and has three implementations:

➤ *DefaultTraceListener class*—An object of this class is automatically added to the `Listeners` collection. Its behavior is to write messages on the Output window.

➤ *TextWriterTraceListener class*—An object of this class writes messages to any class that derives from the `Stream` class that includes the console or a file.

➤ *EventLogTraceListener class*—An object of this class writes messages to the Windows event log.

You can also create a custom listener by inheriting from the `TraceListener` class. When doing so, you must at least implement the `Write()` and `WriteLine()` methods.

Trace Switches

Trace switches are used to control the level of tracing that needs to be done on a program. They can be set via a machinewide (`machine.config`) or applicationwide (`web.config`) configuration files that are Extensible Markup Language (XML) based. The application automatically picks up the changes from the configuration file when it restarts, which is especially useful when the application you are working with is in production mode.

Two predefined classes for creating trace switches are available—the `BooleanSwitch` class and the `TraceSwitch` class. Both of these classes derive from the abstract `Switch` class. You can also define your own trace switch classes by deriving classes from the `Switch` class.

You use the `BooleanSwitch` class to differentiate between two modes of tracing: trace-on or trace-off. Its default value is 0, which corresponds to the trace-off state. If it is set to any non-zero value, it corresponds to the trace-on state.

Unlike `BooleanSwitch`, the `TraceSwitch` class provides five levels of tracing switches. These levels are defined by the `TraceLevel` enumeration and are listed in Table 13.4. The default value of `TraceLevel` for a `TraceSwitch` object is 0 (off).

Table 13.4 The TraceLevel Enumeration		
Enumerated Value	**Integer Value**	**Type of Tracing**
Off	0	None
Error	1	Only error messages
Warning	2	Warning messages and error messages
Info	3	Informational messages, warning messages, and error messages
Verbose	4	Verbose messages, informational messages, warning messages, and error messages

For a **BooleanSwitch** object, if any non-zero (negative or positive) value is specified in the configuration file, the **BooleanSwitch** object's **Enabled** property is set to **true**. For a **TraceSwitch** object, if a value greater than **4** is specified, the **Level** property of the object is set to **TraceLevel.Verbose** (**4**). If a negative value is specified, a **StackOverflowException** exception occurs at runtime.

Take the following steps to learn how to use trace switches in a Web application:

1. Create a new Web application project (Example13_2) with the same user interface as Example13_1.

2. Switch to code view and add the following using directive:

```
using System.Diagnostics;
```

3. Add the following code in the class definition:

```
static TraceSwitch traceSwitch = new TraceSwitch("FactorialTrace",
        "Trace the factorial application");
```

4. Add the following code to the Click event handler of the Calculate Factorial button:

```
private void btnCalculate_Click(object sender, System.EventArgs e)
{
    if (traceSwitch.TraceVerbose)
        // write a debug message
        Debug.WriteLine("Inside Button Click event handler");

    // start indenting messages now
    Debug.Indent();
    int intNumber = Convert.ToInt32(txtNumber.Text);

    if (traceSwitch.TraceError)
    {
        Debug.Assert(intNumber >= 0, "Invalid value",
            "negative value in debug mode");
    }
```

```
        int intFac = 1;
        for (int i = 2; i <= intNumber; i++)
        {
            intFac = intFac * i;
            // write a debug message
            if (traceSwitch.TraceInfo)
                Debug.WriteLine(i, "Factorial Program Debug, Value of i");
        }

        if (traceSwitch.TraceWarning)
            // write a debug message if the condition is true
            Debug.WriteLineIf(intFac < 1, "There was an overflow",
                "Factorial Program Debug");

        lblResult.Text = String.Format(
            "The factorial of {0} is {1}", intNumber, intFac);
        // decrease the indent level
        Debug.Unindent();

        if (traceSwitch.TraceVerbose)
            // write a debug message
            Debug.WriteLine("Done with computations.");
    }
```

5. Open the web.config file of the project; then insert the <system. diagnostics> element in the <configuration> element as shown here:

```
<configuration>
    <system.diagnostics>
        <switches>
            <add name="FactorialTrace" value="4" />
        </switches>
    </system.diagnostics>
    <system.web>
    ...
        </system.web>
</configuration>
```

6. Set the project as the startup project for the solution and run the project using the Debug configuration. Enter a value of 5; note that all messages appear in the Visual Studio .NET Output window. Try again with a negative value and a large value. You see all the errors as well as all the warning messages. Close the form, and then modify the XML file by changing the value of FactorialTrace to 3. You should now see all the messages except the one in the if statement that checks for TraceLevel.Verbose. Repeat the process with the values of FactorialTrace in the configuration file changed to 2, 1, and 0.

7. Modify the program to change all Debug statements to the Trace statements; then run the project using the Release configuration. Change the FactorialTrace switch value to 4 and then repeat the process discussed in step 6.

Debugging

Debugging is the process of finding the causes of errors in a program, locating the lines of code causing those errors, and fixing the errors.

To enable debugging in an ASP.NET application, you need to ensure that the `debug` attribute of the `<compilation>` element in the `web.config` file is set to `true`, like so:

```
<compilation debug="true"/>
```

> **NOTE**
>
> When you deploy your application, be sure that you change the **debug** attribute in the **<compilation>** element in the **web.config** file to **false**. This will improve the application's performance.

Setting Breakpoints and Stepping Through Program Execution

Breakpoints are markers in the code that signal the debugger to pause execution. After the debugger pauses at a breakpoint, you can analyze variables, data records, and other settings in the environment to determine the state of the program.

Follow these steps to learn how to set breakpoints and perform step-by-step execution of a program:

1. Create a new Web application project (`Example13_3`) with the same user interface as `Example13_1`.

2. Switch to code view and add the following `using` directive:

```
using System.Diagnostics;
```

3. Add the following method to the class:

```
private int Factorial(int intNumber)
{
    int intFac = 1;
    for (int i = 2; i <= intNumber; i++)
    {
        intFac = intFac * i;
    }
    return intFac;
}
```

4. Modify the `Click` event handler of `btnCalculate` to the following:

```
private void btnCalculate_Click(object sender, System.EventArgs e)
{
```

```
    int intNumber, intFac;
    try
    {
        intNumber = Convert.ToInt32(txtNumber.Text);
        intFac = Factorial(intNumber);
        lblResult.Text = String.Format
            ("The factorial of {0} is {1}", intNumber, intFac);
    }
    catch(Exception ex)
    {
        Debug.WriteLine(ex.Message);
    }
}
```

5. In the event handler added in step 4, right-click the beginning of the line that makes a call to the `Factorial()` method and select Insert Breakpoint from the context menu. You will note that the line of code is highlighted with red and also that a red dot appears on the left margin. You can alternatively create a breakpoint by clicking the left margin adjacent to a line.

6. Set the project as the startup project for the solution and run the project. Enter a value and click the Calculate Factorial button. Note that execution pauses at the location where you have marked the breakpoint. You should see an arrow on the left margin of the code indicating the next statement to be executed.

7. Select Debug, Step into to step into the code of the `Factorial()` method. Hover the cursor over the various varibles in the `Factorial()` method; you'll see the current values of these variables.

8. Select Debug, Step Out to automatically execute the rest of the `Factorial()` method and restart the step mode in the event handler at the next statement. Step through the execution until you see the form again.

 Breakpoints and other debugging features are available only when you run your project using the Debug configuration.

To set advanced options in a breakpoint, you can choose to create a new breakpoint by selecting the New Breakpoint option from the context menu of the code or from the toolbar in the Breakpoints window. The New Breakpoint dialog box, shown in Figure 13.1, has four tabs. You can use these tabs to set a breakpoint in a method, in a file, at an address in the object code, and when a data value (that is, the value of a variable) changes.

Figure 13.1   The New Breakpoint dialog box enables you to create a new breakpoint.

Clicking the Condition button opens the Breakpoint Condition dialog box, as shown in Figure 13.2.

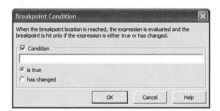

Figure 13.2   The Breakpoint Condition dialog box enables you to set a breakpoint based on the run-time value of an expression.

Clicking the Hit Count button in the New Breakpoint dialog box opens the Breakpoint Hit Count dialog box, shown in Figure 13.3. This dialog box can be especially helpful if you have a breakpoint inside a lengthy loop and want to step-execute the program only near the end of the loop.

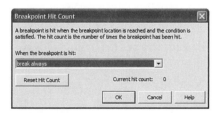

Figure 13.3   The Breakpoint Hit Count dialog box enables you to break the program execution only if the specified breakpoint has been hit a given number of times.

Analyzing Program State to Resolve Errors

When you break the execution of a program, the program is at a particular state in its execution cycle. You can use debugging windows to help you identify the cause of the error you are debugging. Table 13.5 lists the important debugging windows in Visual Studio .NET.

Table 13.5	Important Debugging Windows in Visual Studio .NET
Window	**Description**
Call Stack	Enables you to view the names of methods on the call stack, the parameter types, and their values
This	Enables you to examine the members associated with the current object
Autos	Displays the variables used in the current statement and the previous statement
Locals	Displays the variables local to the current method under execution
Watch	Enables you to evaluate variables and expressions

 You can also perform step-by-step execution of SQL Server Stored Procedures in Visual Studio .NET. To configure a project for SQL Server debugging, access the project properties window. Select the configuration properties for debugging; then in the right pane, under the Debuggers node, select True for Enable SQL Debugging.

Debugging on Exceptions

You can control the way the debugger behaves when it encounters a line of code that throws an exception. You do this through the Exceptions dialog box, which is invoked by selecting Debug, Exceptions.

The two levels at which you can control the behavior of the debugger when it encounters exceptions are as follows:

➤ *When the exception is thrown*—You can instruct the debugger to either continue or break the execution of the program when an exception is thrown.

➤ *If the exception is not handled*—If the program you are debugging fails to handle an exception, you can instruct the debugger to either ignore it and continue or break the execution of the program.

Debugging a Running Process

Visual Studio .NET also enables you to debug the processes running outside the Visual Studio .NET debugging environment. This feature can be helpful for debugging already deployed applications.

When a Web page is requested from the Web server, the ASP.NET worker process (aspnet_wp.exe) serves the request. To debug a running page, you need to attach the Visual Studio .NET debugger to the aspnet_wp.exe process running on the Web server. (You can do so in Visual Studio .NET by selecting Tools, Debug Processes.) In addition, you need to open the source files for the Web page in Visual Studio .NET and set a breakpoint in it at the desired location. After this debugging setup is complete, when you interact with the already running Web page, it will break into the debugger whenever the breakpoint is hit.

When you attach a debugger to the ASP.NET worker process **aspnet_wp.exe**, it freezes the execution of all the other Web applications on that server. This can cause undesirable effects on a production server.

Debugging a Remote Process

The process of debugging a remote process is almost the same as debugging an already running process. The only difference is that, prior to selecting a running process from the Processes dialog box, you need to select the remote machine name. (You can invoke the Processes dialog box by selecting Tools, Debug Processes.)

Before you can remote debug processes, you need to perform a one-time configuration of the remote machine on which the processes are running. To do so, you can use one of the following methods:

➤ Install Visual Studio .NET on the remote machine.

➤ Install the Remote Components Setup on the remote machine. (This can be installed from the Visual Studio .NET Setup Disc 1.)

These methods install the Machine Debug Manager (mdm.exe), which runs as a background service and provides remote debugging support. In addition, these methods add the currently logged-on user to the Debugger Users group; a user must be a member of Debugger Users group to debug. If you want to debug the ASP.NET worker process, you must also have administrative privileges (that is, you should be a member of the Administrators group) on the remote machine.

If you get a DCOM configuration error while debugging, you might not be a member of the Debugger Users group on the remote machine. The local computer and the remote computer must be members of a trusted domain for remote debugging to be possible.

For a different configuration or requirement, you refer to the "Setting Up Remote Debugging" topic in the Visual Studio .NET Combined Help Collection.

Debugging the Code in DLL Files

The process of debugging a DLL file is similar to debugging a Web form. There is one difference, though; the code in a DLL file cannot be directly invoked, so you need to have a Web form that calls various methods from the DLL files.

You typically need to perform the following steps for debugging code in a DLL file:

1. Launch the Web form that uses the methods in the DLL file.

2. Launch Visual Studio .NET and attach the debugger on the Web form. Set a breakpoint where the method in the DLL file is called; then continue with the execution.

3. The execution breaks when the breakpoint is reached. At this point, select Debug, Step into to step into the source code of the DLL file. Execute the code in the DLL file in Step mode while you watch the value of its variables.

Debugging Client-Side Scripts

Visual Studio .NET also enables you to debug client-side scripts. The process is similar to the process discussed earlier for ASP.NET Web forms. However, you must note the following points for client-side scripting:

➤ Client-side debugging works only with Microsoft Internet Explorer.

➤ You have to enable script debugging in Internet Explorer. To do this, select Tools, Internet Options. Then select the Advanced tab and uncheck the Disable Script Debugging option in the Browsing section.

➤ Attach the debugger to the `iexplore.exe` process displaying the Web form. This is required only if you are debugging an already running process. While attaching the process, in the Attach to Process dialog box, select the Script option.

To configure a project for debugging ASP code, access the project properties window. Select the configuration properties for debugging; then in the right pane, under the Debuggers node, select True for Enable ASP Debugging.

Exam Prep Questions

Question 1

> You want to view the trace output for your Web application. The Web application root directory is at **http://localhost/myapplication**. Which of the following URLs would you type in Internet Explorer to view the trace results for this application?
>
> ○ A. **http://localhost/myapplication?trace=true**
> ○ B. **http://localhost/myapplication/trace**
> ○ C. **http://localhost/myapplication?trace=ON**
> ○ D. **http://localhost/myapplication/trace.axd**

The correct answer is D. You can view the trace results by requesting trace.axd from the application directory. Answers A, B, and C are incorrect because these URLs do not reveal trace results for an application.

Question 2

> While debugging your ASP.NET Web form, you want to display the trace messages as part of the page execution details. Which of the following methods should you use? (Select two.)
>
> ❑ A. **TraceContext.Write()**
> ❑ B. **TraceContext.Warn()**
> ❑ C. **System.Diagnostics.Trace.Write()**
> ❑ D. **System.Diagnostics.Debug.Write()**

The correct answers are A and B. The trace messages written using the TraceContext.Write() and TraceContext.Warn() methods can append trace messages to other tracing information in the page output. Answers C and D are incorrect because the trace messages written using the Trace.Write() and Debug.Write() methods of the System.Diagnostics namespace are written to the Output window of Visual Studio .NET by default.

Question 3

You have added the following statement to the **Load** event handler of a single-page Web application:

```
Trace.Listeners.Add(new TextWriterTraceListener
("TraceLog.txt"))
```

Which of the following statements are true with respect to program execution? (Select all that apply.)

❑ A. **TextWriterTraceListner** will listen to all messages generated by the methods of the **Debug** and **Trace** classes.

❑ B. **TextWriterTraceListner** will listen to only the messages generated by the methods of the **Trace** classes.

❑ C. All the trace messages will be stored in a file named **TraceLog.txt**.

❑ D. The trace messages are displayed in the Output window while running the program in either the Debug or Release configuration.

The correct answers are A, C, and D. When the new listener is added to the Trace class, it is also added to the Listeners collection. The Listeners collection already has a DefaultTraceListener object that sends messages to the Output window. Therefore, you have messages in TraceLog.txt as well as in the Output window. Answer B is incorrect because, when you add a listener to the Trace.Listeners collection, it listens to the messages generated by both the Trace and Debug classes.

Question 4

You are asked to implement tracing in a Web application such that the application should display both warning and error messages when the application is run using the Debug configuration and should display only an error message when it is run using the Release configuration of Visual C# .NET. Which of the following code segments best solves this requirement?

○ A.

```
TraceSwitch traceSwitch = new TraceSwitch(
    "MySwitch", "Error and Warning Switch");

#if DEBUG
    traceSwitch.Level = TraceLevel.Warning;
#else
    traceSwitch.Level = TraceLevel.Error;
#endif

Trace.WriteLineIf(traceSwitch.TraceWarning,
"Warning Message");
Trace.WriteLineIf(traceSwitch.TraceError,
"Error Message");
```

○ B.

```
TraceSwitch traceSwitch = new TraceSwitch(
    "MySwitch", "Error and Warning Switch");
#if DEBUG
    traceSwitch.Level = TraceLevel.Warning;
#else
    traceSwitch.Level = TraceLevel.Error;
#endif

Debug.WriteLineIf(traceSwitch.TraceWarning,
"Warning Message");
Debug.WriteLineIf(traceSwitch.TraceError,
"Error Message");
```

○ C.

```
TraceSwitch traceSwitch = new TraceSwitch(
    "MySwitch", "Error and Warning Switch");

#if TRACE
    traceSwitch.Level = TraceLevel.Warning;
#else
    traceSwitch.Level = TraceLevel.Error;
#endif

Trace.WriteLineIf(traceSwitch.TraceWarning,
"Warning Message");
Trace.WriteLineIf(traceSwitch.TraceError,
"Error Message");
```

⭘ D.

```
TraceSwitch traceSwitch = new TraceSwitch(
    "MySwitch", "Error and
    Warning Switch");

#if TRACE
    traceSwitch.Level = TraceLevel.Error;
#else
    traceSwitch.Level = TraceLevel.Warning;
#endif

Trace.WriteLineIf(traceSwitch.TraceWarning,
"Warning Message");
Trace.WriteLineIf(traceSwitch.TraceError,
"Error Message");
```

The correct answer is A. Because the DEBUG symbol is defined in the Debug configuration, the Level property of traceSwitch is set to TraceLevel.Warning. This causes both the TraceWarning and TraceError properties of the TraceSwitch object to evaluate to true, resulting in both of the messages being displayed. In the Release configuration where only the TRACE symbol is defined, the Level property of traceSwitch is set to TraceLevel.Error. This causes the TraceWarning property to return a false value and the TraceError property to return a true value, so only the error messages is displayed. Answer B is incorrect because the Debug class is used to generate the output and therefore no messages is displayed in the Release configuration. Answer C is incorrect because it does the reverse by displaying warning and error messages in the Release configuration and only warning messages in the Debug configuration. Answer D is incorrect because the TRACE symbol is defined in both the Debug and Release configurations, resulting in the display of only error messages for both the Debug and Release configurations.

Question 5

You are developing an ASP.NET Web application, and your application's web.config file has the following code:

```
<system.diagnostics>
    <switches>
        <add name="TraceLevelSwitch" value="3" />
    </switches>
</system.diagnostics>
```

You have written the following tracing code in your program:

```
static TraceSwitch traceSwitch = new TraceSwitch(
    "TraceLevelSwitch", "Trace the application");

[Conditional("DEBUG")]
private void Method1()
{
  Trace.WriteLineIf(traceSwitch.TraceError, "Message 1",
  "Message 2");
}

[Conditional("TRACE")]
private void Method2()
{
    Trace.WriteLine("Message 3");
}

private void btnCalculate_Click(object sender,
System.EventArgs e)
{
    if(traceSwitch.TraceWarning){
        Trace.WriteLine("Message 10");
        Method1();
    }
    else{
        Trace.WriteLineIf(traceSwitch.TraceInfo,
        "Message 20");
        Method2();
    }

    if (traceSwitch.TraceError)
        Trace.WriteLineIf(traceSwitch.TraceInfo,
        "Message 30");
        Trace.WriteLineIf(traceSwitch.TraceVerbose,
        "Message 40");
}
```

Which tracing output will be generated when you run your program in debug mode and click the btnCalculate button?

○ A.

```
Message 10
Message 1
Message 2
Message 30
```

○ B.

```
Message 10
Message 2: Message 1
Message 30
```

○ C.

```
Message 10
Message 2
Message 30
Message 40
```

○ D.

```
Message 20
Message 3
Message 30
Message 40
```

The correct answer is B. The value for the TraceLevelSwitch is 3, which causes the Level property to be set to TraceLevel.Info. This causes the TraceError, TraceWarning, and TraceInfo properties of the traceSwitch to be true; only the TraceVerbose property evaluates to false. Answer A is incorrect because the third parameter of the WriteLineIf() method in the Method1() is used to categorize the output by specifying its value, followed by a colon (:) and then the trace message. Answers C and D are incorrect because the TraceVerbose property evaluates to false, so the string Message 40 will never be displayed.

Question 6

You have following segment of code in your program:

```
EventLogTraceListener traceListener =
    new EventLogTraceListener("TraceLog");

Trace.Listeners.Add(traceListener);
Debug.Listeners.Add(traceListener);

Trace.WriteLine("Sample Message");
Debug.WriteLine("Sample Message");
```

When you debug the program through Visual Studio .NET, how many times would the message **Sample Message** be written to the **TraceLog**?

○ A. 1

○ B. 2

○ C. 3

○ D. 4

The correct answer is D. The message SampleMessage will be written four times. In this question, two instances of EventLogTraceListeners are added to the Listeners collection. Therefore, any message generated by the Trace and Debug classes will be listened to twice because they share the same Listeners collection. Because the program is running in Debug mode, both the Trace and Debug statements will be executed. The net effect is that the messages written by the Trace.WriteLine() and Debug.WriteLine() methods will be both written twice, making four entries in the trace log. Therefore, answers A, B, and C are incorrect.

Question 7

You are debugging a Web form that involves long calculation and iterations. You want to break into the code to watch the values of variables whenever the value of **intValue** changes in the following statement:

```
intValue = ProcessValue(intValue);
```

Which of the following options will quickly allow you to achieve this?

- ○ A. Run the application using step execution mode. Then use the Step Out key to step out of the execution from the **ProcessValue()** method. Use the Immediate window to display the value of **intValue** before and after this line of code executes.

- ○ B. Set a breakpoint at the given statement and set the Hit Count option Break when Hitcount Is Equal to 1.

- ○ C. Set the breakpoint at the given statement. In the Breakpoint Condition dialog box, enter **intValue != intValue** and check the Is True option.

- ○ D. Set the breakpoint at the given statement. In the Breakpoint Condition dialog box, enter **intValue** and check the Has Changed option.

The correct answer is D. When you want to break into the code when the value of a variable changes, the quickest approach is to set a conditional breakpoint and check the Has Changed option. Answer A is incorrect because this solution requires you to constantly monitor the values of the variables. Answer B is incorrect because the hit count counts only the number of times a statement has been executed. Answer C is incorrect because an inequality comparison of a variable with itself always results in a false value and therefore the breakpoint will never be hit.

Question 8

Which of the following statements are true for remote debugging of processes? (Select all that apply.)

❑ A. Both the local as well as the remote machine should have Visual Studio .NET installed.

❑ B. Only the local machine needs Visual Studio .NET.

❑ C. Remote Components Setup is required on the local machine.

❑ D. Remote Components Setup is required on the remote machine.

The correct answers are B and D. You need to have Visual Studio .NET on the local machine to debug the remote processes. In addition, you need to run a Remote Components Setup on the remote machine. Answer A is incorrect because, for remote debugging, Visual Studio .NET is not required on the remote machine. Answer C is incorrect because, for remote debugging, Remote Components Setup is not required on the local machine.

Question 9

While you are debugging in Visual Studio .NET, you want to watch only the values of those variables you are using in the current statement and its previous statement. Which of the following debugger windows is the easiest way to watch these variables?

○ A. Autos

○ B. Locals

○ C. This

○ D. Watch

The correct answer is A. The Autos window gives you the most convenient access because it automatically displays the names and values of all the variables in the current statement and the previous statement at every step. Answer B is incorrect because the Locals window displays the value of all the local variables in the current scope. Answer C is incorrect because the This window displays only the data members of the object associated with the current method. Answer D is incorrect because the Watch window displays only the value of the selected variables and expressions.

Question 10

You have been developing a Web application for an airline's ticketing system. The Web form in the Web application also has some client-side scripting code written in JavaScript. You want to step through this code to understand its execution. Which of the following steps would you take? (Select three.)

❏ A. Set a breakpoint in the client-side scripting code where you want the application to pause execution.

❏ B. Attach the debugger to the **aspnet_wp.exe** process executing the Web form.

❏ C. Attach the debugger to the **iexplore.exe** process displaying the Web form.

❏ D. Enable script debugging in Internet Explorer.

The correct answers are A, C, and D. To enable client-side script debugging, you need to set a breakpoint in the client-side script. In addition to this, you must attach the debugger to the `iexplore.exe` process running the Web form and enable script debugging in Internet Explorer. Answer B is incorrect because client-side scripts execute inside a browser on the client and not on the server.

Need to Know More?

 Kalani, Amit. *MCAD/MCSD Developing and Implementing Web Applications with Visual C# .NET and Visual Studio .NET.* Indianapolis, IN: Que Certification, 2002.

 Review the Microsoft support article titled "Common Errors When You Debug ASP.NET Applications in Visual Studio .NET" at `http://support.microsoft.com/default.aspx?scid=kb;` `en-us;306172`.

 Read the MSDN guide on production debugging for Microsoft .NET Framework applications at `http://www.microsoft.com/` `downloads/release.asp?ReleaseID=45155`.

Deploying a Web Application

Terms you'll need to understand:

✓ Delay signing
✓ Deployment
✓ Global assembly cache
✓ Merge module
✓ Shared assembly

Techniques you'll need to master:

✓ Creating a setup program that installs a Web application and enables the application to be uninstalled
✓ Adding assemblies to the global assembly cache
✓ Planning the deployment of a Web application
✓ Understanding when you should choose to create a Web setup project versus a merge module project

This chapter discusses how to use Visual Studio .NET to create Windows Installer-based Web setup and deployment projects. This chapter also talks about various ways in which an application can be deployed.

Deployment Tools

The .NET Framework simplifies application deployment by making zero-impact installation and xcopy/FTP deployment feasible. You can install a .NET application that uses only managed code and private assemblies by simply copying all the necessary files to the desired destination. No Registry entries need to be created, and no files need to be copied to the Windows system directory (thereby causing zero impact on the configuration of the target machine).

However, some installation tasks, such as those listed here, are difficult or impossible to achieve with xcopy or FTP:

➤ Creating IIS sites or virtual directories

➤ Copying files to relative paths on the target machine that differ from the paths on the source machine

➤ Adding assemblies to the GAC

➤ Creating or configuring databases during the installation

➤ Adding custom event logs or performance counters to the target machine

➤ Checking whether the .NET Framework is installed on the target machine

➤ Allowing license key management and user registration

For these scenarios, the preferred alternative is to use a Microsoft Windows Installer-based installation program. Microsoft's Windows Installer is an installation and configuration service built in to the Windows operating system. It gives you complete control over the installation of an application, a component, or an update.

Deploying a Web Application

Microsoft Visual Studio .NET offers four types of deployment project templates:

➤ *Setup project*—Used to create installation packages for deploying Windows-based applications

➤ *Web setup project*—Used to create installation packages for deploying Web-based applications

➤ *Merge module project*—Used to create installation packages for components that can be shared by multiple applications

➤ *Cab project*—Used to package ActiveX components so they can be downloaded over the Internet

Creating a Web Application for Deployment

Before we delve into the details of creating deployment projects with the help of Visual Studio .NET, you need to create an application that can be deployed. Perform the following steps to create a simple Web application named WebSqlApp that returns the result of any SELECT query from the SQL Server Northwind database. Do the following:

1. Open Visual Studio .NET and create a new blank solution named 315C14 at c:\inetpub\wwwroot\ExamCram. (You might need to change the directory based on your configuration.)

2. Add a new Visual C# ASP.NET Web Application project at the following location: http://localhost/ExamCram/315C14/WebSqlApp.

3. Use Server Explorer to create a data connection to the SQL Server Northwind database. Drag and drop the data connection on the Web form to create a SqlConnection object (sqlConnection1).

4. Place a TextBox control (txtQuery), a Button control (btnExecute), a Label control (lblError), and a DataGrid control (dgResults) on the form. Set the TextMode property of the txtQuery control to MultiLine. Set the Visible property of the lblError control to false.

5. Switch to Code view and add the following line to the using directive:

   ```
   using System.Data.SqlClient;
   ```

6. Enter this code to the event handler of the `btnExecute` control:

```
private void btnExecute_Click(object sender, System.EventArgs e)
{
    SqlCommand cmd = sqlConnection1.CreateCommand();
    cmd.CommandType = CommandType.Text;
    cmd.CommandText = txtQuery.Text;
    SqlDataAdapter da = new SqlDataAdapter();
    da.SelectCommand = cmd;
    DataSet ds = new DataSet();
    try
    {
        da.Fill(ds, "Results");
        dgResults.DataSource = ds;
        dgResults.DataMember = "Results";
        dgResults.DataBind();
    }
    catch (Exception ex)
    {
        lblError.Text = "Error executing query: " + ex.Message;
        lblError.Visible = true;
    }
}
```

7. Change the solution configuration to Release mode and run the solution.

Creating a Web Setup Project

Visual Studio .NET also has a Setup Wizard that helps you interactively create various types of setup and deployment projects. Follow these steps to learn how to use the Setup Wizard to create a simple installer for the `WebSqlApp` application:

1. In the Solution Explorer, right-click Solution and select Add, New Project. Select Setup and Deployment Projects from the Project Types tree; then select Setup Wizard from the list of templates.

2. Name the project `WebSqlSetup`. Click OK, which launches the Setup Wizard. The first screen that appears is the Welcome screen; click Next.

3. The second screen asks you to choose a project type. Select Create a Setup for a Web Application. Then click Next.

4. The third screen of the wizard enables you to choose the project outputs to include in the setup package. Select Primary Output from `WebSqlApp` and Content Files from `WebSqlApp`. Click Next.

5. Open WordPad and create two files: `ReadMe.rtf` and `License.rtf`. Save these files after writing some sample text. The fourth screen of the wizard enables you to choose the files to include in the setup package. Click the Add button and include the ReadMe.rtf and License.rtf files. Click Next.

6. The fifth and last screen of the wizard is the Project Summary screen. Click Finish to create the project.

7. Activate the Properties window for the WebSqlSetup project. Set the manufacturer to WebSql Software, the product name to WebSql, and the title to WebSql Installer.

8. Right-click the WebSqlSetup project in the Solution Explorer and select View, File System. This opens the File System Editor. Select the Web Application Folder node in the File System Editor and change its VirtualDirectory property to WebSql.

9. Set the solution configuration to Release, and then build the WebSqlSetup project. Open Windows Explorer and navigate to the Release folder inside the project folder. Run the setup.exe file. Alternatively, on the development machine, you can install the application by right-clicking the project in the Solution Explorer and selecting the Install option from its context menu. This opens the WebSql Setup Wizard. Accept the default values and complete the installation.

10. Open Internet Explorer and navigate to http://localhost/ExamCram/315C14/WebSql/WebForm1.aspx. Enter a query and click the button to get the results of the query.

11. Select Control Panel, Add or Remove Programs from the Windows Start menu to open the Add or Remove Programs dialog box. Select the WebSql application and click the Remove button to uninstall it. The WebSql application is uninstalled from your computer. Alternatively, on the development machine, you can uninstall it by right-clicking the setup project in the Solution Explorer and selecting the Uninstall option from its context menu.

This setup project works only on the computers on which the .NET Framework runtime has been already installed. For more information on how to redistribute the .NET Framework 1.1 with your application, refer to www.msdn.com/library/en-us/dnnetdep/html/redistdeploy1_1.asp. For more information on how to redistribute the .NET Framework 1.0 with your applications, refer to www.msdn.com/library/en-us/dnnetdep/html/redistdeploy.asp.

You can modify the configuration settings for a Web setup project by selecting the project in the Solution Explorer and selecting Project, Properties from the main menu. This opens the Project Property Pages dialog box, as shown in Figure 14.1.

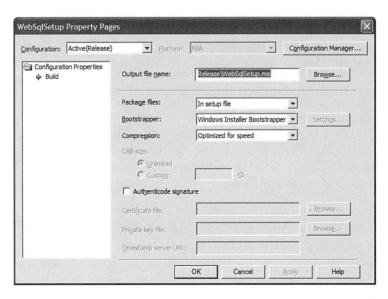

Figure 14.1 The Property Pages dialog box displays the configuration properties of the Web Setup project.

This dialog box has five main configuration properties:

➤ *Output File Name*—Specifies the output filename of the installation package (the .msi file).

➤ *Package Files*—Specifies how to package the files. The options are As Loose Uncompressed Files, In Setup File, and In Cabinet File(s). If the In Cabinet File(s) option is selected, you can also specify the maximum size of the CAB files.

➤ *Bootstrapper*—Specifies whether a Windows Installer bootstrap file needs to be created for launching the installation program.

➤ *Compression*—Specifies whether to optimize the installation files for size or speed or if no optimization is required.

➤ *Authenticode Signature*—Enables you to specify the file containing the Authenticode certificate, private key file, and timestamp server URL (which is provided by the certification authority).

Customizing Web Setup Projects

You might want an installation program to provide custom features and perform custom actions, such as creating Registry entries and providing a customized user interface for installation. Visual Studio .NET provides various editors to customize the installation process, as shown in Figure 14.2.

Figure 14.2   You can launch various editors for a Web setup project via the Solution Explorer.

The File System Editor

The File System Editor specifies where the project output and other files will be installed on the target computer. The File System Editor provides a mapping of the file system on the target machine. For example, at the time of installation, the special folder Web Application Folder is converted to the actual path of the Web application on the target machine.

The Registry Editor

The Registry Editor enables you to specify Registry keys, subkeys, and values that are added to the Registry in the target machine during installation. You can also import Registry files to the Registry Editor.

The File Types Editor

The File Types Editor enables you to associate file extensions and actions with an application.

Using the User Interface Editor

The User Interface Editor enables you to customize the user interface provided during the installation process. The user interface is divided into three stages—start, progress, and end. You can add different types of dialog boxes for each stage, but each stage enables only certain types of dialog boxes to be added.

The User Interface Editor displays the user interface applicable to both the end user and the administrative installations. You can customize the user interface for both of these types of installations. The administrative installation occurs when you run the msiexec command-line tool with the /a option.

Using the Custom Actions Editor

The Custom Actions Editor enables you to run compiled DLL or EXE files, script files, or assemblies at the end of an installation. These files can be used to perform vital custom actions that were not carried out during installation. If the custom action fails, the entire installation process is rolled back. For example, you might have to install the database that is required by your application during the installation process.

The four phases in which custom actions can be performed are install, commit, rollback, and uninstall. Follow these steps to create a simple custom action that launches the WebSqlApp application toward the end of the installation:

1. Add a new, Visual C# Project (LaunchWebSql), based on the Empty Project template, to the solution. Add a new class file (LaunchWebSql.cs) to the project.

2. Modify the class definition as shown here and build the LaunchWebSql project:

```
using System;
using System.Diagnostics;
public class LaunchWebSql
{
  public static void Main(string[] args)
  {
    // Start the process by passing the filename and argument
    Process.Start("iexplore", "http://localhost/ExamCram/315C14/
    WebSqlApp/WebForm1.aspx");
  }
}
```

3. In the Solution Explorer, right-click the WebSqlSetup project and select Add, Project Output from the context menu. This opens the Add

Project Output Group dialog box. Select LaunchWebSql as the project, and select Primary Output from the list box. Click OK.

4. Open the Custom Actions Editor for the WebSqlSetup project. Select the Install node under the Custom Actions node; then select Action, Add Custom Action. This opens the Select Item in Project dialog box. Navigate to the Web Application folder and select Primary Output from LaunchWebSql (Active). Rename the action LaunchWebSql.

5. Select the custom action LaunchWebSql and open the Properties window. Set the InstallerClass property to false.

6. Build the WebSqlSetup project and install the Web application. The WebSqlApp application will be launched after the installation process is completed.

The previous example uses the static Process.Start() method to launch Internet Explorer with the given URL. You also set the InstallerClass property to false because the LaunchWebSql class did not inherit from the Installer class. The .NET Framework supplies the Installer class to provide a base for custom installations.

Using the Launch Conditions Editor

The Launch Conditions Editor enables you to set conditions to be evaluated when the installation begins on the target machine. If the conditions are not met, the installation stops.

The Launch Conditions Editor enables you to perform searches on the target machine for a file, a Registry key, or Windows Installer components. For example, you could add a condition that Microsoft Data Access Components (MDAC) version 2.7 or higher should be installed for the installation to continue.

Shared Assemblies

A shared assembly is shared among multiple applications on a machine. It is therefore stored in a central location called the global assembly cache (GAC) and enjoys special services such as file security, shared location, and side-by-side versioning.

Assigning a Strong Name to an Assembly

An assembly is identified by its text name (usually the name of the file without the file extension), version number, and culture information. A strong name strengthens an assembly's identity by qualifying it with the software publisher's identity. The .NET Framework uses a standard cryptography technique known as *digital signing* to ensure the uniqueness of an assembly.

The process of digital signing involves two related pieces of binary data: a public key and a private key. The *public* key is stored in the assembly manifest, along with other identification information such as the name, version number, and culture of the assembly. To verify that only the legitimate owner of the public key has created the assembly, an assembly is signed using the publisher's private key. The *private* key is assumed to be known only to the publisher of the assembly.

You can generate public/private key pairs using the Strong Name tool (`sn.exe`), which is available in the .NET Framework SDK. For example, the following command creates a pair of public/private keys, both of which are created and stored in a file named `RandNumCorpKeys.snk`:

```
sn -k RandNumCorpKeys.snk
```

Copy this strong name key file to the root directory of the solution, where you will use it for creating strong names for the assemblies. Follow these steps to learn how to create a strong named assembly:

1. Create a new Visual C# .NET Class Library project to the current solution; name it **RandomNumber**.

2. Delete the default `Class1.cs` file. Add a new `Component` class (`RandomNumber.cs`) to the project and add the following code to the `RandomNumber` class:

```
//stores minValue and maxValue
private int minValue=1, maxValue=100;
public int MinValue
{
    get{
        return minValue;
    }
    set{
        minValue = value;
    }
}

public int MaxValue
{
    get{
        return maxValue;
    }
```

```
        set{
            maxValue = value;
        }
    }
    public int GetNext()
    {
        Random r = new Random();
        return r.Next(minValue, maxValue);
    }
```

3. Open the `AssemblyInfo.cs` file. Scroll down in the file and change the `AssemblyVersion` and `AssemblyKeyFile` attributes as shown here:

```
[assembly: AssemblyVersion("1.0")]
[assembly: AssemblyKeyFile(@"..\..\..\RandNumCorpKeys.snk")]
```

4. Build the project. A `RandomNumber.dll` file is generated, and a strong name is assigned to the file based on the specified key file.

In the previous example, you used Visual Studio .NET to attach a strong name to an assembly. If you want to do this manually, you can use the Assembly Linker tool (`al.exe`) with the `-keyfile` option.

Adding an Assembly to the GAC

After you have associated a strong name with an assembly, you can place it in the GAC in several ways, including these:

➤ *Windows Installer*—Microsoft Windows Installer is the preferred way of adding assemblies to the GAC. Windows Installer maintains a reference count for assemblies in the GAC and provides uninstallation support.

➤ *Windows Explorer*—You can open the assembly cache folder (`c:\windows\assembly`, where `c:\windows` is the Windows installation directory) and add an assembly through the drag-and-drop method.

➤ *The .NET Framework Configuration tool*—You can also use the .NET Framework Configuration tool (`mscorcfg.msc`) to add or remove an assembly in the GAC. This tool also helps you configure assemblies and manage their runtime security policies.

➤ *The Global Assembly Cache tool*—The Global Assembly Cache tool (`gacutil.exe`) is a command-line tool that is especially useful for adding and removing assemblies from the GAC via a program script or batch file. To install an assembly, you use the option `/i`, as shown here:

```
gacutil /i RandomNumber.dll
```

To uninstall the assembly, you use the option /u, as shown here:

```
gacutil /u RandomNumber.dll
```

You can also choose to uninstall from the GAC an assembly of a specific version and specific culture by specifying its version, culture, and public key, along with the name of the assembly, like so:

```
gacutil /u RandomNumber,Version=1.0.0.0,
➥Culture=neutral,PublicKeyToken=f26af4dbb33881b1
```

 You need to have administrative privileges on a computer to manage its GAC.

After you have added the RandomNumber.dll to the GAC using any of the methods mentioned previously, perform the following steps to create a Web application that, when executed, loads the component installed in the GAC:

1. Add a new Visual C# ASP.NET Web Application project (RandomNumberApp) to the solution.

2. Use the Add Reference dialog box to add a reference to RandomNumber.dll. Set the Copy Local property of the RandomNumber.dll file to false.

3. Customize the Visual Studio .NET Toolbox to add an icon for the .NET Framework component, RandomNumber.dll.

4. Drag the RandomNumber component from the toolbox and drop it on the form. Change its MaxValue property to 1000 and change its MinValue property to 500.

5. Add a Label control (lblResult) and a Button control (btnGetRandom) to the form. Set the Button control's Text property to Get a Random Number. Then double-click the Button control to add an event handler for its Click event. Add the following code to the event handler:

```
private void btnGetRandom_Click(object sender, System.EventArgs e)
{
    lblResult.Text = String.Format("The next random number is: {0}",
        randomNumber1.GetNext());
}
```

6. Set the project as the startup project and run the application. Click the button and you get a random number between 500 and 1,000 every time you click the button.

In the previous example, the `RandomNumber.dll` assembly is not locally copied to the bin directory of the Web application. Instead, the application loads the assembly from the GAC.

Delay Signing an Assembly

In most companies, the private key is stored securely and only a few people have access to it.

The .NET Framework supports the delay signing technique for developments in such scenarios.

With delay signing, you use only the public key to build an assembly. Associating public keys with an assembly enables you to place the assembly in the GAC and complete most of the development and testing tasks with the assembly. Later, when you are ready to package the assembly, someone who is authorized signs the assembly with the private key. The following list summarizes the various steps involved with delay signing:

1. *Extract a public key from the public/private key pair*—To extract the public key from a file that is storing the public/private key pair, you use the Strong Name tool as follows:

   ```
   sn.exe -p RandNumCorpKeys.snk RandNumCorpPublicKey.snk
   ```

2. *Delay sign an assembly using Visual Studio .NET*—To use delay signing in a Visual Studio .NET project, you need to modify the following two attributes of the project's `AssemblyInfo.cs` file and build the assembly:

   ```
   [assembly: AssemblyDelaySign(true)]
   [assembly: AssemblyKeyFile("RandNumCorpPublicKey.snk")]
   ```

3. *Turn off verification for an assembly in the GAC*—By default, the GAC verifies the strong name of each assembly. If the assembly is not signed using the private key, this verification fails. You can relax this verification for an assembly by issuing the following command:

   ```
   sn.exe -Vr RandomNumber.dll
   ```

   If you execute this command, the GAC always skips the verification for this assembly in the future.

4. *Sign a delay-signed assembly with the private key*—When you are ready to deploy a delay-signed assembly, you need to sign it with the company's private key, like so:

   ```
   sn.exe -R RandomNumber.dll RandNumCorpKeys.snk
   ```

5. *Turn on verification for an assembly in the GAC*—Finally, you can instruct the GAC to turn on verification for an assembly by issuing the following command:

```
sn.exe -Vu RandomNumber.dll
```

Delay Signing Using the Assembly Linker Tool

While generating an assembly, you can also instruct the Assembly Linker tool to sign or delay sign an assembly with the given public/private key file. When you use al.exe for delay signing, you use the arguments listed in Table 14.1 with the command.

Table 14.1 Arguments Passed to al.exe for Delay Signing	
Argument	**Description**
<sourcefiles>	You replace *<sourcefiles>* with the names of one or more complied modules that will be the parts of the resulting assembly.
/delay[sign][+l-]	You can use either the **delay** argument or the **delay[sign]** argument for delay signing. The **+** option is used to delay sign the assembly by storing just the public key manifest in the assembly manifest. The **−** option is used to fully sign an assembly by using both the public and private keys. If you do not use either **+** or **-**, the default value of **−** is assumed.
/keyf[ile]:*<filename>*	You can use either **keyf** or **keyfile** to specify the key file. You replace *<filename>* with the name of the file that stores the key(s).
/out:*<filename>*	You replace *<filename>* with the desired name of the output assembly file.

Assume that you want to create an assembly by linking two modules, Sample1.netmodule and Sample2.netmodule. The public key file is SamplePublicKey.snk, and the desired output assembly is SignedSample.exe. You would use the al.exe command as follows:

```
al.exe Sample1.netmodule,Sample2.netmodule /delaysign+
➥/keyfile:SamplePublicKey.snk /out:SignedSample.exe
```

An assembly signed with a strong name does not automatically assert a company's identity, such as its name. For that purpose, you can use an authenticode signature, in which case the company's identity is asserted by a third-party certification authority (such as Verisign or Thawte). You can use the File Signing tool (**signcode.exe**) to attach an authenticode signature to the assembly.

An important thing to know is the order of commands when signing an assembly using both **sn.exe** and **signcode.exe**. You must sign your assembly with the Strong Name tool (**sn.exe**) before you sign it with the File Signing tool (**signcode.exe**).

Creating a Merge Module Project

The process of packaging a component is different from the process of packaging Web applications. When you have a component such as RandomNumber that will be shared among multiple applications, you should package it as a merge module (.msm file). A merge module includes the actual component, such as a DLL, along with any related setup logic, such as adding resources, Registry entries, custom actions, and launch conditions. Merge modules cannot be directly installed—they need to be merged with the installation program of an application that uses the shared component and packaged into a merge module.

Follow these steps to learn how to create a merge module to package a component:

1. In the Solution Explorer, right-click Solution and select Add, New Project. Select Setup and Deployment Projects from the Project Types tree, and then select Setup Wizard from the list of templates on the right. Name the project **RandomNumberMergeModule.**

2. Bypass the first screen of the wizard. The second screen is the Choose a Project Type screen. Select Create a Merge Module for Windows Installer as an answer to the second question Do you want to create a Redistributable Package?. Click Next.

3. The third screen of the wizard is the Choose Project Outputs to Include screen. Select Primary Output from RandomNumber and click Finish.

4. In the File System Editor, add a new folder named **RandNumCorp** to the Common Files Folder. Move the Primary Output from RandomNumber (Active) file in the Common Files Folder to the RandNumCorp folder.

5. Select the File System on Target Machine node and select Add Special Folder, Global Assembly Cache Folder from the context menu.

6. Select the Global Assembly Cache folder and select Add, Project Output from the context menu. The Add Project Output Group dialog box appears. Select the RandomNumber project, and select Primary Output from the list of items to be added. Then click OK.

7. Build the `RandomNumberMergeModule` project. Open Windows Explorer and navigate to the `Release` folder for the project. Notice that the `RandomNumberMergeModule.msm` merge module has been created.

If you later want to distribute the `RandomNumber` component with a Web application, you can just add the merge module created in the previous example to the Web application's setup project.

Creating Installation Components

The .NET Framework provides the `Installer` class, which is defined in the `System.Configuration.Install` namespace. This class is specifically designed to help you perform customized installation actions.

Understanding the **Installer** Class

The `System.Configuration.Install.Installer` class works as a base class for all the custom installers in the .NET Framework. Some of the important members of the `Installer` class are listed in Table 14.2.

Table 14.2	Important Members of the **Installer** Class	
Member Name	**Type**	**Description**
Commit()	Method	Executes if the **Install()** method executes successfully
Install()	Method	Performs the specified actions during an application's installation
Installers	Property	Specifies a collection of **Installer** objects that are needed for this **Installer** instance to successfully install a component
Rollback()	Method	Is called if the **Install()** method fails for some reason to undo any custom actions performed during the **Install()** method
Uninstall()	Method	Performs the specified actions when a previously installed application is uninstalled

You can derive a class from the `Installer` class and override the methods listed in Table 14.2 to perform any custom actions.

If you want the derived `Installer` class to execute when an assembly is installed by using a Web setup project or the Installer tool (`installutil.exe`), you need to apply the RunInstaller attribute on the class and set its value to true, like so:

```
[RunInstaller(true)]
```

The Installer classes provide the infrastructure for making installation a transactional process. If an error is encountered during the Install() method, the Rollback() method tracks back all the changes and undoes them, leaving the machine in the clean state it was in before the installation process started.

Working with Predefined Installation Components

Most of the components available through Server Explorer have predefined installation components associated with them. For example, when you click the Add Installer link for an EventLog component, a ProjectInstaller class is created in the project and the installation component for the EventLog component is added to this class (see Figure 14.3). If you add more installation components (for example, a PerformanceCounter installation component) to this project, they are all added to this ProjectInstaller class. These installation components are actually added to the Installers collection of the ProjectInstaller class.

Figure 14.3   The Add Installer Link adds a predefined installation component to your project.

When you compile the project to build an EXE or a DLL file, the ProjectInstaller class is part of the output assembly.

Deploying an Assembly That Contains the Installation Components

You can deploy an assembly that contains installation components in two ways. These techniques are covered in the following sections.

Deploying an Installation Component Using the Web Setup Project

To deploy an application that consists of installation components, you need to create a Web setup project as you normally would. However, this time, you use the Custom Actions Editor to deploy the necessary additional resources. At the time of deployment, the deployment project executes the ProjectInstaller class as a part of its custom installation action to create component resources.

Deploying an Installation Component Using the Installer Tool

You can also use the command-line Installer tool (installutil.exe) to install the assemblies that contain additional component resources.

To install the resources contained in an assembly named Assembly1.dll, you could use the following form of the installutil.exe command:

```
installutil.exe Assembly1.dll
```

You can also install resources contained in multiple assemblies, as follows:

```
installutil.exe Assembly1.dll Assembly2.dll Assembly3.dll
```

If you instead wanted to launch the uninstaller for installation classes stored in an assembly, you would use the /u or /uninstall option with the command, as follows:

```
installutil.exe /u Assembly1.dll
```

If you are installing components from multiple assemblies using the **installutil.exe** command, and if any assembly fails to install, **installutil.exe** rolls back the installations of all the other assemblies. However, the process of uninstallation is not transactional.

Working with **Installer** Classes

You can add your own Installer classes to a project to perform custom actions, such as creating a database on a target computer, during installation. These compiled installer classes from the project are then added to the deployment project as custom actions that are run at the end of the installation. The following are typical actions you would perform while creating a custom installer class:

1. Inherit a class from the Installer class.

2. Make sure the RunInstaller attribute is set to true in the derived class.

3. Override the Install(), Commit(), Rollback(), and Uninstall() methods to perform any custom actions.

4. In a setup project, use the Custom Actions Editor to invoke this derived class to perform the required processing.

5. If necessary, pass arguments from the Custom Actions Editor to the custom Installer class using the CustomActionData property.

Scalable and Reliable Deployment

Web applications can be subject to considerable traffic. A popular Web site might have to support hundreds or thousands of simultaneous users. The following sections describe server architectures that help handle this load reliably.

Web Gardens

A *Web garden* is a Web application whose execution is distributed across more than one processor on a multiprocessor computer. For example, suppose that you've installed an ASP.NET application on a computer with eight CPUs. In this case, ASP.NET would automatically launch eight worker processes to handle incoming Web requests and assign one of these processes to each CPU (a procedure known as *setting the affinity* of the process).

Web gardens offer the benefit of faster response times on multiple-CPU computers. In particular, if one worker process becomes hung or slowed down because of programming errors or unexpected input, the Web garden can continue serving requests using the other worker processes.

Web gardening is the default behavior for ASP.NET. However, you might want to configure your Web server to not use every processor for Web gardening. To do this, you can set the value of the following two attributes in the `<processModel>` element of the `web.config` file:

➤ *webGarden*—When set to `true`, this attribute directs Windows to schedule processes to CPUs (thus enabling the default behavior of Web gardening). When set to `false`, this attribute uses the `cpuMask` attribute to determine which processors should participate in a Web garden.

➤ *cpuMask*—This attribute is a bitmask indicating which processors should participate in a Web garden. For example, setting `cpuMask` to `7` (which is binary 111) would indicate that processors 0, 1, and 2 (and no others) should participate in a Web garden.

Web Farms

A *Web farm* takes the concept of a Web garden and extends it to multiple computers. In a Web farm, your application runs on multiple Web servers simultaneously. Some mechanism outside the Web servers is used to distribute requests to the individual servers. Web farms are typically enabled by a technique known as *network load balancing (NLB)*.

Web farms offer the benefits of both scalability and reliability. Your application is more scalable because you can increase its capacity by adding more computers to the Web farm, and your application is more reliable because a failure of any one server does not affect the other servers.

Clusters

Clustering provides a second method of combining multiple computers for a single purpose. The goal of clustering is not to provide additional scalability, but to provide additional reliability. In a cluster, multiple computers are configured using the same software, but only one of these computers is active at any given time. The active server handles all the requests unless it experiences a hardware or software failure. At that point, the clustering software automatically directs requests to the standby server, which becomes the new active server. Clustering is a built-in feature of the Windows Server operating systems. You can also use products such as Microsoft Application Center to make managing software on a cluster easier.

Methods of Deployment

After you have created a setup package, you can deploy your application from any location that's accessible to all its potential users. The Web applications exam requires you to know about the two types of deployment discussed in the following sections.

Deployment via Removable Media

The most common examples of removable media are floppy disks, CD-ROMs, and DVDs. Deployment projects in Visual Studio .NET can be used to create packages divided across multiple files—each with a size specified by the developer. These small files can then be copied to removable media and distributed to users.

To create a Web setup project for removable media, create a Web setup project and in the project's property pages, change the `Package files` option to `In cabinet file(s)`. This action also enables the Cab Size option, where you can specify the size of the cab files depending on your media size.

Web-based Deployment

Web-based deployment is the most popular form of deployment, especially for small applications. With the growth of high-speed Internet connections, this form of deployment is in much higher demand compared to removable media. It offers several advantages over other forms of application deployment, including

➤ It reduces the costs of media, replication, and distribution.

➤ Management of software updates is simple. You can program an application to automatically check for updates on the Web, or you can instruct users to download an update package from a Web page.

For Web-based deployment, after the setup files are created, rather than copying them to a removable media, you copy them to a virtual directory on a Web server. You might also want to password-protect the deployment Web site so that only authorized users can download the application. You can then install the application by navigating to the URL of the `setup.exe` file.

Exam Prep Questions

Question 1

You have created a database-driven Web application. Using Microsoft SQL Server, you have also generated an installation script for your database and stored it in a file named **InstData.sql**. You want to deploy this application on a Web server. When the application is deployed, the database should also be created on the same server. You are creating a Web setup project using Visual Studio .NET. Which of the following actions should you take to create the database while deploying your application on the Web server?

O A. Create a component that derives from the **Installer** class, and override its **Install()** method to create the database. Add the component to the Install node of the Custom Actions Editor in the Web setup project.

O B. Create a component that derives from the **Installer** class, and override its **Install()** method to create the database. Add the component to the Commit node of the Custom Actions Editor in the Web setup project.

O C. Copy the **InstData.sql** file to the Application folder on the target machine's file system using the File System Editor. Add **InstData.sql** to the Install node of the Custom Actions Editor in the Web setup project.

O D. Create a component that derives from the **Installer** class, and override its **Install()** method to create the database. Add the component to the Launch Conditions Editor in the Web setup project.

The correct answer is A. You can use the Custom Actions Editor to perform custom actions such as database installation during the application setup. If you have an Installer class or program that creates a database, it must be added to the Install node of the Custom Actions Editor. Answer B is incorrect because the Commit() method is called after the Install() method has been successfully run. Usually, to avoid raising exceptions, no processing is done in the Commit() method. Answer C is incorrect because only executable or script files can be added to the Custom Actions Editor. Answer D is incorrect because the Launch Conditions Editor is used only to determine whether a prerequisite is met before the installation can continue.

Question 2

You have created a Web application that uses some components not shared by other applications. Each of these components is packaged in its own assembly, each of which has a strong name associated with it. The application that uses these components is not required to load a specific version of these components. You do not want to store the assemblies directly under the application's installation folder. Which of the following options is the best approach for deploying these assembly files?

○ A. Store the components in the GAC.

○ B. Store the components anywhere you like and specify the path to them using the **<codebase>** element in the application's configuration file.

○ C. Store the assemblies in one of the subdirectories under the application's installation directory, and specify this subdirectory as part of the **<probing>** element in the application's configuration file.

○ D. Store the components in the Windows system directory.

The correct answer is C. In the given scenario, the components are not shared between multiple applications and the applications are not specific about versions, so a good place to store the assemblies is a folder inside each application's installation folder, with its location specified via the <probing> element in the application's configuration file. Answer A is incorrect because, if the components are not shared between applications, they don't have to be stored in the GAC. Answer B is incorrect because, although you could use the <codebase> element in the application's configuration file, you would have to specify a certain version for the assembly. Answer D is incorrect because CLR does not search for the assemblies in the Windows system directory.

Question 3

> When you install a Web application on a target machine, you want to store the **Readme.txt** file in the application installation directory selected by the user. You also want to create a shortcut for the **Readme.txt** file on the desktop of the target machine. While creating a Web setup project, which of the following actions will you take in the File System Editor to achieve this? (Select all that apply.)
>
> ❏ A. Move the shortcut to the **Readme.txt** file from the Web Application folder to the user's desktop in the target machine's file system.
>
> ❏ B. Add the **Readme.txt** file to the Web Application Folder node of the target machine's file system.
>
> ❏ C. Create a shortcut to the **Readme.txt** file in the Web Application Folder node of the target machine's file system.
>
> ❏ D. Add the **Readme.txt** file to the user's desktop in the target machine's file system.
>
> ❏ E. Move the shortcut to the **Readme.txt** file from the user's desktop to the Web Application folder in the target machine's file system.

The correct answers are A, B, and C. To copy the Readme.txt file to the installation directory selected by the user at install time, you must add it to the Web Application folder in the target machine's file system. To create a shortcut, you first create a shortcut to the Readme.txt file stored in the Web Application folder in the target machine's file system. Then, you move this shortcut from the Web Application folder to the user's desktop in the target machine's file system. Answer D is incorrect because this action deploys the Readme.txt file, rather than its shortcut, on the user's desktop. Answer E is incorrect because you want to move the shortcut from the Web Application folder to the user's desktop, but this action does just the opposite.

Question 4

You are a developer in a large manufacturing company and are developing a complex inventory control application with a team of 15 other developers. You have written two program modules, **inv1234.cs** and **inv5678.cs**, which are also used with several other applications in the company. You compiled both the program modules using the Visual C# .NET compiler, producing **inv1234. netmodule** and **inv5678.netmodule** files. You now want to link the compiled modules into an assembly that you will install in the GAC to test the Web forms that depend on this assembly. You have decided to keep the name of the assembly as **InvLib.dll**. You have access to your company's public key but not the private key. The public key is stored in a file named **BigCoPublic.snk**. When the testing is completed, your project manager will use the private key (stored in a **BigCoPrivate.snk** file) to fully sign all the assemblies in the accounting software application. Which of the following commands would you choose to successfully sign your assembly?

○ A.
```
al.exe inv1234.netmodule,inv5678.netmodule
➥/delaysign /keyfile:BigCoPublic.snk
➥/out:InvLib.dll
```

○ B.
```
al.exe inv1234.netmodule,inv5678.netmodule
➥/delaysign+
➥/keyfile:BigCoPublic.snk
➥/out:InvLib.dll
```

○ C.
```
al.exe inv1234.netmodule,inv5678.netmodule
➥/delaysign-
➥/keyfile:BigCoPublic.snk
➥/out:InvLib.dll
```

○ D.
```
csc.exe inv1234.cs,inv5678.cs /delaysign
➥/keyfile:BigCoPublic.snk
➥/out:InvLib.dll
```

The correct answer is B. You can use the `al.exe` command to link already compiled modules into an assembly. The process of including a public key in an assembly and signing it with a private key at a later stage is called delay signing. You can perform delay signing on an assembly using `al.exe` with the `/delay+` switch. Answers A and C are incorrect because the `/delaysign` and `/delaysign-` options are equivalent and are used only if you want to fully sign an assembly using both the private key and public key. Answer D is incorrect because the C# compiler (`csc.exe`) does not provide options for the signing of assemblies.

Question 5

> You are using the Installer tool (**installutil.exe**) to install server resources by executing the installer components in three assemblies. You issued the following command:
>
> ```
> installutil Assembly1.exe Assembly2.exe Assembly3.exe
> ```
>
> During the execution of this command, the installation of **Assembly3.exe** failed. Which of the following will happen?
>
> ○ A. Only **Assembly1.exe** will be installed.
>
> ○ B. Only **Assembly2.exe** will be installed.
>
> ○ C. Both **Assembly1.exe** and **Assembly2.exe** will be installed.
>
> ○ D. None of the assemblies will be installed.

The correct answer is D. installutil.exe performs installation in a transactional manner. If one of the assemblies fails to install, it rolls back the installations of all the other assemblies. Answers A, B, and C are incorrect because, if the installation of Assembly3.exe fails, none of the assemblies will be installed.

Question 6

> You have developed a Web custom control that will be used to provide consistent navigation links across all your company's Web applications. These applications will be developed by many developers and deployed across multiple servers. The Web custom control should be installed in the GAC. Which method should you use for deploying this control?
>
> ○ A. Merge module
>
> ○ B. FTP deployment
>
> ○ C. Setup project
>
> ○ D. Web setup project

The correct answer is A. The merge module can be incorporated into the setup projects of other applications and can perform advanced operations such as inserting assemblies in the GAC. Answer B is incorrect because FTP deployment cannot register the control's assembly in the GAC. Answers C and D are incorrect because a setup or Web setup project cannot be merged with other setup projects.

Question 7

You are deploying a mission-critical Web application for your company. Which of these configurations will enable your application to continue functioning even if a critical hardware component such as a power supply fails? (Select two.)

- ❑ A. Single-server deployment
- ❑ B. Web farm deployment
- ❑ C. Web garden deployment
- ❑ D. Cluster deployment

The correct answers are B and D. Web farm and cluster deployments use multiple servers to provide redundancy and hardware fault tolerance to an application. Answers A and C are incorrect because single-server and Web garden installations place the application on a single physical server, where a failure of a critical hardware component can bring down the whole application.

Question 8

You want to create a customized setup program for a Web application. One of the screens shown during installation should be available only from the administrative installation of the Microsoft Windows Installer package. Other setup options are available for regular as well as administrative installations. Which of the following editors will enable you to create such an installation program?

- ○ A. File System Editor
- ○ B. User Interface Editor
- ○ C. Custom Actions Editor
- ○ D. Launch Conditions Editor

The correct answer is B. You can customize the user interface of an installation program using the User Interface Editor for the regular installation and administrative installation. Answer A is incorrect because the File System Editor is useful only for establishing file associations on the target computer. Answer C is incorrect because the Custom Actions Editor is useful only for specifying additional actions to be performed on the target computer at the end of an installation. Answer D is incorrect because the Launch Conditions Editor is useful only for specifying conditions that must be met to successfully run an installation.

Question 9

You work as a software developer for a big pharmacy and are writing some components that will be shared across several applications throughout the company. You want to place an assembly named **CommonComponents.dll** in the GAC for testing purposes. You do not have access to the company's private key, but you have stored the company's public key in the assembly manifest of **CommonComponents.dll**. Which of the following commands are you required to run to place your assembly in the GAC? (Select all that apply.)

❑ A. **sn.exe −Vr CommonComponents.dll**

❑ B. **sn.exe −Vu CommonComponents.dll**

❑ C. **gacutil.exe /i CommonComponents.dll**

❑ D. **gacutil.exe /u CommonComponents**

The correct answers are A and C. You must first turn off the verification for partially signed assemblies. You can do this using the sn.exe tool with the -Vr switch. Next, you install the assembly to the GAC using the /i switch with the gacutil.exe command. Answer B is incorrect because the -Vu option of sn.exe unregisters an assembly for verification skipping, thereby turning on the verification. Answer D is incorrect because the /u option of gacutil.exe is used to uninstall an assembly from the GAC.

Question 10

A Web application is already deployed to your company's production Web server when you discover a logic error in the Visual C# .NET code-behind file for one of the application's Web forms. You have corrected the error and rebuilt the application on the test server. What is the easiest way to transfer the changes to the production server?

○ A. Use FTP to move the changed files to the production server. Then restart the WWW service on the production server.

○ B. Build a Windows Installer project to install the entire application, and run the Installer project on the production server. Then restart the WWW service on the production server.

○ C. Use FTP to move the changed files to the production server. Do not restart the WWW service on the production server.

○ D. Build a Windows Installer project to install the entire application. Then run the Installer project on the production server, but do not restart the WWW service on the production server.

The correct answer is C. If a Web application is already installed on IIS, you can simply replace any updated files. ASP.NET will detect the changed files and automatically recompile the pages as clients request them. Answers A and B are incorrect because there is no need to restart the WWW service on the production server. Answer D is incorrect because the deployment of the code-behind Web forms can be easily done by FTP and building a Windows Installer project is unnecessary.

Need to Know More?

 Ritcher, Jeffery. *Applied Microsoft .NET Framework Programming.* Redmond, WA: Microsoft Press, 2002.

 Read the Deploying .NET Applications: Lifecycle Guide at www.msdn.com/library/en-us/dnbda/html/DALGRoadmap.asp.

 Visit the .NET Framework Deployment and Distributing home page at www.msdn.com/netframework/using/deploying.

 Watch the Microsoft Support WebCast for Deploying Applications with .NET at http://support.microsoft.com/?id=328140.

Maintaining and Supporting a Web Application

Terms you'll need to understand:

✓ Boxing
✓ Event logs
✓ Performance counter
✓ Process
✓ Unboxing

Techniques you'll need to master:

✓ Recording application-specific messages to the Windows event log
✓ Using performance counters to monitor the performance of an executing application
✓ Learning how to design an ASP.NET application for performance

In this chapter, you'll learn about the techniques that enable you to gather execution information for an application. In particular, you'll learn how to get detailed execution information for the ASP.NET worker processes, how to record problems and issues to the event logs, and how to monitor the performance of an application. Finally, you'll also learn various techniques and tips you can use to improve the performance of an ASP.NET application.

Getting Information about the ASP.NET Worker Process

One of the most important processes running on a Web server is the ASP.NET worker process. The ASP.NET worker process handles requests for the execution of the ASP.NET pages. In this section, you'll learn how to retrieve specific execution information for the ASP.NET worker process using the classes of the System.Web namespace.

The ProcessModelInfo class of the System.Web namespace contains two methods that return information about the ASP.NET worker processes. Table 15.1 discusses these methods.

Table 15.1 Static Methods of the ProcessModelInfo Class	
Method	**Description**
GetCurrentProcessInfo()	Returns a **ProcessInfo** object that contains information about the ASP.NET worker process executing the current request
GetHistory()	Returns an array of **ProcessInfo** objects that contain information for the most recent (maximum being 100) ASP.NET worker processes

Both methods listed in Table 15.1 return ProcessInfo objects. The ProcessInfo class provides information for the corresponding ASP.NET worker process. Table 15.2 lists the properties of the ProcessInfo class.

Table 15.2 Properties of the ProcessInfo Class	
Property	**Description**
Age	Gets the length of time the worker process has been running
PeakMemoryUsed	Gets the maximum amount of memory the process has used

(continued)

Table 15.2 Properties of the ProcessInfo Class *(continued)*	
Property	**Description**
ProcessID	Gets the process ID assigned to the process
RequestCount	Gets the number of start requests for the process
ShutdownReason	Specifies a reason why the process was shut down
StartTime	Gets the time at which the process started
Status	Gets the status of the process

Take the following steps to see the ProcessModelInfo and the ProcessInfo classes in action:

1. Open Visual Studio .NET and create a new blank solution named **315C15** at c:\inetpub\wwwroot\ExamCram. (You might need to change the directory based on your configuration.)

2. Add a new Visual C# ASP.NET Web Application at the following location: http://localhost/ExamCram/315C15/Example15_1.

3. Drag a Label control, a DataGrid control (dgProcessHistory), and a Button control (btnRefresh) onto the Web form.

4. Invoke the Properties window and set the AutoGenerateColumns property of the DataGrid control to false. Select the Columns property and click the ellipse (...) button.

5. This opens the DataGrid Properties dialog box. Select the Bound Column from the Available columns list box and click the > button. This adds a bound column in the Selected Columns list box. Enter **ProcessID** in the Header Text and Data Field text boxes, and click the Apply button. Add a few more bound columns with Header Text and Data Field properties set to StartTime, Age, RequestCount, PeakMemoryUsed, Status, and ShutdownReason.

6. Switch to Code view and add the following using directive:
```
using System.Diagnostics;
```

7. Add the following code to the Page_Load() event handler:
```
private void Page_Load(object sender, System.EventArgs e)
{
    // Setting the DataGrid's DataSource to the
    // array of the ProcessInfo objects returned
    dgProcessHistory.DataSource = ProcessModelInfo.GetHistory(100);
    dgProcessHistory.DataBind();
}
```

8. Run the project. You should see the details about the recent ASP.NET worker processes as shown in Figure 15.1.

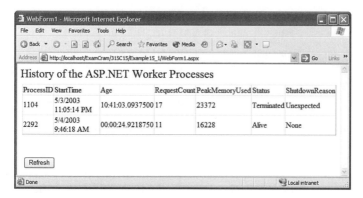

Figure 15.1 The **ProcessModelInfo** and **ProcessInfo** classes provide information about the recent ASP.NET worker processes.

Figure 15.1 shows a list of recent ASP.NET worker processes that started on the Web server since the last IIS reset. Only one of the worker processes is active; the other has been shut down. ASP.NET has a built-in mechanism to detect memory leaks, process crashes, and deadlocks. ASP.NET automatically tracks the problem and recycles the worker process if necessary.

You can configure the parameters ASP.NET uses to recycle the worker process. These settings can be configured in the <processModel> element of the machine.config file.

Working with Event Logs

The event log is the standard destination for applications to record problems and issues. You can easily monitor the behavior of an application by analyzing its messages in the event log. Programmatic access to the event log enables you to automate some of the administrative tasks associated with an application.

By default, three event logs are available: Application, Security, and System. Other applications (including .NET applications) or operating system components such as Active Directory might add other event logs.

Table 15.3 lists the important members of the EventLog class, which belongs to the System.Diagnostics namespace.

Table 15.3 Important Members of the EventLog Class

Member	Type	Description
CreateEventSource()	Method	Opens an event source to write event information
Delete()	Method	Removes a log resource
DeleteEventSource()	Method	Removes an application's event source from the event log
Entries	Property	Gets the contents of the event log
Exists()	Method	Determines whether the specified log exists
GetEventLogs()	Method	Creates an array of the event logs
Log	Property	Specifies the name of the log to read from or write to
MachineName	Property	Specifies the name of the computer on which to read or write events
Source	Property	Specifies the source to register and use when writing to an event log
SourceExists()	Method	Finds whether a given event source exists
WriteEntry()	Method	Writes an entry in the event log

Each application interested in interacting with an event log must register an event source with the log. After an event source is registered, its information is stored in the system Registry and is available across application restarts.

The CreateEventSource() method enables you to register the application with an event log; if the event log does not already exist, this method creates it for you.

The WriteEntry() method of the EventLog object enables you to write messages to the event log specified by the event source. If the event source specified by the Source property of an EventLog object does not exist, the first call to the WriteEntry() method creates the event source before writing the entry to the event log. You can write different types of messages (information, error, warning, success audit, and failure audit) to an event log. These types are specified by the values in the EventLogEntryType enumeration.

Perform the following steps to learn how to record messages to the Application event log from an ASP.NET application:

1. Add a new Visual C# .NET Web application project to the existing solution, and name it Example15_2.

2. Place two Label controls (name one of them lblMessage), one TextBox control (named txtMessage, with its TextMode property set to MultiLine), one Button control (named btnWrite), and five RadioButton controls

(named rbInformation, rbWarning, rbError, rbSuccessAudit, and
rbFailureAudit) on the Web form. Set the GroupName property for each of
the RadioButton controls to EventType. Arrange the controls as shown in
Figure 15.2.

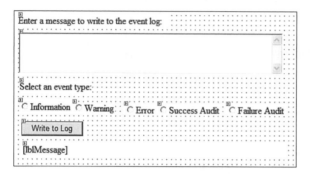

Figure 15.2   The design of an application that enables you to write messages into a custom event
log.

3. Switch to Code view and add the following using directive:

```
using System.Diagnostics;
```

4. Double-click the btnWrite button and add the following code to its
Click event handler:

```
private void btnWrite_Click(object sender, System.EventArgs e)
{
    EventLogEntryType eletEntryType;

    // Set the eletEntryType member
    if (rbWarning.Checked)
        eletEntryType = EventLogEntryType.Warning;
    else if (rbInformation.Checked)
        eletEntryType = EventLogEntryType.Information;
    else if (rbSuccessAudit.Checked)
        eletEntryType = EventLogEntryType.SuccessAudit;
    else if (rbFailureAudit.Checked)
        eletEntryType = EventLogEntryType.FailureAudit;
    else
        eletEntryType = EventLogEntryType.Error;

    string strSourceName = "Example15_2";
    try
    {
```

```
        //If no event source exists, create an event source
        if(!EventLog.SourceExists(strSourceName))
        {
            EventLog.CreateEventSource(strSourceName, "Application");
        }
        // Write an entry into event log
        EventLog.WriteEntry(strSourceName,
                txtMessage.Text, eletEntryType);
        lblMessage.Text = "Entry written to the log successfully";
    }
    catch(Exception ex)
    {
        lblMessage.Text = ex.Message;
    }
}
```

5. Set `Example15_2` as the startup project of the solution and run the project. Enter a message in the message text box and select the type of message from the radio button options. Click the Write to Log button to write to the event log.

6. To view the logged messages, navigate to Server Explorer, expand the Servers node, select the node corresponding to your computer, and expand it. Right-click the Events node and select Launch Event Viewer from its shortcut menu. This action has the same effect as launching the Event Viewer from the Administrative Tools section of the Windows Control Panel.

When executing the program, if you get an error message stating `Requested registry access is not allowed`, it means that the default user for the ASP.NET worker process (`ASPNET`) does not have the correct user rights to create an event source. You can perform the following steps to resolve this problem:

1. Select Start, Run. Type `regedit` to open the Windows Registry Editor.

2. Navigate through the Registry hierarchy to the following Registry subkey:

```
HKEY_LOCAL_MACHINE\SYSTEM\CurrentControlSet\
➥Services\Eventlog\Application
```

3. Right-click the Application subkey; then select New, Key.

4. Type `Example15_2` for the key name.

Of course, when you deploy your application, you do not want the user to manually edit the Windows Registry. In that case, you can create the required Registry keys automatically during the setup process by using the `System.Diagnostics.EventLogInstaller` class.

The Security log is read-only for all users.

Working with Performance Counters

Performance counters are Windows's way of collecting performance data from the running processes. Performance counters are organized into categories, with each category defining a specific set of performance counters. The following two categories of performance counters are specifically dedicated for ASP.NET applications:

➤ *ASP.NET*—The ASP.NET category provides performance counters to monitor the performance for all ASP.NET applications on a Web server, such as Request Execution Time, Request Wait Time, Requests Queued, Requests Rejected, and so on.

➤ *ASP.NET Applications*—The ASP.NET Applications category has various counters that monitor the performance of a single instance of an ASP.NET application, such as Requests/Sec, Sessions Total, Transactions/Sec, and so on.

The PerformanceCounter class enables you to read performance samples for processes running on a machine. By using this class, an application can even publish its own performance counters. Table 15.4 lists the important members of the PerformanceCounter class.

Table 15.4	Important Members of the PerformanceCounter Class	
Member	**Type**	**Description**
CategoryName	Property	Specifies the performance counter category name.
Close()	Method	Closes the performance counter and frees all the resources.
CounterName	Property	Specifies the performance counter name.
CounterType	Property	Specifies the performance counter type.
Decrement()	Method	Decrements the performance counter value by one.
Increment()	Method	Increments the performance counter value by one.
IncrementBy()	Method	Increments or decrements the performance counter value by a specified amount.
InstanceName	Property	Specifies the instance name.

(continued)

Table 15.4	Important Members of the PerformanceCounter Class *(continued)*	
Member	**Type**	**Description**
MachineName	Property	Specifies the computer name.
NextSample()	Method	Returns an object of type **CounterSample** that has properties such as **RawValue**, **BaseValue**, **TimeStamp**, and **SystemFrequency**. These properties provide detailed information on the performance data.
NextValue()	Method	Retrieves the current calculated value (a float type) for a performance counter.
RawValue	Property	Retrieves the raw, or uncalculated, value for a performance counter.
ReadOnly	Property	Indicates whether the **PerformanceCounter** object is in read-only mode.

The process of reading a performance counter value is referred to as *sampling* the performance counter. A good way to analyze a performance counter is to graph sample values over time. Windows provides the Performance Monitoring tool (perfmon.exe) for this very purpose.

Although tools such as perfmon.exe make monitoring the performance of an application simple, it is sometimes also useful to read the values programmatically. This can be useful, for example, when you want a program that monitors the performance of another program and takes actions depending on the performance data from that program. As an example, you might want to allow the download of some large files only when the number of incoming requests on a Web site are below a particular level.

The following steps demonstrate how to use an instance of a PerformanceCounter component to monitor the total number of requests since the ASP.NET worker process was started:

1. Add a new Visual C# Web Application project to the existing solution and name it Example15_3.

2. Place a Label control, a ListBox control (lbPerformance), and a Button control (btnSample) onto the Web form.

3. Open Server Explorer and select the Web server from the Servers node. Select the __Total__ instance of the Requests Total performance counter by navigating to Performance Counters, ASP.NET Applications, Requests Total, __Total__ from the server node. Drag the __Total__ instance of the performance counter to the Web form; then name the counter pcRequests. Change the MachineName property of the counter to a single dot (.) to refer to the Web server on which the code is running.

4. Switch to Code view and add the following `using` directive:

```
using System.Diagnostics;
```

5. Attach an event handler to the `Click` event of the `Button` control and add the following code in the event handler:

```
private void btnSample_Click(object sender,
    System.EventArgs e)
{
    // Get the next performance data
    CounterSample csSample = pcRequests.NextSample();
    // Add the data to the list box
    lbPerformance.Items.Add(pcRequests.CounterName + ": " +
        csSample.RawValue.ToString() + " at " +
        csSample.TimeStamp.ToString());
}
```

6. Set the project as the startup project for the solution and run the project. Each time you click the button, a new performance value is added as a new row to the `ListBox` control.

Designing a Web Application for Performance

You should plan for performance early in the development cycle of an application. It is inexpensive to remove any performance glitches early in the development cycle. As the application moves beyond design, the cost of modifying code or redistributing an application goes up.

The following list includes some of the commonly acknowledged best practices for developing high-performing applications using the .NET Framework:

➤ *Use caching to store content*—ASP.NET enables you to cache entire pages, fragments of pages, or controls. You can also cache variable data by specifying the parameters on which the data depends. Using caching makes it quicker for ASP.NET to return data in response to repeated requests for the same page. On the downside, caching consumes memory. Caching is also not recommended when the application needs to always retrieve the most recent data.

➤ *Avoid session state*—Whether you store it in process, in a State Server, or in a SQL Server database, session state takes memory and requires processing time to store and retrieve values. If a Web form doesn't depend on session state, disable the session state with the `<@% Page`

`EnableSessionState="false" %>` directive. If a Web form only retrieves data but does not update the session state, make the session state read-only with the `<@% Page EnableSessionState="ReadOnly" %>` directive.

> *Avoid view state*—View state lets you persist the contents of a control across trips between the client and server. This comes at the cost of additional bytes traveling in each direction and hence imposes a speed hit. You can avoid this penalty by setting the `EnableViewState` property of controls to `false` when you don't need the control's contents to persist.

> *Use low-cost authentication*—Passport authentication is slower than forms-based authentication, which is slower than Windows authentication. Not authenticating users at all is the fastest choice.

> *Use ASP.NET tracing to know the performance of the Web page*—Tracing provides information on the Web form control tree structure; the size of the view state for each control; different stages of the page processing; and the timing in each of the stages, headers, form variables, sessions and cookies, server variables, and so on. Furthermore, you can include debug messages. Therefore, this great amount of information can be very helpful in knowing the performance of a Web page.

> *Use the `Server.Transfer()` method for server-side page redirection*—You should prefer to use the `Server.Transfer()` method for server-side redirection to ASPX pages in the same application over the `Response.Redirect()` method. This reduces the extra round trip required by the `Response.Redirect()` method to perform client-side redirection.

> *Use Web server controls wisely*—Web server controls need to be processed on the server before they are rendered to the client. Therefore, when the programmable features of the Web form controls are not used, their usage should be avoided. For example, if you place a `Label` Web control on the page that only displays static text and is never used in the server-side code, you should place static HTML text in place of the `Label` Web server control.

> *Avoid frequent boxing and unboxing*—When a value type (such as a structure) is copied to a reference type (such as a class), the compiler needs to create an object on the heap and copy the value of the value type from the stack to this newly created object on the heap. This process is called *boxing*. On the other hand, when you copy a reference type to a value type, the value of the object from the heap is copied to the value type in the stack. This process is called *unboxing*. You should be aware of the overhead involved in boxing and unboxing, and while designing the application, you should choose appropriate data types to minimize this overhead.

➤ *Use the* StringBuilder *class for complex string concatenations and manipulations*—If an application is extensively modifying strings, you should consider using the System.Text.StringBuilder class, which stores the string as an array of characters. The StringBuilder object is mutable and does in-place modification of strings.

➤ *Use* AddRange() *with collections*—A large number of collection classes provide the AddRange() method, which you can use to add an array of items to the collection. Using AddRange() is much faster than adding elements by repeatedly calling the Add() method inside a loop.

➤ *Be careful about throwing exceptions*—Exceptions are cheap, until you throw one using the throw statement. Throwing exceptions is a costly operation. You should use them only to signify exceptional error cases. You should not use exceptions just to manage normal program flow.

➤ *Avoid using unmanaged code*—Calls to unmanaged components involve costly marshaling operations; therefore, the performance of these programs might deteriorate. For maximum performance, you should rewrite the unmanaged components by using one of the languages supported by the CLR. If a rewrite is not possible, you should monitor the use of the unmanaged component to see whether you can reduce the number of calls between the managed and unmanaged code, possibly by doing more work in each call rather than by making frequent calls to do small tasks.

➤ *Make fewer calls across processes*—Working with distributed applications involves the additional overhead of negotiating network- and application-level protocols. Network speed can also be a bottleneck. The best approach is to get more done with fewer calls across the network.

➤ *Compile the application by using the* Release *configuration*—When you are ready to deploy an application, compile it in Release mode rather than in the default Debug mode. Applications compiled using Debug mode might run slowly because of the presence of extra debugging code.

➤ *Use the optimized managed providers*—System.Data.OleDb is a generic provider that can access data exposed by any OleDb provider. Managed providers are specifically optimized for some databases. So, if you are connecting to a SQL Server database, you should use System.Data.SqlClient instead of the generic System.Data.OleDb. Similarly, for Oracle databases you should use classes from the System.Data.OracleClient namespace.

➤ *Use stored procedures instead of SQL statements*—When working with an RDBMS such as SQL Server, you should use stored procedures rather than a set of SQL statements given as a text command because stored procedures are highly optimized for server-side data access and their use usually improves data access performance significantly.

➤ *Tune the database*—Keeping up-to-date indexes greatly helps in improving performance for a database-intensive Web application. You can run SQL Server's Profiler and Index Tuning Wizard to avoid any bottlenecks caused by indexing. In addition, you can use the SQL Server Query Analyzer to optimize a query's performance.

➤ *Use* DataReader *instead of* DataSet *for forward-only sequential access*—If you are reading a table sequentially, you should use DataReader rather than DataSet. DataReader creates a read-only, forward-only stream of data that increases application performance and reduces system overhead because only one row is in memory at a time.

➤ *Use connection pooling for the SQL Server .NET data provider*—The slowest database operation is establishing a connection with the database. The SQL Server .NET Data Provider provides connection pooling to improve performance when connecting to a SQL Server database. In connection pooling, old connection information is stored in a connection pool so it can be reused for the next connection. Making fewer new connections with each request provides significant performance gains. However, if you have dynamic connection strings (that is, you change parameters of the connection strings), you will effectively disallow connection pooling because connections are pooled only on the exact connect string (even whitespaces need to match). To maximize the reuse of connections in a connection pool, you must use the same connection string for all the connections.

➤ *Avoid using auto-generated commands*—The SqlCommandBuilder and OleDbCommandBuilder classes enable you to automatically generate commands used to reconcile changes made to a DataSet. Although automatic generation of INSERT, UPDATE, and DELETE statements for changes to a dataset makes database updates very convenient, it also requires extra trips to the server to get the schema information. Therefore, you should make convenience and performance trade-offs depending on the application's requirements.

➤ *Use short-lived transactions*—Distributed transactions might have significant performance overhead. As a rule of thumb, you should use transactions only when required and keep the transactions as short-lived as possible.

Exam Prep Questions

Question 1

> You have recently deployed an expense reporting system in your company that relies heavily on a SQL Server database. All employees in the company have similar access permissions to the database. You have created the application in such a way that it uses each employee's login name and password in the connection string to connect to SQL Server. Users of the application have reported significantly slow performance, although other applications that use the same database seem to work fine. Your task is to optimize the performance of this application. Which of the following steps should you take?
>
> ○ A. Compile the application to native code using **ngen.exe**.
>
> ○ B. Run the SQL Server Index Tuning Wizard.
>
> ○ C. Increase the maximum size of the connection pool.
>
> ○ D. Use the same connection string for all users.

The correct answer is D. To get the maximum benefit from connection pooling, you must use the same connection string every time you connect to the database. Answer A is incorrect because the application is not slow only during the initial run. Answer B is incorrect because other applications accessing the same database are working well. Answer C is incorrect because you should use the existing connections effectively rather than increasing the size of the connection pool.

Question 2

> You want to determine whether a given event log exists on a remote machine. Which of the following methods is the most efficient way of determining this?
>
> ○ A. **Exists()**
>
> ○ B. **SourceExists()**
>
> ○ C. **GetEventLogs()**
>
> ○ D. **LogNameFromSourceName()**

The correct answer is A. The easiest and most efficient way to determine whether a log exists on a local or remote machine is to use the static Exists() method of the EventLog class. Answer B is incorrect because the SourceExists() method determines the existence of an event source instead of an event log. Answer C is incorrect because the GetEventLogs() method creates an array of all the event logs on a computer, meaning you'll have to do additional programming to search that list and determine the existence of an event log. Answer D is incorrect because the `LogNameFromSourceName()` method is used to determine the name of the event log for the specified event source.

Question 3

You are designing a database-intensive Web application for a large publishing house. You want to get maximum performance from the SQL queries that run to populate a drop-down list from a SQL Server database. Which of the following code segments would give you the fastest performance?

○ A.
```
SqlConnection conn = new
SqlConnection(connStr);
conn.Open();
DataSet ds = new DataSet();
SqlDataAdapter ad = new SqlDataAdapter
("select * from authors", conn);
ad.Fill(ds);
```

○ B.
```
OleDbConnection conn = new
OleDbConnection(connStr);
conn.Open();
DataSet ds = new DataSet();
OleDbDataAdapter ad =
    new OleDbDataAdapter
("select * from authors", conn);
ad.Fill(ds);
```

○ C.
```
SqlConnection conn = new SqlConnection
(connStr);
SqlCommand cmd = new SqlCommand("select *
from authors", connStr);
conn.Open();
SqlDataReader reader;
reader = cmd.ExecuteReader();
```

○ D.
```
OleDbConnection conn = new OleDbConnection
(connStr);
OleDbCommand cmd =
    new OleDbCommand("select * from
authors", connStr);
conn.Open();
OleDbDataReader reader;
reader = cmd.ExecuteReader();
```

The correct answer is C. When you are working with a SQL Server database, using the SQL Server managed provider gives you better performance than its OleDb counterpart. This fact makes answers B and D incorrect. Also, when you are doing sequential read-only operations such as populating a drop-down list, the SqlDataReader object gives better performance than the SqlDataAdapter object. This fact makes answer A incorrect.

Question 4

You create a Web application that enables users to locate the retail stores of your company all across the country. When a user selects a state from a **DropDownList** control, a list of all the stores in that state are displayed. The list is stored in a SQL Server database and changes very infrequently. You are concerned about the performance of the application when the Web server is under heavy load. Which of these actions should you take to improve application performance?

○ A. Use State Server to store the information for each user between requests.

○ B. Use caching to hold the delivered page in memory between requests.

○ C. Use thread pooling to ensure that the application will always have available threads.

○ D. Migrate the results page from ASP.NET to ASP.

The correct answer is B. By using page-level caching, you can cache a separate copy of the results page for each input state. The server can deliver these copies quickly because no database access or other processing is involved in satisfying subsequent requests. Answer A is incorrect because State Server is helpful in sharing the state in a Web farm but does not help in increasing the performance of the Web page. Answer C is incorrect because it is not clear from the question whether the application uses multiple threads. Answer D is incorrect because an ASP.NET page will have better performance compared to an equivalent ASP page.

Question 5

Your application includes a complex Web page with approximately eight **DataGrid** controls. The data in three of these controls is important in determining the proper navigation path when the page is posted back to the server; the other controls' values are changed in every page load. What should you do to improve performance on this page?

○ A. Set the **Enabled** property of the **DataGrid** controls that are changed in every page load to **false**.

○ B. Set the **ViewState** property of the **DataGrid** controls that are changed in every page load to **false**.

○ C. Set the **ViewState** property of the **DataGrid** controls that are not changed in every page load to **false**.

○ D. Set the **Enabled** property of the **DataGrid** controls that are not changed in every page load to **false**.

The correct answer is B. When you set the ViewState property for a DataGrid control to true, the contents of the data grid are passed between the client and server in a hidden form field. Setting ViewState to false removes this information and therefore cuts down on download times. Answers A and D are incorrect because setting the Enabled property of the DataGrid control to false does not have an impact on the view state for the DataGrid control. Answer C is incorrect because, if the DataGrid controls are not changed in every page load, you might actually improve performance by setting its ViewState property to true rather than false.

Question 6

You have developed a database-intensive ASP.NET application for a large pharmaceutical company. The database for the application uses SQL Server 2000. Users of your application are complaining about the consistently slow nature of some reports. Which of the following actions would you take to increase the performance of this application? (Select two.)

❑ A. Compile the application to native code using **ngen.exe**.

❑ B. Run the SQL Server Index Tuning Wizard.

❑ C. Convert all ad hoc SQL statements to SQL Server stored procedures.

❑ D. Add a **PerformanceMonitor** component to the code.

The correct answers are B and C. The SQL Server's Index Tuning Wizard identifies any bottlenecks caused by indexing. SQL Server stored procedures also improve data access performance significantly. Answer A is incorrect because the application is performing slowly consistently rather than only during the initial load. Answer D is incorrect because adding the PerformanceMonitor component helps you monitor the performance of an application but will not help in improving it.

Question 7

Which of the following coding constructs will have a major impact on an application's performance and should therefore be used cautiously?

○ A. **try**

○ B. **catch**

○ C. **finally**

○ D. **throw**

The correct answer is D. The throw statement has the maximum performance penalty and should be used cautiously. Answers A, B, and C are incorrect because they do not have any major impact on the application's performance.

Question 8

Your Web application displays routing and timing information related to your company's network. Each time a new page is loaded, it makes entirely new calculations to determine which information to display. No page in the application passes any information to another page in the application. Which alternative should you use for session state in this application to maximize performance?

○ A. **<@% Page EnableSessionState="false" %>**

○ B. In-process session state

○ C. State Server session state

○ D. SQL Server session state

The correct answer is A. Nothing in this application requires knowledge of session state. To maximize performance, you should disable session state tracking. Answers B, C, and D are incorrect because these are the solutions to store session state and, as noted, session state itself is not required.

Question 9

You have written an application that publishes its own custom performance counter. You want to decrease the value of a performance counter by five. Which of the following methods is the best way to do this?

- ○ A. **Decrement()**
- ○ B. **Increment()**
- ○ C. **IncrementBy()**
- ○ D. **NextValue()**

The correct answer is C. Using the IncrementBy() method is the most efficient way to increase or decrease the value of a counter by the specified amount. Answer A is incorrect because instead of increasing the performance counter, the Decrement() method decreases the performance counter by one. Answer B is incorrect because the Increment() method can increase the performance counter only by one, and you would need to call it several times to increase the counter by multiple units. Answer D is incorrect because, instead of increasing the performance counter, the NextValue() method only returns the next calculated value of a performance counter.

Question 10

Your Web application uses a legacy COM component to perform calculations. Ten values need to be passed to the COM component. You have the choice of several methods to communicate with the COM component. Which method should you select for best performance?

- ○ A. Set individual properties to pass the 10 values. Then call a single method with no parameters that returns the answer.
- ○ B. Call 10 individual methods—each of which takes a single value as a parameter and each of which returns part of the required information.
- ○ C. Call a single method that takes all 10 values as parameters and then returns the required information.
- ○ D. Call one method that takes an array of all 10 values as a parameter, and then call a second method that returns the required information.

The correct answer is C. Communication with legacy COM components must cross process boundaries. To speed up this communication, you need to minimize the number of calls between your application and the COM component. Answers A, B, and D are incorrect because these solutions require making additional method calls to the COM component.

Need to Know More?

 Kalani, Amit. *MCAD/MCSD Developing and Implementing Web Applications with Visual C# .NET and Visual Studio .NET.* Indianapolis, IN: Que Certification, 2002.

 Review the Performance Tips and Tricks in .NET Applications white paper at www.msdn.com/library/en-us/dndotnet/html/dotnetperftips.asp.

 Read the Developing High-Performance ASP.NET Applications topic from the .NET Framework Developer's Guide at www.msdn.com/library/en-us/cpguide/html/cpcondevelopinghigh-performanceaspnetapplications.asp.

Configuring a Web Application

Terms you'll need to understand:

✓ Authentication
✓ Authorization
✓ Caching
✓ Configuration file
✓ Impersonation
✓ Role-based security
✓ Session state

Techniques you'll need to master:

✓ Configuring a Web application by modifying the **web.config** and the **machine.config** files
✓ Implementing and configuring security for a Web application
✓ Implementing and configuring output, fragment, and data caching for a Web application
✓ Configuring and implementing session state in various topologies such as a Web garden and Web farm

In this chapter, you learn how to configure various aspects of an ASP.NET application, including security, performance, and application settings, both as a developer and as an administrator.

Configuration Files

ASP.NET provides extensive support for configuring its behavior with the use of XML-based configuration files. Use of XML files to store configuration makes server-side administration easier for the following reasons:

➤ XML files are plain-text files and can be modified using a simple text editor such as Notepad.

➤ To apply configuration changes, all you need to do is copy these XML files to an appropriate location. The new settings automatically take effect and, in most cases, there's no need to stop and restart the ASP.NET process or reboot the computer.

If you change the **<processModel>** element in the **machine.config** file, you must restart Internet Information Services (IIS) for the changes to take effect. This element controls internal IIS settings such as which processors to use on a multiprocessor computer and the number of threads to allocate to ASP.NET.

Although changes to configuration files are picked up automatically by ASP.NET, it doesn't mean that you can change things without consequences. When you change an application's configuration file, ASP.NET clears all the application state and session state variables for that application. If you change the **web.config** file for a particular site, ASP.NET clears the state settings for every application on the affected site. In addition, if you change the **machine.config** file, you lose all the state settings for every site on the Web server.

Anatomy of a Configuration File

The easiest way to learn about the structure of configuration files is to look inside one. Let's start with the master configuration file that configures ASP.NET's operations on the computer. Its name is machine.config, and you'll find it in the Microsoft .NET installation directory. For example, on Windows Server 2003, this file is at the following location:

```
c:\windows\microsoft.net\framework\v1.1.4322\config\machine.config
```

If you browse through the machine.config file on your computer, you'll get a sense of what you can configure in this fashion. The file includes some comments to show you the allowable options for settings. Table 16.1 lists the various sections you can specify in this (and other) configuration files.

Table 16.1 Configuration File Sections	
Section	Used for
<allow>	Allows access to a resource
<assemblies>	Specifies the assemblies to use for dynamic compilation
<authentication>	Configures authentication
<authorization>	Configures authorization
<browserCaps>	Detects the user's browser type
<clientTarget>	Specifies user agent aliases
<compilation>	Specifies the compiler settings
<compilers>	Specifies the supported compilers
<credentials>	Specifies the name and password credentials for authenticating users
<customErrors>	Specifies the custom error messages
<deny>	Denies access to a resource
<forms>	Configures forms-based authentication
<globalization>	Configures globalization settings
<httpHandlers>	Maps incoming requests to HTTP handlers
<httpModules>	Manages HTTP modules within an application
<httpRuntime>	Configures the HTTP runtime
<identity>	Configures the application identity
<pages>	Specifies the page-specific configuration information
<processModel>	Controls the ASP.NET process model
<protocols>	Contains protocols used to decrypt client data
<securityPolicy>	Maps security levels to policy files
<serviceDescriptionFormatExtensionTypes>	Specifies service description format extensions
<sessionState>	Configures session state options
<soapExtensionTypes>	Specifies SOAP extensions
<trace>	Configures application tracing
<trust>	Configures code access security
<user>	Defines users
<webServices>	Specifies the settings for Web services

For a complete list of what can appear in each element in a configuration file, see **www . m s d n . c o m / l i b r a r y / e n - u s / c p g e n r e f / h t m l / gngrfnetframeworkconfigurationfileschema.asp**.

The Configuration File Hierarchy

Configuration files are treated as a hierarchy by ASP.NET. The machine configuration file (machine.config) controls settings for the entire computer. Settings in machine.config can be overridden for a particular Web site hosted on the computer by a configuration file (web.config) located in the root folder of that Web site. Those settings themselves can be overridden for a particular Web application (virtual directory) by an application-specific configuration file (web.config). These settings, in turn, can be overridden by a configuration file (web.config) that applies to only part of an application.

For example, if you have a URL such as http://localhost/AppDir/ SubDir/default.aspx, the code executing in default.aspx could be affected by the following configuration files, in this order:

1. The machine.config file

2. The web.config file in the root directory of the localhost Web server

3. The web.config file present in the application's root directory AppDir

4. The web.config file present in the subdirectory SubDir

At any time, the web.config file closest in the folder chain to the page being displayed overrides the similar settings defined in the other configuration files. Several other factors complicate this simple picture of how things work, including

➤ *A setting in a configuration file can be marked with a* location *element*—For example, you might tag a particular section with the element <location path="Subdir1">. Settings contained in this element will apply only to pages stored in the Subdir1 subdirectory of the application.

➤ *ASP.NET configuration files apply only to ASP.NET resources*—For example, any HTML page remains unaffected by the settings in the configuration files.

➤ *Any configuration file can mark an element with the* allowOverride="false" *attribute*—In this case, more specific configuration files cannot override this setting.

Reading Configuration Settings from Code

The .NET Framework also provides programmatic access to the configuration files. For example, say you have defined a custom key in the `<appSettings>` element as follows:

```
<appSettings>
  <add key="Custom" value="Custom configuration value" />
</appSettings>
```

You could therefore read it in your program using the following expression:

```
ConfigurationSettings.AppSettings["Custom"]
```

To read one of the built-in values, you need to know which object in the ASP.NET object model consumes that setting. For example, the `Mode` property of the `Session` object exposes the value of the `mode` attribute of the `<sessionState>` element in the configuration file. The `Mode` property can be accessed using the following expression:

```
Session.Mode
```

Configuring Security

When you're developing ASP.NET applications, the two aspects of security you need to configure are authentication and authorization. *Authentication* is the process of obtaining credentials from a user and verifying his identity. After an identity has been authenticated, it can be authorized to use various resources. *Authorization* refers to granting rights based on that identity.

Configuring Authentication

ASP.NET provides flexible alternatives for authentication. You can perform authentication yourself in code or delegate authentication to other authorities. Settings in the `web.config` file control the method of authentication used for any given request.

IIS and ASP.NET Authentication

An ASP.NET application has two separate authentication layers. All requests flow through IIS before they're handed to ASP.NET, and IIS can decide to deny access before the ASP.NET process even knows about the request. Here's how the process works:

1. IIS first checks to ensure that the incoming request comes from an IP address that is allowed access to the domain. If it does not, the request is denied.

2. Next, IIS performs its own user authentication, if it's configured to do so. By default, IIS allows anonymous access, so requests are automatically authenticated.

3. If the request is passed to ASP.NET with an authenticated user, ASP.NET checks to see whether impersonation is enabled. If impersonation is enabled, ASP.NET acts as though it were the authenticated user. If not, ASP.NET acts with its own configured account.

4. Finally, the identity from step 3 is used to request resources from the operating system. If all the necessary resources can be obtained, the user's request is granted; otherwise, it is denied.

Configuring Windows Authentication

The Windows authentication provider allows you to authenticate users based on their Windows accounts. To enable Windows authentication, you use the following entry in the `web.config` file for the application:

```
<authentication mode="Windows" />
```

This provider uses IIS to perform the actual authentication and then passes the authenticated identity to your code. IIS offers four authentication methods:

➤ *Anonymous*—If you select anonymous authentication, IIS does not perform any authentication and anyone is allowed access to the ASP.NET application.

➤ *Basic*—If you select basic authentication, users must provide a Windows username and password to connect. However, this information is sent across the network in clear text, making basic authentication dangerously insecure on the Internet. However, one advantage of basic authentication is that it's supported by most Web servers, proxy servers, and Web browsers.

➤ *Digest*—If you select digest authentication, users must still provide a Windows username and password to connect. However, the password is hashed (scrambled) before being sent across the network. Digest authentication requires that all users be running Internet Explorer 5 or later and that Windows accounts be stored in Active Directory.

➤ *Integrated*—If you select Windows integrated authentication, passwords never cross the network. Users must still have a Windows username and password, but either the Kerberos or challenge/response protocols are used to authenticate the user. Windows integrated authentication requires that all users be running Internet Explorer 3.01 or later.

Passport Authentication

The Microsoft .NET Passport is an online service (www.passport.net) that enables users to use a single email address and a password to sign in to any .NET Passport–participating Web site or service. Users can create free Passport accounts by registering at any .NET Passport–participating Web site or by using the Windows XP/2003 .NET Passport Registration Wizard.

Passport uses an encrypted cookie mechanism to indicate authenticated users. If users have already signed in to Passport when they visit your site, they are considered authenticated by ASP.NET. Otherwise, they are redirected to the Passport servers to log in. To enable Passport authentication, you use the following entry in the web.config file for the application:

```
<authentication mode="Passport" />
```

More information on using .NET Passport with your application can be found at www.microsoft.com/net/services/passport.

Forms Authentication

Forms authentication provides a way to handle authentication using your own custom logic in an ASP.NET application. With forms authentication, the logic of the application is as follows:

1. When a user requests a page from the application, ASP.NET checks for the presence of a special session cookie.

2. If the cookie is present, the request is processed. Otherwise, ASP.NET redirects the user to a Web form you provide.

3. You can carry out whatever authentication checks you want in your form. When the user is authenticated, you indicate this to ASP.NET, which creates the special session cookie to handle subsequent requests.

The following steps show how to implement forms authentication in an ASP.NET Web application:

1. Open Visual Studio .NET and create a new blank solution named 315C16 at c:\inetpub\wwwroot\ExamCram. (You might need to change the directory based on your configuration.)

2. Add a new Visual C# ASP.NET Web Application project at the following location: `http://localhost/ExamCram/315C16/Example16_1`.

3. Add a new Web form (`frmLogin`) to the application. Place a `Label` control that displays a message asking the user whether she wants to log in, two `RadioButton` controls (`rbYes` and `rbNo` with a `GroupName` of `LogIn`), and a `Button` control (`btnSubmit`) on the form.

4. Switch to Code view and add the following `using` directive:

```
using System.Web.Security;
```

5. Add this code to handle the `Button` control's `Click` event:

```
private void btnSubmit_Click(object sender, System.EventArgs e)
{
    if(rbYes.Checked)
        FormsAuthentication.RedirectFromLoginPage("Admin", false);
}
```

6. Edit the `web.config` file to replace both the `<authentication>` and `<authorization>` elements as follows:

```
<authentication mode="Forms">
    <forms loginUrl="frmLogin.aspx" name="315C16" timeout="1" />
</authentication>

<authorization>
    <deny users="?" />
</authorization>
```

7. Set `WebForm1.aspx` as the start page and run the application. Instead of `WebForm1`, the browser displays the custom login form. To proceed further, you must select the Yes radio button and click the Submit button.

Of course, in a real application, you'd likely implement a more sophisticated authentication scheme than just making users select a radio button. You might, for example, store usernames and IP addresses in a database and allow only users who connect from their registered IP addresses. Or you might develop a Web service that allows authenticating users over the Internet.

By default, in the `web.config` file, the `<authorization>` element contains `<allow users="*" />`.

With that authorization setting, ASP.NET allows all users—even unauthenticated users—access to application resources. The * wildcard matches any user. For the previous example, I changed this to a `deny` element, like so:

```
<deny users="?" />
```

The ? wildcard matches only unauthenticated users. The net effect is to allow authenticated users access to all resources, while denying unauthenticated users access to any resources.

The `<forms>` element contains the URL of the form to use for login authentication, the name of the cookie to use, and a `timeout` that controls how long a user can work with the application before being directed back to the login page. (The previous example sets this to the very low value of 1 minute for testing.)

When the user is authenticated, the form calls the `RedirectFromLoginPage()` method of the `FormsAuthentication` object. The two parameters to this method are the name of the authenticated user and a Boolean value that controls whether to save a permanent (cross-session) cookie. If the second parameter is `false`, the cookie is stored in memory and only for the length of the browser session.

To disable authentication for an application, you add the following element to its configuration file:

<authentication mode="None" />

Configuring Authorization

After your application has authenticated users, you can authorize their access to resources.

Implementing Impersonation

ASP.NET impersonation is controlled by entries in the applicable `web.config` file. The default setting is no impersonation, but you can explicitly specify this setting by including this element in the file:

```
<identity impersonate="false"/>
```

With this setting, ASP.NET does not perform user impersonation. What does that mean? It means that ASP.NET always runs with its own privileges. By default, ASP.NET runs as an unprivileged account named `machine`, but you can change this by making a setting in the `<processModel>` element of `machine.config`. This setting can be changed only in `machine.config`, so any change applies to every site on the server when the ASP.NET worker process is restarted. To use a high-privilege system account instead of a low-privilege account, set the `userName` attribute of the `<processModel>` element to `"SYSTEM"`.

The second possible setting is to turn on impersonation, like so:

```
<identity impersonate="true"/>
```

In this case, ASP.NET takes on the identity passed to it by IIS. If you're allowing anonymous access in IIS, ASP.NET impersonates the IUSR_ComputerName account that IIS itself uses. If you're not allowing anonymous access, ASP.NET takes on the credentials of the authenticated user and makes requests for resources as if it were that user.

Finally, you can specify a particular identity to use for all authenticated requests, as shown here:

```
<identity impersonate="true" userName="DOMAIN\username" password="pass-
word"/>
```

With this setting, all requests are made as the specified user (assuming that the password is correct in the configuration file).

Using Role-based Authorization

You can also use Windows's own security mechanisms to authorize access to resources after you've authenticated a user. For example, you can give a Windows account permissions to log on to a SQL Server or open a particular file. These permissions can be granted to the ASP.NET user (if you're not using impersonation) or to individual domain users or groups (if you are using impersonation).

But you can also control access to resources directly in your .NET code using role-based security. Role-based security revolves around two interfaces: IIdentity and IPrincipal. For applications that use Windows accounts in role-based security, these interfaces are implemented by the WindowsIdentity and WindowsPrincipal objects, respectively.

The WindowsIdentity object represents the Windows user who is running the current code. The properties of this object allow you to retrieve information such as the username and his authentication method.

One way to manage role-based security is to use the IsInRole() method of the WindowsPrincipal object to determine whether the current user is in a specific Windows group. The results of this method call can be used to modify your application's user interface or perform other tasks. For example, the following code segment verifies the role membership in the administrators group:

```
// Tell the CLR to use Windows security
AppDomain.CurrentDomain.SetPrincipalPolicy
          (PrincipalPolicy.WindowsPrincipal);
// Get the current principal object
WindowsPrincipal prin = (WindowsPrincipal)Thread.CurrentPrincipal;
```

```
// Determine whether the user is an admin
Boolean admin = prin.IsInRole(WindowsBuiltInRole.Administrator);
// Display the results on the UI
if(admin)
    lblMembership.Text = "You are in the Administrators group";
else
    lblMembership.Text = "You are not in the Administrators group";
```

The three available overloaded forms of the `IsInRole()` method are as follows:

➤ `IsInRole(WindowsBuiltInRole)`—Uses one of the `WindowsBuiltInRole` constants to check for membership in the standard Windows groups.

➤ `IsInRole(String)`—Checks for membership in a group with the specified name.

➤ `IsInRole(Integer)`—Checks for membership in a group by using the specified role identifier (RID). RIDs are assigned by the operating system and provide a language-independent way to identify groups.

Using Caching

Caching refers to storing information for later retrieval, rather than generating it from scratch every time it's requested. For instance, a Web page can be cached so that it's delivered more quickly when it's requested the second time.

By caching, you can ease the load on the server because it does not have to regenerate the output for every page request. But this means that the output sent to a client might not be identical to what the client would have received if no caching were in place. You must balance your needs for current data against server load by specifying an appropriate expiration time for any cached content.

ASP.NET implements three types of caching, which are discussed in the following sections.

Output Caching

Output caching refers to caching the entire output of a page request.

You can specify the cacheability of a page or user control by using the `OutputCache` directive. Table 16.2 lists the attributes of this directive.

Table 16.2 Attributes of the **OutputCache** Directive	
Attribute	**Description**
Duration	Specifies the time in seconds for which the page or user control should be cached.
Location	Specifies the location of the output cache for a page. The possible values are specified by the **OutputCacheLocation enumeration** and include **Any** (the default value, caching can be set at the client browser, proxy server, or Web server), **Client**, **Downstream** (the client browser or proxy server), **None** (no caching), and **Server**. This attribute is not supported when applied to the **OutputCache** directive in user controls because user controls must reside on the Web server to be assembled.
VaryByControl	Specifies a semicolon-separated list of controls in the user control for which to vary the output cache. This attribute is supported only for user controls.
VaryByCustom	Specifies a string that indicates either the **Browser** or a custom string for which to vary the output cache. If the caching is to vary by a custom string, you should provide an overridden version of the **HttpApplication.GetVaryByCustomString()** method in the **global.asax** file to indicate how a page should be cached.
VaryByHeader	Specifies a semicolon-separated list of HTTP headers for which to vary the output cache. This attribute is not supported when applied to the **OutputCache** directive in user controls.
VaryByParam	Specifies a semicolon-separated list of parameters of the Web page for which to vary the output cache. The possible values are **None** (caching does not depend on parameters), ***** (caching for each distinct set of parameters), any query string key names in a **GET** request, or any parameter names in a **POST** request.

When an **OutputCache** directive is applied to an ASPX page, both the **Duration** and **VaryByParam** attributes must be specified. As opposed to this, in the case of user controls, either the **VaryByParam** or the **VaryByControl** attribute must be specified along with the **Duration** attribute. If the required attributes are not supplied, a compile-time error occurs.

Follow these steps to implement output caching for a Web page using the OutputCache directive:

1. Add a new Visual C# ASP.NET Web Application (**Example16_2**) to the solution.

2. Place a `Label` control (`lblTime`) on the Web form. Switch to Code view and add this code in the `Page_Load()` event handler:

```
private void Page_Load(object sender, System.EventArgs e)
{
    lblTime.Text = DateTime.Now.ToLongTimeString();
}
```

3. Set the project as the startup project and run the application. The form is displayed with the current time. Refresh the page several times and note that the displayed time changes every time you refresh the page.

4. Stop the application and switch to HTML view for the Web form. Add an `OutputCache` directive directly after the `Page` directive at the top of the file, like so:

```
<%@ OutputCache Duration="15" VaryByParam="None" %>
```

5. Run the project; the form is displayed with the current time. Refresh the page several times and note that the displayed time does not change until you refresh the page more than 15 seconds after the original request.

In the previous example, note that the `OutputCache` directive requires the `VaryByParam` attribute. If the page output doesn't depend on any input parameters, you can use `None` as the value of this attribute; otherwise, use the name of the parameter to cause caching to be done on a per-parameter value basis.

The `HttpCachePolicy` class enables you to set output caching for a page programmatically. The `Cache` property of the `HttpResponse` object provides access to the `HttpCachePolicy` class. The `HttpResponse` object can be accessed through the `Response` property of the `Page` or `HttpContext` class, as shown in the following code segment:

```
private void Page_Load(object sender, System.EventArgs e)
{
    lblTime.Text = DateTime.Now.ToLongTimeString();
    Response.Cache.SetExpires(DateTime.Now.AddSeconds(15));
    Response.Cache.SetCacheability(HttpCacheability.Public);
    Response.Cache.SetValidUntilExpires(true);
}
```

In this code, manipulating the `HttpCachePolicy` object has exactly the same effect as setting the `OutputCache` directive did in the previous example. This example uses three methods of the `HttpCachePolicy` object. The `SetExpires()` method specifies an expiration time for the cached version of the page; in this case, it's 15 seconds from the time the page is generated. The `SetCacheability()` method specifies where output can be cached through the `HttpCachePolicy` enumeration: `NoCache` for no caching at all, `Private` to allow caching only on the client (the default value), Public to allow caching on any proxy server as well as on the client, and Server to cache the document only on the Web server. Finally, the SetValidUntilExpires() method with its parameter set to true tells the server to ignore client-side attempts to refresh the cached content until it expires.

Caching multiple versions of a page is useful any time you have a page whose output depends on an input parameter. You can base such multiple-version caching on any HTTP header or browser attribute, but most commonly, you'll use the VaryByParam attribute to cache multiple values depending on a query string or form POST parameter.

For example, if you have a page that is accessed using a URL such as http://*ServerName*/GetCountryInfo.aspx?ddlCountries=Brazil and the rendering of this page depends on the query string parameter, you can cache the different versions of that page by using the following OutputCache directive:

```
<%@ OutputCache duration="20" VaryByParam="ddlCountries"%>
```

Here, ddlCountries is the name of a query string parameter and the cache duration is set to 20 minutes. This type of caching involves fewer round trips to the database server. In addition, the Web server can deliver the data from the output cache without dynamically generating the page at every request. As a result, caching helps in creating scalable and high-performance Web applications.

You can also cache the output of a page on the basis of the control's value. For example, consider the following OutputCache directive:

```
<%@ OutputCache duration="20" VaryByControl="ddlCountries"%>
```

This directive caches the output for a page for 20 minutes based on the different values of the ddlCountries control.

Fragment Caching

Fragment caching refers to caching part of a page. You can encapsulate a portion of a page into a user control and cache that portion of the page, while still forcing the rest of the page to be dynamically generated for each request.

Fragment caching is similar to output caching, in which the output of a user control is cached. The OutputCache directive also caches user controls. Refer to Table 16.2 for information on the attributes of the OutputCache directive.

You should specify either the VaryByParam attribute or the VaryByControl attribute in the OutputCache directive of the user control. You should also specify the Duration attribute to indicate how long the user control should be cached. Any number of user controls can exist in a page, and each of these user controls maintains caching on its own.

While caching user controls, you should consider the following points:

➤ Cached user controls are not programmatically accessible. An exception is thrown if you try to access them.

➤ Cached user controls are not added to the control tree.

➤ Cached user controls cannot perform data binding. An exception is thrown if you try to perform data binding on them.

Data Caching

ASP.NET also enables you to cache application data. In a Web application, data can be retrieved through expensive and time-consuming operations. Most of this data can change infrequently but be required often. The caching of arbitrary data is known as *data caching* or *application data caching*.

The Cache class of the System.Web.Caching namespace enables you to cache data. The following lists some important facts about the application cache:

➤ The Cache class enables you to insert any object into the data cache by providing a key and the object to be cached. Later, you can retrieve the object programmatically by supplying its key. You can cache simple strings, array lists, data sets, hash tables, and even custom-created objects.

➤ You can specify a fixed expiration time or a sliding expiration time for the data in the cache.

➤ Data caching enables you to specify any dependencies for the cached item. For example, you could cache a connection string with instructions to re-create the cache if a particular XML file were ever changed. If you set the correct dependencies, you can ensure that users get data as up-to-date as you want.

➤ You can set the priority for the cached item using the CacheItemPriority enumeration to AboveNormal, BelowNormal, Default (Normal), High, Low, Normal, NotRemovable. By setting the priority, you can ensure that data retrieved through an expensive operation is not removed and that data that can be easily retrieved or created is removed in case the memory is running low.

➤ When the memory is running low, ASP.NET can remove data from the cache if the cached data is not used frequently or is unimportant. This operation is called *scavenging*. The scavenging process can save ASP.NET worker processes from being recycled whenever the memory is too scarce to hold the incoming requests.

➤ You can provide a callback method that is called whenever the cached item is removed from the cache. The data item can be removed from the cache due to various options defined by the `CacheItemRemoveReason` enumeration, including `DependencyChanged`, `Expired`, `Removed` (via the `Cache.Remove()` method), and `Underused` (removed when the memory is scarce). The callback method receives notification that the cached item is removed from the cache, and depending on the cache data, this method can be used to perform any cleanup, logging, updating, or recreating data operation.

The `Cache` object can be easily accessed using the `Cache` property of the `Page` object or the `HttpContext` object. You can insert or add items to the data cache using the `Insert()` or `Add()` method of the `Cache` object, respectively. The `Insert()` method has four overloads that provide a choice to insert items in the cache by specifying parameters such as expiration time, sliding expiration time, cache dependency, cache priority, and callback method. The `Add()` method adds an item to the data cache and returns a reference of the added item. The `Remove()` method is called to explicitly remove items from the data cache.

You can also easily insert data items into a data cache using indexers by providing a key and value, like so:

```
Cache["CustomersDataSet"] = dsCustomers;
```

Handling Session State

You already know about the use of session variables to store information in an ASP.NET application. HTTP is, of course, a stateless protocol—meaning that the browser has no way of associating information from one page to another of an ASP.NET application. With session variables, you store this information on the server. The server sends a cookie or appends the session information to the URL with each request and then uses this value to retrieve session state information when the browser returns a new request.

Using Session State in a Process

The default location for Session state storage is in the ASP.NET process itself. If you stop the Web server or restart IIS (or if it crashes for some reason), all this information is lost.

Using Session State Service

As an alternative to using in-process storage for Session state, ASP.NET provides the ASP.NET State Service.

The State Service has two main advantages. First, it is not running in the same process as ASP.NET, so a crash of ASP.NET will not destroy session information. Second, the stateConnectionString used to locate the State Service includes the TCP/IP address of the service, which need not be running on the same computer as ASP.NET. This enables you to share state information across a Web garden (multiple processors on the same computer) or even across a Web farm (multiple servers running the application).

The major disadvantage of using the State Service is that it's an external process, rather than part of ASP.NET. Therefore, reading and writing Session state is slower than it would be if you kept the state in-process.

To enable State Service, you must ensure that a Windows service named ASP.NET State Service is running on the Web server. If the service is not already running, you can manage it using the Services administrative tool of the Windows Control Panel.

To configure an application to use the State Service, you need to edit the `<sessionState>` element of the `web.config` file as shown here:

```
<sessionState mode="StateServer"
    stateConnectionString="tcpip=127.0.0.1:42424"/>
```

Using Microsoft SQL Server to Store Session State

The final choice for storing state information is to save it in a Microsoft SQL Server database.

Similar to the State Service, SQL Server lets you share Session state among the processors in a Web garden or the servers in a Web farm. But you also get the additional benefit of persistent storage. Even if the computer hosting

SQL Server crashes and is restarted, the Session state information will still be present in the database and be available as soon as the database is running again.

To use SQL Server for storing Session state, you must supply the server name, username, and password for a SQL Server account in the `sqlConnectionString` attribute, like so:

```
<sessionState mode="SqlServer"
    sqlConnectionString="data source=SERVERNAME;user
id=alice;password=p@ssw0rd"/>
```

Exam Prep Questions

Question 1

You are adding a section to the **machine.config** file on your ASP.NET Web server. You want to ensure that this section cannot be defined in any other configuration file. Which declaration should you use?

○ A.

```
<section name="customSection"
 type="CustomConfiguration Handler"
allowDefinition="MachineToApplication"/>
```

○ B.

```
<section name="customSection"
 type="CustomConfiguration Handler"
 allowLocation="false"/>
```

○ C.

```
<section name="customSection"
 type="CustomConfiguration Handler" />
```

○ D.

```
<section name="customSection"
 type="CustomConfiguration Handler"
 allowOverride="false"/>
```

The correct answer is B. The `allowLocation` attribute lets you specify that this section should not appear beneath the file where it is defined. Answer A is incorrect because the `allowDefinition` attribute being set to `MachineToApplication` allows this section to be defined on the application level. Answer C is incorrect because omitting all the attributes allows a section to be defined everywhere. Answer D is incorrect because the `allowOverride` attribute applies to actual configuration data, not to section declarations.

Question 2

You have adjusted a setting in one of your ASP.NET application's configuration files by editing the file with Notepad. What must you do to have the new setting take effect?

○ A.   Restart the Web server.

○ B.   Reboot the computer that hosts the Web server.

○ C.   Open the file in Visual Studio .NET.

○ D.   Save the file.

The correct answer is D. Changes to ASP.NET configuration files are automatically picked up by ASP.NET as soon as the files are saved. Answers A and B are incorrect because changes to the application configuration file are automatically picked up by ASP.NET and do not require restarting the Web Server process or the machine. Answer C is incorrect because the application configuration file is a plain-text file and Visual Studio .NET is not needed to either edit or activate it.

Question 3

Your ASP.NET application requires users to be authenticated with a strong identity. You must allow users with any version 4.x or better browser, and you want passwords to cross the network only with secure encryption. Which authentication should you use?

○ A. Windows authentication with basic IIS authentication

○ B. Windows authentication with digest IIS authentication

○ C. Windows authentication with integrated IIS authentication

○ D. Passport authentication with anonymous IIS authentication

The correct answer is D. Only Passport authentication fulfills the requirements stated in the question. Answer A is incorrect because basic IIS authentication does not securely encrypt passwords. Answers B and C are incorrect because digest and Windows integrated authentication require Internet Explorer as the browser.

Question 4

You have implemented forms-based authentication for your ASP.NET application. Some users report that they cannot access any resources on the site, even though you have verified that these users are entering correct authentication information. What could be the most likely cause of this problem?

○ A. These users are using non-Internet Explorer browsers.

○ B. These users have disabled cookies for your Web site.

○ C. These users do not have a Microsoft Passport.

○ D. These users are connecting from the Internet rather than a local intranet.

The correct answer is B. Forms authentication depends on cookies to indicate that a browser session has been authenticated. Answer A is incorrect because form-based authentication is not browser dependent. Answer C is incorrect because users do not need a Microsoft Passport for form-based authentication. Answer D is incorrect because form-based authentication should work well on an intranet as well as the Internet.

Question 5

Your application requires the user to be in the Domain Admins group to activate certain functions. Which ASP.NET security feature should you use to ensure that the user is in this group?

○ A. Passport authentication

○ B. Role-based security

○ C. Encryption

○ D. Type safety

The correct answer is B. Role-based security enables you to check whether a user is in a particular group. Answer A is incorrect because Passport authentication only authenticates the user's identity and does not provide additional information such as role membership. Answer C is incorrect because encryption is a process of protecting messages so that they can be read only via a special algorithm. Encryption is more suitable for protecting data instead of actions. Answer D is incorrect because type safety is an attribute of the code that verifies that the code uses only the memory locations it is allowed to use. Type safety has nothing to do with the functionality of an application.

Question 6

You want to allow any authenticated user access to your ASP.NET application but refuse access to all unauthenticated users. Which setting should you place in the application's **web.config** file?

○ A.

```
<deny users="?" />
```

○ B.

```
<deny users="*" />
```

○ C.

```
<allow users="?" />
```

○ D.

```
<allow users="*" />
```

The correct answer is A. If you deny access to all unauthenticated users, only authenticated users will be able to use the application. Answer B is incorrect because this option denies access to all the users (authenticated or not). Answer C is incorrect because this option allows access to all the unauthenticated users. Answer D is incorrect because this option allows access to all the users (authenticated or not).

Question 7

You are allowing anonymous or Windows integrated authentication on your IIS server. Your ASP.NET application uses Windows authentication with impersonation enabled. Which account will ASP.NET use when a user attempts to retrieve a page from the application?

- O A. The user's own Windows account
- O B. The **ASPNET** account
- O C. The **IUSR_*ComputerName*** account
- O D. An account in the local administrators group

The correct answer is C. ASP.NET impersonates the identity of IIS itself using the IUSR_*ComputerName* account. Answer A is incorrect because, if you allow anonymous authentication in IIS, users are never prompted for their Windows credentials. Answer B is incorrect because the ASPNET account is used when impersonation is disabled. Answer D is incorrect because impersonation is not enabled for a specific identity that belongs to the local administrators group.

Question 8

Your ASP.NET Web form includes a custom user control that displays company information. The rest of the page displays highly volatile stock ticker information. Which type of caching should you use to speed up this page?

- O A. Output
- O B. Varying
- O C. Application data
- O D. Fragment

The correct answer is D. In this case, the user control is a good candidate for caching, but the rest of the page should not be cached. Fragment caching enables you to cache a single user control. Answers A and B are incorrect because output caching and varying caching are useful only for caching the output of the complete page. Answer C is incorrect because application data caching is useful only for caching the data and not for caching page output.

Question 9

Your server is experiencing performance problems because of excessive load. You trace the problem to users overriding the application's caching policy by sending **nocache** headers in their HTTP requests. What should you do?

○ A. Use the **OutputCache** directive to configure caching.

○ B. Use the **HttpCachePolicy.SetExpires()** method to set an extended cache period.

○ C. Use the **HttpCachePolicy.SetCacheability()** method by passing an **HttpCacheability.Private** enumeration value.

○ D. Set the **HttpCache.SetValidUntilExpires()** method by passing **true**.

The correct answer is D. The `HttpCache.SetValidUntilExpires()` method tells the server to ignore client-side refreshes as long as the cache is valid. Answers A, B, and C are incorrect because these options do not override the HTTP `Cache-Control` headers sent by the client.

Question 10

Your ASP.NET application uses a Web farm to maintain confidential financial information. It's critical that Session state be maintained even in case of a server crash. Which alternative should you use for storing state information?

○ A. Session State Service

○ B. In-process storage

○ C. SQL Server storage

○ D. Configuration files

The correct answer is C. By placing Session state information in a SQL Server database, you get the benefit of SQL Server's transactional, logged storage that is guaranteed to keep the data in a consistent state even if the server crashes. Answer A is incorrect because, if the Web server storing the Session state fails, all the session information will be lost. Answer B is incorrect because in-process Session state is not shared between multiple Web servers in a Web farm. Answer D is incorrect because configuration files should be used only for storing configuration information.

Need to Know More?

 Kalani, Amit. *MCAD/MCSD Training Guide (70-315): Developing and Implementing Web-Based Applications with Visual C# and Visual Studio .NET.* Indianapolis, IN: Que Certification, 2002.

 Leinecker, Richard. *Special Edition Using ASP.NET.* Indianapolis, IN: Que Publishing, 2002.

 Onion, Fritz. *Essential ASP.NET with Examples in C#.* Reading, MA: Addison Wesley, 2003.

 Download and read the MSDN guide on building secure ASP.NET applications at www.microsoft.com/downloads/release.asp?ReleaseID=44047.

 Read the .NET security guidance for authentication in ASP.NET at www.msdn.com/library/en-us/dnbda/html/authaspdotnet.asp.

17

Practice Exam #1

Do not read Chapters 17–20 until you have learned and practiced all the material presented in the chapters of this book. These chapters serve a special purpose; they are designed to test whether you are ready to take the Developing and Implementing Web Applications with Microsoft Visual C# .NET and Microsoft Visual Studio .NET exam (70-315). In these chapters, you will find two practice tests, each of which is followed by an answer key and brief explanations of the correct answers and reasons why the other answers are incorrect. Reading these chapters prior to the other chapters is like reading the climax of a story and then going back to find out how the story arrived at that ending. Of course, you don't want to spoil the excitement, do you?

How to Take the Practice Tests

Each practice test in this book consists of 60 questions, and you should complete each test within 120 minutes. The number of questions and the time duration in the actual exam might vary but should be close to these numbers.

After you have read the material presented in the chapters of this book, you should take Practice Exam #1 to check how much you have learned. After the practice test is complete, evaluate yourself using the answer key in Chapter 18, "Answers to Practice Exam #1." When you evaluate yourself, note the questions you answered incorrectly, identify the corresponding chapters in the book, and then reread and understand that material before taking Practice Exam #2. After taking the second exam, evaluate yourself again and reread the material corresponding to any incorrect answers. Finally, take both tests again until you have correctly answered all the questions. The information presented in the following sections should help you prepare for the exams.

Exam-taking Tips

Take these exams under your own circumstances, but I strongly suggest that when you take them, you treat them just as you would treat the actual exam at the test center. Use the following tips to get maximum benefit from the exams:

➤ Before you start, create a quiet, secluded environment where you will be undisturbed for the duration of the exam.

➤ Provide yourself a few empty sheets of paper before you start. Use some of these sheets to write your answers, and use the others to organize your thoughts. At the end of the exam, use your answer sheet to evaluate your exam with the help of the answer key that follows.

➤ Don't use any reference material during the exam.

➤ Some of the questions might be vague and require you to make deductions to come up with the best possible answer from the choices given. Others might be verbose, requiring you to read and process a lot of information before you reach the actual question.

➤ As you progress, keep track of the elapsed time and make sure you'll be able to answer all the questions in the given time limit.

Practice Exam

Question 1

You are developing an ASP.NET application using Visual C# .NET. In your ASPX page, you want to invoke and display a Visual C# .NET method named **DisplayProductNames()** when the page is rendered to the client. Which of the following code blocks should you choose to call the **DisplayProductNames()** method?

O A.
```
<script language="C#" runat="server">
    Response.Write(DisplayProductNames());
</script>
```

O B.
```
<script language="C#" runat="client">
    Response.Write(DisplayProductNames());
</script>
```

O C.
```
<script language="C#">
    Response.Write(DisplayProductNames());
</script>
```

O D.
```
<%= DisplayProductNames()%>
```

O E.
```
<%= DisplayProductNames();%>
```

Question 2

You've used Visual C# .NET to develop an ASP.NET Web form named **Login.aspx**. This Web form allows users to enter their credentials for accessing the Web site. You have defined a code-behind class named **Login** under the **MyCompany** namespace in a file named **Login.aspx.cs** that contains the business logic. You now want to link the user interface file with the code-behind file; you do not want to precompile the code-behind class each time you make modifications. Which of the following **Page** directives would you use in the **Login.aspx** file?

○ A.
```
<%@ Page Language="c#" Codebehind="Login.aspx.cs"
ClassName="MyCompany.Login"%>
```

○ B.
```
<%@ Page Language="c#" Codebehind="Login.aspx.cs"
Inherits="MyCompany.Login"%>
```

○ C.
```
<%@ Page Language="c#" Src="Login.aspx.cs"
Inherits="MyCompany.Login"%>
```

○ D.
```
<%@ Page Language="c#" Src="Login.aspx.cs"
ClassName="MyCompany.Login"%>
```

Question 3

Your Web form allows users to enter a telephone number into a **TextBox** ASP.NET Web server control named **txtPhone**. You use the **RegularExpressionValidator** control to ensure that the phone numbers are in the correct format.

The Web form also includes a **Button** ASP.NET Web server control, **btnReset**, to reset the data entry values. You do not want the validations to occur when the button is clicked. What should you do to ensure this?

○ A. Set the **CausesValidation** property of the **TextBox** control to **true**.

○ B. Set the **CausesValidation** property of the **Button** control to **true**.

○ C. Set the **CausesValidation** property of the **TextBox** control to **false**.

○ D. Set the **CausesValidation** property of the **Button** control to **false**.

Question 4

You have designed a Web form that uses a **DropDownList** control to allow a user to select a state containing her shipping address. You've implemented an event handler for the **SelectedIndexChanged** event to update the sales tax amount displayed on the Web form when a new state is selected.

Users report that the sales tax amount is not updated no matter which state they choose in the **DropDownList** control. What must you do to fix this problem?

○ A. Move the code to the **PreRender** event of the **DropDownList** control.

○ B. Set the **AutoPostBack** property of the **DropDownList** control to **true**.

○ C. Replace the **DropDownList** control with a **ListBox** control.

○ D. Set the **EnableViewState** property of the **DropDownList** control to **true**.

Question 5

You have designed a Web form that includes a **DropDownList** control with an **ID** of **ddlSize**. The **Items** property of the **ddlSize** control contains the following items:

```
-
9
10
11
```

The Web form also contains a **RequiredFieldValidator** control named **rfvSize**. You have set the **ControlToValidate** property of **rfvSize** to **ddlSize**. Your goal is to ensure that a nondefault value is chosen from **ddlSize** before the Web form is posted back to the server. What other property setting must you make on the **rfvSize** control?

○ A. **rfvSize.InitialValue = "-";**

○ B. **rfvSize.Display = ValidatorDisplay.Dynamic;**

○ C. **rfvSize.Visible = true;**

○ D. **rfvSize.EnableClientScript = false;**

Question 6

You have developed an ASP.NET Web page that consists of several Web server controls for data entry. You have placed validation controls to validate the data entered in the Web server controls and have used the **Text** property of the validation controls to display the error messages inline within the validation control. You have deployed the Web page to the testing Web server so that the testers can test your Web page. One of the testers who uses Internet Explorer 4.0 reports that the Web page does not display the error message when he tabs from the control after providing an invalid value. The error messages are displayed only when he clicks the Submit button. How can you solve this problem?

○ A. Set the **Enabled** attribute of the validation controls to **true**.

○ B. Set the **SmartNavigation** attribute to **true** in the **Page** directive.

○ C. Ask the tester to enable client-side scripting before accessing the Web page.

○ D. Ask the tester to upgrade to Internet Explorer 6.0 before accessing the Web page.

Question 7

When a page is restricted in your ASP.NET application (that is, when a 403 error occurs), you want to display a page named **Forbidden.aspx**. For all other errors, you want to display a page named **GeneralError.aspx** to the user. Which settings should you make in the **web.config** file to ensure this?

○ A.
```
<customErrors mode="On"
 defaultRedirect="GeneralError.aspx">
    <error statusCode="403" redirect="Forbidden.aspx" />
</customErrors>
```

○ B.
```
<customErrors mode="RemoteOnly"
 defaultRedirect="GeneralError.aspx">
    <error statusCode="403" redirect="Forbidden.aspx" />
</customErrors>
```

○ C.
```
<customErrors mode="On">
    <error statusCode="403" redirect="Forbidden.aspx" />
    <error statusCode="all" redirect="GeneralError.aspx" />
</customErrors>
```

○ D.
```
<customErrors mode="RemoteOnly">
    <error statusCode="403" redirect="Forbidden.aspx" />
    <error statusCode="all" redirect="GeneralError.aspx" />
</customErrors>
```

Question 8

You have written a Visual C# .NET method that opens a database connection using a **SqlConnection** object, which retrieves some information from the database and then closes the connection. The information is retrieved using a stored procedure that might not always be available because of the maintenance schedules. You have wrapped the code to call the stored procedure in a **try-catch-finally** block. You use two **catch** blocks—one to catch the exceptions of type **SqlException** and the second to catch the exceptions of type **Exception**. Which of the following places should you choose for closing the **SqlConnection** object?

- ○ A. Inside the **try** block, before the first **catch** block
- ○ B. Inside the **catch** block that catches **SqlException** objects
- ○ C. Inside the **catch** block that catches **Exception** objects
- ○ D. Inside the **finally** block

Question 9

Your ASP.NET application includes a Web page named **Errors.htm** that is displayed in response to any error. This page is configured using the following code in the **web.config** file:

```
<customErrors mode="Off"
 defaultRedirect="Errors.htm">
</customErrors>
```

The application includes a detail page named **AccountSummary.aspx**. When an error occurs on the login page, you want to log those errors in the custom log file, **Custom.txt**. What should you do?

- ○ A. Add an **<error>** element as a child of the **<customErrors>** element in **web.config**. Specify the page name as **AccountSummary.aspx** and the redirect page as **Custom.txt** in the new element.
- ○ B. Add an **ErrorPage** attribute to the **Page** directive for **AccountSummary.aspx**. Set the value of this attribute to **Custom.txt**.
- ○ C. Implement the logic in the **Page_Error()** event handler in **AccountSummary.aspx** to store errors into **Custom.txt**.
- ○ D. Implement the logic in the **Application_Error()** event handler in **AccountSummary.aspx** to store errors into **Custom.txt**.

Question 10

You are developing an application to take orders over the Internet. When a user posts back the order form, you first check to see whether she is a registered customer of your company. If not, you must transfer control to the **Register.html** page. Which method should you use to transfer it?

- ○ A. **Response.Redirect("Register.html");**
- ○ B. **Server.Transfer("Register.html");**
- ○ C. **Server.Execute("Register.html");**
- ○ D. **Server.CreateObject("Register.html");**

Question 11

You have deployed an ASP.NET application on your company's intranet. Your company has standardized on Internet Explorer 6.0 as the corporate browser. Users complain that when they use the Submit button to send their expense reports via the application, the focus moves to the first control on the reporting form. This makes it difficult for users to edit their expense reports.

What is the easiest way to maintain focus across postback operations in this application?

- ○ A. Store the name of the current control in session state when the page is posted back, and use this name to set the focus when the page is re-created.
- ○ B. Store the name of the current control in view state when the page is posted back, and use this name to set the focus when the page is re-created.
- ○ C. Write client-side code that stores the focus control in a hidden field and retrieves this information when the page is re-created.
- ○ D. Set the **SmartNavigation** attribute of the **Page** directive to **true**.

Question 12

Your ASP.NET Web application uses session state to track usernames and other user-specific details. Your Web application contains a Web page that displays a greeting to the user—**"Welcome *<UserName>*"**—and the product catalog from a SQL Server database. The product catalog is displayed in a **DataGrid** control that is populated at every page load. Which of the following options should you use in this application to maximize performance? (Select two.)

❑ A. Disable view state for the page.

❑ B. Disable session state for the page.

❑ C. Make the session state read-only for the page.

❑ D. Store the session state in SQL Server.

Question 13

Your ASP.NET application stores sensitive data in the session state. You need to maintain the session state even if the Web server crashes and needs to be restarted. Which mode attribute should you use to configure the **<sessionState>** element for this application?

○ A. **mode="Inproc"**

○ B. **mode="StateServer"**

○ C. **mode="SqlServer"**

○ D. **mode="Off"**

Question 14

You are developing an online bookstore application in Visual C# .NET. Your application needs to store the most recent book viewed by the user and show the recently viewed book's details in the lower part of the Web pages whenever the user accesses the Web site. You do not want to use server-side resources to store the book ISBN. Which of the following state-management techniques will help you accomplish this?

○ A. Hidden fields

○ B. View state

○ C. Cookies

○ D. Sessions

Question 15

You have created an ASP.NET Web page, **Catalog.aspx**, that allows users to purchase products from the catalog. The catalog displays the previously selected item in the lower part of the Web page. This product detail is encapsulated in a **Product** object and is not accessed outside the Web page. The **Product** class is defined as follows:

```
[Serializable]
public class Product
{
    public int ProductCode;
    public string ProductName;
}
```

Which of the following objects should you use to store the **Product** object?

- ○ A. Application state
- ○ B. Session state
- ○ C. View state
- ○ D. Cache object

Question 16

You have developed an ASP.NET Web form that displays product information from a SQL Server 2000 database. The database contains information for about 100 products. Each time the page is displayed, it retrieves information on one product specified by the user. These pages are requested very frequently by users.

Which type of caching can you use to speed up the delivery of this page?

- ○ A. Output
- ○ B. Varying output
- ○ C. Application data
- ○ D. Fragment output

Question 17

You are creating an ASP.NET Web page that reads data from a large XML file (**CustomerInformation.xml**), processes and loads the data in a **DataSet** object, and displays the results to the browser in a **DataGrid** control. The processing of the file data consumes server resources and delays the loading of the Web page. The Web page displays the same data at every request unless the data in the file changes. Which of the following code segments should you use for caching to improve performance?

○ A.
```
<%@ OutputCache VaryByCustom="CustomerInformation.xml" %>
```

○ B.
```
<%@ OutputCache VaryByParam="CustomerInformation.xml" %>
```

○ C.
```
Cache["FileData"] = dsCustomers;
```

○ D.
```
Cache.Insert("CacheValue",
    dsCustomers,
    new CacheDependency(Server.MapPath(
      " CustomerInformation.xml")));
```

Question 18

You are an ASP.NET developer of a company that has a chain of stores selling leather products in the United States. You have developed a user control named **StoreLocator.ascx** that is placed in the main page of the company's Web site. The user control contains a text box named **txtState** that accepts a state name from the user and displays the list of stores in that state. You want to cache different versions of the user control for 600 seconds for each state. Which of the following **OutputCache** directives should you choose to enable caching on the user control?

○ A. **<%@ OutputCache Duration="600" VaryByControl="txtState" %>**

○ B. **<%@ OutputCache Duration="600" VaryByParam="txtState" %>**

○ C. **<%@ OutputCache Duration="600" VaryByControl="*" %>**

○ D. **<%@ OutputCache Duration="600" VaryByParam="*" %>**

Question 19

In your ASP.NET application, you use the data cache to store a **DataSet** object containing a single **DataTable** object named **Customers**. The **Customers DataTable** has all the rows and columns from the **Customers** table in your database. You want to bind only selected columns from the **Customers** table to a **DataGrid** control. You also want a solution that requires minimum programming and that has minimum impact on the functionality and performance of other applications accessing the same SQL Server database. How should you proceed?

○ A.   Create a second **DataTable** object in the **DataSet** object. Copy the desired data to the second **DataTable** object, and bind the second **DataTable** object to the **DataGrid** control.

○ B.   Create a **Command** object to retrieve the desired columns from the **DataTable** object, and bind the **Command** object to the **DataGrid** control.

○ C.   Delete the undesired columns from the **DataTable** object.

○ D.   Create a **DataView** object that retrieves only the desired columns from the **DataTable** object, and bind the **DataGrid** control to the **DataView** object.

Question 20

Your ASP.NET Web application includes a **SqlDataAdapter** object named **sqlDataAdapter1** that was created by dragging and dropping the **Customers** table from a database to your form. Your application also includes a **DataSet** named **dsCustomers1**, based on this **SqlDataAdapter**. Which line of code should you use to load the data from the database into the **DataSet**?

○ A.   **dsCustomers1= sqlDataAdapter1.Fill("Customers");**

○ B.   **sqlDataAdapter1.Fill("dsCustomers1", "Customers");**

○ C.   **sqlDataAdapter1.Fill(dsCustomers1, "Customers");**

○ D.   **sqlDataAdapter1.Fill(dsCustomers1);**

Question 21

You have recently deployed an expense reporting system in your company, and the application relies heavily on its SQL Server database. All employees in the company have similar access permissions to the database. You have created the application in such a way that it uses an employee's logon name and password in the connection string to connect to SQL Server. Users of the application are consistently reporting slow performance of the application. Your task is to optimize the performance of this application. You've noted that another application which uses the same SQL Server database is having good performance. Which of the following steps should you take?

○ A. Compile the application to native code using **ngen.exe**.

○ B. Run the SQL Server Index Tuning Wizard.

○ C. Increase the maximum size of the connection pool.

○ D. Use the same connection string for all users.

Question 22

You are developing an ASP.NET Web application, named **VerifyOrders**, that receives data from the Orders application in XML format. The **VerifyOrders** application enables its users to review the orders and make any changes required. When the users are finished reviewing the orders, the **VerifyOrders** application must create an output XML file, which is returned to the Orders application. The output XML file must contain the original as well as the changed values. Which option should you choose to create such an output XML file?

○ A. Call the **DataSet.WriteXmlSchema()** method and pass an **XmlWriter** object as a parameter.

○ B. Call the **DataSet.WriteXml()** method and set the value for the **XmlWriteMode** parameter to **IgnoreSchema**.

○ C. Call the **DataSet.WriteXml()** method and set the value for the **XmlWriteMode** parameter to **WriteSchema**.

○ D. Call the **DataSet.WriteXml()** method and set the value for the **XmlWriteMode** parameter to **DiffGram**.

Question 23

You are writing a Visual C# .NET Web application that executes several stored procedures to update a SQL Server database. You use database transactions to ensure that either all updates to the database succeed or the changes are rolled back in case of an error. You used the following code segment to create the database connection and the transaction object in your program:

```
SqlConnection sqlConnection1 = new SqlConnection(strConnString);
sqlConnection1.Open();

SqlCommand sqlCommand1 = new SqlCommand();
SqlTransaction sqlTrans;
```

You need to prevent other users from updating or inserting rows into the database until the transaction is complete. Which of the following statements enable you to fulfill this requirement?

○ A.
```
sqlTrans = sqlConnection1.BeginTransaction(
    IsolationLevel.ReadCommitted);
```

○ B.
```
sqlTrans = sqlConnection1.BeginTransaction(
    IsolationLevel.Serializable);
```

○ C.
```
sqlTrans = sqlCommand1.BeginTransaction(
    IsolationLevel.ReadCommitted);
```

○ D.
```
sqlTrans = sqlCommand1.BeginTransaction(
    IsolationLevel.Serializable);
```

Question 24

You need to develop a Web application that exports the contents of the **Customers** table to an XML file. The exported XML file will then be used by a marketing company for various customer relations programs. The marketing company requires that customer data be exported to the XML file in the following format:

```
<Customers CustomerID="ALFKI" ContactName="Maria Anders"
➥Phone="030-0074321" />
<Customers CustomerID="ANATR" ContactName="Ana Trujillo"
➥Phone="(5) 555-4729" />
```

Which of the following code segments would you use to export the **Customers** table to the XML format in the specified format?

○ A.
```
foreach(DataColumn c in dataSet1.Tables["Customers"].Columns)
{
    c.ColumnMapping = MappingType.Attribute;
}
dataSet1.WriteXml("Customers.xml");
```

○ B.
```
foreach(DataColumn c in dataSet1.Tables["Customers"].Columns)
{
    c.ColumnMapping = MappingType.Element;
}
dataSet1.WriteXml("Customers.xml");
```

○ C.
```
foreach(DataColumn c in dataSet1.Tables["Customers"].Columns)
{
    c.ColumnMapping = MappingType.Attribute;
}
dataSet1.WriteXml("Customers.xml", XmlWriteMode.WriteSchema);
```

○ D.
```
foreach(DataColumn c in dataSet1.Tables["Customers"].Columns)
{
    c.ColumnMapping = MappingType.Element;
}
dataSet1.WriteXml("Customers.xml", XmlWriteMode.WriteSchema);
```

Question 25

You are developing a Web application that processes data from a SQL Server 7.0 database. The application reads the data from the database in a forward-only way and does not perform any update operations. You use the **System.Data.SqlClient.SqlConnection** object to connect to the SQL Server database and then use a **System.Data.SqlClient.SqlCommand** object to run a stored procedure and retrieve the results into a **System.Data.SqlClient.SqlDataReader** object. The data returned by the **SqlCommand** object consists of 1,000 rows and 1 column; the column is defined as **nvarchar(20)** in the database. You have written the following code to concatenate the column values of the returned result set into a string variable. What can you do to optimize the application? (Select two answers.)

```
SqlDataReader dr = cmd.ExecuteReader();
String s;
while(dr.Read())
{
    s = s + dr.GetValue(0);
}
```

- ❏ A. Replace the stored procedure with a SQL statement.
- ❏ B. Replace the **SqlDataReader** object with a **DataSet** object.
- ❏ C. Replace the **while** loop with a **for each** loop.
- ❏ D. Replace the **String** variable with a **StringBuilder** object.
- ❏ E. Replace the **GetValue()** method with the **GetString()** method.

Question 26

Your application uses a **SqlDataReader** object to retrieve patient information from a medical records database. When you find a patient who is currently hospitalized, you want to read the names of the patient's caregivers from the same database. You have created a second **SqlDataReader** object, based on a second **SqlCommand** object, to retrieve the caregiver information. When you call the **ExecuteReader()** method of the **SqlCommand** object, you get an error. What is the most likely cause of this error?

- ○ A. You are using the same **SqlConnection** object for both the **SqlDataReader** objects, and the first **SqlDataReader** is still open when you try to execute the **SqlCommand**.
- ○ B. You must use a **SqlDataAdapter** object to retrieve the caregiver information.
- ○ C. You must use the **OleDbDataReader** object to retrieve information instead of the **SqlDataReader** object.
- ○ D. You are using the **ExecuteReader()** method of the **SqlCommand** object and should be using the **ExecuteScalar()** method instead.

Question 27

You've used Visual C# .NET to develop an ASP.NET Web application that will be used by the customer service department. Your application receives data from the Orders application, and users of your application get calls from customers to make changes to their orders. You've written the code that allows them to make changes to the data, but now you want to write code that sends the changed records back to the Orders application. Which of the following methods should you use to accomplish this requirement?

- ○ A. **DataSet.Clone()**
- ○ B. **DataSet.Copy()**
- ○ C. **DataSet.GetChanges()**
- ○ D. **DataSet.Merge()**

Question 28

You are a .NET developer for a large warehousing company and need to develop a Web application that helps users manage the inventory. Inventory data is stored in a SQL Server 2000 database named **WareHouse2** in a database named **Inventory**. You use the **SqlConnection** object and Windows Integrated authentication to connect to the **Inventory** database. Which of the following connection strings should you choose in your Visual C# .NET program?

- ○ A.
  ```
  "Provider=SQLOLEDB;Data Source=WareHouse2;
  ➡Initial Catalog=Inventory;
  ➡Integrated Security=SSPI;"
  ```

- ○ B.
  ```
  "Provider=SQLOLEDB;Data Source=WareHouse2;
  ➡Initial Catalog=Inventory;
  ➡User Id=sa;Password=Ti7uGf1;"
  ```

- ○ C.
  ```
  "Data Source=WareHouse2;
  ➡Initial Catalog=inventory;
  ➡Trusted_Connection=true;"
  ```

- ○ D.
  ```
  "Data Source=WareHouse2;User Id=sa;
  ➡Password=Ti7uikGf1;
  ➡Initial Catalog=inventory;"
  ```

Question 29

You need to develop a database application that interacts with an Oracle database. You need to write code to return the total number of customers from the database, and you need to create the fastest solution. Which of the following actions should you take? (Select all that apply.)

☐ A. Write ad hoc SQL query to return the total number of customers.

☐ B. Create a stored procedure to return the total number of customers.

☐ C. Use the **OleDbCommand.ExecuteScalar()** method.

☐ D. Use the **OleDbCommand.ExecuteReader()** method.

☐ E. Use the **OleDbDataAdapter.Fill()** method.

Question 30

A Web form in your ASP.NET application includes a **ListBox** control named **lbCustomers** that displays a list of customers. The **DataTextField** property of the **ListBox** is bound to the **CompanyName** column of the **Customers** database table. Also, the **DataValueField** property of the **ListBox** is bound to the **CustomerID** column of the **Customers** database table.

Your form also contains a **TextBox** control named **txtCustomerID**, which uses simple data binding to display the **SelectedItem.Value** from the **ListBox** control.

When a user selects a new company name in the **ListBox**, you want to display the corresponding **CustomerID** value in the **txtCustomerID** control. What should you do?

○ A. Call the **DataBind()** method of the **ListBox** control in the **SelectedIndexChanged** event of the **ListBox**.

○ B. Create a public property named **CustomerID** and return the **SelectedItem.Value** property of the **ListBox** as the value of the public property.

○ C. Use simple data binding to bind the **SelectedItem.Value** property of the **ListBox** to the **CustomerID** column of the **Customers** table.

○ D. Call the **DataBind()** method of the **TextBox** control in the **SelectedIndexChanged** event of the **ListBox**.

Question 31

You are developing a sales analysis Web page that displays monthly sales in a **DataGrid** control. Whenever the sales amount increases for average sales, you want to display the sales amount underlined. Which of the following events should you choose to display the sales amount underlined?

○ A. **ItemCreated**

○ B. **ItemCommand**

○ C. **ItemDataBound**

○ D. **DataBinding**

Question 32

You have to develop an ASP.NET Web application that will be used by the order-tracking system of your company. The application must contain a form that displays a list of orders placed by customers for the past year. When an employee selects an order from the list box, you need to display the order status and other information about the selected order in a **DataList** control. You have retrieved the order details in a **DataSet** object named **dsOrders**. The **dsOrders** object contains a table named **Order** that contains the order status and other information. You have set the **DataSource** property of the **DataList** control to **dsOrders** and the **DataMember** property to **Order**. Which snippet of code would you use to bind the text box control to the field named **OrderStatus** in the **Order** table?

○ A.
```
<ItemTemplate>
    <asp:TextBox id="txtOrderID" runat="server"
      text='<%# dsOrders.Order.OrderStatus %>'>
</ItemTemplate>
```

○ B.
```
<SelectedItemTemplate>
    <asp:TextBox id="txtOrderID" runat="server"
      text='<%# dsOrders.Order.OrderStatus %>'>
</SelectedItemTemplate>
```

○ C.
```
<ItemTemplate>
    <asp:TextBox id="txtOrderID" runat="server"
      text='<%# DataBinder.Eval(
        Container.DataItem, "OrderID") %>'>
</ItemTemplate>
```

○ D.
```
<SelectedItemTemplate>
    <asp:TextBox id="txtOrderID" runat="server"
      text='<%# DataBinder.Eval(
        Container.DataItem, "OrderID") %>'>
</SelectedItemTemplate>
```

Question 33

You are designing an application that will enable users to read an XML file from an orders system and convert the XML file into an HTML file using the stylesheet **DisplayOrders.xsl**. Which object should you use to implement this requirement?

- ○ A. **XPathNavigator**
- ○ B. **XslTransform**
- ○ C. **XmlSchema**
- ○ D. **XmlNode**

Question 34

You need to develop an ASP.NET Web application that accesses the Orders XML Web service provided by your company's business partner. You know the URL of the Web service. How can you generate client-side proxy classes for a Web service? (Select two.)

- ❑ A. Use a proxy tool such as the .NET WebService Studio tool.
- ❑ B. Use the Web Services Description Language tool.
- ❑ C. Use the Web Services Discovery Tool.
- ❑ D. Add a Web reference to point to the Web service.

Question 35

You work as a Visual C# .NET programmer for a multinational marketing company. You have been given a task to create a localized version of a Windows form for use in countries where the text is read from right to left. You need to ensure that all the controls in the form are aligned properly for the ease of local users. You need to make minimal changes. Which of the following options should you choose to accomplish this task?

- ○ A. Set the **dir** attribute of each control on the Web form to **rtl**.
- ○ B. Set the **rtl** attribute of each control on the Web form to **true**.
- ○ C. Set the **dir** attribute of the **<HTML>** element to **rtl**.
- ○ D. Set the **rtl** attribute of the **<HTML>** element to **true**.

Question 36

You are converting an existing ASP application to an ASP.NET application. The ASP application uses ADO extensively for data access, and you do not want to convert the ADO code to ADO.NET code yet. You should ensure that the ADO objects continue to function properly on the ASP.NET pages. You also want to achieve the best possible performance from your application. Which of the following solutions should you choose?

○ A. Build a runtime callable wrapper for each ADO object you use.

○ B. Use a **Page** directive to set ASP compatibility mode on the ASP.NET pages, like so:

```
<%@ Page AspCompat="true" %>
```

○ C. Use a **Page** directive to set the ASP.NET page language to **VBScript**, like so:

```
<%@ Page Language="VBScript" %>
```

○ D. Use the Type Library Importer tool to create a primary interop assembly for the ADO objects.

Question 37

You are responsible for maintaining a COM component that is used by numerous applications throughout your company. You are not ready to convert this COM component to .NET-managed code, but you need to make it available to an increasing number of other projects being developed under the .NET Framework. What should you do?

○ A. Set a direct reference to the existing COM component from each .NET project.

○ B. Use the Type Library Importer tool to create and sign an assembly that will use the COM component. Then, you should place the created assembly in the Global Assembly Cache.

○ C. Use the Type Library Importer tool to create an assembly that will use the COM component. Then, you should place the created assembly in the Global Assembly Cache.

○ D. Obtain a primary interop assembly for the COM component.

○ E. Set a direct reference from a single .NET project to the COM component, and include this project in each solution that must make use of the component.

Question 38

You are developing your company's Web site using a Visual C# .NET Web application. The product demo page of the Web site uses PNG graphics to represent the steps involved in using the product. Your company has a strict policy to make Web pages accessible to all readers. What should you do to make this page more accessible?

- ○ A. Use JPG graphics instead of PNG graphics for maximum browser compatibility.

- ○ B. Use the **AccessKey** property for all graphical controls to make them more accessible.

- ○ C. Add ALT text to all graphics to indicate their purpose through the **AlternateText** property.

- ○ D. Add ALT text to all graphics to indicate their purpose through the **ToolTip** property.

Question 39

You've used Visual Studio .NET to create an ASP.NET Web application that interacts with a Microsoft SQL Server database. You've also created a stored procedure, named **CalculateAccessCharges**, to calculate the monthly wireless Internet access charges for customers. When you run the program, the results from the stored procedure are not as expected. You want to debug the **CalculateAccessCharges** stored procedure to find the error. You also want to minimize the time and efforts involved in debugging; which of the following actions should you take?

- ○ A. Use the Tools, Debug Processes menu to attach a debugger to the SQL Server, and then step into the **CalculateAccessCharges** stored procedure.

- ○ B. Place a breakpoint in the **CalculateAccessCharges** stored procedure, and then use the Debug, Step Into menu option to step into the C# program that calls the stored procedure.

- ○ C. Use the SQL Server **Print** command to print the calculated values in the stored procedure.

- ○ D. Use the **Debug.WriteLine()** method to print the calculated values in the stored procedure.

Question 40

You've developed a customer contact management application using a Visual C# ASP.NET Web application. You've used the methods of the **Trace** and **Debug** classes to log serious error messages encountered during program execution. You now want to record all such errors in the Windows event log but do not want any duplicate entries for error messages in the event log. In which two ways can you add a listener to the Windows event log?

❏ A.

```
EventLogTraceListener traceListener =
    new EventLogTraceListener("CustomEventLog");
Trace.Listeners.Add(traceListener);
```

❏ B.

```
EventLogTraceListener traceListener =
    new EventLogTraceListener("CustomEventLog");
Trace.Listeners.Add(traceListener);
Debug.Listeners.Add(traceListener);
```

❏ C.

```
EventLogTraceListener traceListener =
    new EventLogTraceListener("CustomEventLog");
```

❏ D.

```
EventLogTraceListener traceListener =
    new EventLogTraceListener("CustomEventLog");
Debug.Listeners.Add(traceListener);
```

Question 41

Your Web application is failing when a particular variable equals **117**. Unfortunately, you cannot predict when this will happen. You want to write minimal code; which debugging tool should you use to investigate the problem?

○ A. Locals window

○ B. Output window

○ C. Immediate window

○ D. Conditional breakpoint

Question 42

You've developed a Visual Studio .NET application that helps the shipping department in creating mix-and-match pallets. Users of the application complain that the numbers of cases in the pallet are not displayed correctly. To find the location of the error, you place a breakpoint on the **GetCasesInPallet()** method. However, when you execute the program from the Visual Studio .NET environment, the execution does not break at the breakpoint. Which of the following actions should you take to resolve this problem?

- ○ A. Select Exceptions from the Debug menu.
- ○ B. Select Enable All Breakpoints from the Debug menu.
- ○ C. Select Build, Configuration Manager and set the project's configuration to Debug.
- ○ D. Select Build, Configuration Manager and set the project's configuration to Release.

Question 43

You are debugging your ASP.NET Web application and are concerned about the amount of time it's taking to render a particular page. Which class can you use to obtain detailed timing information for the events on the page as it is rendered by the ASP.NET engine?

- ○ A. **System.Diagnostics.Trace**
- ○ B. **System.Diagnostics.Debug**
- ○ C. **System.Web.TraceContext**
- ○ D. **System.Web.UI.Page**

Question 44

You have developed an online shipment tracking Visual C# ASP.NET application. The **ShipmentStatus.aspx** page in your application is displaying incorrect shipping statuses for shipments. You want to view the tracing information for the page. What should you do?

- ○ A. Set the **<trace>** element in the application's **web.config** configuration file to **<trace enabled="false" />**.

- ○ B. Set the **<trace>** element in the application's **web.config** configuration file to **<trace enabled="true" />**.

- ○ C. Set the **<trace>** element in the application's **web.config** configuration file to **<trace enabled="ShipmentStatus.aspx" />**.

- ○ D. Set the **Trace** attribute in the **Page** directive of the **ShipmentStatus.aspx** page to **<%@ Page Trace="true" />**.

- ○ E. Set the **Trace** attribute in the **Page** directive of the **ShipmentStatus.aspx** page to **<%@ Page Trace="false" />**.

Question 45

You've developed an intranet ASP.NET Web application that helps manage production schedules for a manufacturing company. This application uses a library named **Production.dll**. You anticipate that in the future some other applications might use classes from the **Production.dll** library. You also need to maintain multiple versions of **Production.dll**. Which of the following options should you choose to deploy **Production.dll**? (Select all that apply.)

- ❑ A. Sign **Production.dll** with **sn.exe**.

- ❑ B. Sign **Production.dll** with **signcode.exe**.

- ❑ C. Install **Production.dll** in the Windows system directory.

- ❑ D. Install **Production.dll** in the application's bin directory.

- ❑ E. Install **Production.dll** in the Global Assembly Cache.

Question 46

You are a programmer for a popular gaming software publishing company that has recently designed a series of games using the .NET Framework. All these new game applications share some components. Some of these components are shipped in the box with the application, and others are deployed over the Internet. Which of the following commands should you use for these components before packaging them for deployment?

○ A. Use **sn.exe** to sign the components.

○ B. Use **signcode.exe** to sign the components.

○ C. Use **sn.exe** followed by **signcode.exe** to sign the components.

○ D. Use **signcode.exe** followed by **sn.exe** to sign the components.

Question 47

You've used Visual C# .NET to develop an assembly that allows developers in your company to create pie charts in their Web applications. You named the assembly **PieChart.dll** and packaged it as version 1.0.0, which is deployed into the GAC. After two months, you discovered that a bug existed in the assembly. You fixed the bug by releasing a new version of the assembly, named 1.0.1. You then placed the newly created assembly in the GAC. What will happen to the applications written by other developers who use **PieChart.dll**?

○ A. The applications using the **PieChart.dll** assembly will break because the applications will notice two versions of the assembly in the GAC and won't know which one to execute.

○ B. The applications using the **PieChart.dll** assembly will notice a new version of the assembly and will load the new version of the assembly, causing no problems.

○ C. The applications using the **PieChart.dll** assembly will not be bothered by the new version of the assembly in the GAC and will continue to use the older, buggy version of the assembly.

○ D. The applications using the **PieChart.dll** assembly will be requested to select the desired assembly version to run for their applications.

Question 48

You've used Visual C# .NET to develop a component, named **BarGraph**, that enables developers to create bar graphs in their applications. The developers need to deploy the **BarGraph** component with each application that uses the component. How should you package the **BarGraph** component for deployment?

- ○ A. Use a Cab project to package the **BarGraph** component.
- ○ B. Use a Setup project to package the **BarGraph** component.
- ○ C. Use a Web Setup project to package the **BarGraph** component.
- ○ D. Use a Merge Module project to package the **BarGraph** component.
- ○ E. Use a Primary Interop Assembly to package the **BarGraph** component.

Question 49

You have created a database-driven Web application. Using Microsoft SQL Server, you have also generated an installation script for your database. This script is stored in a file named **InstData.sql**. You've created a Web Setup project using Visual Studio .NET to deploy this application on your production Web server. Which of the following editors should you choose to create the database when deploying your application on the client's machine?

- ○ A. Custom Actions Editor
- ○ B. Launch Conditions Editor
- ○ C. File System Editor
- ○ D. User Interface Editor

Question 50

Your ASP.NET application contains this setting in the **web.config** file:

```
<identity impersonate="true"
    userName="CORP\Auditing" password="Auditing"/>
```

You are allowing only digest or Windows-integrated authentication in IIS, and ASP.NET is running under the **SYSTEM** account. Which identity will ASP.NET use to authorize resources if a user with the Windows account **Shirley** in the **CORP** domain logs in via digest authentication?

- ○ A. **CORP\Shirley**
- ○ B. **ASPNET**
- ○ C. **SYSTEM**
- ○ D. **IUSR_***ComputerName*
- ○ E. **CORP\Auditing**

Question 51

You want to give target Web servers the capability to customize your application. In particular, you want to let them specify the file path where the output files, which are generated by the application, need to be placed. You also want to write a minimum of code. How should you add this capability to your application?

○ A. Let the user edit the text in the Registry and use the **Microsoft.Win32.Registry** class to retrieve the value she saves.

○ B. Add another **customconfiguration.xml** file to store the output file path for the application.

○ C. Add an **<outputFilePath>** element to the application configuration file, **web.config**, to store the output file path for the application.

○ D. Add an **<add>** element to the **<appSettings>** element of the application configuration file, **web.config**, to store the output file path for the application.

Question 52

Your ASP.NET application requires users to be authenticated with a strong identity. You must allow users with any version 4.x or better browser, and you want passwords to cross the network only with secure encryption. Which authentication should you use?

○ A. Passport authentication with Anonymous IIS authentication

○ B. Windows authentication with Basic IIS authentication

○ C. Windows authentication with Digest IIS authentication

○ D. Windows authentication with Integrated IIS authentication

Question 53

You have developed an intranet ASP.NET application for your company that uses Microsoft Windows authentication to authenticate the users of the application. After the employee is authenticated, he can access all the Web pages of the intranet application. However, your application contains an **Accounting** directory that has details of employee salaries and paychecks. You want only users of the **Accounting** role to access the pages in this directory. Which of the following pieces of code should you write in the **web.config** file of your application? (Select all that apply.)

❏ A. Add the following **<authorization>** element in the **web.config** file of the application directory:

```
<authentication mode="Windows"/>
<authorization>
    <deny users="?" />
</authorization>
```

❏ B. Add the following **<authorization>** element in the **web.config** file of the application directory:

```
<authentication mode="Windows"/>
<authorization>
    <deny roles="?" />
</authorization>
```

❏ C. Add the following **<authorization>** element in the **web.config** file of the **Accounting** directory:

```
<authorization>
    <allow roles="Accounting" />
    <deny users="*" />
</authorization>
```

❏ D. Add the following **<authorization>** element in the **web.config** file of the **Accounting** directory:

```
<authorization>
    <allow roles="Accounting" />
    <deny users="?" />
</authorization>
```

Question 54

You use Visual Studio .NET to develop an ASP.NET Web application for your state university. You want only members of the **Faculty** or **Admins** role to have access to the **GradesManagement.aspx** Web page of your application. Which of the following options should you choose to implement the security? (Select all that apply.)

❑ A.
```
if (Thread.CurrentPrincipal.IsInRole("Faculty") ||
    Thread.CurrentPrincipal.IsInRole("Admins"))
{
    Transfer();
}
```

❑ B.
```
if (Thread.CurrentPrincipal.IsInRole("Faculty") &&
    Thread.CurrentPrincipal.IsInRole("Admins"))
{
    Transfer();
}
```

❑ C.
```
[PrincipalPermissionAttribute(
    SecurityAction.Demand, Role="Faculty"),
PrincipalPermissionAttribute(
    SecurityAction.Demand, Role="Admins")]
public void Transfer()
{
    ...
}
```

❑ D.
```
PrincipalPermission permCheckFaculty =
      new PrincipalPermission(null, "Faculty");
PrincipalPermission permCheckAdmins =
      new PrincipalPermission(null, "Admins");
permCheckAdmins.Demand();
```

Question 55

One of your colleagues is designing a **Changed** event for his control. He complains to you that his code behaves abnormally: It runs fine some of the time but generates exceptions at other times. Part of his event-handling code follows (line numbers are for reference purpose only):

```
01: public delegate void ChangedEventHandler(
       object sender, CustomerInfoEventArgs args);
02: public event ChangedEventHandler Changed;
03: protected virtual void OnChanged(CustomerInfoEventArgs e)
04: {
05:       Changed(this, e);
06:}
```

Which of the following suggestions will solve his problem?

○ A. The code in line 06 should be replaced with the following:

```
if (ChangedEventHandler != null)
    ChangedEventHandler(this, e);
```

○ B. The code in line 06 should be replaced with the following:

```
if (ChangedEventHandler != null)
    Changed(this, e);
```

○ C. The code in line 06 should be replaced with the following:

```
if (Changed != null)
    ChangedEventHandler(this, e);
```

○ D. The code in line 06 should be replaced with the following:

```
if (Changed != null)
    Changed(this, e);
```

Question 56

You are building a custom control for your company's ASP.NET Web applications. The control will contain the company's privacy policy and copyright notices in a standard set of labels. This control should be shared by multiple applications. Which type of control should you create?

○ A. Web user control

○ B. Composite Web custom control

○ C. Web custom control that inherits from the **Label** control

○ D. Web custom control that inherits from the **WebControl** control

Question 57

Your department is responsible for maintaining the accounting application of your company. You've been assigned the task of creating a standard control to represent credit and debit accounts that will be placed in the Web forms of the accounting application. The control will be made up of a collection of **TextBox** and **ComboBox** controls. You want to write a minimum of code. Which of the following options should you choose to create such a custom control?

○ A. Add a Web custom control to the project and inherit the custom control from the **WebControl** class.

○ B. Add a **Component** class to the project and inherit the custom control from the **Component** class.

○ C. Add a Web user control to the project and inherit the custom control from the **UserControl** class.

○ D. Add a Web form to the project and inherit the custom control from the **Form** class.

Question 58

You are creating a specialized control that will display text rotated at an angle specified at design time. This control must be installed into the Visual Studio .NET toolbox so that it can be used in many projects. The control's user interface will resemble that of a **Label** control, with one additional property named **RotationAngle**. Which type of control should you create?

○ A. Web user control

○ B. Composite Web custom control

○ C. Web custom control that inherits from the **WebControl** control

○ D. Web custom control that inherits from the **Label** control

Question 59

Your colleague has developed a user control in a file named **LogIn.ascx** to prompt for the username and password from the user. She wants to display the **LogIn** control, defined in the **CMI** namespace in the Welcome Web page. Which of the following options would you recommend to your colleague to make the **LogIn** user control available in the Welcome Web page?

○ A.

```
<%@ Register TagPrefix="CMI" TagName="LogIn"
    Src="LogIn.ascx" %>
```

○ B.

```
<%@ Control Namespace="CMI" ClassName="LogIn"
    Src="LogIn.ascx" %>
```

○ C.

```
<%@ Register Namespace="CMI" TagName="LogIn"
    Src="LogIn.ascx" %>
```

○ D.

```
<%@ Control Namespace="CMI" Inherits="LogIn"
    Src="LogIn.ascx" %>
```

Question 60

You are creating a composite control for your ASP.NET Web application that consists of a set of **Label**, **TextBox**, and **DropDownList** Web server controls. Which of the following methods should you override to enable custom rendering for the composite control?

○ A. **CreateControl()**

○ B. **CreateChildControls()**

○ C. **RenderControl()**

○ D. **Render()**

18

Answers to Practice Exam #1

Answer Key

1. D	21. D	41. D
2. C	22. D	42. C
3. D	23. B	43. C
4. B	24. A	44. D
5. A	25. D and E	45. A and E
6. C	26. A	46. C
7. A	27. C	47. C
8. D	28. C	48. D
9. C	29. B and C	49. A
10. A	30. D	50. E
11. D	31. C	51. D
12. A and C	32. C	52. A
13. C	33. B	53. A and C
14. C	34. B and D	54. A and C
15. C	35. C	55. D
16. B	36. B	56. B
17. D	37. B	57. C
18. A	38. C	58. D
19. D	39. B	59. A
20. C	40. A and D	60. B

Question 1

The correct answer is D. The `<% %>` code blocks in an ASPX page are placed inside a method that renders the user interface of an ASPX page. The `<%= %>` construct is used to display values from an ASP.NET code in the resulting Web page. Answer A is incorrect because the `<script runat="server"></script>` code block is used to define class-level methods, properties, and variables. The code in these blocks is directly placed in the class definition when the code is dynamically compiled. Answer B is incorrect because the `runat` attribute of the `<script>` element should have the value `server`. Answer C is incorrect because the `<script>` element without the `runat="server"` attribute is not executed on the server and is passed to the browser. Answer E is incorrect because you should not use a semicolon while calling the method in the `<%= %>` construct.

Question 2

The correct answer is C. The `Inherits` attribute in the `Page` directive specifies a fully qualified name of a code-behind class from which the page should inherit. The `Src` attribute specifies the source filename of the code-behind class; this attribute is used when the code-behind class is not precompiled. Answers A and B are incorrect because the `CodeBehind` attribute is not used by the CLR (Common Language Runtime); it is used internally by Visual Studio .NET to link the ASPX page with the code-behind file. Answer D is incorrect because the `ClassName` attribute specifies the class name for the page that will be dynamically compiled when the page is requested; it does not play any role in linking the ASP.NET page with the code-behind class or file.

Question 3

The correct answer is D. You should set the `CausesValidation` property of the `Button` control to `false` because doing so prevents validation from occurring when the button is clicked. Answers A and C are incorrect because the `TextBox` Web server control does not contain a `CausesValidation` property. Answer B is incorrect because setting the `CausesValidation` property of the `Button` control to `true` causes validation to occur when the button is clicked.

Question 4

The correct answer is B. By default, the SelectedIndexChanged event of the DropDownList control is fired only when the page is posted back to the server. By setting the AutoPostBack property of the control to true, you cause the page to post back as soon as a selection is changed in the list. Answer A is incorrect because the PreRender event does not cause a postback when a selection is changed in the drop-down list. Answer C is incorrect because the ListBox control also does not post back immediately when the selection is changed. Answer D is incorrect because the EnableViewState property indicates only whether the view state should be maintained for the drop-down list.

Question 5

The correct answer is A. The RequiredFieldValidator control ensures whether a value is entered or selected in the control. It can also ensure that the value in a control is different from the original value in the control, if the original value is supplied to the InitialValue property of the RequiredFieldValidator control. Answer B is incorrect because the Display property specifies how to display the inline error message; ValidatorDisplay.Dynamic ensures that the space for the validation control is dynamically added only when the validation fails. Answer C is incorrect because, by default, the Visible property is set to true. The Visible property has no control over the validation; it indicates only whether the control should be rendered on the page. Answer D is incorrect because the EnableClientScript property specifies whether the client-side validation should occur. By setting it to false, the validation occurs only on the server side.

Question 6

The correct answer is C. The ASP.NET validation server controls require client-side scripting support to perform validation on the client side. If the browser does not support scripting, the validation occurs only on the server side when the page is posted. Answer A is incorrect because, if the Enabled attribute had been set to false, the validation would not have occurred on either the client side or server side. Answer B is incorrect because the SmartNavigation attribute is used to enable smart navigation between postbacks and has no control on validation. Answer D is incorrect because client-side validation works with Internet Explorer 4.0 or higher.

Question 7

The correct answer is A. To display custom error pages to all the users, the mode attribute of the <customErrors> element must be set to On. The defaultRedirect attribute of the customErrors element specifies the page to be displayed for any errors not listed. Answers B and D are incorrect because the mode attribute of the <customErrors> element is set to RemoteOnly, which would disable custom error pages for the local computer. Answer C is incorrect because the <error> element specifies an error status code and the resulting page to display.

Question 8

The correct answer is D. The database connection should be closed whether the information can be retrieved or not. The code in the finally block will be executed regardless of whether an exception is thrown. Answer A is incorrect because, if an exception occurs before the code that closes the SqlConnection object in the try block, the code will not be executed. Answer B is incorrect because in this case the SqlConnection object is closed only when a SqlException occurs. Answer C is incorrect because in this case the SqlConnection object is closed only when an exception other than SqlException occurs.

Question 9

The correct answer is C. In a page, to log errors into a custom log file, you need to provide an event handler for the Page.Error event. The Page.Error event occurs whenever an unhandled exception occurs in the page. Answer A is incorrect because the <error> element specifies an error HTTP status code and the redirect page for the HTTP status code. Answer B is incorrect because the ErrorPage attribute specifies the custom error page for an individual page. Answer D is incorrect because the Application_Error() event handler is generated whenever an unhandled exception occurs in the application rather than a page. The Application_Error() event handler should be placed in the global.asax file.

Question 10

The correct answer is A. To transfer execution to a page that is not processed by the ASP.NET process, you must use the `Response.Redirect()` method. Answers B and C are incorrect because these methods are used to redirect control to ASPX pages. Answer D is incorrect because the `CreateObject()` method creates instances of COM components.

Question 11

The correct answer is D. The `SmartNavigation` attribute offers several benefits to users running Internet Explorer 5.0 or higher, including focus persistence, minimized screen flashing, persistent scroll positioning, and better history management. Answers A, B, and C require more efforts because they involve writing code to implement the logic. Thus, none of these answers is "the easiest way."

Question 12

The correct answers are A and C. If the Web page loads the data for the controls at every page load, disabling the view state will make the page size much smaller and maximize performance. If the Web page only reads the data but does not update data in the session state, you can make the session state for the page read-only. This will eliminate the time taken by ASP.NET to store the data in the session state for the Web page. Answer B is incorrect because, by disabling the session state, the Web page will not be capable of displaying the username from the session in the greeting to the user. Answer D is incorrect because storing the session state in the SQL Server creates extra overhead.

Question 13

The correct answer is C. When you store session state data in SQL Server, you can take advantage of the robustness and data protection qualities of SQL Server. This includes the capability to preserve data even across server crashes. Answers A and B are incorrect because storing the session state in the ASP.NET worker process or `StateServer` process would not enable the recovery of data if the Web server were restarted. Answer D is incorrect because it disables session state.

Question 14

The correct answer is C. You want the information to be available across Web pages and browser restarts. Therefore, you should choose cookies because they allow you to store a small amount of information on the user's computer. Answers A, B, and D are incorrect because none of these options (hidden fields, view state, and sessions) can store information across browser restarts.

Question 15

The correct answer is C. You should use view state to store page-specific values. View state can store any type of object as long as it is serializable. Answers A and D are incorrect because both of these techniques store data global to the application and should not be selected for storing user-specific data. Answer B is incorrect because, although the session state is suitable for storing user-specific data, it is not required unless the data is used across pages and is too sensitive to be stored on the client side.

Question 16

The correct answer is B. By using varying output caching, you can store the output of the page for each product in the database. These pages can then quickly deliver information on the individual products without requiring a round trip to the database and creating output for each request. Answer A is incorrect because only varying output caching enables you to save information on each product. Answer C is incorrect because, even though it would save a round trip to the database, it would require the response to be created at each request that can be easily avoided by using varying output caching. Answer D is incorrect because fragment caching is used to cache output of user controls rather than ASPX pages.

Question 17

The correct answer is D. The processing of the file data takes time to load the Web page. Further, the output changes only when the data in the XML file changes; therefore, the best solution is to cache the DataSet object.

This way, you can eliminate the consumption of server resources to create the DataSet object from scratch at every request. Answers A and B are incorrect because output caching cannot be made dependent on a file. Only data stored in the Cache object can be made dependent on other items in the data cache or on an external resource such as a file or directory. Answer C is incorrect because it only adds the DataSet object to the cache and does not set any dependencies.

Question 18

The correct answer is A. You need caching based on the state entered by the user; therefore, you need to set the VaryByControl attribute to txtState to cache different versions of the user control output by state. Answers B and D are incorrect because the VaryByParam attribute specifies the parameters of the Web page, rather than user control, for which the output cache is varied. Answer C is incorrect because the VaryByControl attribute does not work if * is passed—it needs a list of controls in the user control for which the output cache is to vary.

Question 19

The correct answer is D. The DataView object represents a data-bindable, customized view of a data table, which is optimized for sorting, filtering, searching, editing, and navigation. Answers A and C are incorrect because they involve additional programming. Answer B is incorrect because it will impact the SQL Server database with additional hits.

Question 20

The correct answer is C. Although answers C and D both use the correct syntax of the Fill() method, the question clearly states the name of the table; therefore, it is recommended to use the name of the table when filling the DataSet. This is why answer D is incorrect. Answer A is incorrect because there is no overload of the Fill() method that accepts a single string parameter. Answer B is incorrect because there is no overload of the Fill() method that accepts two string parameters.

Question 21

The correct answer is D. Using the same connection string enables ADO.NET to reuse existing pooled database connections instead of creating new ones. This improves performance because creating new database connections is a costly operation. Answer B is incorrect because another application that uses the same database is already performing well. Answer C is incorrect because, if different connection strings are used, each request for the connection will create a new connection pool anyway. Therefore, increasing the maximum size of the pool will not matter. Answer A is incorrect because users are facing slow performance consistently and not just during the first execution.

Question 22

The correct answer is D. When you set the XmlWriteMode parameter of the DataSet.WriteXml() method to DiffGram, the output contains both original and current values. Answer A is incorrect because the DataSet.WriteXmlSchema() method writes the DataSet structure as an XML schema instead of writing XML data. Answers B and C are incorrect because setting the XmlWriteMode parameter to IgnoreSchema or WriteSchema writes only the current value of the data to the XML file.

Question 23

The correct answer is B. IsolationLevel.Serializable places a range lock on the database, thereby preventing other users from updating or inserting rows into the database until the transaction is complete. Answer A is incorrect because IsolationLevel.ReadCommitted holds the lock while the data is being read, but data can be changed before the transaction is complete. Answers C and D are incorrect because the BeginTransaction() method should be called on the SqlConnection object rather than the SqlCommand object.

Question 24

The correct answer is A. The ColumnMapping property determines how a column's values will be written when the WriteXml() method is called on a DataSet to write output to an XML document. When you set the ColumnMapping property of a column to MappingType.Attribute, that column of the table is mapped to an XML attribute. Answer B is incorrect because setting the ColumnMapping property of the column to MappingType.Element maps that column of the table to an XML element. Answers C and D are incorrect because XmlWriteMode.WriteSchema instructs the WriteXml() method to write the current contents of the DataSet as XML data along with the relational structure as an inline XSD schema. Writing an additional schema is not required in the question.

Question 25

The correct answers are D and E. Strings in Visual C# .NET are immutable, so concatenating multiple values into a string requires deleting and re-creating the string many times. The StringBuilder object is optimized for changing textual data. The GetString() method should be used rather than the GetValue() method to retrieve data because the typed methods are faster than the GetValue() method. Answer A is incorrect because stored procedures have much higher performance as compared to SQL statements. Answer B is incorrect because for a forward-only, read-only operation, the SqlDataReader object provides the best performance. Answer C is incorrect because the while loop provides better performance when compared to the for each loop.

Question 26

The correct answer is A. You can have only a single SqlDataReader object open on a single SqlConnection object. If you need a second SqlDataReader object, you must open a second SqlConnection object. Answers B and C are incorrect because the question asks for the likely cause of the error and not just an alternative approach. Answer D is incorrect because you want to retrieve multiple values from the database and the ExecuteScalar() method retrieves only the first column of the first row in the result set.

Question 27

The correct answer is C. Calling the GetChanges() method of a DataSet returns a new DataSet that contains only records that have been changed. Answer A is incorrect because the DataSet.Clone() method copies the structure of the DataSet but does not copy any data. Answer B is incorrect because the DataSet.Copy() method copies all the data instead of only the changed data. Answer D is incorrect because you do not want to merge two DataSet objects.

Question 28

The correct answer is C. To create a connection string for a SqlConnection object that uses Windows Integrated authentication, you need to specify the data source and the initial catalog and indicate that it is a secure connection. You can indicate that it is a secure connection by setting the Trusted_Connection or Integrated Security parameter to true or sspi. Answers A and B are incorrect because you do not specify the provider in the connection string when connecting through the SqlConnection object. Answer D is incorrect because you need to use Windows authentication instead of SQL Server authentication.

Question 29

The correct answers are B and C. To return a single value from the database, you should use the ExecuteScalar() method of the OleDbCommand object. The ExecuteScalar() method executes the query and retrieves the first column of the first row of the result set. You should always use stored procedures rather than the ad hoc SQL statements for speedy delivery. Answer A is incorrect because it uses a SQL query rather than the stored procedure. Answers D and E are incorrect because these solutions involve extra overhead when only a single value needs to be returned from the database.

Question 30

The correct answer is D. The controls already contain all the necessary property settings to transfer the data from the ListBox control to the TextBox control. However, you must call the DataBind method to actually perform the transfer.

Answer A is incorrect because you want to bind the value with a text box and therefore you should call the DataBind() method on the TextBox control instead of the ListBox control. Answers B and C are incorrect because they do not present a solution that binds the value of the TextBox control.

Question 31

The correct answer is C. The best place to display the data underlined is when the sales amount is data bound with the control and before it is rendered. The ItemDataBound event is generated when an item is data bound, and it always occurs before it is rendered for display. The ItemDataBound event passes a DataGridItemEventArgs object to the event handler containing the details about the item that is data bound. Answer A is incorrect because the ItemCreated event is generated when an item is created in the DataGrid control. Answer B is incorrect because the ItemCommand event is generated when any of the buttons are clicked in the DataGrid control. Answer D is incorrect because the DataBinding event is generated when the DataGrid control binds to the data source rather than when individual items are data bound to the data in the data source.

Question 32

The correct answer is C. You have to bind the text box control with a single column of data in the data source control. You have already set the data source and the data member to bind. Therefore, you specify the row to bind using the Container.DataItem and then specify the column to bind. Answer A is incorrect because you have already set the DataSource and DataMember properties; now, you just have to bind to the specific column in the data. Answers B and D are incorrect because SelectedItemTemplate applies only to the selected row in the DataList control.

Question 33

The correct answer is B. You should use the XslTransform object to transform XML data using an XSLT style sheet. Answer A is incorrect because the XPathNavigator object enables you to explore the structure of the XML file. Answer C is incorrect because the XmlSchema object provides the schema definition. Answer D is incorrect because the XmlNode object represents a single node in the document.

Question 34

The correct answers are B and D. Either of these options can generate proxy classes for use in a client application. Answer A is incorrect because the .NET WebService Studio tool is used to invoke a Web service for testing. Answer C is incorrect because the Web Services Discovery Tool can locate files related to a Web service, but it does not generate any proxy classes.

Question 35

The correct answer is C. When the dir attribute is set to rtl, the horizontal alignment of the control's elements is reversed. Answer A is incorrect because you need to make minimal changes. Answers B and D are incorrect because there is no rtl attribute.

Question 36

The correct answer is B. The ADO library and other components developed with Microsoft Visual Basic 6.0 use single-threaded apartment (STA) as their threading model. By setting the AspCompat attribute to true, the .NET Framework allows the page to call STA components. Answer A is incorrect because STA COM components can be directly used only from ASP.NET pages and not from the compiled .NET assemblies. Answer C is incorrect because the Language attribute should be set to any .NET-supported language, such as C# and VB. Answer D is incorrect because, if you convert the STA component to an assembly using the Type Library Importer tool, your application can suffer from poor performance and possible deadlocks.

Question 37

The correct answer is B. Using the Type Library Importer tool (tlbimp.exe) enables you to generate an RCW assembly. To place the RCW assembly in the GAC so that it can be shared by all projects on the computer, you need to sign the assembly using the tlbimp.exe tool. Answers A and E are incorrect because you need to use the component in more than one project. Answer C is incorrect because you also need to sign the RCW assembly while generating it from the Type Library Importer tool. Answer D is incorrect because a Primary Interop Assembly is used for code from other vendors, not for your own code.

Question 38

The correct answer is C. To make the demo page more accessible, you should ensure that you supply all graphics with an `alt` attribute that conveys the important information about the image. The `alt` text information is displayed in place of the image when the image is being downloaded, the image is unavailable, the graphics are turned off in the browser, or the browser doesn't support images. Answer A is incorrect because PNG graphics are widely supported. Answer B is incorrect because providing the short key for the graphics is not as important as providing the `alt` attribute for the image. Answer D is incorrect because the `AlternateText` property is rendered to the browser as an `alt` attribute, unlike the `ToolTip` property.

Question 39

The correct answer is B. You can step into a stored procedure execution directly from within Visual Studio .NET. Answer A is incorrect because the Tools, Debug Processes menu item is useful for debugging running processes—not the stored procedures. Answer C is incorrect because this option takes more time and effort, and the question requires minimal effort and time. Answer D is incorrect because the `Debug.WriteLine()` method cannot directly access the stored procedure values.

Question 40

The correct answers are A and D. The `Debug` and `Trace` classes share the same `Listeners` collection. Therefore, you should add a listener object either to the `Trace.Listeners` collection or to the `Debug.Listeners` collection. Answer B is incorrect because this solution generates double entries in the event log. Answer C is incorrect because the newly created listener object is not attached to the `Listeners` collection of the `Trace` and `Debug` classes.

Question 41

The correct answer is D. A conditional breakpoint lets you pause your code only when a particular condition is true. In this case, you can use that capability to break into the code when the variable has the value of 117. Answers A, B, and C (Locals window, Output window, and Immediate window) are incorrect because they do not work conditionally.

Question 42

The correct answer is C. Breakpoints are invoked only when the project's configuration is in Debug mode. Answer A is incorrect because the Exceptions dialog box is used to configure the breakpoint only in case of an exception. Answer B is incorrect because, when you place a breakpoint, it is enabled by default. Answer D is incorrect because the project's configuration should be Debug instead of Release for debugging to occur (for breakpoints to be executed).

Question 43

The correct answer is C. The `TraceContext` class is responsible for providing detailed timing and other information in the browser window when you activate ASP.NET tracing. Answers A and B are incorrect because the `Debug` and `Trace` classes can be used to display messages about a program's execution but they can't provide detailed timing and other information about a program's execution. Answer D is incorrect because the `Page` class cannot provide timing information for the events on the Web page.

Question 44

The correct answer is D. To enable tracing for a particular page, you should set the `Trace` attribute of the `Page` directive to `true`. Answers A and B are incorrect because the `<trace>` element in the `web.config` file enables or disables tracing for all the Web pages of the application rather than just a single page. Answer C is incorrect because the `enabled` attribute takes a `Boolean` value rather than the name of the Web page. Answer E is incorrect because it disables tracing for the Web page.

Question 45

The correct answers are A and E. You need to sign a shared assembly with the strong name and then install the assembly in the Global Assembly cache. Answer B is incorrect because you use `sn.exe` instead of `signcode.exe` to sign an assembly with a strong name. Answer C is incorrect because the Windows system directory does not allow multiple versions of an assembly to be maintained.

Answer D is incorrect because an assembly that needs to be shared by multiple applications should be stored in a common place, such as the GAC, rather than the bin directory of the Web application. Further, multiple versions of the assembly can be placed only in the GAC.

Question 46

The correct answer is C. Because the components are being used between several games published by your company, they are good candidates to be placed in the GAC of the target machine. However, before a component can be placed in the GAC, it must be signed using a Strong Name Tool (sn.exe). Your company is also deploying software over the Internet, so you should digitally sign your code with a software publisher's certificate obtained by a respected certification authority. After you obtain the certificate, you can use signcode.exe to sign your component. When you are using both sn.exe and signcode.exe with your assembly, you should always use sn.exe before using signcode.exe. Answers A and B are incorrect because you need to use both tools instead of just one of them. Answer D is incorrect because sn.exe should be used before signcode.exe.

Question 47

The correct answer is C. The applications always bind to the assemblies with which they are compiled. Therefore, if you want to execute a new version of the assembly, you either should recompile the application with the new version of the assembly or should modify the application configuration file to redirect to a new version of the assembly. Answers A and B are incorrect because the application will still request the old version of the assembly. Answer D is incorrect because applications will not be requested to choose a particular version of the assembly; instead the applications themselves will request the CLR to locate a specific assembly.

Question 48

The correct answer is D. The Merge Module projects enable you to create reusable setup components by packaging together all the required files, resources, Registry entries, and setup logic necessary to install a component.

Answer A is incorrect because the Cab project creates a cabinet file for downloading from a Web browser. Answer B is incorrect because the Setup project creates an installer for a Web application. Answer C is incorrect because the Web Setup project creates an installer for a Web application. Answer E is incorrect because the Primary Interop Assembly is used for packaging legacy components.

Question 49

The correct answer is A. You can use the Custom Actions Editor to take custom actions such as database installation during the application setup. If you have an installer class or program that can create a database, you must override the Install() method of the base class and you must add the installer program to the Install node of the Custom Actions Editor. Answer B is incorrect because the Launch Conditions Editor is used to specify the prerequisite conditions that must be met to successfully run an installation. Consequently, it cannot be used to execute custom actions. Answer C is incorrect because the File System Editor only provides a mapping of the file system on the target machine and enables you to place files or folders on specific locations on the target machine. However, the File System Editor cannot be used to execute code to create the database. Answer D is incorrect because the User Interface Editor enables you to customize the user interface displayed during the installation process.

Question 50

The correct answer is E. When you enable impersonation by providing a name and password, any authenticated user takes on the credentials of the specified account for purposes of authorizing resources. Answer A is incorrect because the name and password ASP.NET uses to authorize resources are already defined by the <identity> element. Answer B is incorrect because the ASPNET account is used by ASP.NET for requests if impersonation is enabled and ASP.NET runs under a low-privilege account. Answer C is incorrect because the SYSTEM account is used by ASP.NET for requests if impersonation is enabled and ASP.NET runs under a high-privilege account. Answer D is incorrect because the IUSR_ComputerName account, the identity of the IIS, is used by ASP.NET to make requests if the application allows anonymous access.

Question 51

The correct answer is D. You can store your custom settings in the `<appSettings>` element of the application configuration file. The .NET Framework provides the `AppSettings` property of the `System.Configuration.ConfigurationSettings` class to access the value of the custom key added to the `<appSettings>` element. Answer A is incorrect because asking the user to modify the Windows Registry can have undesirable effects. Answers B and C are incorrect because they involve writing additional code.

Question 52

The correct answer is A. Passport authentication enables users to be authenticated with a strong identity using any browser or version. Answer B is incorrect because Basic IIS authentication does not securely encrypt passwords. Answers C and D are incorrect because Digest and Windows-integrated authentication require Internet Explorer as the browser.

Question 53

The correct answers are A and C. You should deny all unauthenticated users with the ? wild character at the application level such that only authenticated users can access the application. In the `web.config` file of the `Accounting` directory, you should allow only members of the `Accounting` role and deny all other users (authenticated as well as unauthenticated) with the * wild character. Answer B is incorrect because you should disallow all unauthenticated users. The `roles` attribute should not contain wild card characters; it should contain only the names of the Windows roles separated by commas. Answer D is incorrect because the `<deny>` element denies only unauthenticated users and provides access to the authenticated users.

Question 54

The correct answers are A and C. These code segments both allow access to the user if he belongs to either the `Admins` or `Faculty` role. Answer B is incorrect because it allows access only for those users who are in both the `Admins` and `Faculty` roles. Answer D is incorrect because, to give access to users in the `Faculty` role, you must call the `permCheckFaculty.Demand()` method.

Question 55

The correct answer is D. The OnChange() method invokes the Changed event to notify all registered objects about the event. If the Changed object is null, no delegate objects have been registered with this event. On the other hand, if the Changed object is not null, the call to the Changed event invokes the registered event handlers. Answers A, B, and C are incorrect because the name of the event is Changed rather than ChangedEventHandler.

Question 56

The correct answer is B. The composite control can easily encapsulate multiple Label controls into a single control. Because it's a custom control, it can be installed into the GAC and shared by multiple applications. Answer A is incorrect because the custom control needs to be used in multiple applications. If you create a Web user control, the user control files need to be included in each application. Answer C is incorrect because the control consists of multiple Label controls. Answer D is incorrect because your control needs to combine existing Web server controls and the WebControl class is used to create Web controls from scratch.

Question 57

The correct answer is C. Web user controls are the best way to reuse common user interface functionality in a Web application. Web user controls are easy to create, just like ASPX pages, and they inherit from the System.Web.UI.UserControl class. They can be easily dragged from Solution Explorer into the Web form. Answer A is incorrect because Web custom controls are precompiled and are best suited for creating custom controls to be used by multiple applications. Answer B is incorrect because using the Component class to create reusable visual components requires additional programming and is therefore better suited for creating nonvisual components. Answer D is incorrect because a Web form cannot be placed inside another Web form.

Question 58

The correct answer is D. Because this control is an extension of the `Label` control, it's easiest to create it by subclassing the existing `Label` control. Answer A is incorrect because a Web user control cannot be added to the Visual Studio .NET toolbox. Answer B is incorrect because composite controls contain more than one control. Answer C is incorrect because, if you derive from the `WebControl` class, you have to write more code.

Question 59

The correct answer is A. The `Register` directive is used to register a Web user control within an ASP.NET Web form. To register a Web user control, you need to specify three attributes: `TagPrefix` to provide an alias to a namespace to which the user control belongs, `TagName` to provide an alias to the user control, and `Src` to provide the path to the user control. Answers B and D are incorrect because the `Control` directive is used to define user-control-specific attributes in the user control file (`.ascx`). Answer C is incorrect because the `Namespace` attribute is used to associate with the `tag` prefix and is not a required attribute to register a user control.

Question 60

The correct answer is B. You should override the `CreateChildControls()` method to create the new controls the composite control will contain. This method is automatically called by ASP.NET when the control is supposed to be rendered. Answers A and C are incorrect because they are not defined as `virtual` methods and cannot be overridden to create child controls. Answer D is incorrect because the `Render()` method is overridden to provide the complete rendering of a Web control; it is used when you are designing a Web custom control from scratch rather than by combining existing controls.

Practice Exam #2

Practice Exam

Question 1

You are developing an accounting application that includes a class named **Transaction**, which is inherited by subclasses such as **DepositTransaction** and **PaymentTransaction**. The **Transaction** class includes a method named **VerifyChecksum()**. The **VerifyChecksum()** method should be available to the **Transaction** class and to all classes derived from the **Transaction** class, but not to any other classes in the application. Which access modifier should you use in the declaration of the **VerifyChecksum()** method?

○ A. **protected**

○ B. **public**

○ C. **private**

○ D. **internal**

Question 2

You have developed an ASP.NET page that contains the following code:

```
<%@ Page Language="c#" AutoEventWireUp="true"
       EnableViewState="true" SmartNavigation="false"%>
<html>
    <script runat="server">
        protected void Page_Load(Object o, EventArgs e)
        {
            if(!Page.IsPostBack)
            {
                // Populate the color drop-down list
                ddlColor.Items.Add("Blue");
                ddlColor.Items.Add("Red");
                ddlColor.Items.Add("Green");
            }
        }
        protected override void OnInit(EventArgs e)
        {
            this.Load += new EventHandler(Page_Load);
            base.OnInit(e);
        }
    </script>
    <body>
        <form runat="server">
            Select a Color:
                <asp:DropDownList id="ddlColor"
                                    runat="server" >
                <asp:Button id="btnSubmit"runat="server" >
        </form>
    </body>
</html>
```

When you view the page in the browser, you find that the color names are displayed twice in the drop-down list. Which of the following options should you choose to solve this problem?

○ A. Modify the **Page** directive as follows:

```
<%@ Page Language="c#"
        AutoEventWireUp="true"
        EnableViewState="false"
        SmartNavigation="false"%>
```

○ B. Modify the **Page** directive as follows:

```
<%@ Page Language="c#"
        AutoEventWireUp="true"
        EnableViewState="true"
        SmartNavigation="true"%>
```

○ C. Modify the **Page** directive as follows:

```
<%@ Page Language="c#"
        AutoEventWireUp="false"
        EnableViewState="true"
        SmartNavigation="false"%>
```

○ D. Modify the **Page_Load()** method as follows:

```
protected void Page_Load(Object o, EventArgs e)
{
    if(Page.IsPostBack)
    {
        // Populate the color drop-down list
        ddlColor.Items.Add("Blue");
        ddlColor.Items.Add("Red");
        ddlColor.Items.Add("Green");
    }
}
```

Question 3

You are designing a Visual C# ASP.NET Web form with a variety of controls on its user interface. Some controls will be infrequently used. For these controls, you do not want the user to be able to tab into the control, but the user should still be able to activate the control by clicking in it. Which of the following options should you use?

○ A. Set the **TabIndex** property of the control to **0**.

○ B. Set the **TabIndex** property of the control to **-1**.

○ C. Set the **AccessKey** property of the control to **null**.

○ D. Set the **Enabled** property of the control to **false**.

Question 4

You have developed a Web page that uses the **Image** ASP.NET Web server control to display images from various sources on the Internet. Sometimes an image might not be available because a Web site might be temporarily down for maintenance. In these situations, you are required to display a description for the image. Which of the following properties of **Image** would you use?

○ A. **ToolTip**

○ B. **Attributes**

○ C. **AlternateText**

○ D. **ImageUrl**

Question 5

You are designing a Web site that is used by your suppliers to quote their pricing for a product that your company will buy over the next quarter. The Web site will use data to calculate the best possible purchase options. Your application displays three text boxes to the suppliers. The first text box (**txtPrevQtrMax**) enables suppliers to enter the maximum value charged by them for this product in the previous quarter. The second text box (**txtPrevQtrMin**) enables suppliers to enter the minimum value charged by them in the previous quarter. The third text box (**txtQuote**) enables suppliers to enter the proposed pricing of the product for the next quarter. You want suppliers to restrict the value of the **txtQuote** field between **txtPrevQtrMin** and **txtPrevQtrMax**. The validation technique you use should utilize the minimum amount of code. Which of the following validation controls would you use to perform the validation?

○ A. **CompareValidator**

○ B. **RangeValidator**

○ C. **CustomValidator**

○ D. **RegularExpressionValidator**

Question 6

Your ASP.NET application enables users to input the URL of a Web page, and then it applies an XSLT file to show how that Web page looks on a mobile device. Which type of control should you use to validate the **TextBox** control where the user inputs the URL? (Select two options; each option presents part of the complete answer.)

- ❑ A. **RequiredFieldValidator**
- ❑ B. **RangeValidator**
- ❑ C. **RegularExpressionValidator**
- ❑ D. **CompareValidator**

Question 7

You are assisting your colleague in solving the compiler error his code is throwing. Following is the problematic portion of his code:

```
try
{
    bool success = GenerateNewtonSeries(500, 0);
    //more code here
}
catch(DivideByZeroException dbze)
{
    //exception handling code
}
catch(NotFiniteNumberException nfne)
{
    //exception handling code
}
catch(ArithmeticException ae)
{
    //exception handling code
}
catch(OverflowException e)
{
    //exception handling code
}
```

To remove the compilation error, which of the following ways would you rearrange the code?

○ A.
```
try
{
    bool success = GenerateNewtonSeries(500, 0);
    //more code here
}
catch(DivideByZeroException dbze)
{
    //exception handling code
}
catch(ArithmeticException ae)
{
    //exception handling code
}
catch(OverflowException e)
{
    //exception handling code
}
```

○ B.
```
try
{
    bool success = GenerateNewtonSeries(500, 0);
    //more code here
}
catch(DivideByZeroException dbze)
{
    //exception handling code
}
catch(Exception ae)
{
    //exception handling code
}
catch(OverflowException e)
{
    //exception handling code
}
```

○ C.
```
try
{
    bool success = GenerateNewtonSeries(500, 0);
    //more code here
}
catch(DivideByZeroException dbze)
{
    //exception handling code
}
catch(NotFiniteNumberException nfne)
{
    //exception handling code
}
catch(OverflowException e)
{
    //exception handling code
}
```

```
    catch(ArithmeticException ae)
    {
        //exception handling code
    }

○ D.
    try
    {
        bool success = GenerateNewtonSeries(500, 0);
        //more code here
    }
    catch(DivideByZeroException dbze)
    {
        //exception handling code
    }
    catch(NotFiniteNumberException nfne)
    {
        //exception handling code
    }
    catch(Exception ae)
    {
        //exception handling code
    }
    catch(ArithmeticException e)
    {
        //exception handling code
    }
```

Question 8

You've developed an ASP.NET Web application that retrieves data from a SQL Server database named Customers. You use the **System.Data.SqlClient** data provider to connect with the database. You need to log the severity level of the errors returned from the SQL Server .NET data provider. Which of the following options should you choose?

○ A. Catch the **SqlException**, which is thrown by the SQL Server .NET data provider. Examine the **Class** property of the **SqlException** object.

○ B. Catch the **SqlException**, which is thrown by the SQL Server .NET data provider. Examine the **Source** property of the **SqlException** object.

○ C. Catch the **SqlException**, which is thrown by the SQL Server .NET data provider. Examine the **Server** property of the **SqlException** object.

○ D. Catch the **SqlException**, which is thrown by the SQL Server .NET data provider. Examine the **State** property of the **SqlException** object.

Question 9

The **machine.config** file on your computer contains this setting:
```
<customErrors mode="RemoteOnly"/>
```

Your application's root directory contains a **web.config** file with this setting:
```
<customErrors mode="On">
    <error statusCode="404" redirect="404.htm" />
</customErrors>
```

Your application's **/custom** directory contains a **web.config** file with this setting:
```
<customErrors mode="Off" />
```

Your application's **/custom/local** directory contains a **web.config** file with this setting:
```
<customErrors mode="On">
    <error statusCode="404" redirect="404.aspx" />
</customErrors>
```

A user at a remote computer requests the file **/custom/remote/ NonExistingPage.aspx**, which does not exist. What is the result?

- ○ A. The **404.aspx** file is displayed.
- ○ B. The default ASP.NET error page is displayed.
- ○ C. The **404.htm** file is displayed.
- ○ D. The stack trace information for the error is displayed.

Question 10

Your ASP.NET application contains a Web form named **login.aspx**. When this page is posted back to the server, you check the entered username and password against your corporate database. If the username and password match, you want to display the **accountdetails.aspx** Web form as the result in the user's browser. Execution of the application will proceed from the **accountdetails.aspx** page. How should you transfer control in this case?

- ○ A. Use the **HyperLink** ASP.NET Web server control.
- ○ B. Use the **Response.Redirect()** method.
- ○ C. Use the **Server.Transfer()** method.
- ○ D. Use the **Server.Execute()** method.

Question 11

You are creating an ASP.NET Web application that reads a text file and displays
its data in the browser. You set the **BufferOutput** property of the **HttpResponse**
object to **true**. You then execute the **CreateHeaders.aspx** page using the
Server.Execute() method to display heading information to the browser. After
this, you read the file and display it in the browser. If the file is not found, you
want to remove any heading information created for the output and you want the
page to continue execution. How can you achieve this?

○ A.   Use **Response.Flush();**.

○ B.   Use **Response.Clear();**.

○ C.   Use **Response.Close();**.

○ D.   Use **Response.End();**.

Question 12

Your ASP.NET Web form displays ordering information for 50 products in
DataGrid and other controls. Your company is unable to accept Web orders, so
there are no controls on the page to post the data back to the server. What can
you do to optimize the delivery of this page?

○ A.   Set the **EnableViewState** attribute to **true** for the **DataGrid** control.

○ B.   Set the **EnableViewState** attribute to **true** for the **Page** directive.

○ C.   Set the **EnableViewState** attribute to **false** for the **DataGrid** control.

○ D.   Set the **EnableViewState** attribute to **false** for the **Page** directive.

Question 13

Your ASP.NET shopping application is deployed and running on a production
server. Web site hits have increased recently, so you are planning to deploy the
ASP.NET Web application to a Web farm, which consists of four servers handling the requests from users. Which of the following steps should you perform
before you move your Web application to a Web farm?

○ A.   Disable session state for the application.

○ B.   Use either the State Service or SQL Server to store session state.

○ C.   Use View state, rather than session, to maintain state.

○ D.   Remove all references to the **Request**, **Response**, and **Server** objects
       from your code.

Question 14

You are in the process of upgrading an existing ASP application to ASP.NET by converting pages one by one to the new architecture. The application currently uses an ASP.NET page to request the user's first name, which is stored in a session variable with this line of code:

```
Session["FirstName"] = txtFirstName.Text;
```

You run the application and enter a first name on the ASP.NET page. When you browse to an existing ASP page that uses the **FirstName** session variable, the first name is blank. What could be the problem?

○ A. You must explicitly use the **Page.Session** property to store shared session state.

○ B. The ASP page needs to explicitly retrieve the **Value** property of the **Session** object.

○ C. The ASP and ASP.NET engines do not share session state or application state.

○ D. You do not have cookies enabled on your computer.

Question 15

You are designing an ASP.NET Web application for a multinational company. When users access the Web site, you want them to be automatically redirected to a page specific to their country. Your colleague has developed a method that determines the user's country from the HTTP request and performs the redirection. Where should you call this method in your application?

○ A. In the **Session_Start()** event handler of the **global.asax** file

○ B. In the **Application_BeginRequest()** event handler of the **global.asax** file

○ C. In the **Page_Load()** event handler of the **default.aspx** file

○ D. In the **Application_Start()** event handler of the **global.asax** file

Question 16

You have created an ASP.NET Web page, **Catalog.aspx**, that enables users to purchase products from the catalog. The product details are fetched in a **DataSet** object from a legacy database over a slow link. The details are displayed in the **Catalog.aspx** page in a **DataGrid** control as per user preferences, which are maintained in the session state. The product details do not change very often; you need to reload the **DataSet** object only every two hours. Which of the following options should you use to store the **DataSet** object?

○ A. Application state

○ B. Session state

○ C. View state

○ D. The **HttpCachePolicy** object

○ E. The **Cache** object

Question 17

You are creating an ASP.NET Web page that performs complex mathematical and scientific calculations and displays the results to the user. The complex calculations use server resources extensively. The calculations change once every 30 minutes. Which of the following **OutputCache** directives should you choose to enable caching on the Web page?

○ A. <%@ OutputCache Duration="30" VaryByParam="None" %>

○ B. <%@ OutputCache Duration="1800" VaryByParam="None" %>

○ C. <%@ OutputCache Duration="30" %>

○ D. <%@ OutputCache Duration="1800" %>

Question 18

You have developed an ASP.NET Web form that displays information on parks by fetching data from a SQL Server 2000 database. The database contains information on approximately 2,500 parks. The user can select a state from the **ddlStates** control and select a park from the **ddlParks** control to get information on the desired park. The page also accepts other information from the user, but this information does not influence the results. Users request these pages very frequently. Which of the following **OutputCache** directives should you use to maximize performance?

○ A. `<%@ OutputCache Duration="120" VaryByParam="*" %>`

○ B. `<%@ OutputCache Duration="120"`
  `VaryByParam="ddlStates;ddlParks" %>`

○ C. `<%@ OutputCache Duration="120" VaryByParam="ddlParks" %>`

○ D. `<%@ OutputCache Duration="120" VaryByControl="ddlParks" %>`

○ E. `<%@ OutputCache Duration="120"`
  `VaryByControl="ddlStates;ddlParks" %>`

○ F. `<%@ OutputCache Duration="120" VaryByControl="*" %>`

Question 19

You've developed a Visual C# ASP.NET Web application that displays supplier data in a **DataGrid** control. The supplier data is stored in a data cache in a table named **Suppliers** within the **dsSuppliers DataSet** object. The primary key for the **Suppliers** table is the **SupplierID** column. You need to display the supplier data in the **DataGrid** control in ascending order of the primary key. You write the following code segment to accomplish this task:

```
DataView dvSuppliers =
➥new DataView(dsSuppliers.Tables["Suppliers"]);
dvSuppliers.Sort = "ASC";
dvSuppliers.ApplyDefaultSort = true;
dataGrid1.DataSource = dvSuppliers;
dataGrid1.DataBind();
```

However, when you run the program, the results are not as expected. How should you change the previous code segment to get the intended results?

○ A. Set the **Sort** property of the **DataView** object to an empty string.

○ B. Set the **ApplyDefaultSort** property of the **DataView** object to **false**.

○ C. Set the **RowFilter** property of the **DataView** object to **SupplierID**.

○ D. The code segment is correct; you need to ensure that the data in the **Suppliers** table is already sorted on the primary key.

Question 20

Your new project is to write a Visual C# ASP.NET Web application that enables professors to maintain the scores of their students. You place a **DataGrid** control on the Web form and bind the data grid to a **DataView** object. You allow professors to make changes in the data grid by adding new rows, modifying existing rows, and deleting existing rows. You now want to insert a command button that enables professors to view the deleted rows from the original data. How should you program the **Click** event of the command button?

○ A. In the event handler for the **Click** event, set the **RowFilter** property of the **DataView** object to **DataViewRowState.Deleted**.

○ B. In the event handler for the **Click** event, set the **RowFilter** property of the **DataView** object to **DataViewRowState.OriginalRows**.

○ C. In the event handler for the **Click** event, set the **RowStateFilter** property of the **DataView** object to **DataViewRowState.Deleted**.

○ D. In the event handler for the **Click** event, set the **RowStateFilter** property of the **DataView** object to **DataViewRowState.OriginalRows**.

Question 21

You have created an array of **Project** objects named **aProjects**. Each **Project** object has a **Name** property and a **Number** property. You want to display all the **Name** values in a **ListBox** Web server control named **lbProjects**. Which code snippet should you use for this purpose?

○ A.
```
lbProjects.DataSource = aProjects;
lbProjects.DataValueField = Name;
lbProjects.DataBind();
```

○ B.
```
lbProjects.DataSource = aProjects;
lbProjects.DataTextField = Name;
lbProjects.DataBind();
```

○ C.
```
lbProjects.DataSource = aProjects;
lbProjects.DataValueField = "Name";
lbProjects.DataBind();
```

○ D.
```
lbProjects.DataSource = aProjects;
lbProjects.DataTextField = "Name";
lbProjects.DataBind();
```

Question 22

You've used Visual Studio .NET to develop an ASP.NET Web application that queries data from a SQL Server database. You used the **SqlConnetion** object to connect to the database. As soon as the database operation is completed, you want to ensure that any pending database transactions are rolled back and connection is returned to the connection pool. You need to reuse the same **SqlConnection** object when your program needs to query the database again. Which of the following actions should you take?

○ A. Call the **Dispose()** method on the **SqlConnection** object.

○ B. Call the destructor of the **SqlConnection** object.

○ C. Call the **Close()** method on the **SqlConnection** object.

○ D. Set the **SqlConnection** object to **null**.

Question 23

You've developed an ASP.NET Web application that enables users to view and modify recently placed orders. Your application needs to display data from the **OrderHeader** and **OrderDetails** data tables. Information from **OrderHeader** is displayed in a **ListBox** control, whereas information from **OrderDetails** is displayed in a **DataGrid** control. Your program must ensure that, as soon as a different order is selected in the **ListBox** control, the **DataGrid** control displays the details corresponding to that order. Which of the following actions will you take to implement this functionality?

○ A. Define primary keys on the **OrderHeader** and **OrderDetails** tables.

○ B. Create a foreign key constraint in the **OrderDetails** table.

○ C. Add a **DataRelation** object to the **Relations** collection of the **DataSet** object.

○ D. Use the **DataSet.Merge()** method.

Question 24

You need to develop an ASP.NET Web application named **ProcessOrders**. This application receives XML data files from various customers, reads the files, and stores them in a SQL Server database for further processing. The **ProcessOrders** application uses an XML schema file to define the format and data types of the XML data files. However, not all customers send the XML data file using the same schema. Your application should parse the incoming data files to ensure that they conform to the XML schema. Which of the following actions should you take to accomplish this requirement?

- A. Implement an **XmlDocument** object to load the document. Pass the schema file to this object to validate and parse the XML document.

- B. Implement an **XmlValidatingReader** object and program an event handler for the **ValidationEventHandler** event to parse the data file that does not conform to the XML schema.

- C. Read the XML file into a **DataSet** object and set its **EnforceConstraints** property to **true**.

- D. Read the XML file and schema into a **DataSet** object. Program the **DataSet.MergeFailed** event handler to parse the data file that does not conform to the XML schema.

Question 25

You are developing a Visual C# ASP.NET Web application to query product information from a SQL Server database. The application specification requires that the users of your application be able to search for a product just by entering the first few characters. You store the characters entered by the user in a variable named **ProdName**. Which of the following SQL statements should you use to retrieve the data from the database?

- A.
```
sqlStatement = "SELECT Name, Description, Price FROM " +
    "Product WHERE Name IN '" + ProdName + "%'";
```

- B.
```
sqlStatement = "SELECT Name, Description, Price FROM " +
    "Product WHERE Name LIKE '" + ProdName + "%'";
```

- C.
```
sqlStatement = "SELECT Name, Description, Price FROM " +
    "Product WHERE Name IN '" + ProdName + "*'";
```

- D.
```
sqlStatement = "SELECT Name, Description, Price FROM " +
    "Product WHERE Name LIKE '" + ProdName + "*'";
```

Question 26

Your Visual C# .NET application needs to read data from a SQL Server 6.5 database and write it to a flat file once every 12 hours. A legacy application accesses this file to update its data. Because the data it will read from the database is huge, you want to retrieve the data with very little impact on the server resources while maximizing performance. Which object should you use to load the data from the database?

○ A. **DataSet**

○ B. **DataTable**

○ C. **SqlDataReader**

○ D. **OleDbDataReader**

Question 27

You allow users to edit product information on a **DataGrid** control bound to a **DataSet** object. When a user clicks the Update button on the form, you call the **SqlDataAdapter.Update()** method to cause the changes from the **DataSet** object to persist to the underlying database. Users report that new records and updated rows are saved properly but deleted rows reappear the next time they run the application. What could be the problem?

○ A. The users do not have permission to update the underlying table.

○ B. The **Update()** method does not delete rows.

○ C. Someone is restoring an old version of the database between the two executions of the program.

○ D. You forgot to set the **DeleteCommand** property of the **SqlDataAdapter** object.

Question 28

Your ASP.NET Web application has two **FileStream** objects. The **fsIn** object is open for reading, and the **fsOut** object is open for writing. Which code snippet would copy the contents of **fsIn** to **fsOut** using a 2KB buffer?

○ A.

```
Int32[] buf = new  Int32[2048];
Int32 intBytesRead;
while((intBytesRead = fsIn.Read(buf, 0, 2048)) > 0)
    fsOut.Write(buf, 0, intBytesRead);
fsOut.Flush();
fsOut.Close();
fsIn.Close();
```

○ B.

```
Int32[] buf = new  Int32[2048];
Int32 intBytesRead;
while((intBytesRead = fsIn.Read(buf, 0, 2048)) > 1)
    fsOut.Write(buf, 0, intBytesRead);
fsOut.Flush();
fsOut.Close();
fsIn.Close();
```

○ C.

```
Byte[] buf = new  Byte[2048];
Int32 intBytesRead;
while((intBytesRead = fsIn.Read(buf, 0, 2048)) > 0)
    fsOut.Write(buf, 0, intBytesRead);
fsOut.Flush();
fsOut.Close();
fsIn.Close();
```

○ D.

```
Byte[] buf = new  Byte[2048];
Int32 intBytesRead;
while((intBytesRead = fsIn.Read(buf, 0, 2048)) > 1)
    fsOut.Write(buf, 0, intBytesRead);
fsOut.Flush();
fsOut.Close();
fsIn.Close();
```

Question 29

Your SQL Server database contains a table, **Sales**, with these columns:

```
SalesID (int, identity)
StoreNumber (int)
Sales (int)
```

You have created the following stored procedure that accepts as inputs the store number and sales, inserts a new row in the table with this information, and returns the new identity value:

```
CREATE PROCEDURE procInsertSales
  @StoreNumber int,
  @Sales int,
  @SalesID int OUTPUT
AS
  INSERT INTO Sales (StoreNumber, Sales)
  VALUES (@StoreNumber, @Sales)
  SELECT @SalesID = @@IDENTITY
```

Which statement should you use to define the **SqlParameter** object for the **@SalesID** parameter for the previous stored procedure?

○ A.
```
SqlParameter paramSalesID = new SqlParameter(
    "@SalesID", SqlDbType.Int);
paramSalesID.Direction = ParameterDirection.Output;
```

○ B.
```
SqlParameter paramSalesID = new SqlParameter(
    "@SalesID", SqlDbType.Int);
paramSalesID.Direction = ParameterDirection.ReturnValue;
```

○ C.
```
SqlParameter paramSalesID = new SqlParameter(
    "@SalesID", Int32);
paramSalesID.Direction = ParameterDirection.Output;
```

○ D.
```
SqlParameter paramSalesID = new SqlParameter(
    "@SalesID", Int32);
paramSalesID.Direction = ParameterDirection.ReturnValue;
```

Question 30

You have defined a method named **DataLoad** that makes a list of suppliers available by returning an **ICollection** interface. You have an ASP.NET Web form with a **ListBox** control named **lbCustomers**. The **Page_Load** event handler for the Web form contains this code:

```
private void Page_Load(object sender, System.EventArgs e)
{
    lbCustomers.DataSource = DataLoad();
    lbCustomers.DataTextField = "CustomerName";
}
```

The Web form opens without error, but no customer names are displayed. What is the problem?

- ○ A. You have neglected to call the **DataBind()** method of the page.
- ○ B. You have neglected to set the **DataValueField** property of the **ListBox** control.
- ○ C. A **ListBox** control cannot be bound to an **ICollection** interface.
- ○ D. The code should be placed in the **Page_Init()** event handler.

Question 31

You are designing a Web form that will use a **Repeater** Web server control to display information from several columns of the **Orders** table in your database. You want to display the column names at the top of the control in **Label** Web server controls. Which template should you include with the column names?

- ○ A. **ItemTemplate**
- ○ B. **AlternatingItemTemplate**
- ○ C. **HeaderTemplate**
- ○ D. **SeparatorTemplate**

Question 32

You are creating a user control that displays employee names whose birthdays fall in the current quarter. The user control is displayed in the activities page of your company's intranet. You have placed a **Repeater** control in the user control and are using data binding to display values from the **dsEmployees DataSet** object into the **Repeater** control. The **Repeater** control contains the following definition:

```
<asp:Repeater id="rptProducts" runat="server"
 DataSource="<%# dsEmployees %>" DataMember="Employees">
```

You want to display the employee's name and the month and day of her birthday in the **Repeater** control. Which of the following options would you choose to maximize performance?

○ A.

```
<ItemTemplate>
    <tr>
        <td><%# DataBinder.Eval(Container.
        ➥DataItem, "Name") %></td>
        <td><%# DataBinder.Eval(
         Container.DataItem, "Date", "{0:m}") %></td>
    </tr>
</ItemTemplate>
```

○ B.

```
<ItemTemplate>
    <tr>
        <td><%# DataBinder.Eval(Container.
        ➥DataItem, "Name") %></td>
        <td><%# DataBinder.Eval(
         Container.DataItem, "Date") %></td>
    </tr>
</ItemTemplate>
```

○ C.

```
<ItemTemplate>
    <tr>
        <td><%# ((DataRowView) Container.DataItem)
        ➥["Name"] %></td>
        <td><%# String.Format("{0:m}",
         ((DataRowView) Container.DataItem)["Date"])
         ➥%></td>
    </tr>
</ItemTemplate>
```

○ D.

```
<ItemTemplate>
    <tr>
        <td><%# ((DataRowView) Container.DataItem)
        ➥["Name"] %></td>
        <td><%# ((DataRowView) Container.DataItem)
        ➥["Date"]) %></td>
    </tr>
</ItemTemplate>
```

Question 33

You've developed an ASP.NET Web application named **ProcessOrder** using Visual C# .NET. Your application receives orders from customers in an XML file named **Orders.xml**, which does not include a schema. Which of the following methods should you use to load data from **Orders.xml** into a **DataSet** object? (Select two.)

❑ A.

```
DataSet ds = new DataSet("Orders");
ds.ReadXml("Orders.xml", XmlReadMode.Auto);
```

❑ B.

```
DataSet ds = new DataSet("Orders");
ds.ReadXml("Orders.xml", XmlReadMode.DiffGram);
```

❑ C.

```
DataSet ds = new DataSet("Orders");
ds.ReadXml("Orders.xml", XmlReadMode.Fragment);
```

❑ D.

```
DataSet ds = new DataSet("Orders");
ds.ReadXml("Orders.xml", XmlReadMode.InferSchema);
```

❑ E.

```
DataSet ds = new DataSet("Orders");
ds.ReadXml("Orders.xml", XmlReadMode.ReadSchema);
```

Question 34

You've created an ASP.NET Web Service project using Visual Studio .NET. The project includes a class named **RefLibrary**, and this class contains the following method:

```
public String Version()
{
    return "1.6";
}
```

You note that you are able to instantiate the **RefLibrary** class from a Web service client project, but the **Version()** method is not available. What could be the problem?

○ A. Only properties can be part of the public interface of a Web service.

○ B. You must mark the method with the **WebService** attribute.

○ C. The methods of a Web service can return only object data.

○ D. You must mark the method with the **WebMethod** attribute.

Question 35

Your ASP.NET application performs various mathematical calculations, and you are beginning to sell this application in multiple countries. How should you ensure that the correct numeric formatting is used in all cases?

- ○ A. Allow the user to select a culture from a list. Create a **CultureInfo** object based on the user's selection and assign it to the **Thread.CurrentThread.CurrentCulture** property. Use the **ToString()** method to format numeric amounts.

- ○ B. Retrieve the value of **Request.UserLanguages(0)** when you're processing the page and assign it to the **Thread.CurrentThread.CurrentCulture** property. Use the **ToString()** method to format numeric amounts.

- ○ C. Allow the user to select a culture from a list. Create a **CultureInfo** object based on the user's selection and assign it to the **Thread.CurrentThread.CurrentUICulture** property. Use the **ToString()** method to format numeric amounts.

- ○ D. Retrieve the value of **Request.UserLanguages(0)** when you're processing the page and assign it to the **Thread.CurrentThread.CurrentUICulture** property. Use the **ToString()** method to format numeric amounts.

Question 36

Your ASP.NET application needs to search for text within longer text passages. You have been assigned to implement this culture-aware feature using Visual C# .NET. What should you use to perform this search?

- ○ A. **CultureInfo.CompareInfo**
- ○ B. **Array.Sort()**
- ○ C. **String.IndexOf()**
- ○ D. **String.IndexOfAny()**

Question 37

You've written a COM component to supply weather information from the weather database to the weather Web page of your Web application. You are porting the Web application to .NET and now want to call the COM component methods from your ASP.NET Web application. The COM component is not used by any other application. Which of the following is the quickest way to use the COM component in the ASP.NET Web application?

- ○ A. Set a direct reference from your .NET client to the COM server.
- ○ B. Use the Type Library Importer to create an unsigned RCW for the COM component.
- ○ C. Use the Type Library Importer to create a signed RCW for the COM component.
- ○ D. Use **PInvoke** to instantiate classes from the COM component.

Question 38

You have designed an ASP.NET Web form that displays inventory information. When a product falls below the reorder level, you need to highlight the product information in a table so that it stands out to the user. Which method of highlighting is most accessible?

- ○ A. **<BGCOLOR>**
- ○ B. **<BLINK>**
- ○ C. **<B>**
- ○ D. **<MARQUEE>**

Question 39

You need to debug an ASP.NET Web application by using Visual Studio .NET, which is installed on your local machine. The Web application is deployed on a remote server. When you attempt to debug the application, you get a DCOM configuration error. Which of the following steps should you take to resolve this problem?

- ○ A. Add your account to the Users group on the local computer.
- ○ B. Add your account to the Users group on the remote computer.
- ○ C. Add your account to the Debugger Users group on the local computer.
- ○ D. Add your account to the Debugger Users group on the remote computer.

Question 40

You've developed a supplier evaluation system using Visual Studio .NET. While testing the program, you notice that the value of the **TotalShipments** variable sometimes becomes **0** and causes an exception in the **CalculateAvgShipDelay()** method. You want your program to check the value of the **TotalShipments** variable and display an error message when the value of **TotalShipments** is **0**. You also want the program to display this error message regardless of how you compile the program. Which of the following code segments should you write before making a call to the **CalculateAvgShipDelay()** method?

- ○ A. Trace.Assert(TotalShipments == 0, "TotalShipments is zero");
- ○ B. Trace.Assert(TotalShipments != 0, "TotalShipments is zero");
- ○ C. Debug.Assert(TotalShipments == 0, "TotalShipments is zero");
- ○ D. Debug.Assert(TotalShipments != 0, "TotalShipments is zero");

Question 41

You've developed an ASP.NET Web application that enables users to generate shipping labels. The program needs to generate thousands of shipping labels each day. You use the **Trace** object to monitor the application and log the results in the Windows event log. You need to monitor errors, warnings, and other informational messages generated by the **Trace** object. You should have flexibility in controlling the amount of information logged for your application, and you want to do this with minimal administrative effort. What should you do?

- ○ A. Compile the application using the **/d:TRACE** switch.
- ○ B. Define an environment variable named **TRACE** and set its value to **true** or **false**. In the program, check the value of the environment variable to indicate the amount of information you want your application to log.
- ○ C. Declare a compilation constant named **TRACE** and set its value to **Error**, **Warning**, or **Info**. In your program, use the **#if**, **#else**, and **#endif** directives to check the level of tracing you want.
- ○ D. Use the **TraceSwitch** class in your program, and then use **TraceSwitch.Level** property to check whether you need to log the performance. Set the level of **TraceSwitch** by using the application's configuration file.

Question 42

The configuration file of a Web application has the following contents:

```
<system.diagnostics>
  <switches>
    <add name="BooleanSwitch" value="-1" />
    <add name="TraceLevelSwitch" value="33" />
  </switches>
</system.diagnostics>
```

You are using the following statements to create switch objects in your code:

```
BooleanSwitch booleanSwitch =
    new BooleanSwitch("BooleanSwitch", "Boolean Switch");
TraceSwitch traceSwitch =
    new TraceSwitch("TraceLevelSwitch", "Trace Switch");
```

Which of the following options is correct regarding the values of these switch objects?

- ○ A. The **booleanSwitch.Enabled** property is set to **false** and **traceSwitch.Level** is set to **TraceLevel.Verbose**.

- ○ B. The **booleanSwitch.Enabled** property is set to **true** and **traceSwitch.Level** is set to **TraceLevel.Verbose**.

- ○ C. The **booleanSwitch.Enabled** property is set to **false** and **traceSwitch.Level** is set to **TraceLevel.Error**.

- ○ D. The **booleanSwitch.Enabled** property is set to **false** and **traceSwitch.Level** is set to **TraceLevel.Info**.

Question 43

You are debugging an ASP.NET Web application you wrote using Visual Studio .NET. Your code uses the **Trace** class to produce the debugging output. In which configuration(s) will this output be enabled?

- ○ A. In the default Release configuration only.
- ○ B. In the default Debug configuration only.
- ○ C. In both the default Release configuration and the default Debug configuration.
- ○ D. In neither the default Release configuration nor the default Debug configuration.

Question 44

You are testing a huge Web application running on the main testing server. Tracing is enabled on the Web application. You have difficulty testing the application from your desktop because the Web application is storing tracing information for only a few requests. You want the Web application to record tracing information for a larger number of requests, and you also want the tracing information to be displayed in the Web page along with the trace viewer. Which of the following options should you choose?

O A. Set the **<trace>** element in the **web.config** application configuration file to the following:

```
<trace enabled="true" pageOutput="true" localOnly=
➥"false" />
```

O B. Set the **<trace>** element in the **web.config** application configuration file to the following:

```
<trace enabled="true" pageOutput="true" localOnly=
➥"true" />
```

O C. Set the **<trace>** element in the **web.config** application configuration file to the following:

```
<trace enabled="false" pageOutput="true" localOnly=
➥"true" />
```

O D. Set the **<trace>** element in the **web.config** application configuration file to the following:

```
<trace enabled="true" pageOutput="true" requestLimit=
➥"50" localOnly="false" />
```

O E. Set the **<trace>** element in the **web.config** application configuration file of the application to the following:

```
<trace enabled="true" pageOutput="true" requestLimit=
➥"50" localOnly="true" />
```

O F. Set the **<trace>** element in the **web.config** application configuration file of the application to the following:

```
<trace enabled="false" pageOutput="true" requestLimit=
➥"50" localOnly="true" />
```

Question 45

You've used Visual C# .NET to create an assembly named **Tracker.dll**, which contains classes for tracking a shipment and is used by several applications, including both managed applications and unmanaged COM applications. The COM applications are already compiled and use late binding to invoke methods from the assembly. Which actions should you take to ensure that the assembly is properly deployed on the target machine? (Select all that apply.)

❑ A. Create a strong name for the assembly using the Strong Name tool (**sn.exe**).

❑ B. Register the assembly using the Assembly Registration tool (**regasm.exe**).

❑ C. Create a type library for the application using the Type Library Exporter tool (**tlbexp.exe**).

❑ D. Import the COM type library definition into an assembly using the Type Library Importer tool (**tlbimp.exe**).

❑ E. Deploy the assembly to the Global Assembly Cache (GAC).

❑ F. Deploy the assembly to the application's bin directory.

❑ G. Deploy the assembly to the Windows system directory.

Question 46

You've used Visual C# .NET to develop a component named **ReplicateWarehouseData**. This component replicates the data used by the Warehousing application developed by the Warehouse Development team of your company. The Warehouse Development team needs to deploy the Warehousing application to its first three customers. How should it deploy the application? (Select two.)

❑ A. Create a Merge module for the **ReplicateWarehouseData** component.

❑ B. Create a Setup project that deploys the application and that includes the Merge module containing the component in the Setup project.

❑ C. Copy the **ReplicateWarehouseData** component into the directory of the Warehousing application.

❑ D. Create a Web Setup project to deploy the application that contains the code for the component.

Question 47

You've used Visual C# .NET to create an assembly named **Tracker.dll**, which contains classes for tracking a shipment. You need to deploy the assembly on the target computer in such a way that it can be accessed by multiple .NET applications. Which of the following actions should you take? (Select all that apply.)

- ❑ A. Create a strong name for the assembly using the Strong Name tool (**sn.exe**).
- ❑ B. Register the assembly using the Assembly Registration tool (**regasm.exe**).
- ❑ C. Use XCOPY to deploy the assembly to the GAC.
- ❑ D. Use FTP to deploy the assembly to the GAC.
- ❑ E. Use the Setup and Deployment project to deploy the assembly to the GAC.

Question 48

You have created and tested an ASP.NET application on your local development server. The application makes heavy use of Web server controls, along with static HTML text. You have deployed the application to your company's production server via FTP. The production server has IIS 5.0 installed on it. The pages in the application are displaying in a jumbled fashion, with text present but none of the Web server controls present. What could be the problem?

- ○ A. Applications containing Web server controls cannot be deployed via FTP.
- ○ B. Web server controls do not function properly on a page that also contains static HTML text.
- ○ C. The ASP.NET worker process is not properly installed on the production server.
- ○ D. ASP.NET requires IIS 6.0 to function properly.

Question 49

You are creating a Web Setup project for a Web application. In the property pages for the Web Setup project, you have set the compression property to **Optimized for speed**. Which of the following options will be true as a result of this configuration option? (Select two.)

- ❑ A. All the assemblies in the application will be precompiled to native code so that they run more quickly.
- ❑ B. Resulting assemblies will be larger in size.
- ❑ C. The setup package will be larger.
- ❑ D. The setup project will run more quickly.

Question 50

Your application requires users to be members of the Accounting role to access a **BalanceSheet** object. Which .NET security feature should you use to ensure that your code has this capability?

○ A. Role-based security

○ B. Code-access security

○ C. SSL encryption

○ D. Type safety

Question 51

You've designed a Visual C# .NET application that uses the following code to check for membership in the Developers group:

```
private void frmSecure_Load(object sender,
➥System.EventArgs e)
{
    // Get the current principal object
    Windows Principal prin = Thread.CurrentPricipal;
    // Determine whether the user is a developer
    Boolean developer = prin.IsInRole("Developers");
    // Display the results on the UI
    if(developer)
        lblMembership.Text = "You are in
        ➥the Developers group";
    else
        lblMembership.Text = "You are not in
        ➥the Developers group";
}
```

Users report that the code claims they are not in the Developers group even when they are. What must you do to fix this problem?

○ A. Use imperative security to ensure that your code has access to the Windows environment variables.

○ B. Create a **WindowsIdentity** object by using the **WindowsIdentity.GetCurrent()** method; then use this object to construct the **WindowsPrincipal** object.

○ C. Use the **WindowsPrincipal.Name** property to retrieve the user's name, and then use that name to call the **IsInRole()** method.

○ D. Call **AppDomain.CurrentDomain.SetPrincipalPolicy (PrincipalPolicy.WindowsPrincipal)** to specify the authentication mode.

Question 52

You've developed a project management system for your company that will be accessed through your company's intranet. The project management system provides an interface to be used by all employees to manage their projects in spite of their diverse nature. All the employees must log on using their Windows domain accounts to access this application. The **web.config** file of the project management application contains the following definition for the **<authentication>** element:

```
<authentication mode="Windows">
```

The Web application runs on IIS 5.0 on Windows 2000 Advanced server. IIS is configured to use Basic authentication to authenticate the users. When you run the application, you notice that all users are allowed access to the application. Which of the following options should you take to allow access to only authenticated users? (Select all that apply.)

❑ A. Add the following code in the **web.config** file of the Web application:

```
<authentication mode="Windows">
<identity impersonate="true" />
```

❑ B. Add the following code in the **web.config** file of the Web application:

```
<authentication mode="Windows">
<authorization>
    <deny users="?" />
</authorization>
```

❑ C. Configure IIS to enable Windows-integrated authentication rather than basic authentication for the Web application.

❑ D. Configure IIS to disable anonymous access for the Web application.

Question 53

You have deployed an ASP.NET application in your company's intranet to manage the timesheets of associates in your company. The application uses Windows-integrated authentication to authenticate users. You allow only authenticated users to access the application. Which account will ASP.NET use to access resources?

○ A. The **ASPNET** account

○ B. The **SYSTEM** account

○ C. The **IUSR_ComputerName** account

○ D. The authenticated user's account

Question 54

You are developing a proof-of-concept program to evaluate role-based security for your .NET Framework application. You write the following code:

```
PrincipalPermission pp1 =
➥new PrincipalPermission("User1", "Role1");
PrincipalPermission pp2 =
➥new PrincipalPermission("User2", "Role2");
PrincipalPermission pp3 =
➥new PrincipalPermission("User3", "Role3");

PrincipalPermission perm1 =
    (PrincipalPermission)pp1.Union(pp2);
PrincipalPermission perm2 =
    (PrincipalPermission)pp3.Union(perm1);
```

Which of the following statements is correct with respect to the previous code? (Select all that apply.)

❑ A. The expression **perm1.IsSubsetOf(perm2)** will evaluate to **true**.

❑ B. The expression **perm1.IsSubsetOf(perm2)** will evaluate to **false**.

❑ C. The expression **perm2.IsSubsetOf(perm1)** will evaluate to **true**.

❑ D. The expression **perm2.IsSubsetOf(perm1)** will evaluate to **false**.

Question 55

You have deployed an ASP.NET application that displays the company's product catalog. Customers can select the product desired from the catalog and place orders. The application has been running successfully, but as the orders increase, you notice that the application is incapable of managing the load and performs slowly. The application also becomes unreachable whenever a hardware failure occurs. This is causing serious side effects in your business. You want to resolve this problem, so which of the following options should you select to deploy your Web application?

○ A. Single-server deployment

○ B. Web garden deployment

○ C. Cluster deployment

○ D. Web farm deployment

Question 56

You have created a Web user control named **signup.ascx** that encapsulates the controls used in your company for newsletter sign-up forms. Now you want to use this control in other Web applications. What must you do?

○ A. Install the control in the GAC.

○ B. Copy the control's files into each application.

○ C. Include the control's project in the solution containing each application.

○ D. Compile the control and copy the compiled assembly into each application's bin folder.

Question 57

You are designing a new control for use in ASP.NET applications. The new control will be used to load an image from a disk file to an **Image** control at runtime. The control will not need a runtime user interface, but it must allow you to select a filename in the Properties window at design time. Which type of control should you create?

○ A. A control that inherits directly from the **WebControl** control

○ B. A control that inherits directly from the **Label** control

○ C. A control that inherits directly from the **Control** class

○ D. A control that inherits directly from the **Component** class

Question 58

You have created a custom component for your application that monitors a bidirectional parallel port for error messages. This component raises an event named **PortError** whenever an error message is detected. At that point, you must make the error code available to the control container. You want to use the best possible coding practices. Which of the following options should you choose to make the error code available to the container?

○ A. Place the error code in a property of the component for the container to retrieve.

○ B. Pass the error code as a parameter to the **PortError** event handler.

○ C. Define a global variable in a separate class and place the value in that variable.

○ D. Define a custom **PortErrorEventArgs** class that inherits from the **EventArgs** class to contain the error code, and pass an instance of the class as a parameter of the **PortError** event handler.

Question 59

Your application contains a Web user control called **LogIn**, which you have defined, in the **LogIn.ascx** file. You want to load this control in the Web page programmatically only if the user is not currently logged in to the Web site. The user control contains the following **Control** directive:

```
<%@ Control ClassName="LogIn"
➥Language="c#" AutoEventWireup="false"
    Codebehind="LogIn.ascx.cs" Inherits="LogIn" %>
```

You have added the following reference to the user control in the home Web page:

```
<%@ Reference Control="LogIn.ascx" %>
```

Which of the following options should you use to load the user control and set its properties in the Web page?

○ A.
```
Control c = new Control("LogIn.ascx");
((LogIn)c).ShowForgotPassword = true;
```

○ B.
```
Control c = new Control("LogIn.ascx");
((LogIn)c).ShowForgotPassword = true;
Controls.Add(c);
```

○ C.
```
Control c = LoadControl("LogIn.ascx");
((LogIn)c).ShowForgotPassword = true;
```

○ D.
```
Control c = LoadControl("LogIn.ascx");
((LogIn)c).ShowForgotPassword = true;
Controls.Add(c);
```

Question 60

You are designing a custom control for monitoring usage patterns of the Web pages. This control will log specific user actions into a SQL Server table. You will place this control on the Web forms, but the control does not require any visual representation at runtime. From which class should you derive this control?

○ A. **Control**

○ B. **UserControl**

○ C. **Form**

○ D. **Component**

Answers to Practice Exam #2

Answer Key

1. A	**21.** D	**41.** D
2. C	**22.** C	**42.** B
3. B	**23.** C	**43.** C
4. C	**24.** B	**44.** D
5. A	**25.** B	**45.** A, B, and E
6. A and C	**26.** D	**46.** C and D
7. C	**27.** D	**47.** A and E
8. A	**28.** C	**48.** C
9. B	**29.** A	**49.** C and D
10. C	**30.** A	**50.** A
11. B	**31.** C	**51.** D
12. D	**32.** C	**52.** B and D
13. B	**33.** A and D	**53.** A
14. C	**34.** D	**54.** A and D
15. A	**35.** A	**55.** D
16. E	**36.** A	**56.** B
17. B	**37.** A	**57.** D
18. B	**38.** C	**58.** D
19. A	**39.** D	**59.** D
20. C	**40.** B	**60.** D

Question 1

The correct answer is A. The `protected` modifier limits member access to the class containing the member and to subclasses of that class. Answer B is incorrect because the `public` modifier allows any class to call the member. Answer C is incorrect because the `private` modifier limits access to the defining class only. Answer D is incorrect because the `internal` modifier limits access to classes within the same project, whether they are derived from the defining class.

Question 2

The correct answer is C. When the `AutoEventWireup` attribute is set to `true`, ASP.NET automatically registers the `Page_Load()` method as an event handler for the `Load` event of the `Page` class. You also explicitly attach the `Page_Load()` method to the `Load` event of the page in the `OnInit()` method. Therefore, the drop-down list is populated twice because the `Page_Load()` method is executed twice. Setting the `AutoEventWireup` to `false` avoids auto-event wiring for `Page` event handlers. Answer A is incorrect because the `EnableViewState` attribute is used to indicate whether the view state should be enabled and has no control over executing the event handlers. Answer B is incorrect because the `SmartNavigation` attribute is used to remember the control focus on a postback and implement other navigation features on a Web page. Answer D is incorrect because, if the drop-down list control is populated on page postback, the drop-down list does not display any values when the page is first displayed; also, multiple postbacks add multiple values in the drop-down list.

Question 3

The correct answer is B. Setting the `TabIndex` property of the control to a negative value removes the control from the tab order. Answer A is incorrect because controls with a `TabIndex` of `0` also participate in the tab order. Answer C is incorrect because `AccessKey` only provides a shortcut key for quick navigation to the control; setting it to `null` has no impact on the tab order. Answer D is incorrect because, if you set the `Enabled` property of the control to `false`, it cannot get the focus under any circumstances.

Question 4

The correct answer is C. The `AlternateText` property specifies the text that is displayed in place of the `Image` Web server control when the image is being downloaded, the image is unavailable, or the browser doesn't support images. Answer A is incorrect because the `ToolTip` property is only used to display ToolTips for the image. Answer B is incorrect because the `Attributes` property represents a collection of name/value pairs that is rendered to the browser in the opening tag of the control. Answer D is incorrect because the `ImageUrl` property is used to specify the URL of the image.

Question 5

The correct answer is A. You would use two `CompareValidator` controls—one control to compare that the value in the control `txtQuote` is greater than or equal to `txtPrevQtrMin`, and the other control to compare that `txtQuote` is less than or equal to `txtPrevQtrMax`. Answer B is incorrect because the `RangeValidator` control is used to perform range validations only on the fixed values set to its `MinimumValue` and `MaximumValue` properties. Only the `CompareValidator` control enables you to compare and validate controls based on the values of other controls. Answer C is incorrect because the `CustomValidator` control requires writing more code. Answer D is incorrect because the `RegularExpressionValidator` control is used to ensure that the input control's value is in a specified pattern.

Question 6

The correct answers are A and C. The `RequiredFieldValidator` control lets you check that the URL is entered in the input control, and the `RegularExpressionValidator` control lets you check that the URL is in the proper format. Answer B is incorrect because the `RangeValidator` control lets you check that the data is within a specific range in the input control. Answer D is incorrect because `CompareValidator` lets you compare the data against a given value or another input control's value.

Question 7

The correct answer is C. When you have multiple catch blocks associated with a try block, you must write them in order from specific to general. The catch block corresponding to the ArithmeticException should come at the end because it is more general compared to the other three. In fact, the DivideByZeroException, NotFiniteNumberException, and OverFlowException classes are derived from ArithmeticException. Answers A, B, and D are incorrect because they do not place the catch blocks in order of specific to general exceptions.

Question 8

The correct answer is A. The SqlException.Class property gets a value from 1 to 25 that indicates the severity level of the error. Answer B is incorrect because the SqlException.Source property gets the name of the provider that generated the error. Answer C is incorrect because the SqlException.Server property gets the name of the computer running the instance of SQL Server that generated the error. Answer D is incorrect because the SqlException.State property gets a numeric error code from SQL Server that represents an error, warning, or "no data found" message.

Question 9

The correct answer is B. The configuration settings most local to the requested page control the response of ASP.NET. In the case of /custom/remote/NonExistingPage.aspx, the configuration file in the /custom directory is applied, which disables custom error pages. Therefore, answers A, C, and D are incorrect.

Question 10

The correct answer is C. The Server.Transfer() method provides a quick way to switch to ASPX pages in the ASP.NET application. Answer A is incorrect because the HyperLink control cannot be used to transfer control to other pages programmatically. Answer B is incorrect because the Response.Redirect() method causes an extra roundtrip between the server and the client to transfer control to another page. Answer D is incorrect because the Server.Execute() method executes the specified ASPX page and returns the control to the calling ASPX page.

Question 11

The correct answer is B. Setting the BufferOutput property to true enables the output to the response stream to be buffered until the entire page is processed. Therefore, you should call the Clear() method to clear the entire response stream buffer created until the file was not found. Answer A is incorrect because the Flush() method flushes the currently buffered content out to the client. Answer C is incorrect because the Close() method closes the HTTP response object and the socket connection to the client. Answer D is incorrect because the End() method stops the execution of the page after flushing the output buffer to the client.

Question 12

The correct answer is D. By default, When ASP.NET executes a page, it saves a copy of all nonpostback controls in the hidden __VIEWSTATE control. Because the page will not be posted back, you don't need this information. Therefore, you can disable view state for the entire page and make the page smaller so that it can be delivered more quickly. Answers A and B are incorrect because they enable the view state, which would store the data of controls in the __VIEWSTATE control and make the page bulky. Answer C is incorrect because it disables view state only for the DataGrid control rather than the whole page.

Question 13

The correct answer is B. Because different computers in a Web farm might serve multiple page requests during a session, you need to store any session state information in a shared repository outside the ASP.NET worker process. Answer A is incorrect because you can use session state in a Web farm configuration. Answer C is incorrect because view state is used to store data related to a page rather than a user session. Answer D is incorrect because the HttpRequest, HttpResponse, and HttpServerUtility objects can be used in a Web farm configuration.

Question 14

The correct answer is C. Session and application state are not shared between ASP and ASP.NET pages. If you set a session or application variable in ASP.NET code, there's no way to retrieve it from ASP code, and vice versa. Answer A is incorrect because the Page.Session property provides only a mechanism to get its value; you cannot set the value of this property. Answer B is incorrect because the ASP.NET Session object is not available in the ASP pages. Answer D is incorrect because cookies are required not just for ASP but also for ASP.NET.

Question 15

The correct answer is A. When a user visits the site, the browser establishes a new session with the Web server. At that time, the Session_Start() event handler is executed. This method is executed only once for the user session and is an appropriate choice for the case in question. Answer B is incorrect because Application_BeginRequest() works for every HTTP request and not just the first request. Answer C is incorrect because the Page_Load() event handler of default.aspx might not work in all cases. This is because the user can enter the Web site through a page other than default.aspx. Answer D is incorrect because the Application_Start() event handler redirects only the first user of the application.

Question 16

The correct answer is E. The DataSet object contains product details that are global to the application and needs to be expired every two hours. The best place to store application data is the application data cache—the Cache object. The data cached in the data cache can be set to expire in a fixed amount of time or by using sliding expiration. Answer A is incorrect because application state is used to store data global to the application but it cannot expire after a fixed amount of time or offer the other features of the Cache object. Answer B is incorrect because session state is used to store user-specific data; if session state is used to store the DataSet object, multiple copies of the DataSet object are created for each user, hindering the performance. Further, the data in session state cannot expire in a fixed amount of time. Answer C is incorrect because it is used to store only page-specific data on the client side. Answer D is incorrect because the HttpCachePolicy object is used to store the HTML output of Web pages rather than the data.

Question 17

The correct answer is B. The Duration and VaryByParam attributes must be specified when an OutputCache directive is applied to an ASPX page. The Duration attribute specifies the period in seconds for which the page should be cached, and if the output does not vary by any parameters, none should be passed to the VaryByParam attribute. Answers A and C are incorrect because the Duration attribute specifies the time in seconds. Answer D is incorrect because the required VaryByParam attribute is missing.

Question 18

The correct answer is B. Because the page accepts other information and the output changes for every state and park selected by the user, you should supply the VaryByParam attribute with ddlStates;ddlParks to cache different versions of the pages for every state and park selected. Answer A is incorrect because the page accepts other information and it would cache all the possible versions of the Web page. Answer C is incorrect because it would cache only on the basis of the park, regardless of the state. Therefore, if two states have parks with the same name, the cache would contain output on only the first park selected by the user. Answers D, E, and F are incorrect because the VaryByControl attribute is applied only in user controls, rather than ASPX pages.

Question 19

The correct answer is A. The ApplyDefaultSort property is used to automatically create a sort order, in ascending order, based on the primary key of the table. The ApplyDefaultSort property applies only when the table has a primary key defined and the Sort property is a null reference or an empty string. Answer B is incorrect because you want to sort using the primary key and for that you should set the ApplyDefaultSort property to true. Answer C is incorrect because you need to sort the data instead of filtering the data. Answer D is incorrect because the given code segment is incorrect: You must specify the name of a column in the Sort property along with ASC or DESC.

Question 20

The correct answer is C. Setting the RowStateFilter property of the DataView object to DataViewRowState.Deleted specifies that you want to view the deleted rows from the original data. Answers A and B are incorrect because the RowFilter property is used to filter rows based on an expression rather than the row states. Answer D is incorrect because setting the RowStateFilter property to DataViewRowState.OriginalRows displays the original data of all the rows, including the deleted rows.

Question 21

The correct answer is D. To display values from an array in a ListBox control, you must set the DataTextField property of the control to a string containing the name of the field. Answers A and C are incorrect because they use the DataValueField property instead of the DataTextField property. The DataValueField property is used to set the value associated with the items in the ListBox control, but this property is not displayed in the control. Answer B is incorrect because the property name of the data source must be specified as a string.

Question 22

The correct answer is C. When you use the Close() method on an SqlConnection object, the connection is closed, all pending database transactions are rolled back, and the connection is returned to the connection pool. Answer A is incorrect because reusing an instance after you have called the Dispose() method can result in undesirable effects. If you think you might want to reuse the connection instance, you should use the Close() method rather than the Dispose() method. Answer B is incorrect because you should call the destructor only when you need to release unmanaged resources. Answer D is incorrect because setting the SqlConnection object to null does not actually close the connection, but the object does continue to exist in memory waiting for garbage collection.

Question 23

The correct answer is C. A DataRelation object is used to relate two DataTable objects to each other. After you create a DataRelation object, you can call the GetChildRows() and GetParentRows() methods of the DataRow object to fetch child rows or parent rows, respectively. Answers A and B are incorrect because just by defining primary keys or foreign keys on the table does not relate the tables. Answer D is incorrect because the DataSet.Merge() method is used to merge two DataSet objects, which is not a requirement in this case.

Question 24

The correct answer is B. The XmlValidatingReader object enables you to validate an XML document. You use its ValidationEventHandler event to set an event handler for receiving information about the schema validation errors. Answer A is incorrect because the XmlDocument object cannot validate the XML document on its own. Answer C is incorrect because the EnforceConstraints property of DataSet is used to specify whether the database constraint rules are followed when attempting any update operation. Answer D is incorrect because the DataSet.MergeFailed event occurs only when a target and source DataRow have the same primary key value and EnforceConstraints is set to true.

Question 25

The correct answer is B. The LIKE clause determines whether a given character string matches a specified pattern. You use the % character as the wildcard character. Answer A is incorrect because you must use the LIKE clause instead of the IN clause for pattern searching. Answers C and D are incorrect because you need to use % as the wildcard character for matching instead of the * character.

Question 26

The correct answer is D. OleDbDataReader enables you to read the data one row at a time in a forward-only fashion; therefore, it occupies less memory and improves the performance of your application. The question requires you to read the data in a sequential fashion and write it to the flat file, so the OleDbDataReader object is the best option. Answer A is incorrect because a DataSet object loads the entire retrieved data in the memory. Answer B is incorrect because you cannot retrieve the data directly in a DataTable object. Answer C is incorrect because the SqlDataReader object is optimized to work with SQL Server 7.0 and later versions.

Question 27

The correct answer is D. Because other operations on the database, such as add and update, are working fine, the DeleteCommand property might not be set. The DeleteCommand property should be set to a command that deletes rows from the database. Answers A and C are incorrect because in these cases, none of the changes would be saved. Answer B is incorrect because, if the DeleteCommand property is correctly set, the Update() method deletes rows.

Question 28

The correct answer is C. The Read() method returns the number of bytes read, so answers B and D fail when there is 1 byte in the file. The Read() method reads to a byte array, so answers A and B fail because the buffer is the incorrect data type.

Question 29

The correct answer is A. While creating a SqlParameter object, you specify SQL Server data types using the SqlDbType enumeration rather than specify the .NET Framework data types. The @SalesID parameter is defined as an output parameter in the stored procedure; therefore, the Direction property of the SqlParameter object should be set to Output. Answers B and D are incorrect because the Direction property is set to ReturnValue, which specifies that the parameter represents a return value from a stored procedure. Answers C and D are incorrect because you should specify SQL Server data types when creating a SqlParameter object.

Question 30

The correct answer is A. You must explicitly call the DataBind method of the page or of the particular control to bind the data. Answer B is incorrect because you can display data in a ListBox even without setting any value for the DataValueField property. Answer C is incorrect because a ListBox control can be bound to an ICollection interface. Answer D is incorrect because you should write data-binding code in the Page_Load() event handler rather than Page_Init().

Question 31

The correct answer is C. The controls in the HeaderTemplate template are rendered once at the start of the Repeater control. Answer A is incorrect because the controls in the ItemTemplate are rendered once for every row of data in the data source of the control. Answer B is incorrect because the controls in the AlternatingItemTemplate are rendered once for every other row instead of the ItemTemplate. Answer D is incorrect because the SeparatorTemplate is rendered once between each row of data in the data source of the control.

Question 32

The correct answer is C. You should use type-casting to display data because the type-casts are evaluated at compile time and therefore do not cause performance penalty as in the case of the DataBinder.Eval() method. To display the month and day, you need to format the date. Answers A and B are incorrect because the DataBinder.Eval() method uses reflection to parse and evaluate a data-binding expression against an object at runtime, which causes a performance penalty. Answer D is incorrect because it does not format the date returned from the database in the desired format.

Question 33

The correct answers are A and D. In this scenario, the XmlReadMode.Auto and XmlReadMode.InferSchema options infer schema from the data. Answer B is incorrect because the data in the Orders.xml file is not a DiffGram. Answer C is incorrect because, when XmlReadMode is set to Fragment, the default namespace is read as the inline schema. Answer E is incorrect because the XML file does not include a schema.

Question 34 ·

The correct answer is D. Adding the WebMethod attribute to a public method makes it callable from remote Web clients. Answer A is incorrect because methods can be part of the public interface of a Web service. Answer B is incorrect because the WebService attribute is applied to the Web service class and not Web methods. Answer C is incorrect because Web service methods can return any data type.

Question 35

The correct answer is A. The CurrentCulture property specifies which culture to use for formatting dates, numbers, currencies, and so on. Answer B is incorrect because allowing the user to choose a culture is better than accepting the value of the UserLanguages string. The UserLanguages property of the HttpRequest object is not a reliable indicator of the end user's preferred language because Web browsers are not required to set this property. Answers C and D are incorrect because the CurrentUICulture property only specifies the culture to use when choosing resources for the user interface.

Question 36

The correct answer is A. Only the CompareInfo object can correctly handle the search in all character sets, including those that use multiple bytes per character. Answer B is incorrect because Array.Sort() does not locate substrings. Answers C and D are incorrect because the String.IndexOf() and String.IndexOfAny() methods can find substrings but are not culture aware.

Question 37

The correct answer is A. Because only one application is using the COM component, the quickest way to create the Runtime Callable Wrapper (RCW) and have the COM component available in your Visual C# .NET project is to use the Add Reference dialog box to add a direct reference to the COM component. Answers B and C are incorrect because the COM component is not shared by multiple applications and you therefore need not use the Type Library Importer tool to generate RCW for the COM component. Answer D is incorrect because the PInvoke feature is used to call functions from unmanaged libraries, such as Win 32 API libraries, rather than the COM component libraries.

Question 38

The correct answer is C. For compatibility with the largest number of accessibility aids, you should use bold or underlining to highlight information. Answer A is incorrect because you shouldn't depend on only color to convey information in an accessible application. Answers B and D are incorrect because they are not accessible ways to highlight information and are not compatible with most of the accessibility aids and Web browsers.

Question 39

The correct answer is D. If you get a DCOM configuration error while debugging, you might not be a member of the Debugger Users group on the remote machine. To resolve this, you must add your account on the remote machine to the Debugger Users group. Answer A is not correct because all users on a local computer are already part of the Users group. Answer B is incorrect because adding an account to the Users group on the remote machine does not allow you to debug a program remotely using Visual Studio .NET. For that, you must be a member of the Debugger Users group. Answer C is incorrect because you need to debug a program remotely, so you should be a member of the Debugger Users group on the remote computer rather than the local computer.

Question 40

The correct answer is B. The Assert() method checks for the given condition and generates an error when the condition evaluates to false. Answer A is incorrect because this code segment generates an error only when the value of TotalShipments is not equal to 0. Answers C and D are incorrect because the Debug.Assert() method is invoked only when the program is complied using the Debug configuration.

Question 41

The correct answer is D. The TraceSwitch class provides a multilevel switch to control tracing output without recompiling your code. Answer A is incorrect because the /d:TRACE option enables the tracing but does not allow multilevel control over tracing output. Answer B is incorrect because modifying environmental variables requires much more administrative effort when compared to a configuration file. Answer C is incorrect because this option requires the program to be recompiled each time the value of TRACE is modified.

Question 42

The correct answer is B. For booleanSwitch, a value of 0 corresponds to Off and any nonzero value corresponds to On. For TraceSwitch, any number greater than 4 is treated as Verbose. From the given values in the configuration file, the booleanSwitch object will have its Enabled property set to true and the traceSwitch object will have its Level property set to TraceLevel.Verbose. Answers A, C, and D are incorrect because the booleanSwitch.Enabled property is set to false instead of true.

Question 43

The correct answer is C. The Trace class is enabled in the default Release configuration as well as the default Debug configuration. Answers A, B, and D are incorrect because the TRACE symbol is defined in both the default Debug and the default Release configurations but the DEBUG symbol is defined only in the default Debug configuration.

Question 44

The correct answer is D. To enable tracing for all the pages of the Web application, you should enable tracing in the application configuration file (web.config). To view the tracing information in the Web page, you should set the pageOuput attribute to true. To store tracing information for more requests, you should set the requestLimit attribute to a larger number. Finally, to access the tracing information from the trace viewer in the tester's desktop, the localOnly attribute should be set to false. Answers A and B are incorrect because the tester wants to view tracing information for a larger number of requests. Answers C and F are incorrect because they disable tracing for the entire Web application. Answer E is incorrect because the localOnly attribute is set to true. The localOnly attribute indicates whether the tracing information should be available only in the hosting Web server or in all the clients (local as well as remote).

Question 45

The correct answers are A, B, and E. Because multiple applications are using this assembly, you need to install the assembly in the GAC. To install the assembly in the GAC, you need to sign the assembly with a strong name before deploying it to the GAC. Finally, to enable COM applications to use the assembly, you must register the assembly in the Windows Registry. Answer C is incorrect because the COM applications don't need to be compiled. Answer D is incorrect because you do not need to use a COM DLL in a .NET application. Answers F and G are incorrect because shared assemblies should be deployed in the GAC. When an assembly is registered in the Windows Registry, COM applications can locate shared assemblies from the GAC.

Question 46

The correct answers are C and D. Because the Warehousing application is the only application using the component, you should copy the component to the Warehousing application. You can now create a Web Setup project to deploy the application and component. Answers A and B are incorrect because the Merge Module projects are useful only for creating reusable setup components.

Question 47

The correct answers are A and E. If you want multiple applications to use an assembly, you need to sign the assembly with a strong name and place the assembly in the GAC. Answer B is incorrect because no COM applications are using the assembly. Answers C and D are incorrect because assemblies cannot be deployed in the GAC with XCOPY or FTP.

Question 48

The correct answer is C. You must install the ASP.NET software on the Web server before accessing ASPX pages. If ASP.NET is not installed, the pages are rendered by IIS as HTML pages and the Web server controls are not displayed. Answer A is incorrect because Web server controls do not require registration in the Windows Registry and can be deployed using the FTP command.

Answer B is incorrect because the Web server controls can easily coexist with static HTML. Answer D is incorrect because even the most basic Web browsers can render ASP.NET pages successfully.

Question 49

The correct answers are C and D. By optimizing the compression of the Web Setup project for speed, the setup program compresses the assemblies using a compression algorithm optimized for speed. The result is a lower compression ratio and a setup package that is larger in size but that executes faster. Answers A and B are incorrect because modifying the Web setup project's properties does not affect the size or speed of the installed assemblies.

Question 50

The correct answer is A. When you want to check whether a particular user belongs to a particular role or whether the user has a particular privilege, you need to perform role-based security. Answer B is incorrect because the application requires access to the BalanceSheet object for specific users. Answer C is incorrect because encryption makes the data more difficult to read but does not restrict the code from performing certain operations. Answer D is incorrect because type safety allows code to access only the primary memory locations that it is authorized to access. Type safety has no control over application-specific operations.

Question 51

The correct answer is D. You must tell the Common Language Runtime (CLR) how users are authenticated, even when you are using a Windows application that automatically employs Windows authentication. Answers A, B, and C are incorrect because they do not specify the authentication mode.

Question 52

The correct answers are B and D. You should configure IIS to disable anonymous access to keep anonymous employees from accessing the system. You can use any of the Windows authentication methods for authenticating employees.

You can also disallow unauthenticated access in the application by using the <deny> element. Answer A is incorrect because it allows access to all users. Answer C is incorrect because you can use any of the Windows authentication methods to implement Windows authentication in your Web application.

Question 53

The correct answer is A. By default, ASP.NET runs under a low privilege account, the ASPNET account. If impersonation is not enabled, all requests are made by ASP.NET using the ASPNET account. Answer B is incorrect because, by default, ASP.NET does not run under the SYSTEM account, which is a high privilege account. Answers C and D are incorrect because impersonation is not enabled with these accounts.

Question 54

The correct answers are A and D. The perm2 object is a union of all three PrincipalPermission objects (pp1, pp2, and pp3). The perm1 object is the union of two PrincipalPermission objects (pp1 and pp2). As a result, perm1 is a subset of perm2, but not vice versa. Answer B is incorrect because perm1 is a subset of perm2. Answer C is incorrect because perm2 is not a subset of perm1.

Question 55

The correct answer is D. To manage the load of your Web application and make the application accessible, you should select Web farm configuration to deploy your application. Web farm configurations make your applications scalable and reliable because they enable you to run multiple Web servers to process the application requests. Therefore, the load is balanced and failure of one server does not affect other servers processing the requests. Answer A is incorrect because the existing deployment is single-server and cannot balance the load of the application or manage a hardware failure in the Web server. Answer B is incorrect because, although Web garden deployment can balance the load of your application by running the application in a multiple-processor computer, it cannot provide a solution in case of server failure. Answer C is incorrect because cluster deployment can make the application more reliable but cannot help in making an application scalable.

Question 56

The correct answer is B. Web user controls can only be shared by copying their files into each application where you want to use them. Answers A and D are incorrect because user controls cannot be precompiled into an assembly and cannot be shared by multiple applications by placing the assembly in the GAC. Answer C is incorrect because the user control files should be included in each application project where they are needed.

Question 57

The correct answer is D. Controls that assist in design view and with no runtime user interface should derive from the Component class. Answers A, B, and C are incorrect because controls derived from the Control, WebControl, and Label classes provide a runtime user interface and therefore are unsuitable for the given requirement.

Question 58

The correct answer is D. Using a class derived from EventArgs to pass event parameters is preferable to using individual arguments because it's more readily extended in case you need to pass additional parameters in the future. Answers A and C are incorrect because event-related data should be passed as an argument to the event handler. Answer B is incorrect because, by convention, event handlers accept only two arguments—the object that received the event and the object containing the event argument. However, according to good programming practices, classes containing event data should derive from the EventArgs class and should have names ending with the suffix EventArgs.

Question 59

The correct answer is D. The LoadControl method of the Page class is used to load a user control programmatically from an .ascx file. Because you want to set the user control properties programmatically, you need to typecast the control to the user control. Answers A and B are incorrect because you cannot create a user control with the constructor of the Control class. Answer C is incorrect because it does not add the user control to the ControlCollection of the parent control.

Question 60

The correct answer is D. When a custom control does not require a runtime user interface, the component class provides the lowest overhead. Answers A, B, and C are incorrect because they are suitable for designing controls with a user interface.

What's on the CD-ROM

This appendix is a brief rundown of what you'll find on the CD-ROM that comes with this book. For a more detailed description of the *PrepLogic Practice Tests, Preview Edition* exam-simulation software, see Appendix B, "Using the *PrepLogic Practice Tests, Preview Edition* Software." In addition to the *PrepLogic Practice Tests, Preview Edition*, the CD-ROM includes the electronic version of this book in Portable Document Format (PDF), and the source code for all the examples used in this book.

PrepLogic Practice Tests, Preview Edition

PrepLogic is a leading provider of certification training tools. Trusted by certification students worldwide, PrepLogic is, we believe, the best practice exam software available. In addition to providing a means of evaluating your knowledge of the Exam Cram 2 material, *PrepLogic Practice Tests, Preview Edition* features several innovations that help you improve your mastery of the subject matter.

For example, the practice tests allow you to check your score by exam area or domain to determine which topics you need to study more. Another feature enables you to obtain immediate feedback on your responses in the form of explanations for the correct and incorrect answers.

PrepLogic Practice Tests, Preview Edition exhibits most of the full functionality of the Premium Edition but offers only a fraction of the total questions. To get the complete set of practice questions and exam functionality, visit PrepLogic.com and order the Premium Edition for this and other challenging exam titles.

Again, for a more detailed description of the *PrepLogic Practice Tests, Preview Edition* features, see Appendix B.

An Exclusive Electronic Version of the Text

The CD-ROM also contains an electronic PDF version of this book. This electronic version comes complete with all figures as they appear in the book. You will find that the search capability of the reader is handy for study and review purposes.

Complete Code Examples

You'll find the complete source code for all the examples used in the book on the CD. Just open any of the solution files in your copy of Visual Studio .NET, and you'll be ready to follow along with the text.

Using the *PrepLogic Practice Tests, Preview Edition* Software

This Exam Cram 2 includes a special version of *PrepLogic Practice Tests*—a revolutionary test engine designed to give you the best in certification exam preparation. PrepLogic offers sample and practice exams for many of today's most in-demand and challenging technical certifications. This special Preview Edition is included with this book as a tool to use in assessing your knowledge of the Exam Cram 2 material while also providing you with the experience of taking an electronic exam.

This appendix describes in detail what *PrepLogic Practice Tests, Preview Edition* is, how it works, and what it can do to help you prepare for the exam. Note that although the Preview Edition includes all the test-simulation functions of the complete retail version, it contains only a single practice test. The Premium Edition, available at PrepLogic.com, contains the complete set of challenging practice exams designed to optimize your learning experience.

Exam Simulation

One of the main functions of *PrepLogic Practice Tests, Preview Edition* is exam simulation. To prepare you to take the actual vendor certification exam, PrepLogic is designed to offer the most effective exam simulation available.

Question Quality

The questions provided in the *PrepLogic Practice Tests, Preview Edition* are written to the highest standards of technical accuracy. The questions tap the content of the Exam Cram 2 chapters and help you review and assess your knowledge before you take the actual exam.

Interface Design

The *PrepLogic Practice Tests, Preview Edition* exam-simulation interface provides the experience of taking an electronic exam. This enables you to effectively prepare for taking the actual exam by making the test experience a familiar one. Using this test simulation can help eliminate the sense of surprise or anxiety you might experience in the testing center because you will already be acquainted with computerized testing.

Effective Learning Environment

The *PrepLogic Practice Tests, Preview Edition* interface provides a learning environment that not only tests you through the computer, but also teaches the material you need to know to pass the certification exam. Each question comes with a detailed explanation of the correct answer and often provides reasons the other options are incorrect. This information helps reinforce the knowledge you already have and also provides practical information you can use on the job.

Software Requirements

PrepLogic Practice Tests, Preview Edition requires a computer with the following:

➤ Microsoft Windows 98, Windows Me, Windows NT 4.0, Windows 2000, or Windows XP.

➤ A 166MHz or faster processor (recommended).

➤ A minimum of 32MB of RAM.

➤ As with any Windows application, the more memory you have, the better your performance will be.

➤ 10MB of hard drive space.

Installing *PrepLogic Practice Tests, Preview Edition*

You install *PrepLogic Practice Tests, Preview Edition* by running the setup program on the *PrepLogic Practice Tests, Preview Edition* CD. Follow these instructions to install the software on your computer:

1. Insert the CD into your CD-ROM drive. The Autorun feature of Windows should launch the software. If you have Autorun disabled, click Start and select Run. Go to the root directory of the CD and select setup.exe. Click Open, and then click OK.

2. The Installation Wizard copies the *PrepLogic Practice Tests, Preview Edition* files to your hard drive; adds *PrepLogic Practice Tests, Preview Edition* to your desktop and Program menu; and installs test engine components in the appropriate system folders.

Removing *PrepLogic Practice Tests, Preview Edition* from Your Computer

If you elect to remove the *PrepLogic Practice Tests, Preview Edition* product from your computer, an uninstall process has been included to ensure that it is removed from your system safely and completely. Follow these instructions to remove *PrepLogic Practice Tests, Preview Edition* from your computer:

1. Select Start, Settings, Control Panel.

2. Double-click the Add/Remove Programs icon.

3. You are presented with a list of software installed on your computer. Select the appropriate *PrepLogic Practice Tests, Preview Edition* title you want to remove, and click the Add/Remove button. The software is then removed from your computer.

Using *PrepLogic Practice Tests, Preview Edition*

PrepLogic is designed to be user friendly and intuitive. Because the software has a smooth learning curve, your time is maximized because you start practicing almost immediately. *PrepLogic Practice Tests, Preview Edition* has two major modes of study: Practice Test and Flash Review.

Using Practice Test mode, you can develop your test-taking abilities as well as your knowledge through the use of the Show Answer option. While you are taking the test, you can expose the answers along with detailed explanations of why the given answers are right or wrong. This gives you the ability to better understand the material presented.

Flash Review mode is designed to reinforce exam topics rather than quiz you. In this mode, you are shown a series of questions but no answer choices. Instead, you are provided with a button that reveals the correct answer to the question and a full explanation for that answer.

Starting a Practice Test Mode Session

Practice Test mode enables you to control the exam experience in ways that actual certification exams do not allow, including

➤ *Enable Show Answer button*—Activates the Show Answer button, allowing you to view the correct answer(s) and full explanation(s) for each question during the exam. When this is not enabled, you must wait until after your exam has been graded to view the correct answer(s) and explanation.

➤ *Enable Item Review button*—Activates the Item Review button, allowing you to view your answer choices and marked questions and facilitating navigation among questions.

➤ *Randomize choices*—Randomizes answer choices from one exam session to the next. This makes memorizing question choices more difficult, thereby keeping questions fresh and challenging longer.

To begin studying in Practice Test mode, click the Practice Test radio button from the main exam-customization screen. This enables the options detailed in the preceding list.

To your left, you are presented with the option of selecting the preconfigured practice test or creating your own custom test. The preconfigured test has a fixed time limit and number of questions. Custom tests enable you to configure the time limit and number of questions in your exam.

The Preview Edition included with this book contains a single preconfigured practice test. You can get the complete set of challenging PrepLogic practice tests at PrepLogic.com and be certain you're ready for the big exam.

Click the Begin Exam button to begin your exam.

Starting a Flash Review Mode Session

Flash Review mode provides an easy way to reinforce topics covered in the practice questions. To begin studying in Flash Review mode, click the Flash Review radio button from the main exam-customization screen. Select either the preconfigured practice test or to create your own custom test.

Click the Begin Exam button to begin your Flash Review of the exam questions.

Standard *PrepLogic Practice Tests, Preview Edition* Options

The following list describes the function of each of the buttons you see. Depending on the options, some of the buttons will be grayed out and inaccessible or missing completely. Buttons that are appropriate are active. The buttons are as follows:

➤ *Exhibit*—This button is visible if an exhibit is provided to support the question. An exhibit is an image that provides supplemental information necessary to answer the question.

➤ *Item Review*—This button closes the question window and opens the Item Review screen. From this screen, you will see all the questions, your answers, and your marked items. You will also see the correct answers listed here when appropriate.

➤ *Show Answer*—This option displays the correct answer with an explanation of why it is correct. If you select this option, the current question is not scored.

➤ *Mark Item*—Check this box to tag a question you need to review further. You can view and navigate your marked items by clicking the Item Review button (if enabled). When grading your exam, you will be notified if you have marked items remaining.

➤ *Previous Item*—View the previous question.

➤ *Next Item*—View the next question.

➤ *Grade Exam*—When you have completed your exam, click this button to end your exam and view your detailed score report. If you have unanswered or marked items remaining, you will be asked whether you want to continue taking your exam or view your exam report.

Time Remaining

If the test is timed, the time remaining is displayed in the upper-right corner of the application screen. It counts down minutes and seconds remaining to complete the test. If you run out of time, you will be asked whether you want to continue taking the test or end your exam.

Your Examination Score Report

The Examination Score Report screen appears when the Practice Test mode ends—as the result of time expiration, completion of all the questions, or your decision to terminate early.

This screen provides a graphical display of your test score, with a breakdown of scores by topic domain. The graphical display at the top of the screen compares your overall score with the PrepLogic Exam Competency Score.

The PrepLogic Exam Competency Score reflects the level of subject competency required to pass this vendor's exam. Although this score does not directly translate to a passing score, consistently matching or exceeding this score does suggest that you possess the knowledge to pass the actual vendor exam.

Review Your Exam

From the Your Score Report screen, you can review the exam you just completed by clicking the View Items button. Navigate through the items, viewing the questions, your answers, the correct answers, and the explanations for those questions. You can return to your score report by clicking the View Items button.

Getting More Exams

Each *PrepLogic Practice Tests, Preview Edition* that accompanies your book contains a single PrepLogic practice test. Certification students worldwide trust PrepLogic practice tests to help them pass their IT certification exams the first time. Purchase the Premium Edition of *PrepLogic Practice Tests* and get the entire set of all-new, challenging practice tests for this exam. *PrepLogic Practice Tests*—because you want to pass the first time.

Contacting PrepLogic

If you want to contact PrepLogic for any reason, including getting information about our extensive line of certification practice tests, we invite you to do so. Please contact us online at www.preplogic.com.

Customer Service

If you have a damaged product and need a replacement or refund, please call the following phone number:

800-858-7674

Product Suggestions and Comments

We value your input! Please email your suggestions and comments to the following address:

feedback@preplogic.com

License Agreement

YOU MUST AGREE TO THE TERMS AND CONDITIONS OUTLINED IN THE END USER LICENSE AGREEMENT ("EULA") PRESENTED TO YOU DURING THE INSTALLATION PROCESS. IF YOU DO NOT AGREE TO THESE TERMS, DO NOT INSTALL THE SOFTWARE.

Glossary

accessibility
The process of making an application more readily usable by users who might have disabilities that interfere with their use of computer hardware or software.

accessor
The code that is enclosed in a get and set block in a property definition. The get accessor is executed when the property value is read, and the set accessor is executed when a value is assigned to the property. A property can contain a get accessor, a set accessor, or both.

ad hoc query
A set of SQL statements that are executed immediately.

application domain (AppDomain)
A secure, versatile, and isolated environment created by the CLR to execute an application.

Application state
A global storage mechanism accessible from all pages in a Web application. Application state is useful for storing information that needs to be maintained between server round trips and that needs to be shared by all the users.

ASP.NET
A subset of the .NET Framework that enables you to develop Web applications and Web services. ASP.NET applications can use the full range of .NET Framework classes and the services provided by the Common Language Runtime.

ASP.NET application
A collection of Web forms, assemblies, and other files stored in a virtual Web directory configured as an IIS application.

assembly
A logical collection of one or more files, which are versioned and deployed as a single unit.

Every type loaded in the CLR belongs to an assembly. *See also* assembly manifest and assembly metadata.

assembly manifest

An integral part of an assembly that stores the assembly's metadata. *See also* assembly metadata.

assembly metadata

A collection of information about the assembly that makes an assembly self-describing. Assembly metadata stores information such as the name of the assembly, the version of the assembly, the files that are part of the assembly and their hash values, and the assemblies' dependencies on other assemblies.

attribute

A declarative tag that can be placed with certain code elements to provide additional information on the corresponding code element at runtime.

authentication

The process of determining the identity of a user based on his credentials.

authorization

The process of allowing a user to use specific resources based on her authenticated identity.

backing store

A place such as memory and hard disk where you can store files.

boxing

The process of converting a value type to a reference type in which the value in the stack is copied into the heap via the creation of a new instance of an object to hold its data. *See also* unboxing.

caching

Storing information for later retrieval, rather than regenerating it every time it's requested.

class

A reference type that encapsulates data (constants and fields) and behavior (methods, properties, indexers, events, operators, instance constructors, static constructors, and destructors). A class is a blueprint from which the objects are created.

CLR (Common Language Runtime)

A program that executes all managed code and provides code with various services at runtime, such as automatic memory management, cross-language integration, code access security, and debugging and profiling support.

column

All the values for one particular property in a table.

complex databinding

Connecting a user interface control to an entire collection of data, rather than to a single data item.

component

A package of reusable code that implements the `IComponent` interface.

configuration file

ASP.NET configuration files are XML files that ASP.NET reads at runtime to determine configuration options.

constructor

A method that allows control over initialization of a type. A constructor is executed when an instance of a type is created.

cookies

A mechanism for storing small pieces of information at the client side. A cookie is associated with a specific domain and is sent along with each request to the associated Web server.

CSS (Cascading Style Sheets)

A collection of styles that can be applied to elements in an HTML document. The CSS styles define how the HTML elements are rendered in the Web browser.

culture

A combination of language and location that is sufficient to dictate the formatting of resources.

culture code

An abbreviation that identifies a particular culture.

data providers

The server-specific ADO.NET classes that supply data.

databinding

The process of connecting the controls on the user interface with the data stored in the data model.

dataset

A server-independent store that can hold multiple tables and their relationships.

debugging

The process of locating logical or runtime errors in an application. Debugging involves finding the causes of the errors and fixing them.

delay signing

A technique that enables a shared assembly to be placed in the global assembly cache (GAC) by signing the assembly with the public key. This enables the assembly to be signed with a private key at a later stage when the development process is complete and the component or assembly is ready to be deployed. This process allows developers to work with shared assemblies as if they were strongly named and yet also prevent the private key of the signature from being accessed at different stages of development.

delegate

A reference type that stores references to a method with a specific signature. A delegate object can be used to dynamically invoke a method at runtime.

deployment

A process by which an application or a component is distributed to be installed on the other computers.

derived control

A control that inherits directly from a specific server control such as the TextBox or Label control.

Disco

A Microsoft standard for Web service discovery.

DOM (document object model)

The DOM class is an in-memory representation of an XML document that enables you to programmatically read, manipulate, and modify an XML document.

encoding

A scheme for representing textual characters as numeric codes.

enumeration

A distinct type that has named constants. Enumeration types are defined by using the enum keyword, and they provide a type-safe way to work with constants.

event

A message sent by an object to signal an action. The action can be a result of user interaction, such as a mouse click, or be triggered by another program.

event handling

The act of responding to an event. Event handling can be accomplished by writing methods called event handlers that are invoked in response to events.

exception

A problem that occurs during the normal execution of a program.

exception handling

The process of handling exceptions raised when the program executes. You can choose to ignore an exception or respond to it by running your own code.

FCL (Framework Class Library)

A library of classes, interfaces, and value types that are included in the Microsoft .NET Framework. This library provides access to the system functionality and is the foundation on which the .NET Framework applications, components, and controls are built.

field

A variable associated with an object or a class.

foreign key

An identifier in a database table that stores values from the primary key in another table. These values indicate to which row in the primary table each row in the other table is related.

GAC (global assembly cache)

A machine-wide code cache that stores assemblies and that is shared by many applications running on that machine.

garbage collection

A process of reclaiming all unused memory and returning it to the heap of available memory. The CLR garbage collector can be invoked when an application gets low on memory resources.

The CLR also compacts the memory that is in use to reduce the working space necessary for the heap.

globalization
The process of identifying the resources to be localized in a particular application.

hidden fields
Input controls that are not visible on the page but are posted to the server along with a page postback.

HTML controls
HTML elements that are used for client-side rendering and are not directly accessible on the Web server.

HTML server controls
HTML elements marked with the `runat="server"` attribute to make them accessible on the Web server.

identity column
A column whose value is automatically assigned by the server when a new row is entered.

IL (intermediate language)
The language into which compilers that support the .NET Framework compile a program. The European Computer Manufacturer's Association (ECMA) ratified IL standard is called Common Intermediate Language (CIL). The Microsoft implementation of CIL is called Microsoft IL (MSIL).

impersonation
ASP.NET uses impersonation to make requests for resources as if those requests were made by the authenticated user.

inheritance
A process through which you create a new type based on an existing type. In an inheritance relationship, the existing type is called the *base* type and the new type is called the *derived* type. When you use inheritance, the derived type automatically gets all the functionality of the base type, without any extra coding.

input validation
A process by which an application examines user input to determine whether it is acceptable for the application.

JIT (just-in-time) compilation
The process of converting IL code into machine code at runtime, just when it is required.

"last one wins" concurrency control
A situation in which an update to a row always succeeds, whether another user has edited the row or not (as long as the row still exists).

localizability
The process of verifying that all localizable resources have been separated from code.

localization
The process of translating resources for another culture.

managed code

The code that runs under the services provided by the CLR. Managed code must expose necessary metadata information to the CLR to enjoy these services. *See also* CLR.

merge module

A merge module enables you to create reusable components that help in deploying shared components. Merge modules cannot be directly installed; they must be merged with installers of applications that use the shared component packed into a merge module.

metadata

Information about elements—such as assembly, type, methods, and so on—that helps the CLR manage garbage collection, object lifetime management, code access security, debugging, and other services for these elements.

namespace

A naming scheme that provides a way to logically group related types. Namespaces have two benefits: They are used to avoid naming conflicts, and they make browsing and locating classes easier.

native compilation

The process of precompiling assemblies in processor-specific machine code. Native compilation can be done with the help of the Native Image Generation tool (ngen.exe).

native image cache

A cache that contains precompiled assemblies.

.NET Framework

A platform for building, deploying, and running distributed applications and XML Web services. The .NET Framework consists of three main parts: the CLR, the FCLs, and a set of language compilers.

OLE DB

A COM-based application programming interface (API) for accessing data. OLE DB supports accessing data stored in any format for which an OLE DB provider is available.

one-way databinding

A process in which the bound property of the control reflects changes to the data model but changes to the control are not written back to the data model.

optimistic concurrency control

A situation in which an update to a row succeeds only if no one else has changed that row after it was loaded into the DataSet object.

OSQL

A SQL Server command-line tool for executing queries.

parameter

A piece of information passed to a stored procedure at runtime.

performance counter

A Windows device that publishes performance-related data for applications and their components.

platform invoke

The feature of the .NET Framework that enables you to call Windows API and other DLL procedures from managed code.

postback

A postback occurs when the user submits a Web form to the server.

primary key

The unique identifier for a row in a database table.

private assembly

An assembly available only to clients in the same directory structure as the assembly.

process

An application under execution.

property

A class member that is similar to a public field but that can also encapsulate additional logic in its get and set accessor methods.

query string

The data appended to the URL; it's separated with a question mark (?). The data attached to the URL is usually a set of key-value pairs, in which each key-value pair is separated by an ampersand (&).

RCW (runtime callable wrapper)

A proxy that enables .NET code to use COM classes and members.

relational database

A database that stores multiple tables and the relationships between them.

relationship

A connection between two tables in a database.

resource file

A file that contains string, bitmap, or other resources that can differ between cultures.

resource-only assembly

An assembly that contains only resources and no executable code.

resultset

A collection of data arranged in rows and columns.

role-based security

A security mechanism in which access to resources is authorized depending on the authenticated identity of the user running the code.

round trip

The combination of a Web page request and a postback operation.

row

All the values in a table that describe one instance of an entity.

satellite assembly

A resource-only assembly that contains culture-specific information.

schema

The structure of a database or an XML file.

session

A sequence of interaction between a client browser and a Web server. Each session is uniquely identified using a SessionID.

session state

Session state information is persisted between individual stateless HTTP requests.

shared assembly

A shared assembly can be referenced by more than one application. An assembly must be explicitly built to be shared by giving it a cryptographically strong name. Shared assemblies are stored in the machinewide GAC.

simple databinding

The process of connecting a single value from the data model to a single property of a control.

SOAP (Simple Object Access Protocol)

A standard for exchanging information and types over the Internet using standards such as XML and HTTP.

SQL Query Analyzer

A SQL Server graphical tool for executing queries.

SQL-92 (Structured Query Language-92)

The official ANSI specification for Structured Query Language.

stored procedure

A set of precompiled Transact-SQL statements stored on the server for later execution.

stream

A file viewed as a stream of bytes.

strong name

A name that globally identifies an assembly. It consists of a simple text name, a version number, culture information (if provided), and a public key and is optionally signed using a digital signature. If the assembly contains more than one file, it is sufficient to generate a strong name just for the file that contains the assembly manifest.

structure

A user-defined value type. Similar to a class, a structure has constructors, fields, methods, properties, and so on. However, structures do not support inheritance.

tab order

The order in which controls receive focus when users navigate on a form by pressing the Tab key.

table

A collection of data about instances of a single entity.

templated control

A control whose display is entirely dictated by templates.

testing

The process of executing programs and determining whether they work as expected. Testing is the process of revealing errors by executing programs with various test cases and test data.

ToolTip

A small pop-up window that displays a brief description of a control's purpose when the mouse hovers over the control.

tracing

The process of displaying informative messages in an application at the time of execution. Tracing messages can be helpful in checking the health of the program or finding errors even though the program is already in production.

T-SQL (Transact Structured Query Language)

The SQL-92 dialect used in Microsoft SQL Server.

two-way databinding

A process in which changes to the control are written back to the data model.

UDDI (Universal Description, Discovery, and Integration)

A standard for discovering details of Web services and other business services available via the Internet.

unboxing

The process of converting a reference type to a value type in which the value from the heap is copied back onto the stack. *See also* boxing.

unhandled exceptions

Exceptions that are not handled in a try...catch block of the program.

Unicode

A universal character set that can represent more than one million characters. Unicode is the default internal language of the .NET Framework.

unmanaged code

Code written in a non-.NET environment that does not benefit from the services of the CLR.

user assistance

Any means of providing information about an application to the user.

UTF-16

A 16-bit Unicode encoding format in which every character is encoded using 2 bytes.

View state

A mechanism used by ASP.NET to maintain the state of controls across page postbacks. View state works only when a page is posted back to itself.

Web custom control

A control that inherits from the WebControl class. Web custom controls can be compiled, and they support advanced features in Visual Studio .NET.

Web Forms Designer

The rich visual environment provided by Visual Studio .NET that allows you to create Web applications.

Web method

A method of a Web service that can be invoked by client applications.

Web server controls (ASP.NET server controls)

A collection of controls that provides varied functionality and a consistent programming model.

Web service

A Web service enables you to instantiate and invoke objects over the Internet.

Web user control

A composite control implemented as an ASCX file with an associated CS file.

WSDL (Web Services Description Language)

An XML language that describes the interface of a Web service.

XML (Extensible Markup Language)

A text-based format that enables developers to describe, deliver, and exchange structured data among a range of applications.

XML attribute

A property of an XML object.

XML declaration

The line in an XML file that identifies the file as XML.

XML element

An XML tag together with its contents.

XML namespace

A set of XML tags that is private to an application.

XML Web services

Applications that expose data and services to other applications using standards such as HTTP, XML, and SOAP.

Index

. . . .

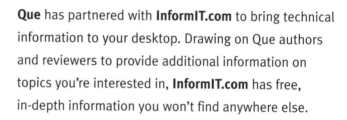